BIKING

THROUGH

EUROPE

BIKING
THROUGH
EUROPE

A ROADSIDE
▪ TRAVEL GUIDE ▪
WITH 17 PLANNED
CYCLE TOURS

Dennis & Tina JAFFE

WILLIAMSON PUBLISHING
CHARLOTTE, VERMONT 05445

Library of Congress Cataloging-in-Publication Data

Jaffe, Dennis.
  Biking through Europe.

  1. Bicycle touring – Europe – Guide-books.
2. Europe – Description and travel – 1971 –
– Guide-books.   I. Jaffe, Tina.   II. Title.
GV1046.E85J34 1987   914   87-8318
ISBN 0-913589-31-4

Cover and interior design: Trezzo-Braren Studio
Typography: Villanti & Sons, Printers, Inc.
Printing: Capital City Press
Cover photo: Steve Morrison

Williamson Publishing Co.
Charlotte, Vermont 05445

Manufactured in the United States of America

First Printing April 1987

ACKNOWLEDGMENTS

Of the many people who have helped in the creation of this book, we would like to give special thanks to Steve and Ruth Morrison, Bob and Donna Snow, Frank and Mary Romary, Basil and Cecilia Jacobs, Mike and Terry Runkel, Brita Alexandersen, Lars Skovenboe, Walt and Willa Halpern, and the many other bikers along the way who were so helpful in providing information.

Contents

Books by Dennis & Tina Jaffee

The Camper's Companion to Northern Europe
A Roadside and Travel Guide

The Camper's Companion to Southern Europe
A Roadside and Travel Guide

INTRODUCTION

Stay another night," said the gray-haired old Greek who had been our host the previous night, "and we'll kill a lamb in your honor." John Rovas and his family were dirt poor country people who lived in a simple farmhouse without electricity. We knew that while the killing of a lamb would be a great honor for us as guests, it would also impose a large financial burden on our new friends. Although the offer was tempting, we had already made reservations to take the boat to Italy, so we decided to forego what surely would have been a wonderful culmination to an already fantastic Greek trip and continue on with our travels. The Greeks are well known for their warm hospitality, and John and his family had, if anything, exceeded our greatest expectations since our arrival at this farm.

It had all started the day before. We had been bicycling through Greece and were shopping for groceries at the open air market in the town of Skotini in the Peloponnese when this small but vigorous old man with a Santa Claus twinkle in his eye approached us with an unusual invitation.

"Ah! You speak English. Wonderful! Then you will be my guests." He told us that he had worked as a waiter at the St. Francis Hotel in San Francisco just before the outbreak of World War I. Although he hadn't been back since then he had retained enough of his English so that with a little effort on everyone's part we were able to at least partially bridge the language gap.

The next thing we knew we were following his dilapidated old moped, which if we hadn't known better we would have thought was a relic from his World War I days, along a bumpy country lane. John lived with his family on a farm at the outskirts of a tiny village that we still haven't been able to find on a map. The whitewashed stone house was without electricity and the floor was of dirt; however, it was a home that exuded a reassuring warmth and friendliness which no hotel could ever hope to duplicate at any price. We were eight people who sat down for dinner at the rickety old kitchen table. Sophia, John's wife, had killed one of their chickens for us, the guests of honor. It was a memorable evening. Eight people, one chicken, and a lot of the throat-searing local wine. In spite of John's rusty English and our non-existent Greek, we had a great time and were able to wade through a series of heady topics, including politics and philosophy. No doubt the wine helped a great deal! We slept like babies in our straw bed, and the next morning John offered to kill the baby lamb for our dinner.

We've done a lot of touring through Europe with our bikes and while that particular trip in Greece will always have a special place in our travel recollections, there have been many other similar encounters in other countries. Somehow the sight of a bike loaded with touring gear seems to evoke an almost universally friendly and hospitable response. A cycling trip will bring you close to the real Europe and offer an opportunity for direct interaction with the natives that no other way of travel can match.

For those of you who are already active cyclists, so much the better! We don't really have to tell you of the thrill of a breathtaking alpine descent or of the satisfaction – call it pride if you will – of having conquered a tough mountain pass or having reached a far-off destination at the end of a hard day's pedaling. Whether you are a newcomer to cycling or an old hand, what we would like to do as this book unfolds is to show you how to superimpose the pleasures of cycling upon a charming, romantic, and often exciting European backdrop.

We have tried to stay away from too many personal reminiscences, which seem to creep into many travel books. It seems a lot more relevant to concentrate on providing as much factual and practical material as possible than it does to burden you with narrative accounts of our own bicycle trips. This book is not the account of just a single bicycle trip, but rather, a compilation of practical information and experiences gathered during the last twelve years that we have spent as Americans living and cycling in Europe.

WHY EUROPE?

The reasons why people travel are often as varied as the people themselves. For some travel is the thrill of seeing different places and making new acquaintances, while for others it is simply a means of getting away from the same old places and people. Whatever your motivations are for traveling, when it comes to the sheer concentration of cultural and historic attractions, romantic hide-a-ways, breathtaking scenery, and outstanding food, there is simply no other place in the world where so much is packed into as small an area as in Europe. The magnificent chateaux of France's Loire Valley, the great museums of Paris, Amsterdam, and London, the splendor of the Swiss alps, the rich canal-laced farmlands of Holland, as well as the romantic castles and half-timbered medieval houses of West Germany are but a few of the wide variety of attractions to be enjoyed within an area that is about one third the size of the United States. Within the range covered by one or two days of cycling, you can pass through areas where different languages are spoken, where the buildings reflect varied architectural styles, and where the cuisine changes as you go from region to region.

Whether you are a veteran of many European tours or have never been overseas before, a bicycle trip is a great way to see and enjoy Europe in depth. If you have traveled in Europe before, zoomed around the high spots by car or in a tour bus and come home dreaming about returning and being able to really get to know a particular country or region, then try a cycling vacation. There is no other way of traveling that will allow you to become more intimate with a region than by pedaling through it on a bicycle.

There is something very disarming and nonintrusive about moving through an area by bike. As a self-propelled, noiseless, nonthreatening visitor, you will find that people will welcome you in a much more sincere and friendly manner than if you were to pull up in your shiny new Mercedes or as part of a boisterous tour group.

Wherever you go you will find that cyclists seem to attract a special welcome that other types of travelers just don't experience. Total strangers will wave and urge you on with their shouts of encouragement. Many times we have been the recipients of some extra courtesy or gesture of friendship just because we happened to be on bikes as we passed through an area.

Once while cycling in the lovely countryside around the French city of Arles, we had stopped to repair a flat. A couple of French cyclists riding sleek racers and decked out in their finest Sunday biking togs stopped to ask if we needed help. Since this was one of those rare occasions when we actually had everything we needed with us, we were able to say "Merci, but no merci!" in our fractured French. Well, it was pretty obvious from the ensuing conversation that we were as American as the proverbial apple pie. "*Vous êtes Americaines?*" asked our French cyclist. "*Oui,*" said we. And so it went. The outcome of this chance international biking encounter was an invitation to ride with them. We gladly accepted, although we felt somewhat out of place with our fat, heavily laden touring machines and our very definitely unchic outfits. It was a great day of inspiring back road cycling which was followed up by one of those dream lunches like you only get in France as guests of our newly made friend Claude and his family. This special camaraderie among cyclists transcends the boundaries of nationality and language and helps to make Europe, where cycling is the national pastime in many countries, a natural goal for a bicycle vacation.

If this is to be your first experience with Europe, and you feel a bit uncertain about venturing out into the great unknown on your own, have no fear; we will take you step by step through the preparations necessary for having a wonderful European trip.

HOW TO USE THIS BOOK

Following the chapters on trip planning, we have taken Europe's eight best cycling countries and provided detailed information for each country. As a special treat we have also included a three country ride around the beautiful Lake Constance. Each chapter includes:

1. A fact sheet listing such useful information as store and bank hours, national holidays, and the addresses of U.S. and Canadian consulates.

2. An in-depth introduction to the country written from a cyclist's perspective, with information about the country and its people, as well as local foods, roads, maps, transporting your bike within the country, and the best times to travel.

3. For each country we have selected routes that combine the most interesting attractions of the country with the best and least congested cycling conditions.

4. Each of the seventeen routes or itineraries follows the same format. An introduction to the route gives an overview of the area traveled through and describes general points of interest, the terrain, and the degree of difficulty. The best maps for cycling the route are also listed.

5. In "Looking Out Over the Handlebars" we take you over the route itself with detailed references to specific landmarks and which roads to follow. Where bicycle paths run adjacent to numbered routes, we have listed the numbered routes for ease in navigation. Distances between the major points along the route are given, along with the elapsed distances. A detailed map of the route shows all the roads and places referred to in the route description. Although we recommend that you enhance this material by purchasing local maps, this section has been designed so that it can be used to navigate by.

6. A section on sights and accommodations parallels the route description, offering a description of the main points of interest along the way. For each place mentioned, suggestions are given for specific hotels, pensions, hostels, and campgrounds. Should you care to make reservations or request more detailed information, we have furnished addresses and telephone numbers. Where the postal code is the same, it is only listed with the first address. The prices quoted are given in local currencies reflecting the costs and exchange rates that were in effect during the summer of 1986. Obviously these will change with inflation and fluctuations in the international currency exchange rates. In some cases a stronger dollar and low inflation rate could mean lower prices. If that sounds like wishful thinking it probably is; but having lived in Europe for the past twelve years, we've gone through this cycle several times and have actually experienced seeing prices getting lower. In any case, these figures will give you a good feeling for the relationship between different modes of travel.

You will find that the material for each route is quite comprehensive. The idea behind using this format was to provide a reference that could be used on the spot for background information, navigation, and for finding accommodations. It's not feasible when touring by bike to carry a library of travel and guidebooks. As you cycle these routes you will find that local tourist offices will be able to furnish a wealth of supplementary material to fill in any gaps we may have left.

Although each of these routes when followed as written will provide a wonderful European cycling experience, they need not be rigidly adhered to. In fact, one of the major problems about furnishing itineraries is the tendency for people to feel obligated to follow them to the letter. If you have just a limited time, you will find that these routes are ideal for a two-week or three-week vacation. If you have some additional time, try to branch out and follow some of the suggestions given regarding additional places to cycle. In any case, we're sure that you will find cycling in Europe to be an exciting and enriching experience. Happy cycling!

BIKING THROUGH EUROPE

BICYCLES AND EQUIPMENT

The one thing that you cannot do without on a European cycling tour is, of course, a bicycle. Sounds simple, doesn't it? Well, it used to be. Then a few years ago, the bicycle boom hit America in a big way. Suddenly the streets have become jammed with riders of all ages, sizes, and shapes decked out in everything from old fashioned "sweats" and tennis shoes to imported cycling outfits and the latest in cycle binding shoes. And these cyclists are riding an absolutely mind-boggling range of styles and types of bicycles.

What to Look for
in a Bicycle

One of the questions we are most frequently asked is, "What kind of bike is best for a European tour?" Actually, there is nothing special that a bike has to have for European touring. If you have a bike and have used it for touring in the States, there is no reason why you can't take it along for a European tour. The only thing to keep in mind is that, with the exception of Great Britain and Ireland, all of Europe is on the metric system, which makes it difficult to obtain nonmetric spare parts and tires on the continent.

In many ways, the purchase of a bike is very much akin to buying a car. While there are tangible considerations, such as performance, technical features, type of driving done, and economics, personal preference also plays a big role.

When choosing a bike, try to keep in mind the purpose for which the bike will be used. Typically a European cycle tour involves, at least to some extent, carrying a heavy load; traveling over some stretches of bad roads including cobblestones, ruts, and potholes; sitting in the saddle for hours; and rain. No matter what kind of bicycle you choose, the following points are particularly important to consider when touring.

1. Heavy loads require sturdy brakes. Cantilever-style brakes have greater stopping power and a more positive feel than the more commonly used caliper-type brakes – although both will serve well when properly adjusted.

2. Sealed hub bearings are important to keep out destructive dirt and water.

3. Drop handlebars have the advantage of offering several riding positions, which helps to minimize fatigue. With your hands placed on the lowest point on the bars, you are most favorably positioned for achieving maximum power when tackling steep hills. This position also offers the least amount of wind resistance on steep descents and when bucking strong headwinds. Flat handlebars force you to sit in a more upright position, which gives slightly better visibility, but it is a less efficient riding position. Your handlebars should be as wide as your shoulders. For additional comfort, you can add foam-padded sleeves to drop handlebars.

4. Pick a saddle that is comfortable since you will be spending a lot of time in close contact with it. The most practical saddles are those of leather-covered foam. Solid leather saddles can be quite comfortable, but they require a long breaking-in period, while those covered with plastic are non-absorbent and will not adapt well to your form. Avoid the narrow racing saddles, which are uncomfortable on long rides. However tempting the idea of having springs under your saddle may appear, resist the temptation as they will reduce your pedaling efficiency and not appreciably increase your comfort.

5. Toe clips and straps hold your feet on the pedals and greatly increase pedaling efficiency.

6. Fenders on a bike may not project a sexy racing image but will be a welcome addition when you ride in the rain.

7. Lights should be carried even if you don't plan to ride at night. Plans often change, and you can easily find yourself out on the road after dark – a dangerous situation without a light. A powerful generator light with a halogen bulb and a red taillight is an excellent investment. Front and rear lights are required in all European countries for cycling after dark. Although opinions vary, we prefer using a generator light over a battery type, even though riding with a generator light on increases the drag on the tire. The drag is minimal and using a generator light will keep you from having to lug around the extra weight of a sufficiently powered battery light or of finding that your batteries are weak just when you need the light most. A disadvantage of a generator light is the fact that when you stop pedaling the light also stops. When loading up the bike, be sure your bags do not cover up the rear light.

8. A kickstand is a handy addition, although it's often difficult to balance a heavily loaded bike. After having our cycles keel over like bowling pins several times, we usually wind up leaning them on whatever is handy.

9. Always carry a tire pump and be sure that the head on the pump is compatible with the valves on your tires. Most European countries use the Presta brand screw-type valve, while the Schrader brand auto tire valve is more common in the U.S. and Britain.

10. With respect to repairs, as a practical matter, if your bike is in good condition and has new tires, the odds are in your favor that on a three-week or four-week trip, the worst that will happen will be a flat tire, and you will most likely escape even that minor inconvenience. However, flat tires can occur at any time or place. Whenever you tour it is always a good idea to carry a tube repair kit and the tools necessary to repair a flat. If you plan to tour extensively, we recommend that you equip your bike with the commonly found European size 700 series tires. If most of your touring is going to be in Great Britain, then stick with the U.S. twenty-six-inch or twenty-seven-inch tires.

Types of Bicycles

The three most popular types of bicycles available on the market are touring bikes, racing bikes, and all-terrain or mountain bikes. Although there are the inevitable hybrids and subclassifications, such as mountain bikes with touring gears and fenders, we will confine our discussion to the three main types.

TOURING BIKES

A good touring bike needs to be able to do one thing better than any other type of bike and that is carry a lot of weight, including the rider, efficiently and comfortably over long distances. Starting with that premise in mind, a touring bike is designed to deliver a soft stable ride, with good cornering and hill climbing performance. Technically this translates into a long wheel base, shallow frame angles, and a long fork rake. This design will minimize fatigue caused by road shock and provide for optimal steering control, even when the bike is heavily ladened with touring gear.

Try to avoid a bike that is too heavy. If possible, the weight of the unloaded bike should not exceed thirty pounds. In most cases, this will be a reflection of the amount of money you are willing to spend. The lighter the bike, the greater the cost.

For touring purposes, wide high-pressure tires mounted on heavy-duty wheels provide stability on poorly maintained streets and cobblestone roads, as well as help to avoid road shocks.

For climbing hills while carrying a heavy load, the low gearing with large intervals between gears that is found on touring bikes makes it possible to climb most hills without getting off the saddle, and provides the wide range of gears necessary to cope with the variety of terrain encountered while touring. In our opinion, a good solid touring bike is the best choice for European touring.

RACING BIKES

Lightweight racing bikes typically have a short wheel base with steep frame angles, high gearing, and small intervals between the gears. The result is a fast, responsive machine well-suited for road racing – and poorly suited for extensive touring. The high gearing makes it difficult to pedal up steep hills, while the short wheel base and stiff frame make the bike difficult to handle, especially when heavily loaded. The shock from every irregularity in the road is transmitted directly by the stiff frame to the rider, which results in an uncomfortable ride. The fragile aluminum wheels commonly found on racing bikes are easily bent, and while thin high-pressure racing tires offer minimal rolling resistance, they produce a jarring ride, have poor traction on loose and wet surfaces, and are easily damaged. This type of bike is best suited for riders in good physical condition who do most of their cycling on roads with smooth surfaces. Using a racing bike on an extensive European tour is a bit like taking a finely tuned Porsche on an off-road tour.

TANDEM BICYCLES

Bicycles built for two sound romantic, but on a long trip they are probably not worth the hassle. In addition to such tour spoilers as the question of who gets the bike if you split up, or what do you do if your partner isn't doing his or her share of the pedaling, a tandem bike just doesn't have the luggage carrying capacity of two single bicycles.

ALL-TERRAIN OR MOUNTAIN BIKES

Developed in the hills of Marin County, California, in the early 70s, the mountain or all-terrain bike, often referred to as an ATB, is the cyclist's equivalent of a jeep or Land Rover. A mountain bike will take you places that you would never consider going with a conventional bicycle. These bikes, which have an extra-long wheel base and low frame angles, are designed to provide maximum comfort and durability. The idea is to have the bike, rather than the rider, absorb the shock of the terrain and to provide optimal stability when riding with heavy loads.

Typically, wide straight handlebars are used to allow the rider to sit upright and have better visibility and control. ATBs are equipped with heavy-duty wide-rimmed wheels and tough, knobby tires. Although these tires will make a sixteenth-century cobblestone street seem like a modern freeway and provide excellent traction under the worst of conditions, they do have a high rolling resistance, which will slow you down considerably on regular roads.

If you are not in a hurry and plan to include a lot of off-road riding, then a mountain bike could be a good choice for European touring. We suggest that you fit the bike with drop handlebars, which will give you the option of having several different riding positions to prevent fatigue.

GEARS

Unless you plan to tour in Holland only, with the wind at your back, having a bike with a sufficient range of gears will make the difference between having an enjoyable trip or a very unhappy and frustrating experience with you spending a lot of time walking your bike up hills. The ideal range of gears should allow you to maintain the same cadence (pedal revolutions per minute) over both level and hilly terrain. Although we see a lot of Europeans touring with single-speed and three-speed cycles, we advise using a bike with ten or more speeds to get the most enjoyment out of your trip. More important than the actual number of gears is the range or difference between the lowest and highest gear. In low gear you should be able to pedal your fully loaded bike up steep hills; conversely, in high gear you should be able to pedal during a descent to gain speed for the next incline. The number of gears or speeds refers to how many steps the range between the highest and lowest gear is divided into. A ten-speed system will have a small and large sprocket on the pedal crank and five smaller sprockets on the rear axle to give ten possible combinations. The lowest gear is obtained by using the smallest front sprocket with the largest rear one and the highest gear is reached with the opposite combination.

The device that disengages and moves the chain between sprockets is called a *derailleur*. The better quality bicycles allow you to select from a variety of interchangeable sprockets with different numbers of teeth, thus making it possible to tailor the bike to your individual requirements.

Some of the newer touring bikes now come with a small third front sprocket, the so-called *granny wheel*. This increases the number of gears from ten or twelve to fifteen or eighteen, depending on the number of rear sprockets present. These are excellent for propelling a heavily loaded bike up steep grades. If you plan to do any hill climbing at all, we recommend that your bike be fitted out with a third front sprocket.

For most continental touring, beginners do best with a front sprocket set of twenty-eight, forty-two, and forty-eight teeth respectively. The better your condition, the fewer teeth you will need on the sprockets. The actual gear ratio is determined by a simple formula. Multiply the number of teeth on the front sprocket by the diameter of the wheel and divide the result by the number of teeth on the rear sprocket.

Before we get bogged down any further with formulas and gear ratios, perhaps we should say that there is no substitute for trying before you buy. Check out a friend's cycle or a dealer demonstration model, preferably with a load similar to what you will be carrying, and get the feel of these different gear ratios for yourself.

Buying, Renting, or
⚡══ Shipping Your Bike ══⚡

The days when you could pick up a fine European machine for practically nothing seem to be a thing of the past, although there are still occasional bargains to be found. If you decide to buy in Europe you really have to know the market well and be willing to spend at least a few days of your vacation shopping around. In most instances you will be better off bringing a bike with you. This will also give you the advantage of having the time to get used to the bike and make any necessary adjustments or repairs prior to coming to Europe.

RENTING ABROAD

For anything other than one-day or two-day local excursions, we recommend that you ride your own bike. If the primary purpose of your trip is going to be cycle touring, you will be spending a lot of hours in the saddle and will find it nice to have a cycle that is compatible with your needs. Although rental bicycles are readily available throughout Europe, most of them are heavyweight one-speed or three-speed clunkers. Good quality ten-speed touring bikes for rent are a rarity.

On the other hand, if bike touring is not your main purpose for being in Europe, then renting a bike to do some local exploring for a day or two is a wonderful way to get to know an area better without having the worry of what to do with your bike when you are not riding. The national railroads in many countries have rental cycles available at a large number of train stations, and rental bikes are also found at most of the popular tourist areas. Check with the local tourist offices for details.

SHIPPING A BIKE

Airline policies regarding the shipping of bicycles seem to be in a constant state of flux; however, while such things as the need for cartons or removing handlebars and pedals vary widely between carriers, practically all foreign and domestic airlines will allow you to take your bike along as part of your baggage allowance. Charter airlines tend to be a bit less flexible. The best policy is to check with the carrier before buying your ticket. If you do have to use a carton, you can usually obtain one from a bicycle shop. You can use the dead space in the carton for storing bulky items such as a tent or sleeping bag. In any case, make certain that your name and address are securely fastened to the bicycle frame. If you have a European address be sure to include this also.

Shipping an unaccompanied bicycle overseas in either direction even by boat is an expensive and complicated proposition requiring a customs agent. It is rarely worth the expense and bother.

Accessories

WATER BOTTLE

The only practical way to carry your water or, for that matter, wine is in a plastic bottle mounted on the frame. When you are thirsty, you don't want to stop, dismount, and then rummage through your panniers to dig out a canteen or water bottle. If you plan to do a lot of hot weather cycling, mount two bottles.

COMPASS

A small compass is a very handy gadget to have along not only for off road riding but also for orientation at unmarked crossroads and even, on occasion, for finding your way out of a city.

RACKS AND BAGS

For any type of touring you will need bags to carry your gear and some way to safely and securely attach them to the bicycle. Riding a bicycle with a backpack might seem like a cheap and simple solution to this problem, but it doesn't work out that way. For one thing, it's unsafe and not very comfortable on a long ride. The whole idea when loading a bike is to keep the center of gravity as low as possible, and riding with a pack just doesn't do it.

To attach bags or *panniers*, as the bags that fit on the sides of the wheels are called in bike lingo, you need a sturdy and securely attached rack or carrier. Be sure that you don't skimp when buying a rear rack. It should have two forward extensions that can be fastened to the seat supports and triangular struts for rigidity to prevent the load from shifting from side to side and upsetting the balance of the bike – not a laughing matter when you're barreling down a steep, winding descent.

If you plan to camp, you will also need to carry a tent, sleeping bag, and cooking gear. The best way to increase your carrying capacity short of having a friend follow you in a van is to attach *low riders*. These twin frames are mounted next to the front hub and can accommodate two good sized panniers. The low center of gravity allows you to carry a lot of weight without it disturbing the bike's handling and steering characteristics. One problem we have encountered when cycling in the city with low riders is the tendency for them to get hung up on high curbstones – in city traffic this is something to watch out for. Handlebar bags are great for easy accessibility, but be careful about putting too much weight in them as the steering is easily affected.

The selection of bags is large, ranging from expensive, color-coordinated, matched sets that can be fastened together for ease in transport when removed from the bike, to do-it-yourself collections of leftover odds and ends. Here are a few things to look for when selecting bags:

1. The material should be a sturdy, heavy-duty, well-stitched waterproof nylon. (Waterproof is perhaps the wrong term since in a heavy downpour there does not seem to be any such thing. In any case, the fabric should be "treated" and as water-resistant as possible.)

2. Multipocket bags that allow you to organize and separate your things by category and frequency of use are the most practical for long trips.

3. The bag should have strong straps, preferably with quick-release buckles, for attaching to the frame.

4. When mounting the rear panniers, be certain that you have enough heel clearance for pedaling.

5. When selecting a handlebar bag, choose one with a sturdy, transparent map pocket that is large enough to show a large section of map. A handlebar bag should leave sufficient room between the bag and the handlebars for you to rest your hands on the handlebars while riding.

BIKE TRAILERS

Towing a specially constructed trailer behind your bike can increase the amount of weight you can carry by as much as eighty pounds. However, before you dash off and spend a few hundred dollars for one, remember that you are the sole and only motor that is going to propel all of this extra gear. From the point of view of efficiency, a trailer doesn't make a whole lot of sense. A trailer weighs about twenty-five pounds compared to about eight pounds for a complete set of empty panniers, which means that you are seventeen pounds behind before you even load up.

A trailer does make sense if you intend to tour with a small child. The Cannondale Bugger III which also comes with a water-repellent canopy is the best of those available on the American market. Another good trailer is made by The Burley Design Cooperative in Eugene, Oregon. We have also seen some interesting designs in Denmark. If you intend to tour with a small child, this is the safest and most comfortable way of traveling. For any undertaking as ambitious as a European tour, the child should be at least two years old and well used to riding in the trailer before you leave for Europe.

CYCLE COMPUTERS

Cycle computers are handy little gadgets that provide a wide range of information, including current speed, average speed, maximum speed, total distance, trip distance, elapsed time, actual time, and cadence. Depending on the model, they can be mechanically powered, battery powered, or solar powered. They clip onto the handlebars and look a lot like oversized digital watches. If you can resist the temptation to spend all of your time playing with it, a cycle computer can be a useful addition to your equipment. For European touring, plan to read distances in kilometers (kms).

LOCKS

Bicycle thieves know no national boundaries and bike theft is a problem in Europe, although it is mostly limited to the major cities. Among these cities, Amsterdam has a particularly bad reputation. Although it's not a good idea to be totally complacent about the theft situation, being paranoid to the point of not enjoying your trip won't help much either. Actually, the incidence of bike theft throughout Europe is far lower than in the U.S. Perhaps the best indication of this is the fact that it's hard to find a really good quality bike lock in Europe. Bring a good lock along, use it, and enjoy your trip.

BELL

Be sure to mount a clearly audible bell. It beats having to shout "Watch out!" in several different languages.

RADIO

If you plan to be away from home for a long time, it's often nice to be able to listen to the news in English as well as to local radio programs. Although carrying a radio adds to your weight, it's now possible to get a compact lightweight radio with AM, FM, and a full range of shortwave bands. The Sony ICF-7600 weighs just over one pound and will receive all local stations, as well as shortwave broadcasts, such as the Voice of America, British Broadcasting Co., and many other English language programs. With a set of earphones you can keep the radio in your handlebar bag and listen to the world as you pedal along or use it at night to bring a little life to a dreary hotel room. A Walkman-type radio and cassette player is lighter but will not receive shortwave, and you'll soon tire of listening to the same few cassettes.

Clothes

lthough there is no need to spend large sums of money getting decked out in the latest biking outfits, there are a few simple things that you can do to make your trip a lot more pleasant. Choose clothing with the idea that you will not be able to have the "proper" attire for every occasion. Take along as many multipurpose items as possible. Clothing should be light and easily folded or rolled into as small an area as possible. Stay with easily washable, drip dry items. For comfort while cycling, avoid stiff materials with heavy seams such as denim, which will chafe your skin. Whatever clothing you choose should be durable enough to withstand the strain of hours of pedaling.

One of your best investments will be a comfortable pair of cycling shorts with a chamois or foam insert sewn into the crotch area. These shorts are now manufactured in attractive styles and colors. Long pants should have some stretchability especially in the knee region. Keep a clip or velcro strap handy to secure your pants legs around your ankles to keep your pants from getting greasy.

A hat is essential for riding in the summer heat of the Mediterranean countries and for keeping your head warm and dry in light rain. Whatever style hat you select, it should sit comfortably without blowing away.

Since you will probably have room for just one jacket, the best choice is one made of a breathable, water-resistant fabric, such as Gore-Tex, which will keep you dry in the rain but is breathable enough to keep you from drowning from the inside out due to accumulated perspiration. As a general principal, try to achieve warmth by multiple layers of thin clothing rather than one large bulky sweater or jacket.

A pair of gloves and a headband will go a long way toward making those early morning starts in spring and autumn a lot more comfortable. Padding in the gloves will absorb much of the vibration and road shock from the handlebars.

A pair of comfortable, securely fitting sunglasses to cut glare and help keep insects out of your eyes are essential for summer touring, especially in the southern countries.

Shoes should be comfortable for long periods of pedaling as well as for walking, hiking, and sightseeing. A good choice for all-around shoes are sturdy jogging shoes. Better yet are the specially designed bicycle touring shoes. Avoid cleated cycle shoes and running shoes with knobby soles. The cleats are impractical for walking and knobby soled jogging shoes often get stuck in the toe clips.

Whether you choose to wear a helmet or not is a lot like deciding whether or not to wear an automobile seat belt. If you have an accident you will be the one to suffer the consequences. Although there is growing support from the various biking groups, helmets are not popular in Europe. In fact, when we see cyclists with helmets we immediately address them in English on the assumption that they are American or Canadian. So far we've been right 99 percent of the time and the one exception was a German who had studied in the U.S.

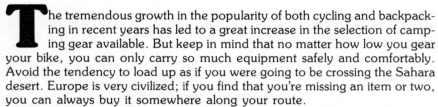

Camping Equipment

The tremendous growth in the popularity of both cycling and backpacking in recent years has led to a great increase in the selection of camping gear available. But keep in mind that no matter how low you gear your bike, you can only carry so much equipment safely and comfortably. Avoid the tendency to load up as if you were going to be crossing the Sahara desert. Europe is very civilized; if you find that you're missing an item or two, you can always buy it somewhere along your route.

If you limit your touring to the Mediterranean coastal regions during the summer months, you can probably get away without taking a tent. But for all practical purposes, including comfort and privacy, even if it doesn't rain, the constant exposure to sun and wind can get very tiring, especially after spending all day in the saddle. If you do any camping at all, you will be happy that you have a tent. With the new lightweight materials, which include fiberglass poles, you can get a one-man tent that weighs about three pounds.

To avoid getting rained on from inside the tent with condensation water, choose a tent with a separate rain fly. If your tent does not have a rain fly, be sure that it at least is well ventilated. For cooking in rainy weather, it's a good idea to have a small vestibule.

Although weight is an important consideration in choosing a tent, don't go to extremes in trying to save on weight. Be sure that you have enough room for yourself and your packs and that the floor material is completely waterproof.

For camping in Europe during the summer, a lightweight sleeping bag will do very nicely. There is no need to spend the extra money and carry the additional weight of a heavy-duty bag that will protect you in below zero weather. Europe in the summer is not that cold. A foam or Ensolite pad provides a comfortable, insulated cushion between you and the ground.

For cooking, use a small one-burner butane stove. They are safer and the fuel is more easily carried on a bike than kerosene. White gas or kerosene is not readily available in Europe, while butane gas cartridges are found everywhere.

Repairs, Spares, and Tools

One of the questions we are often asked is "What do you do if your bike breaks down?" Our immediate answer, which is not as flippant as it might sound, is "The same as we would do in the States – take it to a bike shop!"

Actually the chances of anything major going wrong with your bike are minimal to start with and can be further reduced by making sure that everything is in top condition before your departure. Replace any doubtful parts, such as a worn chain, brake pads, or suspicious looking tires.

Take along a spare tube, patch kit, and, if you plan to doing a lot of cycling especially in rough terrain, bring along an extra tire. Be sure that you know how to remove (and replace) the rear wheel and tire and can fix a flat. Make sure that the bearings are in good shape, and that the wheels are true with no bent spokes. Know how to adjust the brakes and gears.

Should the unlikely occur and you find yourself in need of a repair shop, you will find that with the exception of Eastern Europe and the lesser developed countries, such as Spain, Greece, and Portugal, most towns of any size will have some sort of bike repair facility. Don't be put off by the primitive look of some of these places. It's been our experience that those chaotic establishments where you have to clamber over piles of dismembered cycles, mopeds, and lawnmowers often harbor the most imaginative and resourceful repairmen to be found anywhere.

Get your bike in good shape before you leave, take along a few basics and have a good time. The following items should be taken along on any tour:

Tools
Spare tube (tire optional)
Spare spokes (these can be taped to the frame)
A length of thin-gauge baling wire for emergency repairs
A tube repair kit
A few extra nuts and bolts

Make sure you have a tool that fits every nut bolt and screw. To lighten the load, use multipurpose tools. The baling wire can be carried inside the handlebar tube – simply remove the end cap.

The Art and Science of Packing

One of the most important parts of any cycle tour is not only what you take with you, but how you manage to get everything onto your bike. It's not unusual for first time tourers to return from a trip and find several carefully packed items that they just could not do without lying untouched at the bottom of their panniers. The first step in packing is to carefully and honestly evaluate each item that you want to bring. Be sure that you actually have a valid use for everything that you take along. Do you really need to bring that unread copy of *War and Peace* or your *Trivial Pursuit* game? Keep in mind when making up that list of indispensables that there are very few things which you cannot purchase in Europe.

If you plan to camp, you have a difficult packing task since you must carry shelter, cooking and eating equipment, as well as some food items. Although there is obviously some leeway depending upon the type of bike and your strength, you should try not to exceed carrying a maximum of thirty to thirty-five pounds. If you are traveling with a partner, be sure you don't need-lessly duplicate such items as cooking stoves, tent, or food staples such as sugar, salt, and coffee.

As you go about the business of making up your packing checklist, you will soon discover that there will be little difference in what you will need for a two-week tour and one that lasts for several months. We have included in the appendix a list of items to consider packing.

When you pack, distribute the weight evenly among the panniers, taking care to keep the center of gravity as low as possible. Heavy items and things that will be used infrequently, such as spares and tools, go at the bottom. Use the space inside of cooking gear to hold such items as sugar and spices and soap. Frequently used items such as a camera should be readily at hand, pref-erably in the handlebar bag, while a tent and sleeping bag usually fit best at the top of the rear luggage carrier. Store extra clothes as well as dirty laundry in separate plastic bags. In addition to keeping things organized, this will help keep your clothes dry. Last, but not least, make sure that you leave some room for food and drinks as well as other things that you are sure to purchase along the way.

Before you take off, insure that everything is securely attached to the bike. Do a test run at home with your fully packed bike. Make sure that the load is balanced and that you will feel comfortable riding this way for the dura-tion of your trip. Riding a fully loaded bike is an entirely different experience than just buzzing around with a light handlebar bag.

BIKING THROUGH EUROPE

TRIP PLANNING

As you plan your trip, you might want to keep in mind a quote from our favorite travel book: John Steinbeck's *Travels With Charlie in Search of America*. "Once a journey is designed, equipped, and put in process, a new factor enters and takes over. A trip, a safari, an exploration, is an entity, different from all other journeys. It has personality, temperament, individuality, uniqueness. A journey is a person in itself; no two are alike. And all plans, safeguards, policing, and coercion are fruitless. We find after years of struggle that we do not take a trip; a trip takes us." Keeping that in mind, we would like to offer some suggestions for planning a European cycling tour.

However trite it might seem, one of the first things to decide is where you want to travel and what you would like to see. Although Europe's many attractions are concentrated in a relatively small area, it still takes an awful lot of pedaling power to get from Copenhagen to Lisbon. To save yourself hours or possibly days of unnecessary pedaling, try to develop some idea of the things you would like to see and look over a planning map to get a sense of where these places are in relation to each other. In sorting out where you would like to go, give some thought to just what kind of experience it is you are looking for. Obviously if your main focus is on museums and culture, your itinerary will look a lot different than if your primary reason for going to Europe is to climb mountain passes or to check out some beaches. If yours is to be a city-oriented tour, unless you are going to tour such bicycle friendly cities as Copenhagen, Amsterdam, and Munich, it would be best to plan to store your bike while touring the city and use the excellent public transportation that is found in the major European cities. Most hotels and hostels have places where you can safely leave a bicycle. You can also store your bike for a minimal charge at most railroad stations.

One of the biggest hassles of touring is cycling in and out of a large unfamiliar city. In most cases you will save a lot of time and aggravation by hopping on a train for the last few kilometers into the city and for the few kilometers to the first small town on your route on the way out of the city. This is particularly true in such bicycle unfriendly cities as London, Athens, and Rome.

An important reason for having some idea of which countries you intend to visit is the fact that it is necessary to have a visa to enter some countries. With the exception of France, which just recently introduced a visa requirement on a trial basis, no other western European countries require a visa. Visas are, however, required for all of the Eastern European countries, although some countries, such as Yugoslavia, will issue one at the border. Check for the current requirements with the consulates or national tourist offices of the countries you plan to visit.

The various national tourist offices are one of the best sources of information and can provide a wealth of interesting free material to help you decide where to travel. (For your convenience we have included a list of the national tourist offices in the U.S. in the Appendix.) Once you are in Europe you will find tourist information offices at practically every place that you visit. In addition to providing information on what to see in their region, most offices will also assist in finding accommodations. Many of these offices can also furnish interesting cycling itineraries and maps. The few minutes spent seeking out the local tourist office upon arrival in a new town will be time well spent. These local tourist offices are an especially important source of information for cycle tourers who can't very well carry around a library of travel guidebooks.

MAPS AND ROUTE PLANNING

In the course of our travels we have met cyclists traveling with just about every type of map imaginable, ranging from a large-scale overall map of Europe that was good for showing little more then the fact that Rome was somewhere in Italy and that Great Britain is surrounded by water, to detailed hiking maps that show everything but the cows in the fields. Obviously there has to be a happy medium.

If you use a large-scale map that shows only the heavily traveled main highways, you will be missing out on many of the joys to be found on Europe's vast network of delightful secondary roads. We recently met an American biker in Garmisch-Partenkirchen, in the heart of the Bavarian alps, who was looking all over town for King

Ludwig's Neuschwanstein Castle, the so-called Disneyland castle, one of the finest castles in Europe. On his large-scale map, there was some lettering indicating that Neuschwanstein was somewhere in the vicinity of Garmisch. In fact, Neuschwanstein is just outside of the town of Füssen, some forty hilly kilometers back in the direction that he had just come from. Rather then pedal the extra eighty kilometers to the castle and back, our cyclist friend wound up just buying a postcard with a picture of Neuschwanstein to send to the folks back home. We wondered how many other "Neuschwansteins" he had missed out on by not traveling with a suitable map.

While a detailed map is invaluable in finding your way around the countryside and for avoiding the heavily trafficked main roads, watch out for too much of a good thing! It's easy to get so entranced using such a detailed map that you never see the countryside you are pedaling through. Detailed maps which have you riding across the folded page in just a few minutes can cost $3 or $4 apiece. On a long tour you can find yourself spending several hundred dollars just for maps.

We have had the best experience touring with maps that have a scale of 1:100,000 in areas that we are not familiar with and maps with a scale of 1:200,000 where we have a good feeling for the area.

At this point, a few words about map scales are in order. With the exception of Great Britain where maps are marked in both miles and kilometers, European maps show distances in kilometers. A scale of 1:100,000 indicates that one unit of measure on the map represents 1/100,000th of the actual distance. On a scale of 1:200,000, one centimeter is equal to two kilometers of distance and so forth. The larger the second number, the greater the area represented. The Michelin map #920, which shows all of Europe on a scale of 1:3,000,000 is suitable for planning purposes but is not nearly detailed enough for use on the road.

Michelin maps are available for most but not all of the European countries. Some of these maps are regional and show several countries, while others, such as the Benelux and Swiss series, show sections of individual countries on a scale of 1:200,000. These are the most detailed maps in the Michelin series. For planning purposes the Michelin 900 series of regional maps are excellent. Although it is difficult to find European road maps outside of Europe, some of the larger bookstores in the U.S. and Canada stock the more popular ones. If you can't locate what you are looking for locally, try ordering by mail from **Michelin Guides and Maps** (P.O. Box 5022, New Hyde Park, NY 11042) or the **Banana Republic Travel Bookstore** (P.O. Box 7737, San Francisco, CA 94120; Tel: [800] 772-9977). **Stanfords International Map Centre** (12-14 Long Acre, Covent Garden, London WC2E 9LP, England; Tel: [01] 83 61 321) has one of the best selections of European road maps that is available anywhere. They also have an efficient mail order department.

During the course of a long trip you will find that you will soon accumulate a space-consuming collection of local maps which represent a sizable investment. Rather than just tossing them away when you are done with them, mail them back home. They make great souvenirs and will be invaluable in planning that inevitable next trip.

Detailed maps are best purchased in Europe and, in fact, are often only available in the regions which they cover. The more detailed maps can provide a wealth of useful information and include such features as inclines, scenic routes, and land contours, as well as designating various types of terrain, such as forests and marshes.

Maps can be helpful when choosing the most level routes. Roads that run alongside rivers and railroad tracks are usually devoid of steep grades, as are the roads that run along the crests of ridges. Roads that are more or less perpendicular to rivers tend to rise steeply from the riverbanks.

Once you have decided upon a route, trace it out with a magic marker on the map that you will actually be traveling with. This will save much time and aggravation when you stop at those inevitable crossroads to decide which way to go next.

HOW MANY MILES PER DAY?

When planning a tour it's difficult to avoid having to make at least some estimate of the distances you will be traveling both on an overall and daily basis. If you've already done some bicycle touring, you have no doubt developed a feeling for what constitutes a good day's ride. But if you don't want to miss much of the charm and romance of touring in Europe, it will probably be necessary to cut back on your stateside riding averages. It doesn't make a whole lot of sense to spend the time and money going to Europe only to wind up spending most of your time barreling head down through the countryside to return home with memories of little more than the sight of the top of your front tire spinning along before your eyes.

The distance a person travels when touring is such an individual matter that we hesitate to even raise the subject. Once we see something in print we all seem to have this compulsion to achieve the proscribed standard. However, whenever we get together with other cyclists and start talking about touring, the conversation inevitably gets around to the subject of what constitutes a "good day's cycling." The distance that anyone covers on a given day is influenced by a number of different factors including the terrain, the type of road surface, weather conditions, what there is to see and do along the way, the rider's physical condition and, last, but not least, the rider's mood on that particular day.

Many cyclists seem to measure the "success" of a particular tour in terms of miles covered, as if to say that somehow a person who averages 100 miles per day is having a "better" trip than someone who might be averaging 20 or 30 miles a day. It is very tempting to look at a planning map of Europe where distances between major destinations look deceivingly short and lay out an ambitious tour that has you pedaling the bicyclist's equivalent of that classic travel spoof "If today is Tuesday this must be Belgium." In planning the distance you intend to cover, keep in mind that if you are camping you will need to allocate a certain amount of time to find a suitable campsite, to set up, and take down your tent, and to repack and load your bike. Locating a hotel or hostel can also be a time-consuming business, not something that you want to do at the end of an exhausting day of pedaling. You will also want to set aside time for shopping for food and souvenirs. Whether you eat out in restaurants or prepare your own food, the mere act of consuming three or more meals per day will also take a good-sized chunk out of the time available for actual pedaling. In short, there are many things in the course of a day that will occupy your time besides just pushing pedals.

To give you some yardstick by which to start your planning, we will use ourselves as examples. We are forty and fifty years old respectively, reasonably active, in good health, and are able to play several sets of tennis or jog a few miles without becoming totally exhausted. When we travel with our bikes we find that 30 miles (48 kilometers) per day is a nice, comfortable touring average that allows us time for sightseeing, eating out, picnicking, and occasionally just doing nothing. Hilly terrain, long stretches of cobblestones or poorly surfaced roads, bad weather or a particularly enticing menu at an inviting *auberge* or country inn will easily drop that average.

If you are a newcomer to cycling and are not in especially good shape, you will probably find that 15 to 20 miles per day will be a comfortable average to maintain. If you are in good physical condition and are more concerned with covering distance than sightseeing and visiting cities, you will find 60 (97 kilometers) to 75 (121 kilometers) miles per day to be a comfortable pace. Once again, these numbers are just rough approximations to be used as a guide for planning purposes.

If you are not used to cycling, you will get a lot more enjoyment from your trip if you spend some time before your departure conditioning your cycling muscles and getting your body used to spending several hours at a stretch in the saddle.

When to Go

After you've figured out where you would like to go, it's time to consider when. For many the idea of studying weather patterns and trying to determine just when a particular area is least likely to be crowded so as to arrive at that optimal moment when the sun is shining brightly and there is not another tourist in sight is an impossible dream because of school or work schedules. Although there are "normal" prevailing weather patterns, there often seem to be as many exceptions as there are norms. There are, however, a few things to keep in mind with regard to European weather and seasons.

With the exception of the Mediterranean coastal regions, Portugal, and the interior of Spain, you can and should expect rain during the summer months in the central and northern parts of Europe. Usually the greener the surroundings, the greater the chances of rain. If you plan to climb the high alpine passes, your best bet for having good weather is in July and August, although an occasional summer storm can bring snow to the higher elevations even in August. Before starting your climb, check with the people in the nearest village; usually they have a good feeling for the local weather conditions. In June and September, the traffic on the mountain roads is considerably lighter; however, the chances of hitting a spell of cold wet weather also increase considerably. September is probably the best month for finding the often sought after combination of light traffic and pleasant weather. Although most countries now stagger their school vacations, July and August remain Europe's busiest vacation months. This is the time when beaches throughout southern Europe are packed elbow to elbow with sun-starved northern and central Europeans. Roads are jammed, the sun is blistering hot, and facilities such as campgrounds, hostels, and restaurants are overtaxed.

With so much of the population of northern and central Europe vacationing on the beaches lining the Mediterranean, you can tour the northern and central regions in relative peace and quiet, although there are enough locals and tourists from other countries to keep you from getting lonesome.

About the only places worth cycling in the winter are the coastal regions of southern Spain and Portugal's Algarve province. The climate in this region is very similar to that of southern California. Although you might find the water a bit chilly for swimming, the beaches will be pleasantly uncrowded. This off-season touring will also give you the opportunity to enjoy these lovely areas and the local people at their best.

Traveling Alone, With a Friend, or With a Group

Whether you travel alone, with a friend, or in a group is a very personal decision. There are advantages and disadvantages to each. A person traveling alone has a much greater chance of making friends among the local people, especially those of the opposite sex. If you travel solo, you will not have anyone to share your experiences with in your own language, so you are more likely to make the effort to overcome the language and cultural barriers that so often inhibit travelers from establishing contacts. On the other hand, as a solo traveler, you will experience long periods of solitude and will have to come to grips with occasional bouts of loneliness.

A European cycle tour can be a wonderful family undertaking. Start in one of the countries that has an extensive network of cycle trails so that you won't have to worry about the children riding in traffic. Either Holland or Denmark would be ideal for a first-time family cycling trip. The combination of safe riding conditions and a wealth of attractions ranging from the world-famous museums of Amsterdam to such child pleasers as Copenhagen's fabulous Tivoli and Jutland's Legoland make either of these easy riding countries a natural starting point for a family tour of Europe.

We are often asked what age a child should be for a safe and enjoyable European cycle tour. The answer depends to a great deal on the child and on the attitude of the parents. Young children from the ages of two through five can ride with comfort and safety in a bike trailer, while children from about the age of ten and above should have enough road savvy and stamina to keep up with mom and dad on their own bikes, provided they are not loaded down too heavily. Before embarking upon an ambitious European tour, it is a good idea to take a few lengthy shakedown runs with the entire crew. It makes a lot more sense to find out in your own neighborhood that Johnny isn't quite ready for long sessions in the saddle than it does when you're on the road somewhere between Copenhagen and Amsterdam.

Based on our own experience as well as the impressions we've gathered from talking with other cyclists, there seems to be a general consensus that with the exception of family excursions and organized group tours, two seems to be the magic number. Any more than two people riding together usually leads to problems with people eventually splitting off on their own.

ORGANIZED GROUP TOURS

If you are a bit uncertain about venturing off on your own, you might want to consider taking part in one of the organized cycling tours that are available from a number of U.S. and European based organizations. There are many variations on this theme, ranging from simple guided tours with overnights at youth hostels and campgrounds to luxury tours with stays in elegant chateaux and gourmet meals included. Many tours feature a so-called "sag wagon," which is a van or mini-bus that transports your luggage from hotel to hotel. Should you want to sit out a particular stretch, most tour operators will allow you to ride in the bus. This way of traveling allows you to enjoy touring with a lightly packed bike while still having a full wardrobe wherever you stay. Most tours also include the use of a good quality ten-speed or twelve-speed touring bike and provide for repairs along the way.

The more that you are pampered, the more you can expect to pay. Top of the line tours cost from $150 to $175 per person per day, not including air fare. If you are only able to get away for a short time, a ten-day or two-week tour can serve as a great introduction to European cycling. If you have the time and inclination to make the arrangements yourself and are willing to do without some luxuries such as a sag wagon, you can duplicate most of these tours for about half of the cost.

Although we have never personally taken such a tour, we have on many occasions met up with a variety of cycle tour groups during the course of our travels. In nearly every case participants and guides were enthusiastic and were having a great time. Here is a sampling of just a few of the many tours that are available.

Bicycle France Ltd.
2104 Glenarm Place
Denver, CO 80205
Tel: [303] 296-6972

Offers luxury, gourmet oriented tours through several of France's best cycling regions. Sag wagon and twelve-speed Peugeot cycles furnished.

Ultimate Country Cycling Tours
30 Cedar Avenue
Pointe Claire
Quebec, Canada H9S 4Y1
Tel: [514] 697-9496

A small outfit run by two university professors offering comfortable tours in France. Support vehicle and rental cycles available.

Seven Seas Travel
525 North Michigan Street
South Bend, IN 46601

Runs tours for cycle racers and tourers in Germany and France. Transportation between cycling stretches by a bus that tows a bike trailer. You must furnish your own equipment.

Butterfield & Robinson
70 Bond Street
Toronto, Canada M5B 1X3
Tel: [416] 864-1354

An experienced, well-organized company offering month-long grand tours for students ages sixteen to twenty-one and luxury oriented nine-day adult tours in France, Italy, England, Germany, and Spain. Twelve-speed bikes are provided or you can use your own.

Freewheel Experience
R.D. #1, Box 397
Mohawk, NY 13407
Tel: [315] 866-7842

Specializes in low-cost trips for students. Bicycles are not furnished.

Upper Canada Holidays
Suite 2209
80 St. Clair Avenue East
Toronto, Canada M4T 1N6
Tel: [416] 920-0159

Offers guided or "go-on-your-own" tours from from their own "bike bases" in Switzerland and southern France.

Europeds
Sinex Avenue
Pacific Grove, CA 93950
Tel: [408] 372-1173
 Organizes several six-day to twenty-two-day tours in France and Switzerland. Twelve-speed Peugeot rental bikes are available or you can use your own cycle.

The Cyclists' Touring Club
Cotterell House
69 Meadow
Godalming, Surrey GU7 3HS
England
 An active British-based organization that sponsors a number of reasonably priced tours in England as well as the rest of Europe.

The International Bicycle Touring Society (IBTS)
2115 Passeo Dorado
La Jolla, CA 92037
Tel: [619] 459-8775
 A non-profit organization that sponsors low-cost tours utilizing a sag wagon. Participants must be over twenty-one.

The League of American Wheelmen
Bicycle (USA)
Suite 209
6707 Whitstone Road
Baltimore, MD 21207
Tel: [301] 944-3399
 Publishes an annually updated list of domestic and European bicycle tours.

Travel within *Europe*

TRAINS

For getting from your arrival city to the start of your actual tour, for travel between touring areas, or for bypassing large cities and uninteresting regions, you will find a convenient and efficient transportation network at your disposal. In most countries you can take your bike with you on the train for little or no extra cost, or send it unaccompanied as freight. When shipping a bike as freight in most countries, allow two to three days for it to reach destinations within the country and as long as two weeks to some of the other European countries. Unless you have some compelling reason for shipping your bike separately, it is best to travel on the same train. When a journey requires that you transfer trains, rather than shipping the bike straight through, you can eliminate the chances of

the bike winding up on a different train and possibly even at a different destination if you take care of all of the transfers yourself. Be sure that your name, address, and destination are clearly marked and securely fastened to the frame. Arrive at the station early enough to check out the loading and shipping procedures, which often vary within the same country. If you are going to be loading the bike yourself, find out where the baggage car will be stopping. Trains often only stop for a minute or two and sometimes for even shorter periods. Knowing the location of the baggage car will save you from having to frantically sprint from one end of the platform to the other.
 Although it's a bit of a hassle and probably not absolutely necessary, we always remove all of our bags when loading the bikes ourselves, and when shipping our bikes unaccompanied, we also remove such tempting items as pumps and water bottles. If the conductor will allow it, it's also a good

idea to lock the bike to the side of the baggage car. This will keep the bike from falling, and on trains that make frequent stops, you won't have to worry about someone making off with the bike while you happen to be looking the other way.

Although in some countries the shipping of bikes by trains seems a bit haphazard (which it sometimes is), it's been our experience and the general consensus of most of the travelers we have met that in spite of this, the odds are overwhelmingly in your favor that you will be reunited with your bike at the intended time and place.

FERRIES

In certain parts of Europe, travel by ferry is a way of life. In fact, if you travel in Denmark or through the Norwegian fjord country, you will find it difficult to avoid taking at least one ferry ride. Ferries also provide a comfortable and relaxing way to travel between countries. On some of the longer routes, these boats, which contain movie theaters, discos, and elaborate restaurants, are more like luxury cruise ships than what we commonly think of as a ferry boats.

The cost of transporting a bike is minimal and the loading procedure simple. At the direction of the loading crew just pedal down the ramp onto the car deck. Be certain to securely fasten the bike to a rail or stanchion to prevent damage in rough seas. Some crossings such as the trip from Puttgarden, Germany, to Rødby, Denmark, are just short hops that last an hour or less while others, such as the route across the North Sea connecting Harwich, England, with the German port of Hamburg, or the pleasant Baltic crossing from Stockholm, Sweden, to Turku, Finland, can run twelve to twenty hours or longer.

When traveling in southern Europe you can save a lot of time and hundreds of miles of pedaling by taking the ferry from Italy to Yugoslavia or by going directly to Greece from Italy. For hopping around the crowded Greek islands during the busy summer months, the bike and ferry provide a great combination.

AUTOMOBILES AND CAMPERS

If you are planning to camp with either an automobile and tent or with a camper or motor home, it is still a good idea to take your bike along. You will find that wherever you stop, it will provide excellent local transportation for shopping trips, for touring the area around your campsite, and for getting from campground to town. You will see things from an entirely different perspective when pedaling around a region rather than driving through it. We always enjoy taking our bikes with us on camping trips.

Most camper and automobile rental firms will be able to provide a bicycle rack. Just be sure to specify this when making the rental arrangements. If you are buying a camper or car for delivery in Europe, it is no problem to buy a good rack. We have found the best selection in Germany, Holland, and Denmark.

BUSES

In some countries, such as Austria and Switzerland, it is possible to transport your bike on the extensive post bus network, which provides a useful alternative to the train especially in the alpine regions. In most other countries and when traveling between countries, taking a bicycle on the bus usually proves to be a difficult if not impossible undertaking. On long trips plan to use the train.

Accommodations

In planning your trip, it is a good idea to give some thought as to where you will sleep each night. In many cases how much you can afford to spend will dictate your choices.

For a lot of people it's more important to travel in style for a short period of time, than to skimp and buy more travel time with the savings. The differences can be substantial. For example, by camping and cooking your own meals you can easily travel for a week or longer on what you would spend for a single day and night staying in a quality hotel and eating in plush restaurants.

Although we are always reluctant to give prices in dollars since fluctuations in exchange rates and inflation can quickly change these, they are useful in getting a ball park figure to use for planning purposes. Even though the actual prices may change, the relationships between the different modes of travel will stay constant. For example, it will always be cheaper to camp then to stay at hotels. Just to give some rough approximation of costs, we will list the cost of traveling for two persons through the same region for a two week period using three different styles of traveling. We have chosen France for our example because it is the country that is probably most popular with American cyclists. Plan to spend a bit more in the northern European countries and slightly less in Spain, Portugal, Italy, and Greece. The prices we cite are from summer 1986, at which time $1.00 was equal to about 6.5 French francs.

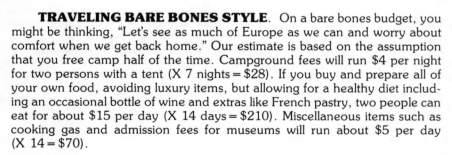

TRAVELING BARE BONES STYLE. On a bare bones budget, you might be thinking, "Let's see as much of Europe as we can and worry about comfort when we get back home." Our estimate is based on the assumption that you free camp half of the time. Campground fees will run $4 per night for two persons with a tent (X 7 nights = $28). If you buy and prepare all of your own food, avoiding luxury items, but allowing for a healthy diet including an occasional bottle of wine and extras like French pastry, two people can eat for about $15 per day (X 14 days = $210). Miscellaneous items such as cooking gas and admission fees for museums will run about $5 per day (X 14 = $70).

Totals for two people for two weeks:

Campground Fees	$28
Food	$210
Miscellaneous	$70
Total:	$308
Average cost per person per day:	$11

TRAVELING BUDGET CLASS. "We have to watch what we spend, but we're not ready to sleep on the ground. We want to enjoy Europe's small restaurants and cafés and we don't mind sharing a bath in a hotel or pension to save money." Two people sharing a room at budget-class hotels (one and two stars) and pensions, which provide clean, comfortable and often very charming accommodations, will pay about $20 per night. On the assumption that you eat breakfast, which is usually not included in French hotel prices, and either lunch or dinner in a modest but respectable restaurant, and picnic for the other meal two persons can eat well and get a good sampling of regional French cuisine for about $45 per day. Assuming that you are going to be a little more liberal with your spending on sightseeing and miscellaneous items than our campers, figure on $10 per day for miscellaneous items.

Totals for two people for two weeks:

Lodging	$280
Food	$630
Miscellaneous	$140
Total:	$1,050
Average cost per person per day:	$38

TRAVELING IN COMFORT. "We earn pretty good money and when we travel we like to sample the best of what a region has to offer. Although we don't have to every night, we do enjoy staying in a chateau or luxury hotel and eating in fine restaurants. Sharing baths in budget hotels is not for us." If you seek out special hotels and chateaux based on their charm and comfort rather than price, but also occasionally stay at a comfortable two-star hotel (with private bath), plan to spend about $55 per night. If you eat all of your meals out, alternating between good restaurants and sometimes great restaurants, and include an afternoon coffee and snack in your routine, you had better plan to do a lot of pedaling or plan on a drastic weight reduction regime when you return home. In any case, figure on spending about $90 per day. For miscellaneous items, including souvenirs that you might like to ship home, figure about $20 per day.

Totals for two people for two weeks:

Lodging	$770
Food	$1,260
Miscellaneous	$280
Total:	$2,310
Average cost per person per day:	$83

CAMPING

In addition to giving you as close to total independence as exists, carrying your own shelter, preparing your own meals, and traveling under your own power is the cheapest way to tour Europe.

Although it might not always be 100 percent legal, free camping is a great way to save money, and if you are discreet about where you set up your tent, the local authorities will rarely hassle you. Europe is full of lovely beaches, forests, and fields where you can set up a small tent for the night, thus saving your money for stays at official campgrounds when you are visiting cities where it's not practical to free camp. Use the facilities at the official campgrounds for taking showers and doing laundry.

When "free camping," it's a good idea wherever possible to ask permission. If there is no one around to ask, try to set up your tent as inconspicuously as possible. Never set up a tent on a plowed or planted field – a sure way to incur the wrath of the natives. When cooking you will attract less attention if you avoid open fires and use a small camping gas stove instead. On the many occasions that we've asked for permission to camp on private property, we've never been turned down. The few times that we've been asked to pay, the amounts asked for have been practically laughable.

Traveling this way, you can get by on surprisingly little money, although the necessity of carrying a tent and cooking gear will insure that you will be carrying a full load. You can keep your food costs to a minimum by purchasing locally made goods and avoiding the expensive imported products. If you plan to do much free camping, you will need to make provisions for carrying a few extra liters of water. Collapsible plastic water containers are best for this purpose.

Of course, just because you are camping doesn't mean that you can't enjoy Europe's fine restaurants and cafés. One night cooking under the stars can be followed the next night by dinner at a fine restaurant. One of the real joys of camping and cycling in Europe is to get up early in the morning, cycle the few kilometers to a little French village, park your bike, and follow your nose to the first enticing *boulangerie*, where you will not be able to resist buying more croissants than you could possibly eat. From there it's on to the *charcuterie* to choose from the mouth-watering assortments of pâtés and cold cuts. Then after a final stop at the cheese shop for another battle with your conscience, it's time to pedal back to the campground with panniers bulging and a well-stimulated appetite to brew up some coffee and enjoy breakfast in the open while contemplating what to do for the rest of the day. That's a lot of what camping and biking in Europe is all about.

One of the great things about camping in Europe is the accessibility of campgrounds. There is just about no place worth visiting that doesn't have at least one nearby campground, and that includes the major cities. Even such metropolitan centers as Paris, Rome, and Munich have campgrounds with good access into the city.

Since campgrounds vary greatly in size and facilities, ranging from small mom-and-pop operations that are little more than a backyard with space for a few campers and tents to huge camping cities accommodating five thousand or more people and providing every conceivable type of amenity including bath tubs, discos, and health spas, it's difficult to speak of a typical European campground. Flush toilets and showers are standard at all Europeans sites. Generally speaking, the more stars a campground has on its sign, the more facilities it will have and the more expensive it will be. Many sites have camp stores, although you will usually pay 10 to 25 percent more for the convenience. An increasing number of sites have installed coin-operated washing machines. Rates, as well as campground regulations, are always posted so you will know in advance what you are getting into.

The whole style of camping in Europe is a bit different from that in the U.S. and Canada. With the exception of a few areas in Scandinavia, wilderness camping doesn't exist. Many Europeans will set up a large two-room or three-room family tent or trailer and spend their entire vacation at one campground, often the same one year after year, developing quite an active social circle along the way.

Even though a number of campgrounds stay open all year, many are seasonal. If you are traveling in the summer, this will not pose any problems; however, when touring in spring and autumn, check with the local tourist authorities for opening and closing times. In our detailed route descriptions, we list campgrounds located at convenient points along each route and include opening and closing dates. These dates will often vary by a few days from year to year, depending on when the weekends fall and sometimes on the whims of the campground operator.

Campground charges are customarily made on a per unit basis; that is, so much per person, per tent, per car, and so on, rather than a flat fee for the use of a campsite. When registering you will be asked to leave your passport or camping carnet at the office. Sometimes when staying for just one night you can avoid this by paying in advance. See the section on Documents in this chapter for details about the international camping carnet.

If you are going to do some serious camping along with your biking, then we must tell you that our two books *The Camper's Companion to Northern Europe* and *The Camper's Companion to Southern Europe* ($13.95 each, plus $1.25 shipping, available from Williamson Publishing, Box 185, Charlotte, VT 05445) are indispensable guides.

YOUTH HOSTELS

The next step up on the accommodations ladder are the youth hostels, which provide inexpensive, basic no-frills facilities, usually in dormitories. Some hostels also provide family accommodations, meals, and cooking facilities. There are more than five thousand hostels in sixty-two countries throughout the world. Hostels, which can be found in such diverse locations as converted ships, castles, and old mansions, are great places for meeting fellow travelers from all over the world.

While youth hostels offer a low-cost alternative to camping and provide a solid roof over your head, they are not to be compared with hotels. In most cases, accommodations are dormitory style with separation of the sexes. Most hostels are closed during the day and have a host of regulations and restrictions. Nearly all hostels require the use of sheet sleeping sacks and do not allow sleeping bags.

A sheet sleep sack is made of bed sheets; its function is protect the mattresses, pillows, and blankets provided by hostels. They can be purchased from the AYH or rented at many hostels. You can make your own by sewing two single sheets together. The official dimensions are seventy inches long by thirty inches wide, with an eighteen-inch-deep pocket to cover the pillow. If you plan to spend a lot of time at hostels, it is best to have your own.

Even though they are called "youth hostels," travelers of all ages are welcome, except at those hostels in the Bavarian section of Germany where travelers who have reached their twenty-seventh birthday are not accepted. Children under five years old are also not allowed, except in family accommodations.

When planning your route, it isn't a good idea to consider visiting only those places that have youth hostels. While there are numerous hostels in Europe, there are not enough in many countries around which to base an entire cycling trip.

In most cases, in order to stay at a IYHF hostel, it is necessary to have a IYHF (International Youth Hostel Federation) membership card. These can be obtained in the U.S. from **American Youth Hostels (AYH)** (National Office, P.O. Box 37613, Washington, D.C. 20013-7613; Tel: [202] 783-6161) or in Canada from the **Canadian Hostelling Association** (Place Vanier, Tower A, 333 River Road, Vanier City, Ottawa, Ontario K1L 8H9; Tel: [613] 746-3844). A junior membership (age seventeen and under) costs $10, a senior membership (age eighteen to fifty-nine) costs $20, and a family membership costs $30. Cards are required for entry to most facilities. It is also possible to obtain an

International Youth Hostel Guest Card at many hostels in Europe. This temporary card, valid throughout Europe, costs the equivalent in local currency of $10 for seniors, $5 for juniors, and $15 for families.

During July and August hostels in the popular tourist regions are usually very crowded and reservations are strongly recommended. The address and telephone numbers of hostels located along the routes we describe are listed under the sights and accommodations section for that route. For a listing of hostels in other parts of Europe, you can obtain the *International Youth Hostel Handbook Volume 1, Europe and the Mediterranean* from the **AYH** travel store (PO Box 37613, Washington, D.C. 20013-7613; Tel: [202] 783-6161). You can also order **Advance Booking Postcards** and **Advance Booking Vouchers** to simplify making reservations. Allow at least six weeks and preferably longer when making reservations by mail. Be sure to enclose an **International Postal Reply Coupon**. These are available from most post offices. Many hostels also accept telephone reservations, which are a lot more practical when you are traveling and don't want to commit yourself to a fixed itinerary so far in advance.

Overnight costs vary with the type of hostel and from country to country and range from a low of $2 to $7 or $8 at the top of the scale.

A youth hostel is known in the French-speaking countries as an *auberge de jeunesse* and in the German-speaking regions as a *Jugendherberge*.

In addition to the official IYHF hostels there are also many inofficial hostels, sleep-ins, and student hotels which offer a wide range of inexpensive accommodations without requiring membership cards and without the curfews and daytime closings found at many IYHF hostels.

HOTELS AND INNS

When it comes to hotel accommodations in Europe, the choices range from scruffy red-light district hotels that rent rooms by the hour to luxurious chateau and castle hotels with a wide range of in between choices. In most countries, although not all, hotels are rated by the government tourist authorities with from one to five stars. Each star indicates additional amenities offered, as well as a higher price. Along the routes which we have chosen we list budget as well as more luxurious accommodations located at convenient intervals along the way. Although the major American hotel chains are well represented, one of the great joys of traveling in Europe is staying at the numerous charming little inns and hotels.

In the budget category, the English **bed and breakfast (B&B)** and the **pensions** found on the continent offer inexpensive accommodations of the type often favored by the Europeans themselves. Such budget-priced rooms usually have a sink with hot and cold running water, while the guests from several rooms share common bathroom and toilet facilities. Many of the older hotels, even some of the more luxurious establishments, offer this arrangement as an alternative to rooms with a private bath and toilet, often at savings of up to 50 percent.

In some cases hotels are less than forthright when it comes to telling you up front about taxes. To avoid unpleasant surprises, ask about additional charges and taxes when checking in.

At most European hotels, a modest continental breakfast of rolls and jelly is included in the room price, while the full English breakfast served at that country's cozy B&B's provides enough fuel to keep you pedaling for most of the rest of the day.

In addition to formal hotels and pensions, most towns with tourist attractions have a number of rooms available in private homes. This is an excellent and inexpensive way to get some insight into how people in other countries live.

Documents

U.S. PASSPORTS

An up-to-date passport is necessary for entering all European countries and for reentry into the U.S. and Canada. Most campgrounds require you to leave your passport when you check in, unless you have a camping carnet. Banks also want to see a passport when you change money or cash traveler's checks.

You can acquire a U.S. passport, valid for ten years (under age eighteen only issued for five years) at any U.S. Passport Agency and at most U.S. post offices, and federal and state courts. The cost is thirty-five dollars. The following items are necessary: 1) proof of U.S. citizenship (previous U.S. passport, birth certificate, or naturalization papers), 2) two identical passport photos, two inches by two inches in size, and 3) identification with your description, photo, and signature, such as a driver's license.

Although a passport can be issued in a few days under extenuating circumstances, it is best to allow at least two months to obtain this document. No passport – no trip!

When you receive your passport make a photocopy of both the information and the photograph pages. Keep this during your travels. It will greatly simplify getting a replacement in the event of loss or theft. If your passport is lost or stolen while you are abroad, notify the local police and the nearest U.S. Consulate or Embassy at once.

Since 1981, family passports are no longer issued. All persons are required to obtain individual passports.

CANADIAN PASSPORTS

Applications for a Canadian passport can be obtained from a passport office, post office, or travel agency. The completed application form, the original copy of your proof of citizenship, two identical photographs (signed in front by you and on the back by your guarantor), and the current fee in cash or certified check can be taken to any one of the eighteen passport offices in Canada. A passport will be issued within three working days. Mailed applications are processed in Ottawa and take considerably longer. The passport is valid for five years.

The Department of External Affairs (Ottawa K1A 0G2) issues a pamphlet on obtaining a passport and a free fact-filled booklet on foreign travel called *Bon Voyage*.

VISAS

With the exception of France, which instituted a visa requirement on a trial basis in 1986, western European countries do not require visas from Americans or Canadians for stays of up to three months. In Portugal, the limit is two months. Obtaining extensions for longer stays is no problem. Border officials rarely even bother to stamp the passports of travelers crossing most western European borders. Custom searches, especially in the summer months, are infrequent.

Visas are required by all Eastern European countries and the Soviet Union. Some Eastern European countries also impose a daily spending minimum. This varies from country to country. Visas for some countries, such as Yugoslavia, can be obtained within a few minutes at the border, while visas for other countries, such as the U.S.S.R., must be obtained in advance at one of their consulates or national tourist agencies. Several weeks or longer may be needed for processing.

Consulates for the Eastern European countries are located in most major North American and European cities. Check with them at least three months in advance to cover contingencies.

If you are planning a trip that will require obtaining several visas, remember that the application process can often take several weeks or longer. In order to avoid being without a passport during this time, you can obtain a second passport to allow you freedom of movement and to provide identification, especially for money changing. This is available from any U.S. Consulate Office. The cost for the additional passport, which is valid for a maximum of one year, is $35 plus a handling fee.

INTERNATIONAL CAMPING CARNET

No one should camp in Europe without an international camping carnet. This valuable document greatly simplifies registering at campgrounds. As part of registerir _____ _____ to leave either a passp _____ tion. the _____ carn _____ carn _____ 716-668-627 pro _____ cau _____ der _____ nly to _____ In No _____ **nal Campers & Hikers** _____ Transit Rd., Buffalo, NY 14221; Tel: [716] 634-5433 or 51 West 22nd Street, Hamilton, Ontario L9C 4N5) and the **American Automobile Association** (AAA) (National Headquarters, 8111 Gatehouse Road, Falls Church, VA 22047; Tel: [703] AAA-6000).

It can also be obtained in Europe from the various automobile clubs, either by joining that club or by being a member of an organization that has a reciprocity agreement with its European counterpart. The following clubs issue camping carnets: in West Germany, the ADAC; in France, the Camping Club International de France; in Great Britain, the Automobile Association and the Camping & Caravanning Club. In each case, a photo is required. The cost varies from $2 to $7. Many European campgrounds grant discounts to holders of the carnet, so it usually pays for itself within a short time.

INTERNATIONAL STUDENT IDENTITY CARD

This card is an excellent investment for students. Holders are eligible for all kinds of discounts, ranging from free museum entry to substantial reductions on many ferry lines. For more information, contact your student union travel office or write to the **Council on International Education Exchange** (CIEE) (205 E. 42nd St., New York, NY 10017 or 236 N. Santa Cruz #314, Los Gatos, CA 95030) or **Canadian Universities Travel Service** (44 St. George St., Toronto, Ontario M5 S2E4).

YOUTH HOSTEL CARD

There may be times when an inexpensive roof over your head will be desirable. A Youth Hostel Card gives you access to over one thousand hostels throughout Europe. A Family Hostel Card is also available. Overnight fees average $7 to $10 per night per person. For further information, write to the **American Youth Hostels** (P.O. Box 37613, Washington, DC 20013-7613; Tel: [202] 783-6161) or the **Canadian Hosteling Association** (333 River Rd., Tower A 3d Floor, Vanier City, Ottawa, Ontario KIL 8H9; Tel: [613] 746-3844).

Money

Despite the fact that in most cases you will have to pay a 1 percent commission to purchase them, traveler's checks provide the majority of tourists with the most convenient way of the handling the monetary aspects of a European biking trip. They are readily convertible into local currency nearly everywhere, although the most favorable exchange rates are usually obtained at banks. Whichever brand of traveler's checks you choose, make sure you keep a separate list of check numbers as well as instructions on replacement procedures. When traveling with others, each person should have a supply of checks so that everyone has access to money in case of an emergency.

Although the use of credit cards in Europe is on the increase, they are not nearly as widespread as in the the U.S. and Canada. While a card, such as the Amex card which allows you to cash personal checks for up to $1,000 every twenty-one days, is handy to have along, you will find that many of the quaint little out-of-the-way country inns and restaurants do not accept credit cards.

Mail

Even if you are away from home for just a short period, receiving mail is a very pleasant experience. The simplest way to receive mail is to use the extensive network of American Express offices. They will keep mail for thirty days at no charge for holders of their traveler's checks. The addresses of American Express offices along the various routes are listed under the individual country headings. For a complete listing of overseas offices, write to **American Express International** (65 Broadway, New York, NY 10006). You can also have your mail sent to any city **c/o Poste Restante** (General Delivery). This can be particularly helpful if you are going to be stopping at towns that don't have American Express offices. In larger cities go to the post office that handles poste restante, usually the main office.

If you know the name and address of a place where you will be staying, you can have your mail sent there. Most hotels, hostels, and campgrounds will hold mail for a reasonable length of time at no charge. In all cases, persons traveling together should have mail addressed jointly so that either person can pick up the mail.

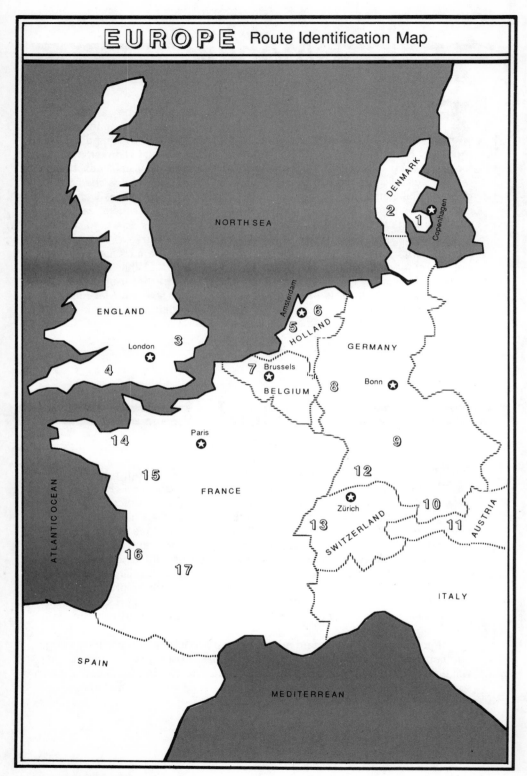

EUROPE Route Identification Map

NORTH SEA

DENMARK

2

1 ★ Copenhagen

ENGLAND

Amsterdam

5 ★ 6

HOLLAND

GERMANY

London ★

3

4

7 Brussels ★

BELGIUM

8

Bonn ★

Paris ★

14

15

9

FRANCE

12

Zürich ★

ATLANTIC OCEAN

13

SWITZERLAND

10

AUSTRIA

11

16

17

ITALY

SPAIN

MEDITERREAN

EUROPE Route Identification Map

1	PAGE 100	DENMARK	Copenhagen and the Islands
2	PAGE 68	DENMARK	Jutland Route
3	PAGE 218	ENGLAND	London and East Anglia
4	PAGE 234	ENGLAND	Through the Heart of England
5	PAGE 252	HOLLAND	Amsterdam and Holland
6	PAGE 266	HOLLAND	Amsterdam and Veluwe
7	PAGE 84	BELGIUM	Brussels and Belgium
8	PAGE 200	GERMANY	Rhine and Moselle Valleys
9	PAGE 184	GERMANY	Castle and Romantic Route
10	PAGE 174	GERMANY	Bavaria Highlights Tour
11	PAGE 52	AUSTRIA	Mountains to Mozart
12	PAGE 292	LAKE CONSTANCE	Switzerland
13	PAGE 280	SWITZERLAND	Zurich to Geneva
14	PAGE 152	FRANCE	Normandy Route
15	PAGE 138	FRANCE	Loire Valley Route
16	PAGE 118	FRANCE	The Wine Country Loop
17	PAGE 128	FRANCE	The Dordogne Route

Riding in Europe

With the exception of something as obvious as the "wrong way" traffic in Great Britain, cycling in Europe is not really very different from riding in the U.S. or Canada. In fact, in most cases, European drivers are more aware of cyclists than their North American counterparts. Here are a few things that you should be aware of when cycling in Europe.

1. Although it is not advisable, you may legally ride side by side (except in Germany) as long as you do not interfere with traffic.

2. Always stay to the right (in Great Britain to the left).

3. Vehicles coming into a traffic circle have the right of way over those vehicles already within the circle, except in Great Britain where the opposite is true. There the approaching vehicle must give way to those already going around the circle.

4. The best approach is to drive defensively and assume that the motorist does not see you or does not care. While this is rarely the case, it's a situation that you don't ever want to test.

5. Riding on the autobahns, motorways, autopistes, and autostradas is prohibited.

6. A round sign with a bicycle on a white field surrounded by a red border means that cycling is not allowed.

7. A round blue sign with a white bicycle in the center indicates the presence of a cycle path whose use is compulsory.

8. Traffic coming from the right has the right of way unless otherwise indicated. The opposite is true in Great Britain.

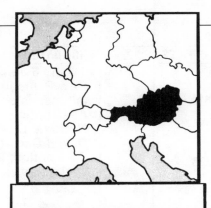

AUSTRIA

POPULATION
7,555,000

RELIGION
90% Roman Catholic

CAPITAL
Vienna (Wien)

CURRENCY
Schilling (S); divided into 100 groschen

OFFICIAL LANGUAGE
German; English is widely spoken, especially in tourist areas

BANKING HOURS
M T W F 0830–1200
        1300–1500
    TH 0800–1230
        1330–1730
Exchange offices at major airports and train stations are open evenings and weekends.

STORE HOURS
M–F 0800–1200
      1400–1800
Sat 0800–1200

EMERGENCY PHONES
Police   *133*
Fire   122
Ambulance 144

TO CALL USA AND CANADA
Dial 001; area code and number

U.S.A. CONSULATES
Giselakai 51
5020 SALZBURG
Tel: [0662] 28 601
Telex: 6333164

Boltzmanngasse 16
1091 VIENNA
Tel: [0222] 31 55 11
Telex: 144634

CANADIAN CONSULATE
Dr. Karl-Lüger Ring 10
1010 VIENNA
Tel: [0222] 63 66 26 or
     [0222] 63 36 91

HOLIDAYS

1 Jan.; 6 Jan.; 1 May; Ascension Day, Pentecost, Corpus Christi (all movable); 15 Aug., Assumption Day; 26 Oct., National Day; 1 Nov., All Saint's Day; 8 Dec., Immaculate Conception; 25 and 26 Dec., Christmas.

MAPS

The best overall map of Austria is the Michelin #426, Austria/Österreich (scale 1:400,000; 1 cm = 4 kms). For cycling purposes, we like the Die General Karte series (scale 1:200,000; 1 cm = 2 kms) published by Mair. The entire country is covered in eight maps. Steep hills are indicated by arrows, elevation contours are shown, and a number of off-road tracks and hiking trails are indicated. The back of the map has useful tourist information (in German only). The legend is in English.

For super detail, the somewhat unwieldy and expensive Wanderkarten series (scale 1:100,000; 1 cm = 1 km) published by Freytag and Berndt covers the country in fifty-two separate sheets. These are primarily hiking maps, best used for local off-road touring. The Kompass Wanderkarten are highly detailed hiking maps on a scale of 1:50,000 (1 cm = .5 kms); they are best for off-road touring over a limited distance.

TRANSPORTATION WITHIN THE COUNTRY

The ÖBB or Austrian National Railway has an extensive network which makes it possible to take your bike to just about any part of the country without having to pedal up a single alp. With a valid ticket you can take your bike on the train with you at a cost of 20 S. Unfortunately, not all trains have baggage cars. We found the system used to indicate which trains carry bicycles confusing – and we speak fluent German. Your best bet is to ask at the station. In most cases you can load and unload the bike yourself. Just to be sure ask permission. Shipped as unaccompanied baggage, the bike can take as long as three days to reach its destination.

In many cases you can also take your bike with you on the excellent postbus system. This is especially useful in reaching remote mountain villages. If the bike fits into the baggage compartment, there is no charge. If you take it on the bus with you, the charge is 3 S for the first 20 kms and 6 S for longer distances. Bikes are not allowed on chair lifts.

BIKING
THROUGH
EUROPE

AUSTRIA

When the allied powers dismantled the old Austro-Hungarian Empire at the end of World War I, they didn't leave very much of the mighty empire that once controlled a huge chunk of central and eastern Europe. But what they did leave, at least from the point of view of tourists, is nothing short of sensational. Austria – even the Austria of the 80s – really does look like the scenery in *The Sound of Music*.

If ever there were a country designed for vacationing, it has to be Austria. With the exception of sandy beaches, which were given up when the Hapsburgs lost control over large portions of the Italian and Yugoslavian coast, the country has everything that a vacationer could hope for: spectacular alpine scenery, picturesque villages with painted houses and onion-domed churches, inviting clear lakes, and two of Europe's most beloved cities – the old Hapsburg capital of Vienna (Wien) and, of course, Salzburg, the *Sound of Music* city. And with some of Europe's finest baroque architecture and a musical heritage that claims such giants as Mozart, Haydn, Schubert, and Bruckner there is plenty to stimulate the senses while resting up for the next high alpine pass.

Even though mountains make up nearly three quarters of the country, there are enough valleys and flatlands to offer enjoyable touring for even the most timid cyclist. Careful use of the country's extensive and efficient rail system will allow you to bypass the nasty stretches. The province of Burgenland, which encompasses the region to the east and south of Vienna, lacks the spectacular mountains of western Austria, but is nevertheless delightful touring country. The infrequently visited area around the Neusiedler See, one of Europe's largest lakes, is dotted with wonderful castles, elegant manor houses, and quaint villages – and it is all flat. On the other hand, if you thrive on gobbling up alps as though they were the proverbial molehills, then save your schillings and forget about the train. There is enough in Austria to keep your pulse pounding above 130 for as long as you like. The country is full of roads that make you think you are pedaling up the alpine version of a coil spring!

One of the nicest things about Austria – besides the fantastic scenery – is the Austrians themselves. Over the years they have perfected the art and science of making their many guests feel right at home in a manner that few countries can match. Although tourism is big business, accounting for a substantial portion of this tiny neutral republic's foreign currency earnings, it is all done with charm and *Gemütlichkeit*. The Viennese, who exude a special charm of their own, have a phrase for it: *Küss die Hand*, which literally translated means "kiss the hand." Perhaps it is best described as being akin to fawning all over you with kindness and service but at the same time still maintaining a certain flair and dignity.

ROADS

Unfortunately, so many mountains and narrow valleys do not leave a lot of room for the luxury of an extensive network of side roads such as those found in England or the Netherlands. The roads that you will encounter generally are in good condition, although the extreme weather conditions in the higher elevations often tear up the road surfaces pretty badly. Occasionally you will come across cycle paths, usually near the cities, but generally they are rare occurrences.

The traffic density is high, and main roads are crowded, especially during the peak months of July and August and during German holidays, when the country is invaded by hordes of tourists from neighboring Bavaria. In recent years the Austrians have greatly increased their autobahn network. This has helped to relieve some of the traffic on adjacent roads.

For those with mountain bikes, Austria has miles of forest roads and hiking trails that are ideal for off-road touring. Before heading off into the countryside, be sure to get detailed maps. The Wanderkarten hiking maps (scale 1:50,000) for the local area are your best bet for keeping on course. One good all-terrain bike stretch with some alpine scenery runs from Schnarnitz at the Austrian German border near Mittenwald north of Innsbruck, through the Karwendeltal to the Hinterissand, then over into Germany to Vorderiss. There it meets up with our "Best of Bavaria Route" by following hwy B307

into the village of Fall, and from there traveling on to Bad Tölz. There is a grade of 23 percent approaching the Hochalmsattel.

Up until a few years ago when the Arlberg tunnel was opened, traffic on the Arlberg Pass Road was enough to discourage all but the most determined cyclists. Now that the tunnel and highway that leads up to it have siphoned off a good part of the traffic, this is a very interesting and rewarding climb with a 12 percent grade as you approach the summit. *Note*: This route is only for experienced cyclists in *good condition*. The road snakes up through the famous ski resorts of St. Anton and St. Christoph to reach the summit – under 1,800 meters. From there it's downhill all the way into Switzerland. This is a great way to combine the "Best of Bavaria Route" with the "Three Country Tour" around Lake Constance. To do this: from Garmisch-Partenkirchen, cross the border at Griesen. Then head over the Fern Pass (elevation 1,200 meters) and follow Arlberg signs. Watch out for weather changes! We once got caught in a driving snowstorm at the top of the Arlberg in mid-August. The approaches to high mountain passes are posted with signs showing if the pass is open or closed. For more information on Austrian alpine passes, consult the *Austrian Pass Directory*, available from **L'Ordre des Cols Dur** (39 Delahays Road, Hale, Altrincham, Cheshire WA 15 8DT, England; Tel: [061] 98 05 03 30). This interesting outfit also publishes information on mountain passes in other countries.

BICYCLE SHOPS AND RENTALS

Although many Austrians ride bikes, Austria is not a cycling country in the sense that France and Holland are. Although larger cities have cycle shops, many smaller towns and villages do not. Check you bike carefully and be sure that you have whatever spares you think you might need before setting off. Don't forget that Austria is on the metric system.

It is possible to rent bicycles from nearly one hundred stations of the Austrian National Railway between 1 April and 2 November. The cycle can be returned to any participating station. These bikes generally are not suitable for long-distance touring. There are numerous private rental firms in the popular tourist areas, such as Salzburg. Again these bikes are great for taking a spin around the local area, but for any kind of serious touring, you will do best with your own wheels.

ACCOMMODATIONS

This small "tourist friendly" country has some 70,000 establishments offering beds to tourists, and that doesn't even include the youth hostels and many campgrounds. It's not really a problem finding a place to spend the night in Austria – except, of course, in high season (July and August and holiday weekends) in the popular tourist areas. Just about any place you are likely to visit will have a tourist office which, for a few schillings, can find a comfortable room for you in a private home even in the busiest of times. A tourist office in Austria is known as a *"Fremden-verkehrsamt," "Verkehrsamt," "Verkehrsverein,"* or simply "Tourist Information."

Austria has some really fine romantic castle hotels that will fulfill any royalist fantasies you might be harboring. But one of the joys of touring in Austria is stopping at a friendly little geranium-bedecked pension to sample Austrian *Gemütlichkeit* firsthand and to rest your cycle-weary bones in a fluffy feather bed – and all this at prices that make the sterile, impersonal motels at home seem outrageously expensive! Look for signs reading: *"Pension," "Frühstucks-pension," "Fremdenzimmer,"* or*"Zimmer Frei"* (which means room free, not free room!).

There are approximately one hundred IYHA hostels distributed throughout the country. Many are concentrated in the region east of Salzburg called the Salzkammergut. The density of IYHA hostels is not great enough to allow you to do any substantial amount of touring staying only at hostels.

In addition to the IYHA hostels, there are a number of other hostel-type accommodations to be had. A list of these is available from the Austrian National Tourist Office. For details on youth hostels, check with local tourist offices or contact **Öster-reichischer Jugendherbergsverband** (Schottenring 28, A-1010 Vienna; Tel: [0222] 63 53 53) or the **Öster-reichisches Jugendherbergswerk** (Freyung 6-11, A-1010 Vienna; Tel: [0222] 63 18 33).

Campers have their choice of a wide variety of often very nicely situated campgrounds around most of the tourist areas. In some areas off the beaten path you will have no problem finding a patch of forest in which to pitch your tent. If anyone is around, be sure to get permission. The same holds true for camping on farmland. We've done a lot of free camping and have never been turned down when we asked. We always sleep a little better when we know that we are "legal."

FOOD AND DRINK

Food and drink in Austria is cause in itself for scheduling a vacation to this alpine Disneyland. Think of all the eating you can justify by pedaling the alps. *Strudel* (apple pastry like you never get at home) tastes out of this world served hot with vanilla sauce or whipped cream, and *schlagsahne* is whipped cream only like the Austrians can make it. Be sure to include at least a few stops at a roadside café or *konditorei* to sample the excellent Austrian cakes and pastries. Some other good reasons for coming to Austria are the delicious game dishes. In season, in the fall, look on the menu for *reh* or *hirsch* (venison) and *wildschwein* (wild boar). *Knödel* (the translation would be dumplings but the taste defies translation) is wonderful; when you see it on a menu order it.

Austrian wines are generally excellent; however, at this writing, their reputation is still suffering from a series of scandals concerning antifreeze in the wine which severely rocked the industry.

Tips and service are usually included in restaurant bills, although it is customary to add a few schillings for good service.

Austria is also an ideal country if you are on a budget or simply enjoy a good picnic. All the ingredients are there: great bread and rolls, tasty cheeses, all kinds of delicious sausage and cold cuts. And the whole country is one big picnic table; wherever you go you will find scenic spots for picnicking and gathering strength for the next stage of your tour.

SOURCES OF ADDITIONAL INFORMATION

The **Austrian National Tourist Office (ANTO)** has offices in New York (500 Fifth Ave., Suite 2009, New York, NY 10110; Tel: [212] 944-6880) and Los Angeles (3440 Wilshire Blvd., Suite 906, Los Angeles, CA 90010; Tel: [213] 380-3309). They will provide general information and maps good for planning and will also furnish the addresses of the regional tourist offices which can provide detailed information about their particular areas.

Österreichischer Fahrradverband (Hasnerstrasse 12, A-1040 Vienna; Tel: [222] 65 73 39) is the national cycling organization.

MOUNTAINS TO MOZART ROUTE

START	FINISH
SALZBURG	SALZBURG

DISTANCE KM
545 kms/339 miles

MAIR MAPS
Die General Karte #7
(scale: 1:100,000; 1 cm = 1 km)

No cycle tour through Austria would be complete without pedaling through the magnificent countryside where Julie Andrews romped and sang in *The Sound of Music*. Salzkammergut is one of the most enchanting regions in all of Austria. From prehistoric times until recently, the Salzkammergut was closely tied to the production and trading of salt. *Salz* is the German word for salt, and you will notice a great many place names beginning either with this word or its synonym, *Hall*.

A glorious composite of lakes, mountains, and picturesque villages, the Salzkammergut is an ideal place if you want to check into a quiet little pension and spend a few days vacationing as the Europeans do. The lakes are perfect for swimming, the mountains made for hiking, and even the smallest towns are amply provided with cozy little bars and comfortable, atmosphere-packed restaurants. Stash your bags in your room and enjoy the feeling of exploring this idyllic landscape on your "lightweight" bike. (The last time that we tried this we had an enjoyable break from the routine of touring. The only problem was getting used to having the weight on the bikes again.) The route includes the fashionable resort of Bad Ischl, a favorite spot of the Emperor Franz Joseph, and the salt mines at Halstatt which skirt the huge wall formed by the Dachstein Massif, whose highest peak reaches nearly 3,000 meters. With two of the country's most interesting cities at either end, the route offers a pleasant mixture of city sightseeing and countryside touring.

Although there are some tough sections – in particular the Gerlos Pass on the stretch between Zell am See and Innsbruck (which can be avoided by taking the train from Zell am See to Kitzbühel, or by cycling from Zell to Kitzbühel via Saalfelden) – the remainder of the route is of moderate difficulty with some hilly stretches. There are also some very lovely level sections.

Because of the city's popularity and ease of access, we have started our route in Salzburg. From Munich, Salzburg is just under 200 kms by road, and there is regular train service between Munich and Salzburg.

There are several places along this route that can be easily linked to our "Best of Bavaria Route." From Bad Reichenhall, it is interesting cycling by way of Ruhpolding to join up with the Bavarian route at Lake Chiemsee. From Innsbruck, it is only about 50 kms over the Zirler Berg to Garmisch-Partenkirchen. To avoid this steep climb, you can take the train from Innsbruck to Mittenwald and proceed from there either to Garmisch or to Bad Tolz in the other direction.

One of the classic alpine cycle climbs is over the Grossglockner High Alpine Road. Rest up in Zell am See before tackling this 2,500-meter-high twisting and winding pass road. The scenery is spectacular and the run down into Heiligenblut is an unforgettable experience.

With the many lakes and rivers that are ideal for taking a refreshing dip along the way, this route is best enjoyed in the summer. Except for the fact that a lot of other people have the same idea, July and August are very pleasant months for touring this part of Austria. As is the case throughout the alpine region, you can expect the weather to change very quickly. Sudden summer thunderstorms are a regular occurrence, although they usually don't last very long. Snow can fall in the higher elevations at any time of the year. September and even early October when the crowds have thinned out and the autumn colors are starting to transform the face of the landscape can be an ideal time to cycle this route. If you are there in late September, you may see the brightly decorated cows being brought down from the high alpine meadows into the valleys for the winter. May and June when the wild flowers are blossoming and the tourist onslaught has not yet begun are also excellent months for seeing Austria.

In the region described by this route, there are plenty of small hotels and pensions, as well as a good number of luxury hotels. There are also campgrounds located at regular intervals along the route, as well as an abundance of sites for free camping.

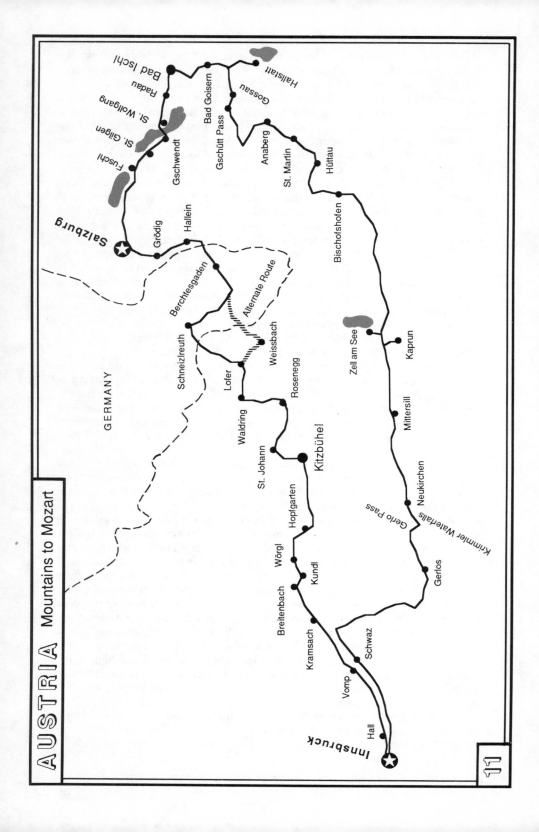

MOUNTAINS TO MOZART

CITY
SALZBURG

ROUTE
158

DISTANCE KM	TOTAL KM
37	0

ROUTE DESCRIPTION
From the main train station, head out of the city taking the Gabelsbergerstrasse, and then the Sterneckstrasse, following the signs to Graz. At the east edge of town, pick up hwy 158. The road climbs up the Kühlberg and offers a good view of Salzburg. Continue on 158 past the idyllic little lake of Fuschl to the larger St. Wolfgang See. Turn off at Gschwendt and head down to the lake. Take the ferry across to St. Wolfgang.

CITY
ST. WOLFGANG

ROUTE
145 166

DISTANCE KM	TOTAL KM
38	37

ROUTE DESCRIPTION
From St. Wolfgang, take the road that runs along the lake, passing through the little settlement of Radau to Bad Ischl. From Bad Ischl, take the small road that runs parallel to the main hwy 145. At Bad Goisern, turn off onto hwy 166 and follow the road along the lake to Hallstatt.

CITY
HALLSTATT

ROUTE
166 99 159

DISTANCE KM	TOTAL KM
64	75

ROUTE DESCRIPTION
Return to the junction with hwy 166, passing under the old salt aqueduct, and follow this scenic road over the Gschutt Pass (969 meters). For a spectacular view of the mountains, just before the pass summit, take the turn off at Gossau to the Lake of Gossau. The massive mountains are the Dachsteingruppe. At the junction with hwy 162, stay with 166 through Anaberg and St. Martin to meet up with the autobahn and hwy 99 near Hüttau. This is a beautiful stretch of mountain cycling with some grades of up to 17 percent. Take hwy 99 to intersect with hwy 159 for the last few kms to Bischofshofen for a well-deserved rest.

CITY
BISCHOFSHOFEN

ROUTE
311

DISTANCE KM	TOTAL KM
46	139

ROUTE DESCRIPTION
Leave Bischofshofen heading south on hwy 311, which follows the course of the Salzach River most of the way into Zell am See.

CITY
ZELL AM SEE

ROUTE
311 168 165

DISTANCE KM	TOTAL KM
49	185

ROUTE DESCRIPTION
Take hwy 311 from Zell toward Kaprun. At the junction with hwy 168, take 168 along the Salzach to Mittersill. Then pick up hwy 165, which continues along the Salzach to Neukirchen am Grossvenediger.

CITY
NEUKIRCHEN

ROUTE
165

DISTANCE KM	TOTAL KM
48	234

ROUTE DESCRIPTION
From Neukirchen, continue along hwy 165 and enjoy some outstanding views of the imposing Kleinvenediger and Grossvenediger. The narrow, winding Gerlos Pass Road opens up some spectacular scenery, including the Krimmler Waterfalls, which crash down some 400 meters into the Salzach Valley. The descent from the 1,507-meter-high summit down to Gerlos is equally spectacular.

CITY
GERLOS

ROUTE
165 169 171

DISTANCE KM	TOTAL KM
43	282

ROUTE DESCRIPTION
From Gerlos, follow hwy 165 to the junction with hwy 169. Continue on 169, which runs along the Ziller River down into the Inn Valley. At the intersection with hwy 171, turn off and follow 171 to Schwaz.

CITY	ROUTE
SCHWAZ	171

DISTANCE KM	TOTAL KM
25	325

ROUTE DESCRIPTION
Take hwy 171, which runs through the beautiful Inn Valley into Innsbruck.

CITY	ROUTE
INNSBRUCK	171

DISTANCE KM	TOTAL KM
60	350

ROUTE DESCRIPTION
Leave Innsbruck on hwy 171 and follow a series of small roads on the north side of the Inn River, passing through Hall, Vomp, and Kramsach. Cross over the Inn at Breitenbach to Kundl and then continue on to Wörgl on hwy 171.

CITY	ROUTE
WÖRGL	170

DISTANCE KM	TOTAL KM
30	410

ROUTE DESCRIPTION

Take hwy 170 from Wörgl along the Brixentaler Ache through Hopfgarten and into the resort town of Kitzbühel, surrounded by the beautiful backdrop formed by the rounded, green-covered slopes of the Kitzbüheler Alps.

CITY
KITZBÜHEL

ROUTE
161 164 312

DISTANCE KM	TOTAL KM
41	440

ROUTE DESCRIPTION

Leave Kitzbühel on hwy 161 to St. Johann in Tirol. Then continue on hwy 164 to the village of Rosenegg. A pleasant little-traveled road runs through the quiet Pillerseetal to meet up with hwy 312 at Waidring. Continue on 312 over the Strub Pass to Lofer.

CITY
LOFER

ROUTE
312 305

DISTANCE KM	TOTAL KM
42	481

ROUTE DESCRIPTION

From Lofer, take hwy 312 across the border into Germany. At Schneizlreuth, turn off and follow hwy 305 on a long, winding climb through the Alpine Park into Berchtesgaden.

Note: As an alternative route from Lofer to Berchtesgaden, there is a rough road closed to auto traffic, which has grades up to 28 percent. The road climbs up from Weissbach, which is 10 kms south of Lofer, on hwy 311 and then runs through the Watzman Berchtesgaden National Park. This is a good test for your all-terrain bike.

CITY
BERCHTESGADEN

ROUTE
305 159

DISTANCE KM	TOTAL KM
22	523

ROUTE DESCRIPTION

Take hwy 305 from Berchtesgaden to the junction with hwy 319, from there follow the signs toward Hallein, crossing back into Austria at Oberau. From Hallein, take hwy 159 toward Salzburg. To avoid the heavy traffic into the city, turn off to Grodig and from there follow the signs into Salzburg.

CITY
SALZBURG

DISTANCE KM	TOTAL KM
0	545

FROM MOUNTAINS TO MOZART SIGHTS AND ACCOMMODATIONS

SALZBURG. Even though it has been over-publicized, over-described, and over-visited, there is one thing that Salzburg is not – and that is over-rated! As famous cities go, it is not a big city. In fact, its population ranks it similar in size to Greensboro, North Carolina. There, with all due respects to our friends from North Carolina, comparisons cease.

Salzburg is located in an idyllic setting, nestled in the mountains and occupying both sides of the **Salzach River**. It has a long association with the church, going back some twelve centuries. It was the archbishops of Salzburg who were largely responsible for developing the city and giving it such an attractive face, all with revenues gained from the lucrative salt trade. Salzburg in German means "salt fortress," and although tourism has replaced salt as the basis of the local economy, the surrounding region is full of reminders of this once important industry. Aside from the fact that it enjoys such a favored location and serves as the gateway to the **Salzkammergut**, one of the country's most favored vacation regions, Salzburg is a pleasure to visit. The area most worth seeing, the old section of the city, is surprisingly small. The larger, modern part of Salzburg is rather uninteresting.

From its perch four hundred feet above the old town, the **Fortress Hohensalzburg** is Salzburg's most dominant feature. Begun in 1077 and successively enlarged and fortified until 1681, it is the largest completely preserved medieval fortress in central Europe. It served to protect and sometimes house the archbishops of Salzburg. Be sure to take in the fine panorama of the city and the surrounding **Salzburger Alps** from the castle walls. An interesting museum, the **Burgmuseum**, has a series of exhibits tracing the development of the town.

Down in the **Old Town**, the lively **Getreidegasse**, a narrow shopping street lined with fine old houses and scores of souvenir shops, is one of the main attractions. The house at number 9 is where Salzburg's most famous native son was born. You can't miss it. Written in large letters across the otherwise fine facade is **"Mozarts Geburtshaus."** In the apartment in which he was born is a small museum with mementos of his life. You can also visit the **Mozart Family Home** (Mozarts Wohnhaus) at 8 Marktplatz. The elaborately decorated **Residenz** was the palace of the archbishops, and it was here that the young Mozart often played for important guests.

Salzburg boasts of several interesting churches, including the rather austere early baroque **cathedral** (Dom) in the heart of the Old Town and the **Church of the Holy Trinity** (Dreifaltigkeitskirche) and the **Collegiankirche** on the other side of the river. These two masterpieces were by one of Austria's most famous architects, Fisher von Erlach. Also on the same side of the river is the elaborate baroque **Mirabell Palace**, where candlelit chamber music concerts are held. **Hellbrunn Castle**, just south of the city, is worth pedaling the 5 kms in order to see the rich interiors, elaborate gardens, and trick water fountains.

No visit to Salzburg, which practically owes its existence to the salt trade, would be complete without a visit to a **salt mine**. **Hallein**, about 12 kms south of the city has been producing salt since the thirteenth century. Take the tour of the underground caves and galleries of the **Durrnberg Salt Mines**. For an added bit of trivia: the home and tomb of **Franz Xaver Gruber**, composer of "Silent Night," are located in Hallein.

As you might imagine in a town as popular as Salzburg, the choice of accommodations is wide, ranging from simple rooms in private homes to luxury reminiscent of the days of the Empire. For pampered, old-world luxury right in the heart of the Old Town, the traditional atmosphere and the fine restaurant of the

HOTEL GOLDENER HIRSCH
(Getreidegasse 35 & 37, 5021 Salzburg;
Tel: [0622] 84 85 11) can't be beat. The
HOTEL ÖSTERREICHISCHER HOF
(Schwarzstrasse 5; Tel: [0622] 72 541)
looking across the river at the old town is
another one of the best of Salzburg's
traditional hosteleries. In the budget
category, there are a number of fine, small,
atmosphere-packed Old Town hotels,
including the conveniently located HOTEL
BLAUE GANS (Getreidegasse 43; Tel:
[0662] 41 317). For a comfortable pension,
try the PENSION KOCH (Gaisbergstrasse
37; Tel: [0662] 20 402). If you arrive in
high season and have trouble getting a
room, the Tourist Office (Mozartplatz 5) in
the center of the Old Town will help you
out.

There are several youth hostels in the
Salzburg area, including the 370-bed
JUGENDHERBERGE NONNTAL (Josef-
Preis-Allee 18; Tel: [0662] 42 670) and the
recently opened JUGENDHERBERGE
(Hauerspergstrasse 27; Tel: [0662] 75 030)
located near the train station. Inexpensive
dormitory beds are also available at the
INSTITUT ST. SEBASTIAN (Linzergasse
41; Tel: [0662] 71 386).

There are several good campgrounds
within the immediate vincinity of Salzburg
and many scattered throughout the
Salzkammergut. The most convenient site
from which to visit the city is STADT
CAMPING on the Bayerhammerstrasse at
the north end of town. Amenities include
washing machines, restaurants nearby, and
a camp store. It is open 15 May to 15
October.

ST. WOLFGANG. Located on the lake
of the same name, St. Wolfgang fulfills all
of the requirements of a stereotypical
Austrian alpine village. There are quaint
chalets with flower-bedecked balconies that
look out over the lake to the snow-capped
alps in the distance and a charming onion-
domed pilgrimage church. This small village
is one of the most widely visited spots in
the entire Salzkammergut. The **White
Horse Inn** (Weisses Rössl), made famous
in a romantic operetta, is one of the town's
most popular attractions.

There are other equally charming and
much less commercialized villages in the
region. In particular, **Fuschl** on the tiny
Fuschlsee and **St. Gilgen** at the tip of
the **Wolfgangsee** are worth visiting. **Bad
Ischl**, a bit further down the road, is in the
heart of the Salzkammergut. During the
reign of Emperor Franz-Josef, it was one of
the most fashionable centers of European
social life. While there stop and visit the
Imperial Villa.

From St. Wolfgang, you can take the cog
railway to the top of the nearly 1,800-meter
Schafberg, the highest peak in the
Salzkammergut. Locals claim that from the
summit you can see thirteen lakes. We only
counted ten, but it was an overcast day!

One of our favorite places to stay in all of
Europe is the SCHLOSSHOTEL FUSCHL
on the small lake of the same name.
Unfortunately the last time we were there, it
was closed. Perhaps when you pedal by
this way it will have reopened. One of the
most romantic places to stay in the whole
Salzkammergut is none other than St.
Wolfgang's famous WHITE HORSE INN
(5360 St. Wolfgang; Tel: [06138] 2306),
located right on the lake.

Accommodations in St. Gilgen and
Strobl, at the opposite end of the lake just
5 kms from St. Wolfgang, are much more
reasonably priced than in busy St.
Wolfgang. The HOTEL ZUM GOLDENEN
OCHSEN (5340 St. Gilgen; Tel: [06627]
223) is a comfortable, moderately priced
hotel. Doubles without a bath go from 400
S. For an inexpensive pension in St.
Gilgen, try the PENSION FERSTL (Tel:
[06627] 216).

There is a IYHF hostel in St. Gilgen,
HAUS SCHAFBERGBLICK (Mondsee-
strasse 7-11; Tel: [06227] 365), and also
one in Mondsee on the other side of the
Schafberg, JUGENDGÄSTEHAUS (Kran-
kenhausstrasse 9, 5310 Mondsee; Tel:
[06232] 2418).

There are a number of nicely situated
campgrounds throughout the region, but
you can count on them being very crowded
in July and August. One of the most
convenient is CAMPING BERAU, located
on the lake between St. Wolfgang and
Strobl. It is open 15 April to 30 September.

HALLSTATT. Clinging to the steep slopes that rise up from the darkness of the **Hallstätter See**, the picturesque village of Hallstatt occupies a site that has been inhabited since neolithic times. The attraction has been the mining of that ever-precious commodity, salt. The ancient **salt mines** in the Valley of the Salzburg can be visited. Also of interest are the **Dachstein Ice Caves**, which are accessible by cog train from nearby Obertraun, and the small **Museum of Prehistory** in Hallstatt.

In an inspiring setting overlooking the lake, SEEHOTEL GRÜNER BAUM (Marktplatz 104, 4830 Hallstatt; Tel: [06134] 263) makes a great base for doing some local touring. HAUS SARSTEIN (Gosaumuhlstrasse 83; Tel: [06134] 217) is one of those gernaium-bedecked Austrian pensions that belong in everyone's European trip.

The rather spartan local youth hostel IYHF JUGENDHERBERG HALSTATT (Salzbergstrasse 22; Tel: [06134] 297) is less inspiring.

Of the several campgrounds in the area, the fine view and easy access to the lake make CAMPING HOLL a good choice. It is located just south of Hallstatt in Lahn. The facilities include a washing machine, camp store, and nearby restaurant. It is open 1 May to 30 September.

BISCHOFSHOFEN. Located at the intersection of several major roads, the small industrial town of Bischofshofen makes a convenient stopping point. Surprisingly, the **parish church** in this otherwise rather uninteresting town is one of the finest Gothic churches in the Austrian Alps.

The town's most comfortable hotel and best place to eat is the moderately priced GASTHOF ALTE POST (5500 Bischofshofen; Tel: [06462] 2207). Doubles with bath are priced from 450 S. For a quiet room in a good pension, try PENSION FEITZINGER (Tel: [06462] 2231).

There is a pleasant campground in a meadow just off hwy 311 in St. Johann im Pongau 6 kms south of Bischofshofen. Called CAMPING WIESHOF, it is open all year. There are also a number of attractive pensions and small inns should you find

Bischofshofen not to your liking. Frau Huber's *gemütlich* PENSION ALPENBLICK (5600 St. Johann im Pongau; Tel: [06412] 6234) is especially appealing and inexpensive – about 300 S for a double without bath.

ZELL AM SEE. Beautifully situated overlooking the **Zeller See**, the little town of Zell am See is a popular all-year resort town. This is excellent hiking country with good access to the higher elevations by a series of lifts that open up a wide area for good skiing in winter. There is skiing all year on the glacier at nearby Kaprun.

The choice of small hotels and pensions in this little resort town is overwhelming. In the luxury category, the traditional alpine decor makes the HOTEL ST. GEORG (5700 Zell am See; Tel: [06542] 3533) our number one choice. One of the nicest of the many pensions is the PENSION TIROLERHEIM (Tel: [06542] 2884). Another pleasant and convenient place to spend a night or two is Frau Gadenstätter's PENSION MIRABELL (Tel: [06542] 2665).

CAMPING PRIELAU is a pleasant site located on the north shore of the lake just a few minutes cycling distance from the center of Zell. It is open 1 May to 31 October.

NEUKIRCHEN AM GROSSVENE-DIGER. Neukirchen is a small town at the eastern approach to the **Gerlos Pass** in a popular hiking and skiing area. The "Grossvenediger" in the town's name refers to the block of mountains that rise up to nearly 3,700 meters just to the south of the town.

The town's top lodgings are to be found at the GASTHOF KAMMERLÄNDER (5741 Neukirchen am Grossvenediger; Tel: [06565] 6263). Inexpensive rooms are to be found at Herr Pichler's small GASTHAUS POSTALM (Tel: [06565] 6520) where you can get a double for under 300 S.

Campers looking for a place to pitch a tent in the woods should have no problems in this rugged area. There is a scenically located all-year campground in Hollersbach about 10 kms east on hwy 165. It is called CAMPING HOLLERSBACH. There is also a small campground in Pinzgau on the way up to the pass.

GERLOS. A pleasant small village at the western gateway to the **Gerlos Pass**, Gerlos attracts many vacationers interested in pursuing water sports on the nearby artificial lake behind the **Durlassboden Dam**. The **parish church of St. Leonard** erected in 1735 has some interesting ceiling frescoes.

For a first-class little village inn, try the GASTHOF GERLOSERHOF (6281 Gerlos; Tel: [05284] 5224). The PENSION DORFBLICK (6281 Gerlos; Tel: [05284] 5272) is a charming little country pension.

The closest campground, CAMPING ZELL AM ZILLER, is an all-year site with full facilities. It is located 16 kms down the road at Zell am Ziller.

SCHWAZ. Beginning in the early fifteenth century, Schwaz developed as an important center for the mining of copper and silver. In fact, it was the wealth gained from this region that helped finance a good part of the expansion of the Hapsburg Empire under the emperors Maximilian I and Charles V. Although much of the town was destroyed in a dispute with the Bavarians in 1809, there are still some fine fifteenth-century and sixteenth-century buildings left. The parish church is one of the largest Gothic churches in Tirol. The vast roof is decked with 15,000 copper tiles.

There are numerous small *pensionen* and *gasthäuser* all along the remaining 25-kms stretch into Innsbruck. For a cozy *gasthäus* with a good kitchen, try the GOLDENER LÖWE (6130 Schwaz; Tel: [05242] 2373). For a budget room, stop at the VILLA ARZBERG (Tel: [05242] 3720).

CAMPING PLANKENHOF is on a pleasant meadow next to the gasthöf of the same name, just off hwy 171. It is open 1 April to 31 October.

INNSBRUCK. With a population of over 100,000, Innsbruck, the cultural and tourist capital of the Tirol, is the largest city in the western part of Austria. Although the old town center is quite attractive and contains some interesting sights, Innsbruck's greatest appeal lies in its magnificent location. In a broad valley on the Inn River, the city is surrounded by a beautiful alpine panorama. An ideal location for both summer hiking and winter sports, Innsbruck has twice hosted the winter Olympics (1964 and 1976).

One of the city's main attractions is the **Hofburg** (Imperial Palace), an impressive baroque structure built by the Empress Maria Theresa. While in the old town be sure to see the **Goldenes Dachl** (golden roof), an intriguing building dating from the reign of Maximilian and symbolizing the wealth and power of the Hapsburgs. Next to the Goldenes Dachl is the ornate stucco facade of the **Helblinghaus**. The Tomb of Maximilian, located in the **Imperial Chapel** (Hofkirche), is surrounded by a ring of statues composed of the protective saints of the Hapsburg family. The **Tiroler Landesmuseum**, also known as the **Ferdinandeum**, is concerned primarily with showing the development of the fine arts in Tirol. **Ambras Castle** at the south end of town near the autobahn, the favorite residence of Archduke Ferdinand, has a great collection of arms and armor that includes a fine display of jousting equipment.

Located in the heart of the old town, the HOTEL GOLDENER ADLER (Herzog-Friedrich-Strasse 6, 6021 Innsbruck; Tel: [05222] 26334) is a cozy traditional inn. It has been caring for visitors to Innsbruck for more than six hundred years. Another first-class hotel in the traditional style is the HOTEL SCHWARZER ADLER (Kaiser-jagerstrasse 2; Tel: [05222] 27109). In the budget department, there are a number of good reasonably priced *gasthäuser* and *pensionen*, including the GASTHÖF GOLDENER WINKEL (Tel: [05222] 46 368) and the peaceful PENSION PAULA (Weiherburggasse 15; Tel: [05222] 37 795). Doubles with bath go for about 400 S.

Youth hostelers have a number of choices in and around Innsbruck. The IYHF JUGENDHERBERGE INNSBRUCK (Reichenauerstrasse 147; Tel: [05222] 46 179) is a modern 190-bed hostel at the east edge of town. There is also a campground next to the hostel, CAMPING REICHENAU, the most convenient of all the Innsbruck area campgrounds. It is open 15 April to 15 October.

WÖRGL. Wörgl is an important Inn valley road and rail junction. The town's top hotel is the HOTEL LINDE (6300 Wörgl; Tel: [05332] 2359). The WÖRGLER HOF (Tel: [05332] 2303) is a good inexpensive *gasthöf*. There is a nice campground located next to the Itter Castle, in Itter just past Hopfgarten off hwy 170 on the way to Kitzbühel. It is a well-equipped all-year site.

KITZBÜHEL. Beautifully set amidst the Kitzbüheler Alps, Kitzbühel is one of Austria's most popular ski resorts and attracts a large international crowd. In spite of all the growth accompanying this fame, Kitzbühel, which dates back to 1271, has managed to maintain its traditional Tirolean old town center.

Although ski season prices are among the steepest in Austria, the summer season brings reductions. But this is not a town noted for its great bargains. A popular stopping-off place is the PENSION TONI SAILER (6370 Kitzbühel; Tel: [05356] 3041). Toni Sailer is the hometown boy who took all the skiing honors in the 1956 Olympics. The HOTEL MONTANA (Tel: [05356] 2526) is a solid medium-priced hotel.

CAMPING SCHWARZSEE is a first-rate, fully equipped, all-year campground located at the edge of town on the Schwarzsee.

LOFER. With its onion-domed church set against the background of the heavily wooded foothills of the **Ochsenhorn Mountain**, Lofer is one of the region's most picturesque towns.

For a comfortable room and hearty meal, settle in for the night at the GASTHÖF SALZBURGERHOF (5090 Lofer; Tel: [06588] 333), where a double without a bath will cost just under 500 S.

The closest campground is in St. Martin, only 1 km south of Lofer on hwy 311. PARKCAMPING GRUBHOF is a fully equipped campground in a beautiful wooded setting with magnificent mountain vistas. It is open 1 May to 30 September.

BERCHTESGADEN (Germany). A small town dwarfed by its surroundings, Berchtesgaden sits in one of the alpine region's prime locations. The town owes its early prosperity to the rich salt deposits in the surrounding mountains. Although salt is still mined in the region, the prime industry today is tourism. In summer, Berchtesgaden is a favorite for hikers and climbers; in the winter, it is one of Germany's most popular ski resorts. A visit to the **salt mines** where you don miner's garb and explore underground galleries, ride on a subterranean lake, and slide down a chute is without a doubt one of the highlights of a visit to Berchtesgaden. Nearby **Kehlstein** is the site of Hitler's famous **Eagle's Nest retreat**. The **Königsee** just south of Berchtesgaden – even with the tourist mobs – is one of the most beautiful of the alpine lakes.

The HOTEL WITTELSBACH (Maximilianstrasse 16, 8240 Berchtesgaden; Tel: [08652] 5061), a classic old hotel completely remodeled a few years ago, is conveniently located right in the heart of town. Another place with loads of atmosphere in an idyllic country location is the LANDHAUS BRANDNER (Salzbergstrasse 6; Tel: [08652] 63 058) on the road to Obersalzberg. Inexpensive bed and breakfast accommodations are also available at the TOURISTTENHEIM HOTEL KÖNIGSEE (Seestrasse 29, Tel: [08652] 5046) located directly next to the beautiful Königsee about 5 kms from Berchtesgaden.

The IYHA youth hostel, DEUTSCHE JUGENDGERBERGE (Gebirgsjägerstrasse 52, Tel: [08652] 2190), is located in Strub just a few kms southwest of the center of Berchtesgaden.

There is a large campground in a beautiful natural setting near the lake. Facilities include a washing machine, camp store, and restaurant. It is open all year.

Additional Recommended Routes

Austria offers the cyclist with a little extra time several interesting and rewarding touring possibilities. The region around Vienna, although flat, can hardly be described as uninteresting. If you are anywhere in the vincinity of the Austrian capital, be sure to budget a few days to enjoy the beauties of this still great city. Although Vienna itself is not much for cycling, the famous **Wienerwald** (Vienna Woods) with its forested, rolling hills to the south and west of the city provides a wonderful opportunity for mingling with the Viennese who often frequent the many lively *heuringen* (wine taverns). The Wienerwald is laced with numerous trails ideal for cycling.

Vienna also makes a great base for touring the **Danube Valley** (in Austria and Germany this great river is known as the Donau). It is beautiful, mostly level riding along the river to the historic city of **Krems**, and then on to **Melk**, site of one of the finest baroque abbeys in southern Europe. The stretch between the village of **Grien** and **Krems** is the most picturesque section of the Danube Valley.

If you are curious about what lies behind the Iron Curtain, it is just a few hours cycling from Vienna to the Hungarian border. Hungary provides a great introduction to Eastern Europe. Visas can be obtained from the Hungarian consulate in Vienna or at the highway border crossings.

Another area rich in touring possibilities and one seldom visited by Americans is the province of **Kärnten** (Corinthia). The region is rich in scenic attractions, with many beautiful lakes, hilltop castles, and historic old towns. The mountains, while not as spectacular as in Tirol or the Vorarlberg, nevertheless present some formidable challenges. Traffic is not as heavy as in some other parts of the country and there are more secondary roads.

The **Wörthersee** near **Klagenfurt** and the **Ossiachersee** near **Villach** make a pleasant combination for a lake and town tour. You can easily circle both lakes and tour the towns in a couple of days. From Villach, it is great cycling over the little-traveled **Wurzen Pass** into Yugoslavia. At some points this narrow winding road reaches a grade of 19 percent. Visas can be obtained at the border.

BELGIUM

POPULATION
9,863,000

RELIGION
Primarily Catholic

CAPITAL
Brussels

CURRENCY
Belgian franc (BFr.); divided into 100 centimes

OFFICIAL LANGUAGE
Flemish (Dutch); 32% French — English is widely understood

BANKING HOURS
M-TH 0900–1530
   F 0900–1500
Train station exchange in Brussels is open 0600–2200; in Zaventem Airport from 0730–2200.

STORE HOURS
Food: 0800–1800
Others: 0900–2100 or 2200
(All shops must close by 2200)

EMERGENCY TELEPHONE NUMBERS
Police
   (in greater Brussels area)   901
      Elsewhere   906
Ambulance   900

TO CALL USA OR CANADA
Dial 001; area code and number

USA CONSULATES
Boulevard du Regent 27
1000 BRUSSELS
Tel: [02] 51 34 450
Telex: 84621336
Rubens Center
Nationalstraat 5
2000 ANTWERP
Tel: [03] 23 21 800
Telex: 31966

CANADIAN CONSULATE

Rue de Loxum 6
1000 BRUSSELS
Tel: [02] 51 37 940

AMERICAN EXPRESS OFFICES

Meir 87
ANTWERP
Tel: [03] 23 25 920

pl. Louise 2
BRUSSELS
Tel: [02] 51 21 740

HOLIDAYS

1 Jan.; Easter Monday; 1 May, Labor Day; Ascension Day, movable; Pentecost, movable; 21 July, Independence Day; 15 Aug., Assumption Day; 11 Nov., Armistice Day; 25 Dec., Christmas Day.

ROADS

This country has more registered motor vehicles per kilometer of road than any other European country. A few years ago a popular magazine ran a survey of European drivers; it rated Belgian drivers as the worst in Europe. Not surprisingly, Belgium has one of the highest accident rates in Europe. Belgian roads are often crowded with cyclists. What all this adds up to is when you cycle in Belgium, extra caution is advised. Fortunately, there is a good network of secondary roads and cycle paths, and since so many Belgians are themselves cyclists, most motorists have some comprehension of what it is like to be out there on a bike.

While surfaces on the main roads are good, many less-traveled secondary roads can be rough. Most of the major roads have cycle lanes, although there are fewer of these in the region of the Ardennes. Where cycle paths are present, the law requires that they be used. However, the surfaces are often less than ideal, especially for a thin-wheeled racer. We have often observed the locals bypassing the trails in favor of the better road surface. No one seems to mind.

The Ardennes forest has a number of hiking trails, dirt tracks, and gravel roads well suited for mountain bike touring. In Flanders there are many possibilities for cycling along the canal towpaths.

Next to Monaco and Holland, Belgium has the highest population density in the world, which means that you will rarely be very far from a town or village. In the towns and villages you will often have to put up with bone-jarring cobblestones.

MAPS

For overall planning, Michelin map #409, Belgique, Luxembourg (scale 1:350,000; 1 cm = 3.5 kms), which shows scenic routes, some contour features, and most secondary roads, is excellent. The less-detailed (scale 1:400,000) free map issued by the Belgian National Tourist Office indicates the most interesting places to visit. It may also be useful for laying out your Belgian tour.

The best maps to use when you are actually cycling are Michelin maps #213, Oostende-Bruxelles-Liège, and #214, Mons-Luxembourg (scale for both is 1:200,000; 1 cm = 2 kms). Both show all surfaced roads, some unsurfaced lanes, some cycle trails, as well as scenic roads and inclines.

BIKING THROUGH EUROPE

BELGIUM

Applying a cyclist's eye to Belgium, we like what we see. For one thing, it is nice to know that should we so desire we can pedal across the entire country in a couple of days. However, when we look at Belgium as a place to spend a few weeks of cycling, it is amazing what this little kingdom by the sea has to offer.

A constitutional monarchy since 1831, the country is split roughly in half along ethnic lines. The French-speaking Walloons live in the southern part of the kingdom and the Flemings, who occupy the northern part of the country known as Flanders, speak Flemish, a Dutch dialect. Although officially classified as bilingual, Brussels is primarily a French-speaking enclave in Flemish territory. Thickening this polyglot brew are the people in the eastern part of the country near Eupen and Arlon whose native tongue is German. In effect, Belgium is a trilingual country. As you cycle through the different linguistic areas you will be pleased to note that English is widely understood, especially in the cities and among the younger people.

The variety that Belgium offers its visitors is not restricted to languages. In the North there is a flat region of fens, canals, and rivers, which are a natural extension of the Netherlands. The sea coast, although only 60 kilometers long, contains some fine sandy beaches and dunes, as well as Ostend, the country's most important seaport. Much of the land along the North Sea coast, as in Holland, has been reclaimed from the sea. The central and southern plains, the least interesting for cycle touring, are rich agricultural regions with broad fields of wheat and sugar beets.

Belgium has some suprisingly challenging cycling country, particularly in the Ardennes, a region of steep hills and dense forests along the border with Germany and Luxembourg. It was in the Ardennes forest near the town of Bastogne that the famous World War II Battle of the Bulge took place.

During both world wars Belgium was the scene of heavy fighting and suffered extensive damage. In spite of this destruction, there are still some outstanding old cities to be seen, in particular, the medieval beauties of Bruges and Ghent.

Belgians on bicycles are a very common sight. Most Belgians seem to be primarily interested in racing and recreational cycling; cycle touring is not as popular a pastime as in neighboring Holland or Denmark. Belgian cyclists have claimed more international titles over the past half-century than cyclists from any other country, and such champions as Eddie Merckx have become national heroes.

Because the country is multilingual, towns and cities will often have more than one name. Nowadays most maps and road signs will show the alternate names; however, it wasn't very long ago that we completely passed up a town because we knew it by the "other name." In our route descriptions, we will try to give all of the alternate names.

TRANSPORTATION WITHIN THE COUNTRY

In Belgium the national rail system is called **SNCB**, short for *Societe Nationale des Chemins de fer Belge*. This efficient operation rivals the Swiss SBB, bringing dependable rail service to all parts of the country. You may take your bike along on most trains, although not on international trains if your journey is within the country. For travel with a bike within the country, you pay a flat rate and are responsible for loading and unloading it yourself. Bicycle tickets are sold at the baggage counter. If you are shipping the bike as unaccompanied luggage, allow up to two days for the bike to reach its destination. The bicycle will be loaded by the station personnel.

You may not transport your bike on the Belgian bus system.

ACCOMMODATIONS

One of the advantages of touring in a country with such a high population density is that you are never very far from a town or village and a place to stay. The hotels and inns have a typically Dutch flavor in the North and a strong French flavor in the South. Belgian hotels are rated by the tourist authorities with from one to five stars according to the Benelux standard, which is also in use in Luxembourg and the Netherlands. Costs are based on the room rather than per person, and outside of Brussels, Belgian hotel prices are not unreasonable.

For travelers on a budget, there are some one hundred youth hostels and more than five hundred campgrounds scattered throughout the country. For further information concerning youth hostels in Flanders, contact **Vlaamse Jeugdherbergcentrale** (Van Stralenstraat 40, B-2008 Antwerp; Tel [03] 23 27 218). For information on hostels in Brussels and the French-speaking southern and eastern provinces, contact **Centrale Wallonne des Auberges de Jeunesse (CWAJ)** (rue Van Oost 52, 1030 Bruxelles; Tel: [02] 21 53 100).

BICYCLE SHOPS AND RENTALS

Just about every town in Belgium has a cycle shop. In all there are some six thousand scattered about the country. Metric parts are stocked, and even though many shops specialize in racing machines, local mechanics are resourceful. You should have no trouble getting your touring or mountain bike repaired if the need arises.

As in many other countries, the national railway system operates a train and bike rental scheme. You can rent a bicycle at any one of some sixty participating stations and return it to any of the other participating stations. There are also several "hand in" stations that receive bikes but do not rent them. The details of this plan are explained in the booklet *Train + Velo* (in Flemish, *Trein + Fiets*) available at SNCB stations. There are also a number of private firms that rent cycles. Check with local tourist offices for details.

FOOD AND DRINK

Belgian cuisine is strongly influenced by France, its neighbor to the south, and many gourmets are convinced that the fare in Belgium's top restaurants sets the standard for the world. In any case, we've always eaten extremely well whether we are picnicking or dining in restaurants. A few tasty Belgian specialties include *waterzooi de volaille*, pieces of chicken and vegetables served in a creamy broth, and *karbonaden*, a Flemish beef stew cooked in beer. For a special treat, try a heaping plate of Belgian mussels steamed in white wine; they always taste better here than anywhere else. Beer is the favorite drink, and per capita consumption comes close to that of neighboring Germany. Belgian street foods are delicacies, especially the *frites* (French fries) served with thick mayonnaise and the waffles served with all sorts of toppings. Many chocolate connoisseurs swear that the Belgian chocolates, especially the Godiva brand, are the world's best.

SOURCES OF ADDITIONAL INFORMATION

The main office of the **Belgian National Tourist Office** in Brussels (rue Marché-aux-Herbes 61, 1000 Brussels; Tel: [02] 51 23 030) just around the corner from the Grand' Place, can supply you with a wealth of information about Brussels and the rest of the country.

The **Belgian Tourist Office** (745 Fifth Ave., New York, NY 10151; Tel: (212) 758-8130) in the States can also supply plenty of information.

In Belgium, local tourist offices are called *Syndicat d'Initiative* in the French-speaking provinces and *Dienst voor Toerisme* in the Flemish regions. Most of the larger towns have special youth information offices called *Info-Jeugd* in Flemish and *Info-Jeunes* in French.

The national cyclist's organization, **Ligue Velocipedique Belge** (ave. du Globe 49, 1190 Brussel; Tel: [02] 34 3-0 008), is mostly concerned with racing.

BRUSSELS AND ONCE AROUND BELGIUM

START	FINISH	MICHELIN MAPS
BRUSSELS	BRUSSELS	#214, Mons-Luxembourg; #213, Oostende-Bruxelles-Liège (scale 1:200,000; 1 cm = 2 kms)

DISTANCE	
666 kms/414 miles	

Starting in the cosmopolitan capital of Brussels, our route takes in Antwerp, Belgium's second most populous city, and makes a circle through the flat western provinces. The highlight of this part of Belgium is Bruges, a jewel of a medieval city. Approaching the North Sea coast, the route crosses the reclaimed polders, then runs down along the beaches and dunes to the seaport of Ostend before returning to Brussels by way of the ancient city of Ghent. Just south of Brussels is the famous battlefield at Waterloo where Wellington's defeat of Napoleon changed the course of European history. The entire region west of Brussels is totally flat and cycling it requires no exertion, unless the wind is blowing in off the North Sea. In that case, at least for part of the way, you will be traveling head down, pedaling in low gear. If you are lucky, you will be able to use that same wind to push you effortlessly back to Brussels. The eastern part of the route crosses into the Ardennes and requires a ten-speed and a bit of pumping to negotiate the sometimes steep hills. This is not mountain country, but you should be in good shape to get the maximum enjoyment out of this portion of the route. Although it is not to be compared with Bruges, Namur, the gateway to the Ardennes, has an old citadel that is worth a stop.

Although our route starts and ends in Brussels, which has excellent rail connections with the rest of Europe, it can be easily picked up or left anywhere along the way. There are good ferry connections across the Channel to England from Zeebruge and Ostend or from the French port of Dunkerque just across the border about 30 kilometers from Ostend. By taking the ferry from either Zeebruge or Ostend to the English port of Felixstowe, you can link up nicely with the "East Anglia Route" or take the train into London and tour "The Heart of England." From Liège at the eastern edge of this route, it is only about 40 kilometers to join up with the "Rhine-Moselle Route" at Aachen or Monshau.

Even though you might run into some crowds and heavy traffic, your best chances for hitting good weather are in July and August. With its close proximity to the North Sea, Flanders is rainier and more susceptible to strong winds than the more sheltered Ardennes. Cycling the Ardennes in autumn when the leaves begin to turn and the tourists have departed can be a delightful experience, providing you have some luck with the weather.

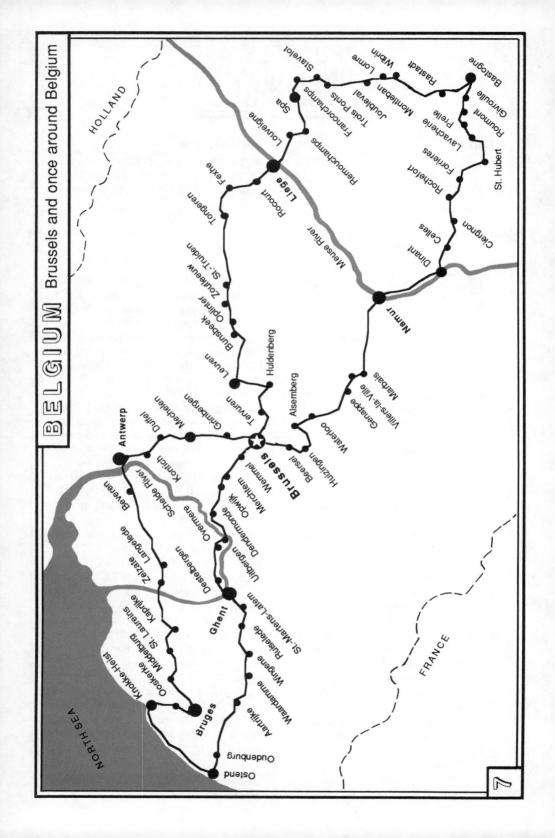

BELGIUM Brussels and once around Belgium

7

BRUSSELS AND ONCE AROUND BELGIUM

CITY

BRUSSELS (Bruxelles)

DISTANCE KM	TOTAL KM
45	0

ROUTE DESCRIPTION

From Brussels' Gare du Nord (train station) cross over the river and head for the Atomium and Royal Palace. Then follow the road north to Grimbergen. From there, continue 10 kms to Mechelen (Malines), the religious capital of the country, which has a fine medieval old town square and cathedral. From Mechelen, take the winding back roads into Antwerp by way of Duffel and Kontich.

Note: To avoid heavy traffic getting out of Brussels, it is best to take the train from the Gare du Nord to Mechelen.

CITY

ANTWERP (Antwerpen, Anvers)

ROUTE

N70 N445 N436

DISTANCE KM	TOTAL KM
78	45

ROUTE DESCRIPTION

From the center of town, take the tunnel under the river Schelde. The entrance is by the Platin-Moretus Museum. Follow N70 to Beveren. Continue west on N445 toward Zelzate. Just before Zelzate, turn north along the Wangelede River to the town of Langelede and then continue to Sas-van-Gent, passing through a few kilometers of Dutch territory. Cross the river and continue heading across this flat region of Flanders on N436 to Kaprijke. From Kaprijke, follow the road that winds along the Dutch border, passing through St. Laureins and Middelburg into Bruges.

CITY

BRUGES (Brugge)

DISTANCE KM	TOTAL KM
52	123

ROUTE DESCRIPTION

Leave Bruges and take the path along the scenic Brugge-Damme canal to Ooskerke. Then head across the dunes to the seaside resort of Knokke-Heist. Continue along the resort-lined North Sea coast down to the seaport of Ostend.

CITY

OSTEND (Oostende, Ostende)

ROUTE

N368

DISTANCE	TOTAL KM
69	175

ROUTE DESCRIPTION

The route to Ghent follows N368 a good portion of the way across the flat Flanders plain, passing through Oudenburg and Aartrijke to Waardamme. From Waardamme, continue to Wingene, Ruiselede, and St. Martens Latem, crossing over the autobahn into Ghent.

CITY
GHENT (Gent, Gand)

ROUTE
N445 N416

DISTANCE KM	TOTAL KM
52	244

ROUTE DESCRIPTION
Leave Ghent on N445 at Destelbergen. The road runs under and then over the autobahn and continues to Overmere. At Overmere, head south to cross the Schelde at Uitbergen. Take N416 into Dendermonde (Termonde). From there head back into Brussels by way of Opwijk, Merchtem, and Wemmel.

CITY
BRUSSELS (Bruxelles)

ROUTE
N5 N275 N93

DISTANCE KM	TOTAL KM
68	296

ROUTE DESCRIPTION
Head south out of Brussels to Beersel, the site of a medieval water castle. From there continue through the woods and attractive gardens at Huizingen to Alsemberg. From Alsemberg, continue on to visit the museum and battlefield at Waterloo. From Waterloo, head south on N5 to Genappe. From Genappe go to Villers la-Ville, stopping to visit the ancient abbey just north of Villers. Then take N275 to the intersection with N93 at Marbais. Follow N93 into Namur.

CITY
NAMUR (Namen)

ROUTE
N47 N48 N511

DISTANCE KM	TOTAL KM
48	364

ROUTE DESCRIPTION
Take N47 south from Namur along this scenic stretch of the Meuse River to Dinant. From Dinant, climb up on N48 past the autobahn. Continue on to Celles and then on to Ciergnon. Turn onto N511 and pedal into Rochefort.

CITY
ROCHEFORT

ROUTE
N49 N46

DISTANCE KM	TOTAL KM
49	412

ROUTE DESCRIPTION
From Rochefort, take N49 through Forrieres and continue up the long hill (14 percent grade) to St. Hubert. From St. Hubert, take N46 south. After about 3 kms, turn north on the road to Lavacherie, and continue through the forest and marshlands passing through Prelle, Roumont, and Givroulle to Bastogne.

CITY
BASTOGNE (Bastenaken, Bastaken)

ROUTE
N34 N560 N812 N23

DISTANCE KM	TOTAL KM
57	461

ROUTE DESCRIPTION
Take N34 out of Bastogne to Longchamps. Turn off and head north through Rastadt, to N560. Take N560 about 1 km to Mormont, and then turn off to Wibrin. Continue through Wilognne. Cross N15 and pick up N812 to Montleban and continue through the village of Lomre and on to Joubleval at the intersection with N28. Pick up a narrow, winding road that roughly parallels N28, passing through the Forest of Hodinfosse to the town of Trois Ponts. Pick up N23 and continue the 6 kms to Stavelot.

CITY
STAVELOT

ROUTE
N422 N62 N697 N666 N62

DISTANCE KM	TOTAL KM
46	518

ROUTE DESCRIPTION
Leave Stavelot on N422 to Francorchamps. Then take N62 to Spa. From Spa, follow N697 to the autobahn N666 at Remouchamps. Then continue north on N666 to Louveigne. Take N62 into Liège.

CITY
LIÈGE (Luik, Lüttich)

ROUTE
N79

DISTANCE KM	TOTAL KM
40	564

ROUTE DESCRIPTION
From the north edge of the city in the suburb of Rocourt, take the road to Tongeren by way of Fexhe. Follow N79 to St.-Truiden.

CITY
ST.-TRUIDEN (Sint-Truiden, Saint-Trond)

ROUTE
N79 N253

DISTANCE KM	TOTAL KM
62	604

ROUTE DESCRIPTION
From St.-Truiden, take the winding back roads through Zoutleeuw, Oplinter, and Bunsbeek to rejoin N79 for the 15 kms to Leuven (Louvain). From Leuven, head south on N253 to Huldenberg. From there return to Brussels by way of Tervuren.

CITY
BRUSSELS

DISTANCE KM	TOTAL KM
0	666

BELGIUM SIGHTS AND ACCOMMODATIONS

BRUSSELS (Bruxelles). Brussels is definitely worth a visit, but don't plan to spend too much time in this modern city. The best of Belgium is to found in the countryside. The cosmopolitan Belgium capital has a population of just over a million and is home to several major international organizations, including **NATO** and the **EEC** (European Economic Community).

Your first stop in Brussels should be at the tourist office, **Tourisme Information Bruxelles** (rue Marché-aux-Herbes 61) just off of the Grand' Place. In addition to the usual city map and brochures, they can book hotel rooms, provide listings of current Brussels' happenings, as well as reserve theater and concert tickets. The tourist office distributes a booklet, *Gourmet Restaurants*, which lists and rates more than 100 of the best of the city's 1,500 restaurants, for a small fee.

The main attraction is the incredibly ornate **Grand' Place**. Located in the center of the Old Town, this huge square (80,500 square feet) is lined with a pleasant mixture of Gothic and baroque facades. One of the most interesting is the **Hotel de Ville** (Town Hall), the most beautiful example of fifteenth-century architecture in Belgium. The **Broodhuis** (Maison du Roi) opposite the Town Hall houses the **Museum of the City of Brussels**, which contains exhibits that illustrate the history of the city. Another interesting house on the Grand' Place is the **Maison des Brasseurs**, the site of the old Brewer's Guild. It contains a **Brewery Museum** with a collection of old beer-making implements. A glass of beer is included in the entry price. Be sure to schedule an evening visit to the Grand' Place in your plans; the play of lights upon the intricate stone facades lends a magical note to the area.

Brussels is an easy city for sightseeing as most of the main attractions are within convenient walking distance of the main square. The **Manneken-Pis**, the irreverent seventeenth-century statue of a little boy urinating, has over the years become the symbol of the city. The most plausible of the many tales concerning its origin is that it was placed just behind the Hotel de Ville off the Grand' Place by the mayor of Brussels in 1619 to commemorate the finding of his lost son.

Of the city's more than twenty museums, highlights include the **Musée d'Art Ancien**, which has a fine collection of paintings by the early Flemish masters, including some by Rubens and Brueghel. The **Musée d'Art Moderne** is a new museum that opened in 1984 to feature the works of a number of nineteenth-century and twentieth-century painters, including Ensor and Magritte.

The thirteenth-century Gothic **St. Michael's Cathedral**, atop a hill near the center of the city, is one of Brussels' oldest buildings and the national cathedral. **The Parc de Bruxelles** at the east edge of the old town separating the Parliament and the Royal Palace is a lovely garden laid out in the classic French style. In earlier times it was the hunting ground of the dukes of Brabant.

One of the most interesting excursions from Brussels is to the suburb of **Waterloo**, about 10 miles south of the capital. There are several museums in the area that describe the famous 1815 battle between Napoleon and Wellington. Climb to the top of the **Butte du Lion** (Lion's Mound) for a bird's-eye view of the battlefield.

Tervuren, an ancient village about 8 miles east of Brussels, is the site of one of the finest collections of African art in the world, the **Musée Royale de l'Afrique Centrale** (Museum of Central Africa). The museum is situated in a beautiful park and contains a wealth of magnificent exhibits from the days when the large chunk of Africa, now called Zaire, was the Belgian Congo, a Belgian colony.

Castle aficionados should pedal out into the countryside just southwest of Brussels to visit the historic thirteenth-century **Gaasbeek Castle**, which is located in a beautiful park. Also worth visiting is the imposing, three-towered, moated, red brick fortress at **Beersel**.

With so many diplomats running around on expense accounts, there are few restaurant and accommodation bargains to be found in this sophisticated European capital. The HOTEL METROPOLE (place de Brouckere 1, 1000 Brussels; Tel: [02] 21 72 300) is a fine, conveniently located hotel in the nineteenth-century tradition, one of the better values in the luxury category. For a good inexpensive hotel, try the HOTEL BERCKMANS (rue Berckmanns 12, Berckmansstraat, 1060 Brussels; Tel: [02] 57 89 48).

Brussels also has several inexpensive hostels and sleep-ins. The best of the lot is the IYHF AUBERGE DE JEUNESSE BRUEGEL (rue de St. Esprit 2; Tel: [02] 51 10 436), a large, modern, well-equipped hostel, conveniently located close to the Central Station.

Although there are no campgrounds directly in the city, there is a good site about 10 kilometers south of the city in Beersel (on our route to Waterloo). CAMPING DE BEERSEL is open all year.

ANTWERP (Antwerpen, Anvers). Lying on the Schelde River nearly at the Dutch border, Antwerp is Belgium's second largest city and one of the most cosmopolitan in Europe. The city has a centuries-long tradition of being a major banking and trade center, as well as being one of the world's most important diamond-cutting centers. You can watch the diamond cutters working at their fascinating trade at the **Vieligheidsmuseum** (Diamond Museum) (Jezusstraat 28-30). Antwerp also is home to Europe's largest community of Orthodox Jews. A stroll along Pelikaanstraat in the heart of the **Jewish Quarter**, where many of the residents are clad in the traditional black garb of the Orthodox Jew, is reminiscent of street scenes that were commonplace throughout central Europe prior to World War II.

As the birthplace of the painter Peter Paul Rubens, Antwerp has a longstanding tradition as a fine art center. The artist's house, where he lived and painted for close to thirty years, has been preserved as a museum. Unlike so many famous artists, Rubens achieved recognition and wealth early in his career and was able to live in quite a fashionable manner. His house at Wapper 9, one of the best museums of its kind, is packed full of the works of Rubens and his contemporaries. The massive **Royal Museum of Fine Arts** has a splendid collection of Flemish masters, including the works of Rubens, Frans Hals, Van Dyck, and Van der Weyden. Another unique museum not far from the Rubens house is the **Plantin-Moretus Museum**, site of the famous sixteenth-century Plantin print shop. The richly furnished interior includes some fine tapestries and several Gutenberg Bibles. Round out your Antwerp museum tour with a visit to the **Marine Museum** housed in the Steen, a tenth-century fortress, the city's oldest building. The museum contains an interesting assortment of ancient maps, ship models, and relics.

Dominating the center of the old city, the **Cathedral of Our Lady**, the country's largest church, has a cavernous interior, richly adorned and containing several very good Rubens. The sixteenth-century **Stadhuis** (Town Hall), facing the main square, is a sparkling example of Renaissance architecture.

For a change of pace, cycle out to the suburban estate of **Middelheim**. There in a lovely setting in the gardens of the estate is an outstanding array of fine sculpture, including pieces of such diverse artists as Rodin and Henry Moore.

The **Tourist Information Office** just in front of the central train station can provide you with a city map and a number of useful brochures, including a monthly listing of concerts and other events.

The HOTEL WALDORF (Belgielei 36-38, 2018 Antwerp; Tel: [03] 23 09 950) is a good quality downtown hotel. Doubles run from 2,500 BFr. At the other end of the scale, you can get a double with bath down the hall for 900 BFr. at RUBENSHOF (Amerikalei 115-117; Tel: [03] 23 70 789).

The 124-bed IYHF hostel is the modern and comfortable OP SINJOURKE (Erik Sassonlaanz; Tel: [03] 23 80 273).

CAMPING DE MOLEN is a pleasant small site located in the suburb of Linkeroever. It is open 1 April to 30 September.

BRUGES (Brugge). If you have time to visit only one city in Belgium, make sure that it is Bruges. Virtually a living open-air museum, the city has retained a medieval mood and presence matched by practically no other town in northern Europe. This is one place where you must get off your bike and explore the city on foot. Even if you have no eye for photography, you will come home from Bruges with prize-winning photos.

During the Middle Ages, the town was an important seaport, connected with the sea at Zeebrugge by the Zwin. The boat excursion along the old canals is a delightful way to get a feel for the city. For a birds-eye view, climb the **belfry** that rises some three hundred feet above the thirteenth-century marketplace in the center of the old town. It is here that the traditional *Play of the Golden Tree*, depicting the history of Flanders and Bruges, is performed every five years (next performance: 1990). The colorful **Holy Blood Procession**, dating back to the time of the Crusades, is held every year on Ascension Day.

Although the entire city can be considered a museum, there are several indoor museums worth visiting. The **Groeninge Museum** has a good collection of Flemish masters and some interesting Brueghels. The **Memling Museum** located in the medieval **St. Jans Hospital** houses the most important works of Hans Memling. For a glimpse into the lives of the old nobles of Bruges, visit the **Gruuthuse Museum**, formerly the home of one of the lords of Bruges; it contains a collection of armor, weapons, and furniture.

The **Prinselijk Begijnhof Ten Wijngaardee** (Princely Béguinage) founded in 1245, a delightful area of white cottages surrounding a tree-lined courtyard, is still inhabited by traditionally garbed Benedictine sisters.

The **Tourist Office** (Dienst voor Toerisme) is in the center of the old town at Markt 7. Be sure to get a copy of their monthly program, *Agenda Brugge*. The town is especially lively during the boisterous **Festival of Flanders**, an international music fest held during the first half of August.

The BOURGOENSCH HOF (Wollestraat 39; Tel: [050] 33 16 45) is a comfortable traditional hotel. For a good budget hotel, try the 'T SPEELMANSHUYS, ('t Zand 3; Tel: [050] 33 95 52).

The Bruges youth hostel is the 218-bed EUROPA JEUGDHERBERG (Baron Ruzettelaan 143; Tel: [050] 35 26 79).

Campers have a choice of several good campgrounds in the Bruges region. The most convenient is CAMPING ST. MICHIELS, a large all-year site about 2 kilometers southwest of the town center in the suburb of St. Michiels.

OSTEND (Ostende, Oostende). Originally a village at the east end of the coastal strip called Ter Streep, Ostend is now a fashionable beach resort. It is also Belgium's most important seaport. A large part of the city is protected from the ravages of the North Sea by a huge dike, the **Zeedijk**. There is regular ferry service between Ostend and the English ports of Dover and Folkestone.

This busy beach resort offers a large selection of accommodations at every level. The town's top hotel with doubles starting at 2,500 BFr. is the HOTEL ANDROMEDA (Kursaal Westhelling 5, 8400 Ostend; Tel: [059] 50 68 11). Of the many inexpensive small hotels, one of the town's best bargains is to be found at the HOTEL PALM BEACH (Koningstraat 90; Tel: [059] 70 54 77).

The 96-bed youth hostel, DE PLOATE (Langestraat 82; Tel: [059] 70 54 84), is located just a short distance from the train station.

K.A.C.B. CAMPING is a large all-year campground located at the north end of town.

GHENT (Gent, Gand). A thriving industrial city of 250,000, Ghent is the capital of the province of East Flanders. Rich in tradition and with an old town containing more historic buildings than any other Belgian city, Ghent is deserving of a visit; however, don't expect all of the charm of her sister city Bruges.

The main attractions are located within a short radius of the center of the old town. Castle and torture chamber fans should not pass up the foreboding **'s Gravensteen** (the castle of the Count of Flanders). The stone castle has walls six feet thick, and the interior contains several dungeons, as well as a collection of instruments of torture and execution. On a somewhat lighter vein, the **Museum Voor Schone Kunsten** (Fine Arts Museum), located in the **Citadel Park**, has a good collection of both classical Flemish masterpieces and the works of modern Belgian artists. The **Cathedral of St. Baaf** is an interesting combination of Gothic and Renaissance architecture. The interior is embellished with some fine pieces of art, including an intricately carved pulpit and Van Eyck's *Adoration of the Mystic Lamb*.

The main **Tourist Office** is located at Belforstraat 9, in the center of the old town across from the Town Hall.

For an old-world hotel loaded with tradition and atmosphere (Napoleon Bonaparte stayed there), try the more than seven-hundred-year-old SINT JORISHOF (Botermarkt 2, 9000 Ghent; Tel: [091] 24 24 24).

The spacious two-hundred-bed youth hostel, DE DRAEKE (St. Pietersplein 12; Tel: [091] 22 50 67), has plenty of atmosphere. It is located in an old abbey.

Campers should head for CAMPING BLAARMEERSEN, part of a sports complex at the western edge of town. It is open 1 March to 15 October.

NAMUR (Namen). Tucked into the rising hills that mark the beginning of the Ardennes country, Namur is a charming fortified old town situated at the junction of the Meuse and Sambre rivers. The imposing old **citadel**, strategically perched on a hill overlooking the valley and scene of countless battles, offers a splendid overview of the town and its surroundings. Be sure to take the underground train ride and see the film describing the history of the fortress.

Within the town itself, the eighteenth-century **Cathedral of St. Aubain**, a museum of religious treasures, and the **Archaeological Museum** are worth seeing.

For a good, comfortable hotel close to the train station, check into the HOTEL VICTORIA (ave. de la Gare 11-12, 5000 Namur; Tel: [081] 22 29 71) or the HOTEL PORTE DE FER (ave. de la Gare 4-5; Tel: [081] 23 13 45).

The youth hostel at Namur is one of the most congenial we have ever run into. AUBERGE DE JEUNESSE NAMUR (rue Felicien Rops, 8 La Plante, 5000 Namur; Tel: [081] 22 36 88) is located just outside of town along the river Meuse on the way to Dinant.

There is no campground in Namur itself. The closest is the small CAMPING 4 FILS AYMON CHAUSSEE DE LIÈGE located at the river about 7 kms east of Namur off N17 in the direction of Liège. It is open 1 April to 30 September.

ROCHEFORT. An attractive little Ardennes town dominated in the south by the ruins of an old castle, Rochefort makes a good base from which to explore the extensive grottoes in Rochefort and in nearby **Han-sur-Lesse**.

This small town has several surprisingly good hotels, the most attractive of which is the six-room AUBERGE LES FALIZES (rue de France 70, 5430 Rochefort; Tel: [084] 21 12 82).

AUBERGE DE JEUNESSE LE VIEUX MOULIN (rue du Hableau; Tel: [02] 21 53 100) is a pleasant, newly remodeled sixty-six-bed youth hostel.

The closest campground is CAMPING DE LA LESSE at the river in nearby **Han-sur-Lesse**. It is open 1 May to 31 August.

BASTOGNE (Bastenaken, Bastaken). Located near the border with the Grand Duchy of Luxembourg, Bastogne was the site of the historic Battle of the Bulge. In 1944 the Germans launched a massive attack trapping a large contingent of American troops. The German demand for surrender was met by the now-legendary reply of "Nuts" by the U.S. Forces Commander Gen. McCauliffe. There are several interesting museums and monuments in the town, including a **Nuts Museum**, commemorating this famous World War II battle.

You can spend a relaxing evening and enjoy a good meal at the **HOTEL LEBRUN** (rue de Marche 8, 6650 Bastogne; Tel: [062] 21 54 21).

There is an all-year campground at the northeast edge of town. From Bastogne, take the road toward Marche and turn off by the Esso station.

STAVELOT. This ancient town is situated on the river Ambleve. Until the French revolution, Stavelot was the seat of the **Benedictine Abbey** founded in 651 by St. Remaclus. Only the tower of the church and some small buildings remain. Just east of the city are the ruins of a fifteenth-century castle from which there is a good view of the surrounding countryside. This is a good base for exploring the **Hautes Fagnes Nature Reserve**, which contains Belgium's highest point, the observation tower at the **Signal de Botrange** (694 meters). Not exactly the Alps, but the contrast with the lowlands to the west is striking.

Comfortable rooms at reasonable prices are available at the HOTEL VAL D'AMBLEVE (route de Malmedy 9, 4970 Stavelot; Tel: [080] 86 23 53) where a double without a private bath will cost about 1,000 BFr.

CAMPING L'EAU ROUGE is a large all-year site located near the river.

LIÈGE (Luik, Lüttich). With a population of nearly a half million, Liège is Belgium's third largest city, the capital of the province of Walloon, and a major industrial center.

The city has concentrated in its old town core many vestiges from its l,300-year history. The river Meuse seems to meander through just about every part of the city, making a stroll through town a delightful succession of encounters with countless little bridges and winding streets. Liège has one of the largest pedestrian zones on the continent, making it particularly well suited for a walking tour.

The center of the city is formed by three adjacent squares: Place St.-Lambert, Place du Marche, and the Place de la Republique Francaise. Most of the town's main attractions are within easy walking or cycling distance from there. Of the many churches (over one hundred steeples dot the city's skyline), the fine Romanesque **Church of St. Barthelémy** is one of the most interesting. The intricate twelfth-century **font** by Renier de Huy, which rests on a pedestal of bronze bulls, is one of the "Seven Wonders of Belgium."

Le Musée de la Vie Walloone (The Museum of Walloon Life) housed in a former seventeenth-century convent displays exhibits depicting the many aspects of Walloon life. There is an outstanding collection of **marionettes**, as well as a replica of a nineteenth-century coal mine. Although the mines have been shut down, Liège was the first town in Europe to mine coal on a large scale. The fine collection at the **Museum of Modern Art** chronicles the development of painting and sculpture from the 1850s up to the present and includes the works of contemporary Belgian artists. If you have an interest in firearms, be sure to visit the **Musée d'Armes** (Weapons Museum). With more than eight thousand weapons, this is one of the best collections of its kind in the world. Liège has a long-standing tradition as a center for the manufacture of quality firearms.

From the **Parc de la Citadelle** atop a five-hundred-foot hill in the north of the town, you can enjoy an excellent vista of Liège and the surrounding countryside. Climb the some four hundred steps leading up from the Law Courts or hop on your bike and drive up via the rue de L'Academies.

Although the American chains Holiday Inn and Ramada Inn are well represented, we prefer the more authentic (and cheaper) HOTEL LE CYGNE D'ARGENT (rue Beeckman 49, 4000 Liège; Tel: [041] 23 70 01).

Although there is no IYHF hostel in Liège itself, students can stay at the inexpensive FOYER INTERNATIONAL DES ETUDIANTS (rue du Vertbois 29; Tel: [041] 23 50 98).

The closest campsite is in Jupille about 8 kms northeast of Liège. CAMPING FAYEN-BOIS is a small all-year site.

ST.-TRUIDEN (Sint-Truiden, Saint-Trond). An important market town in the fruit-producing region of **Hesbaye**, Sint-Truiden developed around an ancient abbey founded in 657 by Saint Trudo. The **seminary** north of the Grote Markt has incorporated some of the remnants of the original abbey.

The town's most comfortable hotel is the small HOTEL CICINDRIA (Abdijstraat 6, 3800 St.-Truiden; Tel: [011] 68 13 44).

CAMPING DE EGEL (Bautershoven 95) is located on the edge of town. It is open 1 April to 31 October.

POPULATION
5,123,989

RELIGION
97% Lutheran

CAPITAL
Copenhagen

CURRENCY
Danish Krone (DKr.); divided into 100 ore

OFFICIAL LANGUAGE
Danish; English widely spoken

BANKING HOURS
M T W F 0830–1600
      Th 0930–1800

STORE HOURS
M–Th 0900–1730
   F 0900–1900 or 2000
   S 0900–1200 or 1400

EMERGENCY TELEPHONE NUMBERS
Ambulance, Fire, or Police: 000
(no coin required)

TO CALL USA OR CANADA
Dial 0091; area code and number

HOLIDAYS
1 Jan.; Green Thursday; Good Friday; Easter Sunday and Monday; 3 May; 16 May; 5 June (from noon); 26 & 27 May; 25 & 26 December

USA CONSULATE
1 Kristen Bernikosgade
1105 COPENHAGEN
Tel: [01] 12 22 99

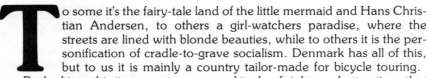

BIKING THROUGH EUROPE

DENMARK

To some it's the fairy-tale land of the little mermaid and Hans Christian Andersen, to others a girl-watchers paradise, where the streets are lined with blonde beauties, while to others it is the personification of cradle-to-grave socialism. Denmark has all of this, but to us it is mainly a country tailor-made for bicycle touring.

Packed into this tiny country are a multitude of sights and attractions that range from Copenhagen, the country's rollicking capital, to the broad beaches and dunes of the Jutland peninsula, to historic castles such as Kronbørg – inspiration for Shakespeare's Hamlet – to tiny picture-postcard villages with thatched-roofed cottages. One of the great things about touring a small country like Denmark is the fact that within a two-week or three-week period, you can pretty well cover the highlights of the entire country with some time left over for relaxing and mingling with the natives.

With a population less than that of greater Los Angeles, Denmark, a member of NATO and the European Common Market, is an active participant in the mainstream of twentieth century European life. It is a spotlessly clean country where everything seems to function efficiently, and yet it is a country where the people have not sacrificed warmth and friendliness for efficiency.

With an area approximately equal to that of land-locked Switzerland divided among some four hundred islands (only one hundred are inhabited) and bordered by more than four thousand miles of coastline, Denmark has a proud Viking heritage and is dominated by the sea. In fact, you will never have to travel more than forty miles or so to reach the ocean.

The Danes are a friendly, fun-loving, industrious people who present a marked contrast to their more dour northern neighbors – the Swedes and Norwegians. Europe's oldest kingdom, Denmark has been a constitutional monarchy since 1849. Wide-ranging social legislation and high taxes have provided for many far-reaching social welfare programs and one of Europe's highest living standards. Tourism is one of the country's leading kroner earners, and as a foreigner you will be made to feel welcome wherever you go. English is understood just about everywhere, especially among the younger Danes.

With 2.5 million bicycles distributed among its 5 million residents, Denmark definitely qualifies as a "bicycle friendly" country. Many Danes commute to work by bike, and many also mount their cycles in their leisure time to enjoy their own beautiful country. Although the loftiest peak in all of Denmark, Jutland's Yding Skovhoj, rises to just 550 feet above sea level, the countryside will present enough in the way of rolling hills to make a ten-speed worthwhile.

Denmark is super touring for all but hard-core alpine cyclists. The large Jutland (Jylland) peninsula, the only portion of the country with a land connection to the European continent, is a sparsely populated region of broad sandy beaches, grassy dunes, and attractive lakes and fjords – all interspersed with rolling hills and pleasant wooded areas.

The island of Zealand (Sjaelland), a popular cycling area, includes the capital city of Copenhagen, as well as excellent beaches, a number of historic towns and castles, magnificent parks, beech forests, and long stretches of undulating hills and fields.

Fünen (Fyn), the birthplace of Hans Christian Andersen, is another popular island destination. Fünen's fertile soil has earned it the nickname of "Denmark's garden." The island's hilly southern portion is a favorite cycling region for locals and tourists alike.

Regular, inexpensive ferry connections between the numerous islands make island hopping with a bike a joy. It's great fun to wheel your bike to the head of the long lines of cars assembled at the dock and know that you are paying just a fraction of what the motorists are paying to flit from island to island.

TRANSPORTATION WITHIN THE COUNTRY

The Danish National Railroad (DSB) runs one of the most efficient operations in Europe; unfortunately, their efficiency drops off considerably when it comes to transporting bicycles. In recent years, largely due to the aggressive tactics of the Danish Cycling Federation, there has been some improvement in the situation. It is now possible to take your bike with you on a number of trains between major Danish cities. The charge is 30 DKr.; reservations are necessary and must be made at least three hours prior to the train's departure. These "bike friendly" trains are listed on the back of the *Denmark By Bicycle* map. It is also possible to take your bike on some commuter trains. The charge is 10 to 20 DKr.; reservations are recommended but not required. Only four bikes per train are carried, and bikes are not accepted during rush-hour periods (Monday to Friday before 9 A.M. and between 3 and 6 P.M.). If you send your bike as freight on a different train, it will cost you 20 DKr. for under 100 kms and 40 DKr. for over 100 kms. Not bad, but the DSB will guarantee only that your bike will arrive within two to three working days of shipment.

ROADS

Many of Denmark's main roads are accompanied by bike paths, plus there are some 50,000 kms of little-used secondary roads. In many parts of the country it is possible to cycle for hours without encountering more than a few cars. Where cycle paths are present, Danish law requires that they be used. In a country where so many people ride bicycles, it is hardly surprising to find that Danish motorists are very aware and considerate of cyclists on the roads.

The law requires that cyclists keep to the right and make left turns at intersections in two steps:
1. Stay to the right and first cross the street that you want to turn into.
2. Cross the street which you had been riding on.

It sounds confusing and a bit of a hassle, but it is really practical, especially when traffic is heavy.

Roads and towns are well marked and signs are easily read. Major international highways are denoted with the letter E and one or two digits on a green background; primary highways are marked with one or two digits on a yellow background; and secondary roads are marked with three digits on a white background. Bicycles are not allowed on the freeways.

Although they still exist in some rural areas and small villages, cobblestones – every biker's bane – generally have been eliminated. Road maintenance is kept to a high standard; potholes and badly surfaced roads even in outlying areas are a rarity.

MAPS

For such a small country, it is amazing what a large variety of suitable cycling maps are available. For tour planning and an overall view of the country, the *Cykelferiekort (Denmark by Bicycle)* issued by the Danish Cyclist Federation is the best. Cycle routes throughout the country are shown on a scale of 1:510,000 (1 cm = 5.1 kms). The flip side of this very useful publication (it is too bad that such maps aren't available for other countries) contains a wealth of information in Danish, English, and German, specifically aimed at cycle tourists. It includes details on ferries, trains, and youth hostels. The map, which costs 42 DKr. can be ordered directly from **Dansk Cyklist Forbund** (Kjeld Langes Gade 14, 1367 Kopenhagen K, Denmark; Tel: [01] 14 42 12). All orders must be paid in Danish kroners and include a 15 DKr. handling charge.

Depending on what level of detail you like for your touring and how much you are willing to spend, you can navigate your way across Denmark utilizing any one of three different series of maps.

There is a series of maps issued by the Geodaetisk Institut that covers the country in 110 separate maps (scale 1:50,000; 1 cm = 5 km). These are so detailed that they are better suited for hiking and are not really practical for cycling. After all, if you spend all of your time pouring over detailed maps, you will wind up seeing very little of the actual country. Then there is the cost and hassle of traveling with so many maps.

The Geodaetisk Institut also offers a series of thirty-three maps which cover the country in excellent detail, showing all paved roads and many tracks, as well as every small settlement (scale 1:100,000; 1 cm = 1 km). These are the best maps to use for touring as long as cost is not a big factor. Each map costs 33 DKr. and a two-week to three-week tour could easily eat up fifteen or more maps. The maps are available directly from Dansk Cyklist Forbund and at many Danish bookstores.

Denmark at a scale of 1:200,000 (1 cm = 2 km) covers the country in four sheets. These maps show most roads and denote the major tourist attractions. Height contours are not shown, but in Denmark that's not really a problem. We've used these maps and found them to be quite adequate for touring purposes. They are available under the Geodaetisk Institut's and the "Mair die General Karte" label. They can be found in bookstores in Denmark, Germany, and England, or ordered from Dansk Cyklist Forbund.

For cycling in and around Copenhagen, the Cyklist Forbund puts out a map showing all the city streets that have marked bikeways. *Copenhagen by Bicycle* issued by "Use It," Youth Information Copenhagen (Radhusstraede 13, 1466 Copenhagen K; Tel: [01] 15 65 18), shows the major biking streets·and is packed with useful tips for biking in the Danish capital.

Cyklistkort for Fyn is a detailed map (scale 1:100,000) for cycle tours of the island of Fünen. It is available from Dansk Cyklist Forbund.

The intercity bus network is quite extensive. In most cases buses will transport bikes on a space available basis. The only problem is that space is often not available. Baby buggies have preference, so be prepared to be "bumped." City buses do not transport bicycles.

As you might imagine in a country with more than four hundred islands, ferries are an important means of transportation. It's pretty hard to do any significant amount of touring in Denmark without using the ferries, which range from large ocean-going vessels that transport trains and trucks along with your bike to quaint little boats where your bicycle will be the largest vehicle aboard. In any case, a ferry ride provides a pleasant way to rest your weary legs and enjoy the scenery. In most cases there is a small charge for transporting a bicycle, although some ferries make no additional charge. The Danish Cyclist Federation cycling map lists the details for the most important routes.

BICYCLE SHOPS AND RENTALS

With a ratio of one bike for every two inhabitants, Denmark is well-outfitted with bicycle shops. Practically every small town has at least one. Danish mechanics are resourceful and very helpful. Most speak English.

Spare parts are usually stocked for the major European and Japanese makes, but don't expect to find a wide selection of Schwinn or Cannondale parts. Twenty-four-inch, twenty-six-inch, twenty-seven-inch, and twenty-eight-inch tubes and tires, as well as the French size 700 C, are available at most of the larger shops.

Rental cycles are widely available at the major train stations and through local tourist offices and cycle shops. Unfortunately, most of these are heavy clunkers. Daily rental costs are 20 to 30 DKr. and weekly rentals cost 100 to 175 DKr., depending on the type and location. Identification and a deposit are required. To avoid disappointment, book ahead. Most rental places are closed on Sundays.

ACCOMMODATIONS

Denmark has an efficient tourist infrastructure which provides a large variety of pleasant, clean accommodations ranging from campgrounds and youth hostels to plush castle hotels.

Unlike most European countries, hotels in Denmark are not classified, so price usually becomes the determining factor in choosing a hotel. A comprehensive listing of hotels, pensions, inns, and youth hostels showing prices and describing facilities is available free from the Danish National Tourist Office and most tourist offices in the country. In many cases, even in high season, discounts and special deals are available. Don't hesitate to ask. With the exception of hotels in Copenhagen, an inexpensive hotel without a private bath will set you back about 150 to 210 DKr. In most towns the local tourist office will be able to find you an inexpensive, comfortable room in a private home or pension for a small fee. The English-style bed and breakfast is not commonly found in Denmark. When searching for a private room, look for signs reading "Vaerelser."

Another interesting possibility is to stay on a working farm for a few days or longer and use this as a base from which to explore the local area. In many cases, home-cooked meals are provided. On some farms, accommodations with cooking facilities are provided. Approximate costs per person/per night including two meals is 160 DKr. Figure on paying a total of about 1,400 DKr. per week for a four-person to six-person farm apartment. For further information contact the Danish National Tourist Office or your travel agent.

The kro is a Danish institution. These small rural inns scattered throughout the countryside are often in romantic old half-timbered houses. Well known for fine traditional food and warm hospitality, these are great places to rest up after a hard day's cycling. Average overnight price for a double without bath or meals is 150 to 325 DKr. A promotional deal offering substantial discounts utilizing "Kro Checks" is available from travel agents or the **Dansk Kroferie** (Horsens Turistbureau, Kongensgade 25, Dk-8700, Horsens; Tel: [05] 62 38 22).

The ninety-five youth hostels spread throughout the country offer a reasonably priced alternative to camping. Many of the hostels are located in old remodeled houses, some in old schools or farmhouses, while several are brand new. In all cases the high Danish standard of cleanliness is maintained, and facilities are comfortable but not luxurious. Family rooms with hot and cold running water are available, and many hostels serve reasonably priced meals or provide cooking facilities. Upon request the next day's take-away lunch often will be provided. Costs for a bed are about 40 to 43 DKr. per person per night. A youth hostel card (I.Y.H.A.) is required. A guest card valid at all Danish hostels can be purchased at most hostels or from the **Danish Youth Hostel Association** (Vesterbrogade 39, DK-1620 Kopenhagen V; Tel: [01] 31 36 12) for 110 DKr. The

Danish Youth Hostel Association also will provide a guide to all the Danish hostels for 22 DKr.

There are some five hundred official camping sites located primarily along the coast and at most places you will visit. Sites are classified by the tourist authorities with from one to three stars depending on amenities provided. In general, standards of cleanliness and service are high. You can count on most three-star sites to have a swimming pool and coin-operated laundry facilities.

To stay at a Danish campground it is necessary to present either an International Camping Carnet or a Danish Camping Pass. The camping pass can be purchased at any campground in the country. The average cost for a one-night stay is about 28 DKr. per person and bicycle.

A free map and listing of official campsites is available from the Danish National Tourist Office. The *Official Danish Campground Guide* is available from **Campingradet** (Skjoldsgade 10, DK-2100 Kopenhagen 0) for 32 DKr. plus 20 DKr. for postage. Most sites are open from 1 May to 1 September, and seventy are open all year.

Free camping is illegal, so be careful where you decide to pitch your tent. Enforcement is particularly stringent around beach and dune areas. Offenders are often fined on the spot. If possible, get a local farmer to give you permission to set up your tent. If you decide to "free camp," be discreet!

FOOD AND DRINK

Whether you eat out in restaurants all the time or picnic your way through the country, rest assured you will eat very well! A number of Danish delectables are familiar sights on American supermarket shelves and restaurant menus.

The traditional Danish lunch consists of an assortment of smorrebrod (open-faced sandwiches) made of meats, fish, cheeses, eggs, and vegetables. According to a Danish friend, there are some 250 possible varieties of smorrebrod. Danish pastry is different from the American version and is scrumptious. *Polser*, the tasty Danish version of the hot dog, is found at stands everywhere. It is little surprise that sea food plays such an important role in the diet. Delicious herring, smoked salmon, mussels, lobster, shrimp and smoked eel are widely eaten. Danish cheeses such as blue, havarti, and danbo are world renowned and make a great combination with any one of the fine Danish beers. Alcohol, in general, is very expensive, with the exception of beer and aquavit, a potent, locally produced schnapps. Wines must be imported and are priced out of sight. Save your wine drinking for countries where the wine is homegrown. Fresh fruits and vegetables are relatively scarce and quite expensive.

Denmark is a nation of small shops and open-air markets. Small supermarkets are found in most middle or larger sized towns. Food quality is uniformly good. Butcher shops have a good variety of prepared meat, fish, and vegetable salads. Add some of the excellent bread and rolls from a *bageri* (bakery), top it all off with a bottle of Carlsberg beer, and you have the makings of a super picnic. *Konditori* and bakeries seem to be everywhere, and we always have a hard time pedaling past them. Danish cakes and pastries come in a mouth-watering assortment of sizes, shapes, and tastes.

One of the best places to eat out in Denmark is at a *kro*. These atmosphere-rich country inns are found throughout the country, many in out-of-the-way locations on just the kind of roads that are ideal for cycling. Tradition has it that every Danish town of any size has a *kro* for the residents and their guests. These *kros* feature some of the best traditional regional cooking in the country.

When searching for a restaurant, look for the *"Dan Menu"* sign. More than seven hundred participating restaurants and *kros* offer a two-course traditional meal at a fixed price including tax and service of 68 DKr. A budget version is the Tourist Cafeteria Menu. Participating cafeterias offer a two-course meal for 45 DKr.

In addition to the many cafés and restaurants, there are numerous *polser* stands and take-out *smorrebrod* places.

PACKAGE TOURS

There are a number of tours available that encompass all parts of the country and run from several days to two weeks. A variety of accommodations are offered, ranging from youth hostels to comfortable hotels. Bicycles and meals are included. (There is a price reduction if you use your own bike.) Unlike so many other package deals, you can cycle on your own and set your own pace. For detailed information, contact **Dansk Cykelferie** (C/O DVL Rejser, Kultorvet 7, DK-1175 Copenhagen K; Tel: [01] 13 27 27).

SOURCES OF ADDITIONAL INFORMATION

Tourist Information Offices are conspicuously located in all tourist areas throughout the country. Full service offices are identified with the international "i" sign. Many offices can provide bicycle itineraries for their respective areas. The main **National Tourist Office** is in Copenhagen (H.C. Andersens Boulevard 22, DK-1253 Copenhagen K; Tel: [01] 11 13 25). It is a well-organized center with information about all major Danish tourist attractions.

Dansk Cyklist Forbund (Danish Cyclist Federation) (Kjeld Langes Gade 14, DK-Copenhagen K; Tel: [01] 14 42 12) is one of Europe's most active cycling organizations. A voluntary group financed by membership fees, they have been instrumental in achieving many improvements in cycling conditions for Danish and foreign cyclist alike. If there is anything you would like to know about biking in Denmark, these are the people to contact. They are also an excellent source of maps. The federation office is located just a few minutes' walk from Tivoli in Copenhagen.

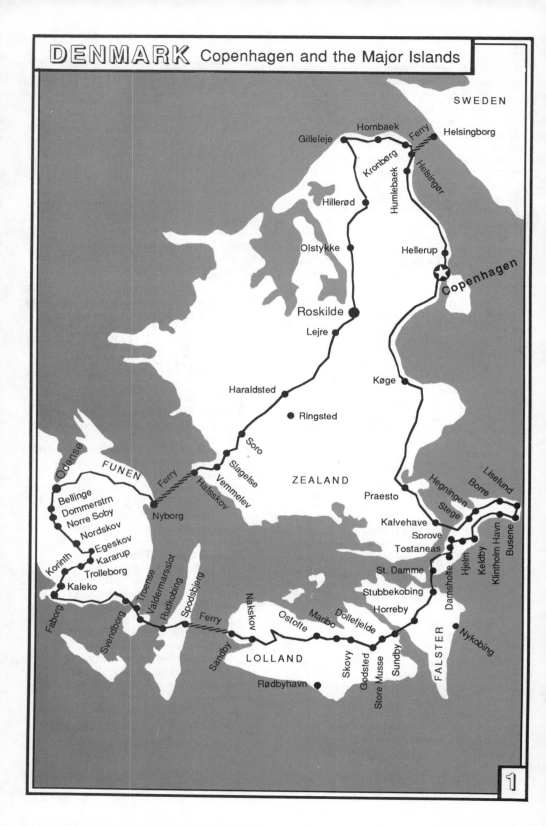

DENMARK Copenhagen and the Major Islands

SWEDEN

Hornbaek
Gilleleje
Ferry
Helsingborg
Kronbørg
Helsingør
Humlebaek
Hillerød
Olstykke
Hellerup
Copenhagen
Roskilde
Lejre
Køge
Haraldsted
Ringsted
Soro
Odense
FUNEN
Ferry
Slagelse
Halsskov
Vemmelev
ZEALAND
Praesto
Hegningen
Liselund
Borre
Bellinge
Dommerstrn
Norre Soby
Nyborg
Stege
Nordskov
Kalvehave
Sprove
Egeskov
Tostaneas
Klintholm Havn
Busene
Kararup
St. Damme
Hjelm
Keldby
Korinth
Trolleborg
Troense
Valdermarsslot
Stubbekobing
Damsholte
Kaleko
Rudkobing
Horreby
Faborg
Spodsbjerg
Ferry
Nakskov
Maribo
Dollefjelde
Svendborg
Ostofte
Sundby
FALSTER
Nykobing
Sandby
LOLLAND
Skovy
Godsted
Store Musse
Rødbyhavn

1

Copenhagen and the Major Islands

Quaint thatched-roofed, half-timbered farmhouses; elegant manor houses; historic castles; clean, sandy beaches; lonely stretches of grass-covered dunes; Viking relics; Tivoli, Copenhagen's unique fun park; ferry rides; and the birthplace of Hans Christian Andersen are all part of the route we have chosen to show off the best of Denmark's many attractions.

Cycling is easy, and with the exception of a few hilly areas, presents no great challenge. This route can be negotiated with a three-speed bike, but a ten-speed will make your life a bit easier. Most visitors coming to Denmark want to check out Copenhagen first, and for that reason we have chosen to begin our route there. However, the route is laid out so that it can be started at any point along the way and pedaled in either direction.

If you are coming by bike from Germany, take the one-hour ferry ride from Puttgarden in Schleswig Holstein to the Danish port of Rødby. This 600-km route will take you through all of the major touring regions of Denmark, with the exception of Jutland, which forms the major portion of our other Danish route. To do this comfortably and allow sufficient time to enjoy the many interesting attractions along the way, you should allow a good two weeks.

COPENHAGEN AND THE MAJOR ISLANDS LOOP

DISTANCE
597 kms/370 miles

MAIRS DIE GENERAL MAPS
Denmark #3, #4
 (scale 1:200,000)

GEODAETISK INSTITUT MAPS
#1212, #1312, #1313, #1411,
#1412, #1413, #1414, #1511,
#1512, #1513, #1514
 (scale 1:100,000)

Note: The *Cykilistkort for Fyn*
 (scale 1:100,000) can be used
 in place of Geodaetisk maps
 #1212, #1312, and #1313

This route covers a variety of terrain, passing through dense forests, rolling farmlands, and beach areas. It includes several picturesque ferry crossings. This is great country for a first European cycling tour, and cyclists of all ages will find this an interesting route.

The influence of the Gulf Stream helps to provide Denmark with the mildest climate in Scandinavia. The touring season runs from May through September, with the best chances of having good weather coming in June and July. August is the rainiest month, with the greatest amount of rainfall occurring in the western portion of the Jutland peninsula. Temperatures vary little within this small country. The average temperature in July is about 60° F. It rarely gets very hot and you can usually plan on encountering a fair amount of wind. The prevailing winds are westerlies.

Although some of the major tourist attractions can be quite crowded in July and August, crowds are nothing like those experienced in southern Europe. The best times for a cycle tour are late June, July, August, and early September.

In such a highly developed, densely populated small country, you will never be more than a few hours pedaling time from a campground, youth hostel, or *kro*.

★ *LOOKING OUT OVER THE HANDLEBARS* ★

COPENHAGEN AND THE MAJOR ISLANDS

CITY	ROUTE
COPENHAGEN	152

DISTANCE KM	TOTAL KM
35	0

ROUTE DESCRIPTION

From the Town Hall Square, take H. C. Andersen Blvd. to Norre Sogade following the signs to Helsingør. There are bike paths all along the route out of town and most of the way to Helsingør. Norre Sogade runs into Oster Sogade. Turn left at the intersection with Osterbrogade, which continues as Strandvejen. Route 152 hugs the coast most of the way to Helsingør and, except for a few kms, is lined with bike paths. At the edge of town just before Hellerup, the route passes the Tuborg brewery.

CITY
HUMLEBAEK

ROUTE
152

DISTANCE KM	TOTAL KM
23	35

ROUTE DESCRIPTION

Stay on 152 along the coast to Helsingør, site of Hamlet's castle at Kronbørg.

CITY
HELSINGØR

ROUTE
237

DISTANCE KM	TOTAL KM
24	58

ROUTE DESCRIPTION
From Helsingør, the road follows the north coast of the island with scenic views out over the Øresund to nearby Sweden. This stretch of wooded coastline contains some fine sandy beaches and the quaint seaside resorts of Hornbaek and Gilleleje.

CITY
GILLELEJE

ROUTE
Bike path

DISTANCE KM	TOTAL KM
39	82

ROUTE DESCRIPTION
From the Gilleleje train station, take the delightful bike path, which runs past the ruins of Soberg Castle and through the pleasant forest of Gribskov to end at Hillerød.

CITY
HILLERØD

ROUTE
6

DISTANCE KM	TOTAL KM
35	121

ROUTE DESCRIPTION
Leave Hillerød heading south on 233 toward Nr. Herley. Turn right at the intersection with hwy 6 and follow this all the way to Roskilde. Although there is a cycle path for most of the way, it is necessary to leave hwy 6 just north of Olstykke for a few kms before rejoining the cycle path for the remaining 14 kms to the former Danish capital of Roskilde.

CITY
ROSKILDE

ROUTE
14

DISTANCE KM	TOTAL KM
15	156

ROUTE DESCRIPTION
Take hwy 14 under the freeway toward Ringsted. About 1 km outside of Roskilde, follow the signs along Ledreborg Alle to Lejre. From Lejre continue on to Soro, following a series of little-traveled winding country lanes through the rolling dairy lands and quiet villages. Your best bet for navigating this back country stretch to Soro is to follow the signs from village to village, passing through Lejre, Saerlose, Ny Tolstrup, Mortenstrup, Haraldsted, Estrup, Gyrstinge, St. Ebberup, Fulby, and Pedersborg. Don't be misled by main city signs which will lead you to the busy main highway.

CITY
SORO

ROUTE
E66

DISTANCE KM	TOTAL KM
18	171

ROUTE DESCRIPTION
In Soro, take the good bike path that runs alongside the main highway E66 to Slagelse.

CITY
SLAGELSE

ROUTE
150

DISTANCE KM	TOTAL KM
34	189

ROUTE DESCRIPTION
From Slagelse take hwy 150, crossing the main road E66 to Vemmelev. Pick up the bike trail and follow the signs to the ferry at Halsskov.

CITY
KORSER/HALSSKOV

ROUTE
FERRY

ROUTE DESCRIPTION
Take the one-hour crossing. There are twenty to thirty crossings daily. The fare for one way with a bike is 50 DKr.

CITY
TO KUNDSHOVED/NYBORG, ISLAND OF FÜNEN

ROUTE
160

DISTANCE KM	TOTAL KM
27	223

ROUTE DESCRIPTION
From the harbor, take the bike path to Nyborg; then follow the path that accompanies hwy 160 most of the way into Odense.

CITY
ODENSE

DISTANCE KM	TOTAL KM
10	250

ROUTE DESCRIPTION
From the center of Odense, head south to the Open Air Museum, then continue on the bike path toward Bellinge. At Svenstrup, turn onto the road to Dammestrup. Stay on this back country road past a small lake into Norre Soby. Cross hwy 43 and continue through the quiet villages of Nordskov and Gestelev to hwy 323. Cross this and go through Herringe to Rudme. At Rudme, turn right and follow the signs to Egeskov.

CITY
EGESKOV

ROUTE
8

DISTANCE KM	TOTAL KM
10	260

ROUTE DESCRIPTION
From the castle at Egeskov, take hwy 8 through the village of Kararup to Brahetrolleborg Castle.

CITY
BRAHETROLLEBORG

ROUTE
8

DISTANCE KM	TOTAL KM
24	270

ROUTE DESCRIPTION
Leave the castle park and stay on hwy 8 to the town of Korinth. Go through the town and pick up the road (on the left) through the village of Diernaes, past the six-hundred-year-old windmill at Kaleko into the historic city of Fåborg.

Note: At this point you may follow the rest of this route back to Copenhagen or continue on with the Jutland (western) loop. The Jutland route continues along the south coast of Fünen, crosses over to the Jutland Peninsula, runs down along the west coast beaches, and then skirts the German border before returning by ferry to Fünen to link back up with this route to return to Copenhagen.

CITY	ROUTE
FÅBORG	44

DISTANCE KM	TOTAL KM
15	294

ROUTE DESCRIPTION
From Fåborg, take hwy 44 to the little settlement of Bogentved. Turn off to the right in the direction of the sea, and follow the winding road along the romantic coastal stretch into Svendborg.

CITY	ROUTE
SVENDBORG	9

DISTANCE KM	TOTAL KM
3	309

ROUTE DESCRIPTION
Cross the Svendborg bridge onto the tiny island of Tasinge. Follow the signs to Troense and Valdermarsslot, an impressive seventeenth-century palace with a maritime museum. Pick up hwy 9 at Lundby, and follow the bike path over the bridge into the port of Rudkobing on the island of Langeland, which is noted for its many fine beech trees.

CITY
RUDKOBING

ROUTE
9

DISTANCE KM	TOTAL KM
35	312

ROUTE DESCRIPTION
It is just 3 kms across the island to the ferry terminal at Spodsbjerg.

CITY
SPODSBJERG/TARS

ROUTE
FERRY

ROUTE DESCRIPTION
Take the forty-five-minute crossing; there are eighteen crossings daily. The fare for one person with a bike is 45 DKr.

CITY
TARS/NAKSKOV

ROUTE
291

DISTANCE KM	TOTAL KM
34	347

ROUTE DESCRIPTION
From the ferry, follow the signs to Sandby. Bikes are not allowed on hwy 9 to Nakskov. From Sandby, continue into Nakskov, then take hwy 291 across the flat farmlands (sugar beets) toward Maribo. Just before the junction with hwy 9, turn off and follow the road to Ostofte and then into Maribo.

Note: Rødbyhavn, some 15 kms south of Maribo, is the main ferry terminal for crossings to Germany. The sixty-minute trip to Puttgarten costs 60 DKr. for one person with a bike. There are twenty-two to thirty crossings daily.

CITY	ROUTE
MARIBO	297

DISTANCE KM	TOTAL KM
20	381

ROUTE DESCRIPTION
Head out of Maribo along the Sonderso (lake), passing through Revshale. Continue on to the stately Engestofte Manor House. The little-traveled road continues through the little villages of Skovby, Godsted, Hejrede, Store Musse, Dollefjelde, and Krattet before joining up with hwy 297 at the Fuglsang Manor House. Take hwy 297 5 kms into Sundby. Then cross the bridge to Nykobing on the island of Falster.

CITY	ROUTE
NYKOBING	271

DISTANCE KM	TOTAL KM
40	401

ROUTE DESCRIPTION
From Nykobing, follow the road to Horreby. Then stay on 271 through the fertile farmland to Stubbekobing.

CITY
STUBBEKOBING/BOGO

ROUTE
FERRY

ROUTE DESCRIPTION
The crossing time is thirteen minutes; there are fourteen crossings daily. The fare for one person with a bike is 13 DKr.

CITY
BOGO/NYBY

DISTANCE KM	TOTAL KM
25	441

ROUTE DESCRIPTION
Take the causeway onto the island of Møn and follow a series of small roads around this tiny island to Møn Klint. You will pass through St. Damme, Tostaneas, Sprove, Damsholte, Hjelm, Bissinge, Keldby Busemarke, Klintholm Havn, Kraneled, and Busene.

CITY
MØN/KLINET

DISTANCE KM	TOTAL KM
26	466

ROUTE DESCRIPTION
Continue along the north side of the island to Stege by way of Liselund, Borre, Ostermark Ullemarke, Udby, and Hegningen.

CITY	ROUTE
STEGE	59 265

DISTANCE KM	TOTAL KM
45	492

ROUTE DESCRIPTION
Take hwy 59 from Stege. Follow this over the bridge to the island of Zealand. At Kalvehave, continue north on hwy 265 to the pleasantly located city of Praesto.

CITY
PRAESTO

ROUTE
209

DISTANCE KM	TOTAL KM
30	537

ROUTE DESCRIPTION
From Praesto, continue along hwy 209 to the beach resort of Køge.

CITY
KØGE

ROUTE
151

DISTANCE KM	TOTAL KM
30	567

ROUTE DESCRIPTION
A good bike path follows the beach front road past a number of seaside resorts into the center of Copenhagen.

CITY
COPENHAGEN

TOTAL KM
597

COPENHAGEN AND THE MAJOR ISLANDS SIGHTS AND ACCOMMODATIONS

COPENHAGEN. The Danish capital is one of the great cities of Europe, offering visitors a rich assortment of delights and diversions. Its fantastic amusement park, Tivoli, broad boulevards, street performers, bustling shopping streets, royal palace, fine museums, and swinging night life are all concentrated in an area easily covered on foot.

Without a doubt, the main attraction is fabulous **Tivoli**, a package of fun and fantasy that no visitor to Copenhagen should pass up. There's something for everyone – exciting rides; a gambling casino; gourmet restaurants and polser stands, discos; circus acts; jazz, classical, and rock music – and all of this in a magical setting of thousands of twinkling colored lights and fresh blossoms – right in the heart of the city! The park is best enjoyed at night. It is open 1 May to mid-September.

Be sure to take the time to wander around **Ströget**, the main shopping street. It is packed with people, performers, and plush shops. For museum-goers, the **Ny Carlsberg Glypotek**, one of Scandinavia's major art museums, and the **Frihedsmuseet** (World War II Resistance Museum) are worth a visit.

A harbor and canal cruise is a great way to see the city's highlights, but Copenhagen is a city for walking. Stroll the harbor district, **Nyhavn**, once a favorite haunt of Hans Christian Andersen, and wander through **Christiania**, a living testament to Danish tolerance. This sprawling district was taken over by masses of young people and drop-outs in the 1970s; today it is a haven for those experimenting with alternative life styles. Beer connoisseurs should be sure to make the pilgrimage to Mecca, which in Copenhagen means either the **Tuborg** or **Carlsberg brewery**.

Of all the major cities in Europe, Copenhagen ranks high on the list of "bicycle friendly" cities. An extensive network of heavily utilized cycle lanes extends to all sections of the Danish capital. An excellent cycling map of Copenhagen is available from **Dansk Cyklist Forbund** (Kjeld Langes Gade 14, 1367 Copenhagen K; Tel: [01] 14 42 12).

There are a few places that rent bikes, among them: KOBENHAVNS CYKEL-BARS (Gothersgade 157-159; Tel: [01] 14 07 17), JET CYKLER (Istedgde 100; Tel: [01] 23 17 60), DAN WHEEL (Colbjorn-sensgade 3; Tel: [01] 21 22 27), LYNGBY TRAIN STATIONS (Tel: [02] 87 02 65), and KLAMPENBORG STATION (Tel: [01] 64 08 60). Don't expect fancy touring or racing machines, but they do have sturdy basic cycles suitable for touring most parts of the country. Figure on paying about 30 DKr. for one day and 250 DKr. for a two-week rental.

There is a place to stay to fit everyone's budget from swank hotels to a "sleep in" in a converted ice hockey stadium. Hotel rooms generally are expensive. For tips on finding inexpensive lodging and a young people's perspective on this fun city, check in with "Use It" at **Huset, Youth Information Center** (13 Radhusstraede, Copenhagen K; Tel: [01] 15 65 18). While you are there, pick up a free copy of their useful pamphlet *Copenhagen by Bicycle*.

Even the "inexpensive" hotels in Copenhagen will provide clean and very adequate accommodations. The biggest concentration of hotels is within a few block radius of the Central Station. Tucked in amidst the raunchy bars and sex shops are some quite decent hotels. Breakfast is usually, but not always, included. Ask when registering.

HOTEL DANIA (Istedgade 3, 1650 Copenhagen V; Tel: [01] 22 11 00) is a good, clean relatively inexpensive hotel – a five-minute walk to Tivoli. The PARK HOTEL (Jarmers Plads 3, 1551 Copenhagen V; Tel: [01] 13 30 00) is a pleasant, moderately priced hotel in a good, convenient neighborhood. HOTEL D'ANGLE-TERRE (Kongens Nytorv 34, 1050 Copenhagen K; Tel: [01] 12 00 95) is the classiest hotel in town. Doubles run about $200 per night. The food in the dining room is excellent and actually quite reasonably priced.

A good way to beat the high cost of hotel accommodations is to rent a room in a private home. Many are conveniently located in easy-to-reach suburbs and also give you a glimpse into everyday Danish life. The helpful staff at **Kiosk P** located in the Central Train Station will assist in finding a room in a private home for a small fee. "Use It" (see above) will also provide the same service.

There are three youth hostels in the Copenhagen area, all located on the outskirts of the city but with good access to the town via public transportation or cycle paths. A Youth Hostel Association card is required. Accommodations are in dormitories or two-person and four-person rooms.

BELLAHOJ VANDRERHJEM (Herbergsvejen 8, 2700 Bronshoj; Tel: [01] 28 97 15) has 308 beds in an apartment building about 5 kms from town center. Meals are served, but there are no cooking facilities. COPENHAGEN HOSTEL (Sjaellandsbroen 55, 2300 Copenhagen S; Tel: [01] 52 29 08) has 448 beds in a sprawling modern complex. There are fifty rooms with two beds each. Meals are served, but there are no cooking facilities. LYNGBY VANDRERHJEM (Radvad 1, 2800 Lyngby; Tel: [02] 80 30 74) has ninety-four beds in a pleasant old building about 15 kms north of city center. It offers meals and kitchen facilities.

Another low-cost option for convenient, albeit bare bones, accommodations is VESTERBRO UNGDOMSGARD (Absalonsgade 8, 1658 Copenhagen V). It has 160 beds, plus one dormitory with sixty additional beds. It is conveniently located and no membership card is required. It is open 5 May to 1 September. COPENHAGEN SLEEP IN (Per Henrik Lings Alle 6, 2100 Copenhagen O; Tel: [01] 28 50 59) offers 432 beds (4 beds to a cubicle) in a partitioned-off ice hockey stadium. Showers and lockers are available. Sleeping bags are required. Bed and breakfast costs 50 DKr. It is hard to beat this place for both price and novelty! It is open 27 June to 1 September.

Of the many campgrounds in the Copenhagen vicinity, two are the most convenient and best equipped. BELLAHOJ CAMPING (Hvidkildevej, 2400 Copenhagen) is in a park 5 kms from town center. It is open 1 June to 1 September. ABSALON CAMPING (132 Korsdalsvej, 2610 Rodovre) is a huge parklike site with good facilities and access to the city center. It is located 9 kms from Copenhagen and is open all year.

HUMLEBAEK. Just a few hours ride north of Copenhagen is the site of the **Louisiana Museum**. In a beautiful park setting with a fantastic sculpture garden overlooking the Øresund, this intriguing museum has one of northern Europe's best collections of modern art.

HELSINGØR (Elsinore). This old trading port is best known as the site of **Kronbørg Castle**, which served as the inspiration for the setting of Shakespeare's famous play *Hamlet*. From the castle there's a great view over to the Swedish coast. In case you want to add Sweden to your list of countries cycled, it is only a twenty-minute ferry ride across the Øresund to the Swedish city of Helsingborg. In addition to the castle, Helsingør has some fine old houses and is the home of the **Danish Museum of Technology**. The tourist office is at the harbor (Havnepladsen 3).

HOTEL SKANDIA (Bramstraede 1, 3000 Helsingør; Tel: [02] 21 09 02) is moderately priced and conveniently situated. If you are attracted by names, then there is no better place to stay in Elsinore than at the HOTEL HAMLET (Bramstraede 5; Tel: [02] 21 05 91). For first-class lodgings, the HOTEL MARIENLYS (Ndr. Strandvej Tel: 21 18 01) on the coast road just outside of town has a view of Kronbørg in the distance and is one of the finest hotels in the entire region. It has an excellent dining room.

The youth hostel, HELSINGØR VANDRERHJEM (Ndr. Strandvej 24, 3000 Helsingør; Tel: [02] 21 16 40), is a pleasant old pink mansion located right at the beach. It has two hundred beds, as well as family accommodations, meals, and cooking facilities. It is very popular in the summer so reservations are recommended.

GRONNEHAVE CAMPING is on the road to Hornbaek in a large grassy field. It is a ten-minute walk to Kronbørg Castle. The campground has a camp store. It is open all year.

GILLELEJE. A quaint little fishing town, Gilleleje has become a popular summer refuge for Copenhageners. Try to catch the colorful early morning fish auction.

If you want a hotel room in this town, try PENSION GILLELEJE (Tel: [02] 30 07 59). It is well situated, has twenty-eight rooms, some with bath, is reasonably priced.

For tenters, the best site in the area is NAKKEHOVED CAMPING, located just off hwy 237 (coast road) by the lighthouse, about 2 kms from Gilleleje. It is a nice grassy site, at the beach with a restaurant and camp store. It is open 1 April to 1 October.

ROSKILDE. Its origins steeped in legend, Roskilde was the capital of Denmark until the early sixteenth century. It is now the principal center for touring the region west of Copenhagen. Scenically situated at the head of the Roskilde Fjord, the city has a number of worthwhile attractions, including the impressive 880-year-old **Roskilde Cathedral**, burial place of Danish kings and queens, and the **Viking Ship Museum**, a modern structure housing the remnants of five Viking ships recovered from the Roskilde Fjord. The tourist office is on Fondens Bro, just down the street from the cathedral. In July, Roskilde is the site of one of Europe's most important music festivals.

At the Lejre Research Center in Lejre, a few kms beyond Roskilde, is interesting reconstruction of the past – Iron Age houses have been constructed and people actually live under Iron Age conditions during the summer. Located in the delightful countryside surrounding Lejre are several interesting Stone Age megaliths and one of the largest Viking tombs in Scandinavia.

There is an interesting **Trolley Museum** at Haraldsted on Lake Langeso.

If you want to stay in a hotel, SVOGERSLEV KRO (Svogerslev, 4000 Roskilde; Tel: [02] 38 30 05] is a friendly country inn, with a cozy ambiance, outstanding food, and moderate prices. It is located just 3 kms west of Roskilde center. HOTEL PRINDSEN (Algade 13; Tel: [02] 35 80 10) is a stately one-hundred-year-old building in the center of town with all the modern conveniences. The rooms are expensive.

The youth hostel, ROSKILDE VANDRERHJEM ("Horgarden" Horhusene 61, 4000 Roskilde; Tel: [02] 35 21 84), is an eighty-four-bed modern house in a park at the west edge of town. Family rooms, meals, and cooking facilities are available. It is open all year.

Campers have a first-class, well-equipped site at their disposal. It is only 2.5 kms from the center of town via a well-marked cycle path. CAMPING VEDDELEV is beautifully situated on the Roskilde Fjord in Veddelev. It is open 12 April to 14 September.

HILLERØD. One of North Zealand's principal towns, Hillerød's main attraction is **Frederiksborg Castle**, one of the finest Renaissance structures in all of Europe. Set in a beautiful park, the castle has a labyrinth of richly decorated rooms and houses the **National Historical Museum**. Be sure to set aside a few hours to tour the castle and grounds. This is one of Denmark's top attractions.

KFUM MISSIONHOTEL (Slotsgade 5A; Tel: [02] 26 01 89) is a small, pleasant, modestly priced hotel just a short walk to the castle.

HILLERØD CAMPINGPLADS is a first-class, nicely shaded camping site, only 1 km from the castle. It is open Easter to 15 September.

HALSKOV/KORSER. Used as a harbor since the eleventh century, Halskov has become a busy modern ferry port. Although it is now an important industrial center, the town has preserved a good deal of its old charm.

For a reasonably priced hotel room, check in at the small HOTEL TARN-BORGKROEN (Tarnborgvej 16, 4220 Korser; Tel [03] 57 10 69). A peg above in price is the more modern KLARSKOV-GARD (Tel: [03] 57 23 22) at the edge of town in the suburb of Klarskov.

Campers stopping off before taking the ferry to the island of Fünen have two municipal campgrounds to choose from. LYSTSKOVE CAMPING is just beyond the junction of hwys 150 and 265 into Korser. There are plenty of shade trees, a camp store, restaurant, and washing machine. It is open 15 May to 15 September. HALS-SKOVHAVN CAMPING, close to the Fünen ferry terminal, offers swimming nearby, a camp store, and a washing machine. It is open Easter to 30 September.

SORO. This is a pleasant little country town. Its **Abbey Church** – the largest in Denmark – contains the remains of Bishop Absalon, founder of Copenhagen.

KREBSHUSET (Ringstedvej 87, 4180 Soro; Tel: [03] 63 01 80) is a pleasant little guest house with just five reasonably priced doubles and a good restaurant right in town. HOTEL POSTGAARDEN (Storgade 25-27; Tel [03] 63 22 22) is an attractive, modestly priced hotel.

UDBYHOJ CAMPING is a three-star all-year site, pleasantly located on the lake at the edge of town. There is a camp store and washer and dryer on the premises.

SLAGELSE. During the Middle Ages, Slagelse was an important trading center. Of interest is the Gothic-style **St. Michael's Church**. The old barn adjacent to the church was once used as a school, which Hans Christian Andersen attended from 1822 to 1826. About 7 kms west of town lies **Trelleborg**, a Viking stronghold dating from the years 1000 to 1050. Adjacent to the site is a reconstructed Viking house.

For a good small town hotel, try HOTEL SLAGELSE (Sdr. Stationsvej 19; Tel: [03] 52 01 72).

SLAGELSE VANDRERHJEM (Bjergbygade 78, 4200 Slagelse; Tel [03] 52 25 28) is the local youth hostel, a modern two-story brick building with 120 beds. Family accommodations, meals, and cooking facilities are available. It is open 6 January to 20 December.

Campers can check in at the municipal campground: SLAGELSE KOMMUNES CAMPINGPLADS. It is conveniently located in town; the site is well marked. There is a coin-operated laundry on the premises and it is open 1 April to 1 November.

FÜNEN. In English it's called Fünen, and the Danes refer to it as *Fyn*. Whichever, it is the country's second largest island and it lies between the Jutland peninsula and the island of Zealand. It is a rich soil agricultural area. The island's southern portion is hilly and has picturesque fishing villages and elegant old manor houses which draw cyclists from all over. Fünen is our favorite part of Denmark.

NYBORG/KUNDSHOVED. This pleasantly situated port city was a royal capital between 1200 and 1430. The royal castle was built in the twelfth century with impressive defenses to control access to the eastern part of the island.

HOTEL NYBORG STRAND (Osterovej 2; Tel: [09] 31 31 31) is an expansive, moderately priced hotel nicely located in a wooded area at the beach. Some bicycle touring groups use the hotel as a base. The best low-priced rooms in the area are at the MISSIONSHOTELLET (Ostervolgade 44; Tel: [09] 31 01 88).

You can get information about the youth hostel, STOREBAELT (Ostervej; Tel: [09] 31 02 80) through the Nyborg tourist office. It has one hundred beds with twenty family rooms and is open 1 July to 31 August.

NYBORG CAMPING, a large, well-equipped site, is pleasantly situated at the beach between the ferry terminal at Kundshoved and the town of Nyborg. Facilities include a camp store and laundromat. It is open from Easter to 25 August.

ODENSE. Although it is Denmark's third largest city and will celebrate its 1,000 year birthday in 1988, Odense is best known as the birthplace of that enchanting storyteller, Hans Christian Andersen. Andersen used the city and its surroundings as the setting for many of his tales. Despite the fact that Odense is home to many industries and is an important trading center, the well-preserved old town and many parks and gardens make this a delightful place to visit.

The city's main attraction is the famous storyteller's birth house. The charming half-timbered house in the center of the old town contains many interesting artifacts which belonged to the author. Just a few blocks away on Munkemøllestraede, in the house in which Andersen lived from the age of two to fourteen, is another small museum depicting the living conditions of a family of modest means in the early nineteenth century.

The Fünen Village (*Den Fynske Landsby*) on Sejerskovvej at the south edge of town is one of the country's largest open air museums. A complete typically Fünen village has been built to portray rural life on the island in the eighteenth and nineteenth centuries. Theater performances are held here during the summer. We enjoyed a delightful performance of *The Princess and the Pea* during our last visit.

If you are in need of a bike rental or repair, stop at CYKELCENTRET (Allegade 72; Tel: [09] 13 88 94) or GEORGS CYKLER (Skovgyden 6; Tel: [09] 11 88 58).

For pleasant dining in a quaint seventeenth century inn, try DEN GAMLE KRO (Overgade 23) in the center of the old town.

For budget hotel accommodations, we like the small (fourteen-room), but clean and friendly HOTEL KAHEMA (Dronningensgade 5, 5000 Odense C; Tel: [09] 12 28 21) near the train station and the comfortable HOTEL FANGEL KRO (Fangelvej 55; Tel: [09] 96 10 11). For plusher digs, the modern and most appropriately named HOTEL H. C. ANDERSEN (Claus Bergsgade 7; Tel: [09] 14 78 00) around the corner from H. C. Andersen's birthplace, will take good care of you, but plan to spend about 750 DKr. for a double. The GRAND HOTEL (Jernbanegade 18; Tel: [09] 11 71 71) is a big, old, traditional-style hotel with period furnishings. It is a bit less pricey.

ODENSE VANDRERHJEM (Kragsbjerggarden, Kragsgjergvej 121, 5230 Odense M; Tel: [09] 13 04 25) is a pleasant 280-bed youth hostel with family rooms located in a sprawling half-timbered building only a few minutes pedaling from the town center. Meals and cooking facilities are available.

Campers have easy access to an excellent well-equipped site situated in a lovely park just across the street from the open air museum: ODENSE CAMPINGPLADS. It is open 26 April to 14 September. If you do not have a tent, they will rent you a hut. There is also a good site at the west end of the city. CAMPINGPLADS BLOMMENS-LYST is 9 kms from the city center. It is open 1 June to 1 September.

EGESKOV. Looking like something out of a book of fairy tales, the sixteenth-century **Egeskov Castle** is built on pilings and surrounded by a formidable moat. It is one of Denmark's most impressive castles. The interior of the castle has recently been opened to visitors. Round out your tour of Egeskov by strolling the magnificent gardens and visiting the unique collection of old autos and aircraft at the museum adjacent to the castle.

For a comfortable stay in a pleasant country inn, we like the little KVAERN-DRUP KRO (Bojdenvej 1, 5772 Kvaern-drup; Tel: [09] 27 10 05) in the nearby town of Kvaerndrup. The food is quite good and reasonably priced.

BRAHETROLLEBORG CASTLE.
Dating in part back to the twelfth century, Brahetrolleborg Castle is located in a lovely park. Be sure to stop in at the HUMLEVE RESTAURANT at the entrance to the park. Besides offering a selection of tasty dishes, the restaurant has a fine collection of antiques and modern art. The interior of the castle, once a Cistercian monastery is presently closed to the public.

The KORINTH KRO (Reventlowsvej 10; Tel: [09] 65 10 23) is a pleasant out-of-the-way country inn in the nearby town of Korinth.

FÅBORG. A quiet eighteenth-century market town, Fåborg has a number of well-preserved houses. The local **art museum** and **bell tower** are of particular interest.

Budget watchers should seek out the HOTEL FAERGEGARDEN (Christian IX's vej 31, 5600 Fåborg; Tel: [09] 61 00 59). One of their seven doubles, with a bath down the hall, will set you back about 250 DKr. The FALSLED KRO in nearby Millinge (3 kms) (Tel: [09] 68 11 11) is one of the island's most charming and luxurious inns. There are just twenty beds, so you better reserve one if you plan to pedal by there in July or August.

FÅBORG VANDRERHJEM (Gronnegade 72-37, 5600 Fåborg; Tel: [09] 61 12 03) is a cozy fifty-eight-bed hostel with six family rooms. Meals and cooking facilities are available. It is open 1 April to 1 November.

Of the several campgrounds located in this popular vacation and cycling region, the most convenient is HOLMS CAMPING in the town of Odensevej on hwy 43, the main road to Odense. Rental huts, washing machines, and a camp store are all available. It is open 15 May to 1 September.

SVENDBORG. Scenically poised on the Svendborg Sound, this ancient market town has preserved a great deal of its old character. The bridge crossing the sound to Vindeby on the island of Tasinge affords an impressive view from its one-hundred-foot height. Be sure to stop by **Valdemar's Castle**, an elegant seventeenth-century manor house built by King Christian IV for his son Valdemar. It is located in Troense, a cute little fishing village only a few minutes from Svendborg. Summer activities include treasure hunts (for children only!). There is a fine restaurant in the castle cellar and an interesting **Maritime Museum** with a great collection of models.

For a reasonably priced hotel room, the PENSION VILLA STRANDBO (Borges Alle 13, 5700 Svendborg; Tel: [09] 21 12 74) is a good bet. Call ahead in the summer, they only have five rooms. Also recommended are the moderately priced HOTEL AERO (Brogade 1; Tel: [09] 21 07 60 (try their dining room; you'll be pleasantly surprised) and the plush HOTEL TROENSE (Strandgade 5-7; Tel: [09] 22 54 12), a first-class hotel at the yacht harbor.

SVENDBORG VANDRERHJEM (Villa Soro, Christiansmindevej 6, 5700 Svendborg; Tel: [09] 21 26 16) is a small friendly youth hostel in a big old white house on the sound. Family rooms, meals, and cooking facilities are provided.

There are a number of good campgrounds in and around Svendborg. We especially enjoy stopping at VINDEBYORE CAMPING on Tasinge. It is a nice grassy site right on the water. There are rental huts, as well as a washing machine and camp store. It is open 15 May to 1 September.

RUDKOBING. At the end of a mile-long causeway leading to the island of Langeland, Rudkobing is a popular town with many old houses and streets. The **Langeland Museum** has an interesting Viking grave.

Of the town's several small hotels, the HOTEL SKANDINAVIAN (Brogade 13, 5900 Rudkobing; Tel: [09] 51 36 18) is the best.

RUDKOBING VANDRERHJEM (Dyrs-kuepladsen, 5900 Rudkoping; Tel: [09] 51 18 30) is a modern eighty-two-bed hostel with seven family rooms. It is open 1 May to 15 September.

RUDKOBING CAMPING is a small site with limited facilities. It is located at the south edge of town.

NAKSKOV/TARS. Although the port city of Naskov lying on the fjord of the same name is an important industrial town with Denmark's largest sugar refinery located there, there are nevertheless some interesting parts of town. We wouldn't suggest that you make special plans to stop here. However, should you find yourself in Naskov with time on your hands, be sure to wander or pedal through the old town with its well-preserved pharmacy and half-timbered houses.

THOMSENS HOTEL GARNI (Tilgade 53, 4900 Naskov; Tel: [03] 92 04 00) is a solid, medium-priced hotel with a good restaurant. The leading hotel in Naskov is the HOTEL HARMONIEN (Nybrogade 2; Tel: [03] 91 21 00).

The local youth hostel is NASKOV VANNDRERHJEM (Blegen 4, 4900 Naskov; Tel: [09] 92 09 43). Located in a small modern building, the hostel has fifty-two beds but no family rooms. Meals and cooking facilities are available. It is open 15 May to 1 September.

CAMPING HESTEHOVEDET is a first-class municipal facility located between Naskov and the ferry terminal at Tars. Facilities include a restaurant, washing machine, and a small camp store. It is open 27 April to 2 September.

MARIBO. Beautifully situated on the Sonderso in the heart of the island of Lolland, the town has an interesting historical museum as well as an open air museum. Just 5 kms to the north is **Knuthenborg Safari Park**, the largest manor-house park in Scandinavia. In addition to a large collection of exotic animals, the park contains seven miniature castles and an extensive variety of trees from all over the world.

In the hotel budget category, the nine rooms at the JERNBANEHOTELLET (Jernbanegade 20; Tel: [03] 88 02 87) are good value for the money. If you are in the market for a first-class hotel, then the HOTEL HVIDE HUS (Vestergade 27-29; Tel: [03] 88 10 11) is the best in the area.

MARIBO VANDRERHJEM (Skelstrupvej 19, 4930 Maribo; Tel: [03] 88 33 14) provides pleasant accommodations in a big traditional-style house. The hostel offers sixty beds, nine family rooms, meals, and cooking facilities. It is open 1 February to 20 December.

MARIBO CAMPING, a good municipal site, is pleasantly situated on the Sonderso. Facilities include a washing machine, camp store, and restaurant. It is open 15 May to 1 September.

NYKOBING. Beautifully placed on the Guldborg Sound is the principal town on the island of Falster. Although now a prosperous industrial town, Nykobing still has a number of well-preserved old streets and half-timbered houses. The **Falster Museum** is housed in a building called Czarens Hus, in which the Russian czar Peter the Great lived in 1716.

Either the HOTEL BALTIC (Jernbanegade 43-47, 4800 Nykobing; Tel: [03] 85 30 66) or the TEATERHOTELLET (Torvet 3; Tel: [03] 85 32 77) are good choices for an overnight stay.

NYKOBING CAMPING is a large grassy site with a full range of facilities conveniently located in the town. It is open 1 May to 15 September.

STUBBEKOBING. A charming, ancient little town, Stubbekobing is beautifully placed on the Gronsund. The **twelfth-century church** is the oldest on the island. From Stubbekobing it is only a twelve-minute ferry ride to Bogo, from which a bridge connects to the island of Møn.

There's not much in the way of hotels in this small town. Your best bet is the ELVERKROEN (Vestergade 35, 4850 Stubbekobing; Tel: [03] 84 12 50).

STUBBEKOBING CAMPING is a well-shaded, pleasantly located site with a washing machine and small camp store. It is open 29 April to 2 September.

THE ISLAND OF MØN. The island is best known for its steep white **chalk cliffs**. Located at the eastern end of the island, these impressive formations are one of the country's principal tourist attractions. When touring the island to view the cliffs, you will be rewarded with some fine sandy beaches, beautiful scenery, and lovely old village churches. Stege, the island's main town, has a particularly fine church whose interior is adorned with rich **medieval frescoes**. The island also contains a number of interesting prehistoric remains.

In Stege, the HOTEL STEGE BUGT (Langelinie, 4780 Stege; Tel: [03] 81 54 54, is a pleasant, small hotel located on the bay. HOTEL PRAESTEKILDE (Klintvej 116, Keldby; Tel: [03] 81 34 43) is an attractive, small country hotel in the nearby village of Keldby. There are several good small hotels at the eastern end of the island. For a low-cost room, try PENSION BAKKEGARDEN (Busenvej 64, Busene; Tel: [03] 81 90 86) or HOTEL STORE KLINT (Stengardsvej 6, 4791 Borre; Tel: [03] 81 90 08).

Of the several campgrounds on the island, CAMPING MØNS KLINT, beautifully situated near the cliffs, is the best. Located off hwy 287 between Borre and the cliffs, it offers a full range of facilities, including laundromat, camp store, and restaurant. It is open 1 April to 31 October. CAMPING STEGE in the town of Stege is a small, conveniently located site with limited facilities. It is open 1 May to 30 September.

PRAESTO. A pretty little town surrounded by forests, Praesto is nicely situated on the Praesto Fjord. The main attraction is the collection of **sculpture by Thorvaldsen**, Denmark's greatest sculptor, located in the baroque manor house of Nyso.

The HOTEL SVEND GONGES KRO (Adelgade 82, 4720 Praesto; Tel: [03] 79 10 27) is a reasonably priced *kro* with a good restaurant and lots of atmosphere.

PRAESTO CAMPINGPLADS is a small wooded site with a small camp store. It is open 1 May to 15 September.

KØGE. A picturesque port town, Køge is noted for its well-preserved half-timbered houses, some dating back to the early sixteenth century. In the surrounding countryside are several fine castles, including the sixteenth-century Renaissance mansion of Vallo, 7 kms south of Køge just off hwy 209.

Inexpensive hotel rooms are hard to come by since Køge is practically a suburb of Copenhagen. The CENTRALHOTELLET (Vestergade 3, 4600 Køge; Tel: [03] 65 06 96) is a solid, moderately priced small hotel. For a first-class modern hotel, try the HOTEL HVIDE HUS (Strandvejen 111; Tel: [03] 65 36 90).

KØGE VANDRERHJEM (Lille Køgegaard, Vamdrupvej 1, 4600 Køge; Tel: [03] 65 14 74) is a large, efficiently run one-hundred-bed hostel. Meals are available, but there are no cooking facilities.

There are two conveniently located campgrounds. The three-star VALLO CAMPING at the south end of town off hwy 209 offers a full range of facilities. It is open 1 April to 30 September. CAMPING KØGE SYDSTRAND, located right at the beach, is a small, often crowded site. It is open 1 May to 30 September.

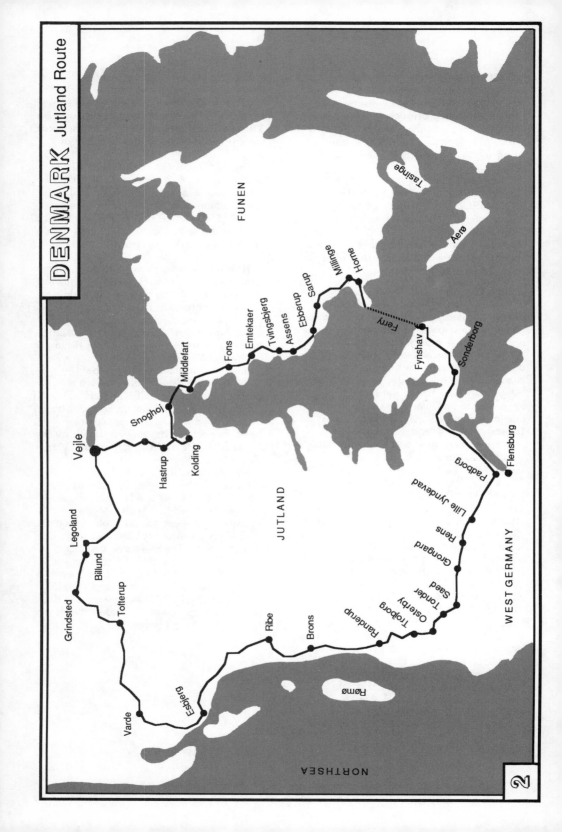

DENMARK Jutland Route

FUNEN

Tåsinge

Ærø

Millinge
Horne

Emtekaer
Tvingsbjerg
Assens
Ebberup
Sarup

Fons

Ferry

Middlefart

Fynshav

Sonderborg

Snoghoj

Kolding

Vejle
Hastrup

Flensburg

Padborg

Lille Jyndevad

JUTLAND

Grongard
Rens

Legoland

Billund

Saed
Tonder
Osterby
Trojborg

Grindsted

Tofterup

Randerup

WEST GERMANY

Ribe

Brons

Esbjerg

Varde

Rømø

NORTHSEA

2

The Jutland Peninsula
═══ and the ═══
South Coast of Fünen

When you tire of big city crowds, museums, and cathedrals and are looking for lonely roads that wind through gentle, sparsely populated countrysides and along quiet broad sandy beaches, consider cycling through the Jutland Peninsula and along the southern coast of the island of Fünen. The route offers just that, along with all of the bonuses of cycling in Denmark: quaint fishing villages, centuries-old inns, warm Danish hospitality, and a special treat – a visit to Legoland.

For practical purposes, we have started this route in Fåborg on the south coast of the island of Fünen. This is a convenient point for joining up with the Copenhagen route. By combining the two routes you will spend a very pleasant and rewarding 949 kms of Danish cycling.

From Germany's northernmost state of Schleswig Holstein, it's a simple matter to link up with this route by crossing the border at Flensburg or further west near the Danish city of Tonder. There is regular ferry service from the west coast port of Esbjerg to the English city of Harwich. This provides a pleasant way to combine Danish touring with one or both of our English routes.

THE JUTLAND PENINSULA ROUTE

DISTANCE
352 kms/218 miles

MAIRS DIE GENERAL KARTEN MAPS
Denmark #3 and #4
  (scale 1:200,000)

GEODAETISK INSTITUT MAPS
#1111, #1112, #1113, #1211,
#1212, #1213 (scale 1:100,000)

This route covers a variety of terrain, passing through dense forests, rolling farmlands, and along a number of fine beaches. By no stretch of the imagination can you call Denmark mountainous, but there are a few hilly sections of Jutland and southern Fünen that will make you happy to have a ten-speed bike. Exposed to the North Sea as it is, the Jutland Peninsula bears the brunt of the strong westerly winds that often sweep across the land.

These same winds are often the bearer of the heavy rains that account for the fact that the beautiful Jutland beaches are not very crowded even in the summer. Jutland's rainiest month is August, with the heaviest rainfall occurring in the western portion of the peninsula.

Since a good portion of this route runs through a sparsely settled portion of the country, the network of inns and hotels is not as dense as in other parts of the country. There are numerous opportunities for free camping along the way; however, in recent years the Danish police have been strict in enforcing the ban on free camping. If you do decide to spend the night among the dunes or in the forest, be sure to keep your tent out of sight.

★ *LOOKING OUT OVER THE HANDLEBARS* ★

THE JUTLAND ROUTE

★

CITY	
FÅBORG	

ROUTE	
8	

DISTANCE KM	TOTAL KM
4	0

ROUTE DESCRIPTION

Follow hwy 8 out of Fåborg to Horne.

★

CITY	ROUTE
HORNE	329 323

DISTANCE KM	TOTAL KM
35	4

ROUTE DESCRIPTION

From Horne, take the road to Millinge, intersecting with hwy 329. Stay on 329 until just south of Jordlose. Then follow a series of winding country lanes through the hilly coastal region, passing the villages of Strandby, Sarup, and Snave. Continue past the elegant manor house at Hagenskov and cycle on to Ebberup. At Ebberup, take hwy 323 into Assens.

Note: As an alternate to the route described above, it is possible to follow the network of narrow seldom-traveled roads that wind along the coast from Strandby to Assens.

CITY
ASSENS

DISTANCE KM	TOTAL KM
20	39

ROUTE DESCRIPTION
From Assens, it is a pleasant 35 kms along a series of country roads that pass through some lovely little villages to Middelfart. Leave Assens via Korsgade and "village hop" up the coast, passing through Tvingsbjerg, Sandager, Emtekaer, Wedellsborg Manor House, Eskor, Tybrind, Rud, Fons, Ronaes, Gamborg, and Svenstrup.

CITY
MIDDELFART

ROUTE
161

DISTANCE KM	TOTAL KM
25	59

ROUTE DESCRIPTION
Take hwy 161 over the bridge to Snoghoj on the Jutland Peninsula. Stay on 161 into Kolding.

CITY
KOLDING

DISTANCE KM	TOTAL KM
12	84

ROUTE DESCRIPTION
Leave Kolding on hwy 161, heading back toward Middelfart. Just past Norre Bjert turn off to Eltang. Continue on crossing the freeway to Mosvra. Follow the sign to Hastrup. The road continues on to Vejle, paralleling the freeway part of the way and passing through Tiufkaer, Horsted, and Klattrup into Vejle.

CITY
VEJLE

ROUTE
28 176

DISTANCE KM	TOTAL KM
48	96

ROUTE DESCRIPTION
Leave Vejle on the cycle path that follows hwy 28 toward Grindsted. After a few kms (at Skibet), the path veers off to the left. Stay on the cycle path and continue to hwy 176. Take 176 the remaining 13 kms to Legoland.

CITY
LEGOLAND/BILLUND

ROUTE
28 30 475

DISTANCE KM	TOTAL KM
20	144

ROUTE DESCRIPTION
From Billund, take the bike path that runs alongside hwy 28 into Grindsted. The bike path continues along hwy 30 to Tofterup and then for part of the way along hwy 475 into Varde.

CITY
VARDE

ROUTE
475

DISTANCE KM	TOTAL KM
30	164

ROUTE DESCRIPTION
Another bike route leaves Varde along hwy 475 and then turns off into the port city of Esbjerg.

CITY
ESBJERG

DISTANCE KM	TOTAL KM
60	194

ROUTE DESCRIPTION
From the Jerne section of Esbjerg, follow the road to Novrup and Tjaereborg. Continue on to Ribe via the marked cycle route.

CITY
RIBE

DISTANCE KM	TOTAL KM
50	254

ROUTE DESCRIPTION
The stretch from Ribe to Tonder passes through a marsh area with large sections protected by dikes. Some of the finest beaches and dunes in Denmark are found along this stretch. Although often windy, this is pleasant cycling country. Work your way down the coast through the villages of Oster Vedsted, Vester Vedsted, Rahede, Hogsbro, Rejsby Brons, Astrup, Ballum Enge, Forballum, Randerup, Harres, Trojborg Visby, Oster Gammelby, Gaerup, Osterby, Gallehus, and then into Tonder.

Note: About halfway between Ribe and Tonder is a causeway to the island of Rømø, a popular vacation spot with excellent, wide sandy beaches. If you're looking for a day or so of beach time, this is the place, weather permitting, of course!

CITY
TONDER

ROUTE
8 11

DISTANCE KM	TOTAL KM
33	294

ROUTE DESCRIPTION
Leave Tonder on hwy 8. After 3 kms, turn off onto hwy 11 to the border town of Saed. Then follow the road along the border with Germany to Padborg. Crossing the rich farmlands, pass through the villages of Grongard, Lydersholm, Rens, Lille-Jyndevad, and Sofiedal. Then cross the freeway into Padborg.

Note: Padborg borders on the German city of Flensborg, which is an excellent gateway for touring Schleswig Holstein.

CITY
PADBORG

ROUTE
8 481

DISTANCE KM	TOTAL KM
15	327

ROUTE DESCRIPTION
From Padborg it is just a few kms to Kursa. From there take the coast road which runs along the shore of the Flensberg Fjord. The cliffs on the other side are in Germany. From Rinkenaes, take hwy 481 past Grasten into Sonderborg.

CITY
SONDERBORG

ROUTE
8

DISTANCE KM	TOTAL KM
10	342

ROUTE DESCRIPTION
Continue on hwy 8 to the ferry terminal at Fynshav.

CITY
FYNSHAV/BOJDEN

ROUTE
FERRY

ROUTE DESCRIPTION
The crossing time is fifty minutes; there are eight crossings daily. The fare for one person with a bike is 33 DKr.

CITY
BOJDEN

ROUTE
8

TOTAL KM
352

ROUTE DESCRIPTION
From the ferry, follow hwy 8 through Horne into Fåborg.

Note: From Fåborg, continue with Copenhagen and the Major Islands Loop, as described earlier in this chapter for the return trip to Copenhagen.

THE JUTLAND ROUTE SIGHTS AND ACCOMMODATIONS

ASSENS. A pleasant old town on Fünen's west coast, Assens overlooks the Lillebaelt, which separates Fünen from the Jutland Peninsula. The town contains a number of fine sixteenth-century and seventeenth-century **half-timbered houses** and an interesting fifteenth-century **church**.

The STUBBERUP KRO (Middelfartvej 113; Tel: [09] 79 10 11) in nearby Stubberup is a small quaint country inn. MARCUSSENS HOTEL (Strandgade 22, 5610 Assens; Tel: [09] 71 10 89), a stately well-run small town hotel, is Assen's best. It is located at the harbor.

ASSENS VANDRERHJEM (Ungdommens Hus, Adelgade 26, 5610 Assens; Tel: [09] 71 13 57) is a youth hostel with seventy-six beds and six family rooms. It is located in the city in a rather gloomy old building. Meals and cooking facilities are available. It is open 1 April to 1 November.

CAMPING WILLEMOES is a nice, fully equipped, well-shaded site located at the harbor. It has a laundromat and camp store and is open Easter to 16 September.

MIDDELFART. This busy small town is where two bridges connect the island of Fünen with Jutland. The principal point of interest is the old royal **castle of Hindsgavl** on the peninsula of the same name. The main building of the castle, now used as a lecture center, dates back to 1784.

Particularly attractive lodgings are to be found on a farm that has been restored and modernized in the nearby town of Norre Aby. It's called FONSVANG RONAES-BROVEJ (5 Fons, 5580 Nr. Aby; Tel: [09] 42 18 14). HOTEL HINDSGAVL SLOT (Hindsgavl Alle; Tel: [09] 41 18 18) is an elegant old manor house in delightful surroundings on the grounds of the old castle. A double runs about 500 DKr. For more modest, down-to-earth lodgings, try the KONGEBROGARDEN Kongebrovej 60, 5500 Middelfart; Tel: [09] 41 03 60) where a double will set you back about 200 DKr.

GLAS KLINT CAMPING is a large wooded site at the beach on the peninsula near the bridge to Snoghoj. It has a camp store and is open 19 April to 16 September.

KOLDING. Located on a fjord of the same name, Kolding has been an important trading center since the early fourteenth century. **Kolding Hus**, the city's most notable structure, was built in the thirteenth century as a fortress for the Danish kings. Accidentally destroyed during the Napoleonic Wars, the castle has since been restored. Of interest also is the **Geographical Garden**, an impressive collection of plants from all over the world. The town center contains a number of well-preserved sixteenth-century and seventeenth-century houses.

Low-priced rooms are available at HOTEL MOLLEGARDEN (Dyrehavevej 198, 6000 Kolding; Tel: [05] 52 09 18), while the attractive HOTEL TRE ROSER (Byparken; Tel: [05] 53 21 22) offers a full range of hotel services at twice the price.

KOLDING VANDRERHJEM (Ornsborgvej 10, 6000 Kolding; Tel: [05] 52 76 84) is a hostel with eighty-eight beds in a one-story building that looks like a motel. Family accommodations, meals, and cooking facilities are available. It is open 15 January to 15 December.

KOLDING CAMPINGPLADS provides camp sites in a wooded area conveniently located near Koldinghus. It has a camp store and basic facilities, but not much in the way of luxury. It is open 1 April to 1 October.

VEJLE. A popular resort town as well as an important industrial center, Vejle is beautifully situated at the head of the Vejle Fjord. A few kms northwest is Jelling, site of the **burial mounds** of King Gorm and Queen Thyra, Denmark's first rulers. The local church contains the oldest **frescoes** in the country.

The BREDAL KRO & MOTEL (Horsensvej 581, 7120 Vejle; Tel: [05] 89 57 99) is a comfortable modernized country inn. Located 6 kms east of Vejle on the fjord amid the hills and forest is the MUNKEBJERGVEJ HOTEL (Munkebjergvej 125; Tel: [05] 82 75 00), a super international-class resort hotel with prices to match. Doubles run from 600 to 1,150 DKr. At the other end of the spectrum, a double with bath down the hall will cost 300 DKr. at the PARK HOTEL (Oria Lehmannsgade 5, Vejle; Tel: [05] 82 24 66).

VEJLE VANDRERHJEM (Gl. Landevej 80, 7100 Vejle; Tel: [05] 82 51 88) is a youth hostel with 116 beds and some family rooms. It is open 15 January to 15 December.

VEJLE KOMMUNALE CAMPINGPLADS is a well-equipped, nicely situated site near the Vejle Fjord. It has a laundromat and camp store. It is open 15 April to 15 September.

BILLUND/LEGOLAND. The headquarters of the Lego Company is the site of one of the world's most unique amusement parks. An entire miniature town, along with replicas of some of the world's best-known buildings, has been constructed out of millions of the famous Lego plastic building blocks.

Of the several hotels in the area, the HOTEL ANTIQUE (Vejlevej 10; Tel: [05] 33 16 55), in spite of its name, offers pleasant accommodations at moderate prices.

BILLUND CAMPING is a well-equipped camping site, popular with visitors from all over the world who come to visit Legoland. It is located near the airport and has a washing machine, small camp store, and nearby restaurant. It is open 28 April to 16 September.

VARDE. A small industrial town, Varde has an interesting local **museum** and a number of fine **old houses**.

For a hotel room, try HOJSKOLEHJEMMET (Storegade 56, 6800 Varde; Tel: [05] 22 01 40).

The closest hostel is in Oksbol, about 13 kms west of Varde. OKSBOL VANDRERHJEM (Praestegardsvej 21, 6840 Oksbol; Tel: [05] 27 18 77) is a low modern building with one hundred beds and fifteen family rooms. Meals and cooking facilities are available. It is open 1 January to 22 December.

There is no campground in Varde; however, there is a site on the coast 13 kms southwest of Varde at Sjelborg. VORBASSE CAMPING is a large, well-equipped site with little shade. It is open 14 April to 16 September.

ESBJERG. The country's largest fishing port is also an important ferry terminal for connections with Great Britain and the Faroe Islands. In recent times it has gained importance as the base for Danish oil and natural gas exploration in the North Sea. Along the waterfront there is an interesting **Fishery and Seafaring Museum**. From the harbor, it is only a twenty-minute ferry ride to the offshore island of Fanø. The island's sandy beach extends for some 16 kms.

This busy town has a good selection of hotels. For plenty of atmosphere at reasonable prices, try the GULDAGER KRO (Stationsvej 104, Guldager; Tel: [05] 16 70 08) located in Guldager, about 5 kms northwest of Esbjerg center. Another pleasant, moderately priced hotel is KORSKROEN (Skads Hovedvej 116; Tel: [05] 16 02 73).

The youth hostel, ESBJERG VANDRERHJEM (Gl. Vardevej 80, 6700 Esbjerg; Tel: [05] 12 42 58), is a stately multi-story brick building with 124 beds and 33 family rooms. Meals and cooking facilities are provided. It is open 8 January to 8 December.

STRANDSKOVENS CAMPING is a nice well-equipped site located near the youth hostel. Facilities include a washing machine and camp store. It is open 15 May to 15 September.

RIBE. The town's history dates back to the mid-ninth century and Ribe lays claim, rightfully so, to being Denmark's best-preserved medieval town. During the early Middle Ages, when sea routes linked it to a good part of the known world, Ribe was the country's most important town. A walk through Ribe's old town is a trip into history. Winding cobblestone streets and scores of quaint half-timbered houses provide tangible links with the past. Of particular interest is the **Domkirke**, an impressive cathedral built during the twelfth century and combining Romanesque and early Gothic styles. Cycling across the flat marshlands, the towers of the cathedral are the first glimpse of Ribe that you will encounter.

For a hotel room, take your choice between the tiny and charming five-room WEIS' STUE (Torvet 2, 6760 Ribe; Tel: [05] 42 07 00), where a double costs 240 DKr., and HOTEL DAGMAR (Torvet 1; Tel: [05] 42 00 33), the town's fanciest hotel right next door.

RIBE VANDRERHJEM (Ribehallen, Hovedengen, 6760 Ribe; Tel: [05] 42 06 20) is a small, conveniently located hostel with eighty-six beds and nine family rooms. Meals and cooking facilities are provided. It is open 1 May to 15 September.

RIBE CAMPINGPLADS is a first-rate camping site located about 1 km north of the city. It is surrounded by trees and offers many facilities, including a laundromat and camp store. The campground is open Easter to 15 September.

TONDER. Now more than 10 kms from the sea, Tonder was once a port town, prior to the building of a series of dikes in the sixteenth century. The town, which has retained and preserved many old buildings, is also the center of an important lace making industry.

HOSTERUPS HOTEL (Sondergade 30, 6270 Tonder; Tel: [04] 72 21 29) is a moderately priced hotel on the main road to Ribe.

TONDER VANDRERHJEM (Kogsgarden, Sonderport 4, 6270 Tonder; Tel: [04] 72 35 00) is a sprawling complex of barracks with 116 beds and 30 family rooms. Meals and cooking facilities are available. The hostel is open 1 February to 22 December.

TONDER CAMPINGPLADS is a large open field. Campground facilities include a washing machine and camp store. It is open Easter to 30 September.

PADBORG. Just across the border from the German city of Flensburg, Padborg is the marketing center for Southern Jutland's agricultural industry.

For a touch of old-world atmosphere, check in at the BOV KRO (Haervejen 25, Bov; Tel: [04] 67 13 32) just north of Padborg.

The closest hostel is in Kollund, 5 kms east of Padborg. KOLLUND VANDRER-HJEM (Graensehjemmet, Fjordvejen 44, 6340 Krusa) is located in a wooded area at the beach. It has 174 beds with 45 family rooms. Meals and cooking facilities are available.

FRIGAARD CAMPING, in nearby Kollund, is a large field near the beach. The facilities include a washing machine and camp store and is open all year.

SONDERBORG. Located on the fertile island of Als, Sonderborg is a busy commercial and industrial center. Particularly interesting is the **Sonderborg Slot**, a thirteenth-century castle that was altered in the fifteenth and early eighteenth centuries. The historical museum has exhibits documenting the Schleswig Wars.

For a good, inexpensive hotel try the HOTEL BALTIC (Tel: [04] 44 52 00) in nearby Horuphav. The HOTEL ANSGAR (Norrebro 2; Tel: [04] 42 24 72) is a good choice for a moderately priced city hotel.

SONDERBORG VANDRERHJEM (Kaer-vej 70, 6400 Sonderborg; Tel: [04] 42 31 12) is a two-hundred-bed hostel. It also has thirty-four family rooms in its sprawling complex. Meals and cooking facilities are provided. It is open 1 February to 22 December.

SONDERBORG CAMPING RINGGADE is a large site near the water with a laundromat and camp store. It is open 1 May to 15 September.

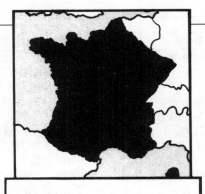

FRANCE

POPULATION
53,963,000

RELIGION
Mainly Roman Catholic;
4% Moslem

CAPITAL
Paris

CURRENCY
French franc (Fr.); divided into
100 centimes

EXCHANGE RATE (1986)
$1.00 = 6.5
1 = $ .15

OFFICIAL LANGUAGE
French; Breton in Brittany;
German in Alsace and Lorraine

BANKING HOURS
M-F 0900-1200
    1400-1600
    (in larger towns)
T-S 0900-1200
    1400-1600
  M Closed
    (in provinces)
Note: Banque Transatlantic,
1 Boulevard des Capucines,
Paris, is open Saturdays
0900-1200 and 1400-1700

STORE HOURS
Food: T-S 0800-1200
           1400-1900
       (Some open Sunday and
       Monday afternoons)
Shops: T-S Same as above;
       many large department
       stores open on Sundays

EMERGENCY TELEPHONE NUMBERS
Police 17

ROADS

The fact that France has the thickest network of roads in all of Europe can be taken as either a curse or a blessing for cyclists. So many roads must mean a lot of cars and trucks; on the other hand, the existence of a large number of minor roads and country lanes offers cyclists the opportunity to escape most of the heavy traffic, which tends to concentrate on the major arteries.

In a country where bicycling is so popular, there are surprisingly few bicycle paths. Where present their use is obligatory. Look for the sign *"Piste Cycliste Obligatoire."*

As in all countries, the autoroutes (tollroads) are off limits to cyclists. The major highways are designated with the letter "N" (*Route Nationale*) and are colored red on the Michelin and most other maps. Generally speaking, these are heavily utilized and carry most of the truck traffic.

Some "N" roads have shoulders suitable for bicycles; however, where possible we try to avoid these in favor of the "D" roads. "D" stands for *Route Departmental* and the countryside is liberally laced with these. Recently a number of "N" roads have been reclassified as "D" roads, which may lead to some confusion if you are using older maps. Although some "D" roads are shown in red on the Michelin maps, most are colored yellow or white. The "white" roads are the least heavily traveled and wherever possible we use these. It is the "D" roads that will take you through the heart of rural France.

In general, roads tend to be well maintained, and the jarring potholes and quaint cobblestones that will loosen all of the nuts and bolts on your bike as well as shake the fillings out of your teeth are seldom encountered. Probably because so many of them ride bicycles themselves, French drivers are particularly courteous to cyclists. Roads and towns are well marked.

BIKING
THROUGH
EUROPE

FRANCE

Probably no other country in the world offers such an interesting amalgamation of the past, present, and future as does France – Europe's largest nation. Wherever you travel you will encounter reminders of the country's incredibly rich history: prehistoric megoliths in Brittany; 30,000-year-old cave paintings in the Dordogne; the well-preserved Roman amphitheaters of Arles, Nimes, and Orange; the sumptuous palace of Versailles and the imposing chateaux and mansions of the Loire Valley; and the World War II invasion beaches and monuments of Normandy.

Don't get the idea, however, that France is a nation wallowing in its past. France is very much involved in the present and future. After all, the term *avant garde* is very definitely French, and such projects as the supersonic Concorde, the high speed TGV (Train Grande Vitesse), and the proposed tunnel link with Great Britain are in the very forefront of modern technology.

For cycle tourists, France has attractions to suit all tastes. The country's natural beauties include the broad sandy beaches and dunes of the Atlantic coast, the rugged cliffs and delightful coves of Brittany and Normandy, as well as the magnificent Alps and Pyrenees.

Quaint villages, cities with manicured tree-lined boulevards, sidewalk cafés wherever you go, opulent palaces, elegant chateaux, towering cathedrals, and intriguing ancient walled cities such as Carcassone and Aigues Morte, all combine to make a visit to France a unique and fascinating experience. Although Paris is far from the ideal city for cycling, if time and budget allow, a visit to the "city of light" should be a part of your trip to France.

Volumes have been written trying to explain the characteristics of the French. They have been described as haughty, arrogant, romantic, charming, and just about every other adjective in the dictionary. Over the years we've managed to spend a lot of time in different parts of the country – camping, cycling, and skiing – and have had nothing but positive encounters with the French. We've also had the opportunity to quietly observe many American tourists in their encounters with the French. If there is one bit of advice we can offer it is to learn at least a few key words and phrases of French.

Nothing seems to go further in establishing friendly contact with the French than addressing them in their own language.

Cyclists in this country of bicycle fanatics have a decided advantage over fellow travelers when it comes to meeting people. On a recent cycle trip we were slowly pedaling through a small village in the Bordeaux wine country. A little old man, the stereotypical Frenchman complete with beret, waved at us and motioned for us to stop. A careful inspection of our heavily loaded bicycles and the exchange of a few phrases in our very broken French and his halting English were followed by an invitation to visit the wine cellars of our new acquaintance, Monsieur Prunier.

"Why not?" we said, and followed him into a cave that looked like something out of an old Vincent Price movie. In a corner of the stone-arched, cobweb-filled cellar were several carefully covered very fine Peugeot bikes. Our common bond!

After exchanging a few pleasantries about biking, out came the wine. About two hours later, having sampled new wine, old wine, and Monsieur Prunier's special brandy, and after having solved the problems of the world in a language that would have made any French or English teacher wince with pain, we emerged from that delightful cellar, embraced our new friend, mounted our bikes, and somewhat unsteadily negotiated the few kilometers to the nearest campground.

A common interest – in France biking is a national pastime – a few words of French, and you have the basis for many such enjoyable encounters. You can't plan these things; but spend enough time pedaling through the French countryside and you'll have your share of pleasant experiences to tell to the folks back home.

Of all the countries in Europe, France, with its variety of attractions and dense network of small country roads, is a natural for cycle touring. Bicycling as a sport is extremely popular, and on weekends thousands of natives of all ages are out on the roads decked out in their colorful cycling togs.

MAPS

For overall planning and obtaining a good perspective of the entire country, the best map to use is the **Michelin #989, France** (scale 1:1,000,000; 1 cm = 10 km). For actual cycling, the Michelin Yellow Series covers the entire country including the island of Corsica in forty detailed regional maps (scale 1:200,000; 1 cm = 2 km). These are suitable for cycling purposes. Steep inclines are denoted with arrows, and those maps marked *avec relief* also show contour shading. Michelin maps are readily available and reasonably priced at bookstores throughout France. Selected bookstores in some other countries and in the U.S. carry them at higher prices. Your best bet is to buy a Michelin #989 for planning and then pick up the detailed maps when you get to France.

IGN (Institut Geographique National) **Serie Rouge Maps** (scale 1:250,000; 1 cm = 2.5 km) cover the country in sixteen maps and are very good for cycling. Tourist attractions, height shading, and scenic roads are shown.

IGN SERIE VERTE MAPS (scale 1:100,000; 1 cm = 1 km) cover the country in seventy-four individual maps. They are very detailed maps, showing every road and practically every farmhouse, as well as height contours. In our opinion, they are *the best maps* available for cycling in France. Each map covers an area of 225 by 275 kms. Readily available throughout France, they are difficult to find elsewhere.

TRANSPORTATION WITHIN THE COUNTRY

The French rail system, **SNCF (Societé Nationale des Chemins de Fer)** is one of the largest and best in Europe. In this nation of avid cyclists, SNCF makes an honest and generally successful attempt to provide efficient transportation for cyclers. You can take your bike with you as baggage at no charge on some two thousand trains daily. These trains are indicated with a bicycle symbol on the schedules posted in the train stations. In most cases you will be expected to load and unload your bike yourself. Play it safe and remove all bags from the bike.

On trains where it is not possible to take your bike along as hand baggage (most long distance and international routes), it will be necessary to register the bike as unaccompanied baggage. Take your bike to the *bagages* counter at the train station at least thirty minutes prior to the train's departure. Be sure to have your ticket with you. For 5 Fr. SNCF will provide a carton in which to pack your bicycle. Insurance against loss or damage is also available at a modest price.

Loading and unloading is done by the SNCF staff. In most instances you can expect to claim your bike within twenty-four hours of your arrival. On international routes there can be a delay of several days. Inquire in advance so that you can plan for any delays.

Most train stations will provide storage for a bicycle for a charge of 19 Fr. The brochure *Guide du Train et du Velo* available at all train stations and from the French National Tourist Offices, provides all the details of shipping a bike in France.

Most buses do not take bicycles; however, there seems to be no set policy. Inquire locally, as in many cases it's up to the driver.

There are a number of restrictions on transporting a bicycle in and around Paris. These generally apply on weekdays during the rush hours: 0630 to 0930 and 1630 to 1900.

BICYCLE SHOPS AND RENTALS

There is practically no town or village in France that doesn't have at least some sort of a bike repair shop. French-made bikes and parts conform to the metric system, which can lead to difficulties in repairing some American cycles. French mechanics, however, are quite resourceful and usually accommodating to foreign tourists.

Bicycles are available for rental at some 280 train stations. Conventional, six-speed and ten-speed bikes are available. In many cases it is possible to drop off the bike at another station opening up interesting touring possibilities. Most popular resort areas have bicycle rental shops; however, for any serious touring it's best to have your own wheels.

ACCOMMODATIONS

Whether you are merely looking for a place to pitch a tent for the night, or you are planning to nurse your saddle sores at an elegant chateau or romantic auberge, the scope and availability of accommodations is extensive. For each of the routes described we have tried to include a broad range of accommodation suggestions.

Chambres d'hote are the French equivalent of that venerable institution, the bed and breakfast. These are furnished rooms in private homes, usually in rural areas, where breakfast is provided. You will often see small "*Chambre d'Hote*" signs posted along the roads. Don't hesitate to follow one of these signs in search of lodging; more likely than not, you will be in for a pleasant and inexpensive experience. Detailed information can be obtained at local tourist offices.

Scattered throughout the country are thousands of low-priced, government-sponsored inns, or *auberges* and *logis*. They provide a reliable, basic, comfortable standard of accommodation. Most have restaurants that feature regional cooking. It is often expected that meals be eaten on the premises. Be sure to clarify this point when you register. For more information, contact the **Federation Nationale des Logis et Auberges de France** (25 rue Jean Mermoz, 75008 Paris) or the French National Tourist Office.

Hotels in France are graded by the government with from one to five stars depending on the type and standard of facilities. For an overnight stay, the one-star and two-star establishments are quite adequate. In fact, many of the "no star" non-rated hotels are very acceptable. Another inexpensive option is provided by the *Relais Routiers* frequented by long-distance truck drivers and denoted by the red and blue "Routiers" disc.

Cyclists looking for luxurious accommodations in romantic settings will find a generous number of stately mansions, elegant chateaux, and romantic country inns are available if they are willing to part with the extra francs. A cycle tour doesn't have to be an exercise in spartan living. There is nothing quite like spending the day pedaling through the delightful Bordeaux wine country or the magnificent Loire valley and then rolling up to an imposing chateau late in the afternoon and parking your bike among the assembled Mercedes and Jags, then indulging in a hot bath, an aperitif in the swank bar, some fine regional cuisine, and finally sinking off to sleep in a fluffy down bed. Compared to prevailing U.S. prices, French style luxury, while not exactly cheap, is still a bargain.

Breakfast in most hotels of all classes is not usually included; however, it is often assumed that you will be breakfasting at the hotel, and, in some cases, also eating an additional meal. Be sure to clarify this when you register. We generally prefer to pedal a bit before breakfast and stop along the way at a *boulangerie* or café for fresh croissants.

During July and August hotels are often full. To avoid disappointment, try to reserve in advance. Many hotels will grant substantial discounts in the off season. Don't be afraid to ask. **Accueil de France** is a reservation service provided by the tourist offices in forty-one major cities. For the cost of a telex or telephone call, they will obtain a confirmed room reservation for you. There are also several chains of particularly attractive hotels including: **Relais et Chateaux** (10 place de la Concorde, 75008 Paris) and **Chateaux Hotels et Hostelleries d'Atmosphere** (Chateau dePray, Charge, 37400 Ambroise).

There are some two hundred youth hostels (**Auberges de Jeunesse**) affiliated with the International Youth Hostel Federation (I.Y.H.F.) spread throughout the country. Depending on the type of hostel, overnight rates run from 17 to 30 Fr. per night/per person. Many also offer reasonably priced meals and cooking facilities. Membership cards are required (I.Y.H.F. cards honored). A number of hostels also provide space where you can pitch a tent. During July and August, reservations are recommended in the popular resort areas; however, in most cases finding a bed for the night is not a problem. Generally speaking, the distances between hostels is too great to plan on using these as the sole source of lodging.

For further information, contact the **American Youth Hostels** (1332 I St. NW, Suite 800, Washington D.C. 20005; Tel: [202] 783-6161), **Canadian Hostelling Association** (Place Vanier, Tower A, 333 River Road, Vanier City, Ottawa, Ont. K1L 8H9; Tel: [613] 748-5638), **Federation Unie Des Auberges De Jeunesse** (6 rue Mesnil, 75116 Paris; Tel: [45] 05 13 14), and **Ligue Francaise pour les Auberges de la Jeunesse** (38 bd. Raspail, 75007 Paris; Tel: [45] 48 69 84).

More than any other European nation, France is camper country. *The Official French Campsite Guide* lists approximately eight thousand campgrounds. Additionally there are two thousand CL type sites, which are farms that allow up to eight camping units on their property.

You are never very far from a campground in most parts of France. In the principal tourist areas just about every town has a municipal campground. Many of these are well equipped and reasonably priced. Figure on paying approximately 15 to 25 Fr. per night. Although the Camping Carnet is rarely required, it will save you from having to surrender your passport; at many campsites it is good for a 10 to 20 percent discount.

Most sites are well posted and easy to find. The French countryside is particularly well suited to free camping. Just watch out for signs that say "Camping sauvage interdit": French for "No Camping."

In rural areas you will often see signs reading "Camping a là Ferme". When we first encountered these with our limited French we were sure this meant campground closed. We now know better. These signs indicate camping possibilities on a local farm or, in some cases, in someone's large yard. Facilities are usually simple but adequate, and these rural sites are rarely crowded even in the height of summer.

Another possibility are the Gites Ruraux de France – small, usually out-of-the-way sites located on working farms. During the summer months, stays are normally on a weekly basis only. These inexpensive sites make a good base for touring individual regions in depth. Another excellent possibility for inexpensive accommodations are the Gites d'Etape. There are four hundred of these gites, which range from fully equipped chalets to rudimentary refuges and shelters. They are available to cyclists on an overnight basis. For more information on gites, contact the French Government Tourist Office or the **Federation Nationale des Gites Ruraux de France** (34 rue Godot de Mauroy, 75009 Paris).

FOOD AND DRINK

For many, the enjoyment of the country's gastronomic specialties is closely akin to religious fanaticism. As a cyclist touring France you can have it any way you like it. Stop in at the many fine roadside inns and restaurants and partake of the excellent regional cuisine, or load up on the enticingly displayed pâtés, cheeses, and salads in the local shops, and picnic along the route; or eat baloney sandwiches and granola bars – the choice is yours! If you opt for the baloney and granola route, you don't need our help. However, if you'd like to experience some of the delights of French food here are a few helpful hints.

Although supermarkets (supermarché) are becoming increasingly prevalent, much of the fun of eating and traveling in France comes from shopping at the many small shops whose display windows and counters are truly works of art. These are great places to stock up for picnics or on the spot refreshment. There is hardly a village you will cycle through that won't have a seductive selection of foodshops. Whenever we bike in France we have a hard time getting past the seemingly endless array of charcuteries and patisseries. One of the advantages cyclists have over the motorist or bus traveler is the opportunity to see all that good food in the store windows.

A charcuterie, the French equivalent of a delicatessen, is the place to get pâtés of all sorts, a variety of cold cuts, as well as a dazzling assortment of tasty meat, fish, or vegetable salads. A boucherie is a butcher shop, which sells fresh meats and some pâtés and salads. Cremeries, in addition to selling milk and butter, usually carry a wide assortment of delicious French cheeses. Don't be afraid to experiment! They are all good. A bakery is called a boulangerie, and it is the place to get that good crisp French bread (baked fresh several times daily), as well as croissants and some pastries. A patisserie will rarely have bread but offers some of the best pastries anywhere. An epicerie is a grocery store which usually carries a little bit of everything from wine to toilet paper.

If you want to linger over a coffee, a glass of wine or a coke, and perhaps eat a snack while soaking up some atmosphere, then plant yourself at a café. No place in France is very far from a café, and they make a great refuge on a rainy day. Table service can cost up to 50 percent more than standing at the bar. A brasserie is the place for simple inexpensive food while a restaurant can mean anything from McDonald's to Maxim's. At most restaurants, the prix fixe menu of the day is the best deal. A 15 percent service charge (service compris) is usually included in the price. If the service is good, most people leave an additional 5 percent. Be sure to sample the various regional dishes such as bouillabaisse in Marseille, the excellent seafood in Brittany, and cassoulet in the Languedoc. The local wines are almost always excellent.

SOURCES OF ADDITIONAL INFORMATION

In France, **tourist offices** are called *Syndicat d'Inititive* or *Office de Tourisme*. Located in all areas of interest to travelers, these are the best sources for information on local attractions, accommodations, and restaurants. Many offices also can provide bicycle itineraries for in depth local touring and will often have information not available at the French National Tourist Office. In France, contact the **Bureau National des Renseignements Touristique** (127 Champs-Elysees, 75008 Paris; Tel: [47] 23 61 72). See the appendix for U.S. addresses.

Federation Francaise de Cycletourisme (FFCT) is a private, member-supported organization that represents some two thousand local cycle touring clubs (8 rue Jean-Marie Jego, 75013 Paris; Tel: [45] 80 30 21). They can provide a wealth of useful information on bicycle touring in France (some in English).

Wine Country

If you are looking for a cycle touring route that combines the charm and beauty of rural France, the enjoyment of fine wine and outrageously tasty food, quiet country roads with few hills, broad stretches of pine forests and fine sandy beaches then search no further – Bordeaux and the surrounding wine country offer all of this and much more. Little wonder that this region in the southwest corner of France is a favorite touring destination.

In spite of the area's popularity, the prevailing feeling of the countryside is one of calmness and serenity. You won't find thousand bed Hilton hotels or fast food restaurants on every corner. The Bordelais, as the people who inhabit this region are called, are known for their contented manner.

Bordeaux, one of France's great cities, is the hub of this pleasant region. The city itself is large enough to offer everything that a great city should, but it is still a manageable size. Serving as the center of the world's greatest wine producing district, Bordeaux has attracted a fine collection of chefs who produce cuisine on a par with the region's outstanding wines. Regional specialties include excellent duck, tender *entrecôtes* and *foie gras*, (a delicious goose liver pâté), as well as superb fish, oysters, mussels, and eel from the local rivers and the nearby ocean. The surrounding countryside is dotted with villages and chateaux whose names grace the wine lists of fine restaurants throughout the world – St. Émilion, Médoc, or Rothschild.

For more information about this great wine region inquire at the Maison du Vin in Bordeaux or at the **Maison du Vin** (Place La Tremoille, Margaux; Tel: [56] 58 40 82). Most chateaux graciously welcome visitors and many offer free samples. Look for signs reading "*degustation*." Pack a picnic lunch, pick up a bottle of fine wine, and pedal off into the vineyards or search out a quiet spot along the river to enjoy *le picnique* French style. There's something very special about drinking wine right at the source.

On a recent tour through the area while gathering material for this book, we fell prey to one of the more pleasant hazards of touring in France. It was a hot June afternoon and after several hours of hard pedaling we stopped

at a small chateau in the Médoc to take one of those "educational" wine chateau tours. At the end of the tour it was time for a bit of "*degustation*." The
people at the chateau were so nice that after a few free glasses of lovely red
wine, we felt obliged to show our appreciation and wound up buying several
bottles of that same lovely red wine, giving no thought at all as to where we
would store these precious souvenirs. Our panniers were stuffed full. The solution was actually quite simple – what you can't carry you can always drink.
It was quite a party! We parked our bikes in a clump of bushes at the edge
of the vineyard and proceeded to solve our storage problem. We did such
a good job that we decided in the interest of highway safety as well as keeping
our bikes and selves intact that we should not venture out of our vineyard retreat until the situation had cleared some. We pitched our tent in the bushes
and enjoyed a lovely evening watching the grapes grow under the shadow
of the old chateau. Ever since that June night we've had a very special association with the wines of the Médoc.

Of course, there is a lot more to cycling here than food and wine. The
countryside is varied and always attractive. The coastal region has miles of
nearly deserted beaches, massive dunes, and relaxing pine forests, while the
rather sparsely populated Médoc region with its famous chateaux is level and
literally carpeted with vineyards. On the other side of the Gironde river,
which is formed by the confluence of the Garonne and Dordogne, the terrain
is more hilly and the villages closer together.

BORDEAUX TO
BORDEAUX LOOP

START	FINISH	DISTANCE
BORDEAUX	BORDEAUX	365 kms/227 miles

MICHELIN MAPS	IGN MAPS
#71 La Rochelle-Bordeaux, #75 Bordeaux-Tulle (scale 1:200,000)	Carte Touristique, Gironde (scale 1:125,000) or #46 Bordeaux-Royan, #47 Bordeaux-Perigueux (scale 1:100,000)

The portion of the route covering the Médoc peninsula and the coastal
stretch is almost completely level and can be cycled easily with just
about anything that has two wheels, handlebars, and a chain. For
added comfort on windy days we recommend at least a three-speed bicycle.
This is not a physically demanding route; in fact, the most demanding aspect
may be successfully negotiating your way past all of the *degustation* places!
The countryside in the St. Émilion region is hilly, but the hills are short and
not all that steep. A good multi-gear bike will go a long way in helping you
enjoy this region.

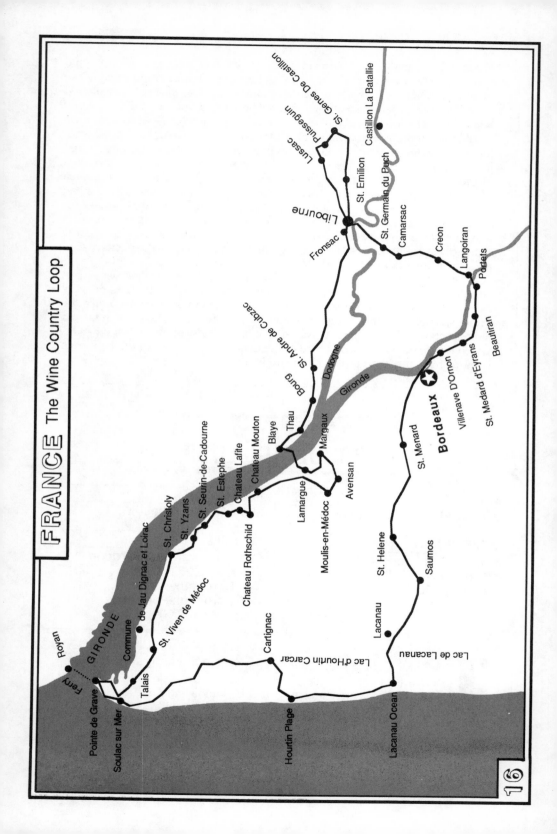

FRANCE The Wine Country Loop

Bordeaux

GIRONDE

Royan
Ferry
Pointe de Grave
Soulac sur Mer
Talais
de Jau Dignac et Loirac
Commune
St. Viven de Médoc
St. Christoly
St. Yzans
St. Seurin-de-Cadourne
St. Estephe
Chateau Lafite
Chateau Mouton
Chateau Rothschild
Cartignac
Houtin Plage
Lac d'Hourtin Carcar
Lacanau Ocean
Lac de Lacanau
Lacanau
St. Helene
Saumos
St. Menard
Villenave D'Ornon
St. Medard d'Eyrans
Beautiran
Portets
Langoiran
Creon
Camarsac
St. Germain du Puch
St. Emilion
Castillon La Batallie
Puisseguin
Lussac
St. Genes De Castillon
Libourne
Fronsac
St. Andre de Cubzac
Dordogne
Bourg
Gironde
Thau
Blaye
Margaux
Lamargue
Moulis-en-Médoc
Avensan

16

Beginners should not hesitate to cycle here. Villages are close together and you're never very far from an inviting café or *patisserie*. The problem we always encounter when cycling this region is exerting enough energy pedaling to justify our enormous caloric intake.

The route we describe is basically divided into two loops with Bordeaux as the center. The shorter of the two loops takes in the port of Libourne and the Libournais region, encompassing such famous wine producing districts as St. Émilion and Pomerol. If you only have a few days allocated for the wine country, you can terminate this route at Libourne or return to Bordeaux, depending on your future plans and train connections.

To continue with the second portion of the route, follow the Gironde up to Blaye and take the ferry across to the Médoc Peninsula. The route winds through some of the most famous wine-producing vineyards in the world, passing Chateau Margaux and Chateau Lafite-Rothschild. The most impressive of the hundreds of wine-producing chateaux in the Bordeaux region are found on this side of the river. (For details on visiting the individual chateaux, check with the tourist office or the Maison Du Vin in Bordeaux). Leaving the vineyards, the route follows the coast through a little developed stretch of fine sandy beaches and dunes backed by extensive pine forests. Much of this part of the route is on bicycle trails. With the exception of only a few kilometers, the route avoids heavily traveled main roads.

Although the route can be started at any point, we advise beginning in Bordeaux. The city is easily reached by train, and a stay of a day or two will serve as a good introduction to the flavor and character of the entire region.

There are several points where the route can be continued to link up with other intersting cycling routes. For example, the St. Émilion portion links up nicely with the Dordogne route. The coastal portion of the route can be extended down to the international resort of Biarritz and from there on into Spain. By taking the ferry from the tip of the Médoc Peninsula to Royan and continuing north, you can join up with the Loire Valley route or continue on to Brittany and Normandy.

The Médoc region is not densely populated, and many tourists make their excursions in this region using Bordeaux as a base. There are, however, sufficient inns and small hotels so cyclists need not worry about finding accommodations. As is the case throughout France, campgrounds abound. The only youth hostel on the route is in Bordeaux.

This is good country for summer touring. Although the months of July and August bring a large influx of tourists into the region, crowds are nothing like those found on the Mediterranean coast of France. The weather can be hot, but not oppressive, and it is generally tempered with a cooling sea breeze.

May, June, and September are excellent times for touring. During these months there are few tourists. You can just about have the roads to yourself and the beaches are virtually deserted. The bathing season is relatively short. Outside of July, August, and early September the water is pretty cold.

One of the best ways to enjoy the color and romance of the wine country is to cycle through it during harvest time when the vineyards are alive with workers and villages hold their wine festivals. Depending on weather conditions, the Bordeaux harvest usually takes place in late September and early October.

THE WINE COUNTRY LOOP

CITY
BORDEAUX

ROUTE
D108 D214 D13 D20 D121
D14 D115 D20 N89

DISTANCE KM	TOTAL KM
50	0

ROUTE DESCRIPTION
From the Gare St. Jean at the south end of Bordeaux, follow signs S to the suburb of Begles. From there continue past several small ponds to Villenave D'Ornon. At this point, pick up hwy D108, and follow it south along the train tracks to St. Medard d'Eyrans. The hwy splits at the train station, continue on D214 to Beautiran and then to Portets. Cross the Garonne to Langoiran. Take D13 toward Creon; after a few kms this runs into D20. On this side of the river you will encounter some hills, but the route levels out approaching Libourne. Just before St. Genes de Lombaud, turn off to the left and take D121 and then D14 into Creon. Leave Creon via D121, which winds through the hilly countryside, changing into D115 for the last few kms and passing a chateau before reaching Camarsac. Follow the signs to St. Germain du Puch via Le Grande Puch. From there it's a straight shot via D20 and N89, crossing the Dordogne to Libourne.

CITY
LIBOURNE

ROUTE
D243

DISTANCE KM	TOTAL KM
8	50

ROUTE DESCRIPTION
From the Libourne train station, follow the signs to St. Émilion via D243.

CITY
ST. ÉMILION

ROUTE
D243 D17 D122 D224

DISTANCE KM	TOTAL KM
40	58

ROUTE DESCRIPTION
Leave St. Émilion on D243 and pass through the rolling vineyard-covered hills to St. Genes de Castillon. Then take D17 through Puisseguin to the little wine village of Lussac. From Lussac, it is an easy pedal back to Libourne on D244.

Note: To link up with the Dordogne Route, from St. Genes de Castillon take D17 down to Castillon la Batallie. Then either take the train or pedal about 45 kms along the Dordogne to Bergerac.

Note: If at this point you wish to return to Bordeaux rather than continue with the Médoc and beach portion of the route, you can follow the main hwy N89 back into Bordeaux.

CITY
LIBOURNE

ROUTE
D670 D669

DISTANCE KM	TOTAL KM
32	98

ROUTE DESCRIPTION
From Libourne, cross L'Isle and follow the signs toward Fronsac. Continue on D670 through a series of small towns to St. Andre de Cubzac. The road passes through vineyards and offers occasional glimpses of the Dordogne into Bourg.

CITY
BOURG

ROUTE
D669

DISTANCE KM	TOTAL KM
15	130

ROUTE DESCRIPTION
Leave Bourg and take the road that winds along the river bank and offers a number of fine picnic spots. After passing the Chateau du Thau, pick up D669 for the remaining 6 kms to Blaye.

CITY
BLAYE/LAMARGUE

ROUTE DESCRIPTION
From Blaye, a small ferry crosses the river to Port de Lamargue. Crossing time about 10 minutes. In July and August: 11 crossings daily; off season: 5 to 6. Cost for 1 person with bike about 20 Fr.

CITY
LAMARGUE

ROUTE
D5 D2

DISTANCE KM	TOTAL KM
11	145

ROUTE DESCRIPTION
From the ferry dock, it is a slight climb through the town of Lamargue to the main road—D2—which runs along the Médoc side of the Gironde. Turn left toward Bordeaux. The road is flanked on both sides by vineyards.

CITY
MARGAUX

ROUTE
D105 D208 D5 D2

DISTANCE KM	TOTAL KM
11	156

ROUTE DESCRIPTION
From Margaux, take D105 to Avensan, then follow the winding D208 through the vineyards to Moulis-en Médoc. Continue on D5 back to the intersection with D2. Now head north and pass through several delightful small villages, often little more than a few old stone houses, a tiny market, and a lovely old church. On the way to Pauillac you will pass several famous chateaux, including Chateau de-Beychevelle.

CITY
PAUILLAC

ROUTE
D2 D1

DISTANCE KM	TOTAL KM
55	187

ROUTE DESCRIPTION
Leave Pauillac via D2. Just after crossing the train tracks, turn off on the road to Chateau Mouton, then down the narrow track leading to the other famous Rothschild property, Chateau Lafite. Continue on the pleasant winding road to yet another quaint village whose name adorns wine bottles in fine restaurants throughout the world, St. Estephe, passing the ornate castle-like Chateau Cos. Continue north along the "Médoc Touristique Circuit Nord." The road offers some fine views of the Gironde River. Past the town of St. Christoly, the vineyards and chateaux end and the route passes through flat dairylands joining up with D1 at St. Viven de Médoc. From there it is just under 15 kms to the delightful Atlantic coast resort of Soulac-sur-Mer. This last stretch approaches the ocean across the open fields and is often plagued by strong headwinds.

Note: From Soulac there is a bike path through the forest to the tip of the peninsula at Pointe de Grave. There is regular ferry service across the mouth of the Gironde to Royan on the mainland with continuous crossings in the summer. The cost for the 30-minute trip: 20 Fr. for 1 person with bike. This is a good jumping off point for the Loire Valley, Brittany, and Normandy. It is about 180 kms to Nantes, the gateway to the Loire and Brittany.

CITY
SOULAC-SUR-MER

ROUTE
D101 D101E

DISTANCE KM	TOTAL KM
35	242

ROUTE DESCRIPTION
Although there are plans to complete a cycle trail from Soulac all the way down the coast to Cape Ferret, as of summer '86 the trail had not been completed. The best cycling route south is to follow the posted *"Route du Lac."* This is a level, little traveled road passing through a pleasant wind-sheltered forest to the tiny settlement of Cartignac. From there turn off to the beach at Hourtin Plage.

CITY
HOURTIN/HOURTIN PLAGE

ROUTE
BT

DISTANCE KM	TOTAL KM
38	277

ROUTE DESCRIPTION
From Hourtin Plage there is an excellent bike trail leading through the dunes and forest to Lacanau Ocean. Along this stretch are miles of virtually deserted beach.

CITY	
LACANAU/LACANAU OCEAN	

ROUTE	
BT	

DISTANCE KM	TOTAL KM
50	315

CITY	
BORDEAUX	

TOTAL KM	
365	

ROUTE DESCRIPTION

From Lacanau, a well-marked bicycle trail leads through the forest all the way back to the northern outskirts of Bordeaux.

Note: If you're not quite ready to head back to the big city continue the additional 40 kms from Lacanau Ocean along the bike way through the Foret du Dom Porge to the popular resort town of Cape Ferret, which stretches out along the mouth of the enormous Bassin D'Arcachon. The entire region around the Bassin D'Arcachon is well suited for all types of water sports. There are plenty of campgrounds, a youth hostel, and hotels in all categories.

To return to Bordeaux, pedal along the east shore of the Bassin to the Village of Lege, then head north on D3 to Le Porge. From there take D5E northeast to pick up the Lacanau-Bordeaux bike trail at Saumos.

From Arcachon to the plush international resort Biarritz is approximately 150 kms. Most of the route is level and along little traveled roads through wooded areas with access to long stretches of excellent beaches. There are ample accommodations along the way.

From Biarritz it is approximately 20 kms of hilly going to the Spanish border.

WINE COUNTRY SIGHTS AND ACCOMMODATIONS

BORDEAUX. Pleasantly situated on the Garonne River in the southwest corner of France, Bordeaux lays claim to the title of "wine capital of the world." It is one of France's most attractive large cities. At one time an English colony, Bordeaux's star ascended during the reign of Louis XV when the city experienced a building boom that left it heir to some of the finest examples of eighteenth-century architecture found anywhere in the country. Although the city does have some bicycle lanes, Bordeaux is best explored on foot.

The expansive **Esplanade des Quinconces** laid out in 1820 overlooks the river with its gardens and impressive monuments; it is Europe's largest formal square. The city's rich architectural heritage is reflected in such outstanding buildings as the Grand Theater, the Bourse, and the Hotel de Ville. The **Cathédrale St. André**, a stunning edifice with sections dating back to the eleventh century, is Bordeaux's principal church. Museum goers should not pass up the excellent fine arts museum, **Musée des Beaux Arts**, and the **Musée Jean Moulin**, which documents the French Resistance movement during World War II.

Before venturing out into the adjacent wine country, be sure to stop in at the **Maison du Vin** (House of Wine) across from the tourist office (1 cours du XX Juillet) for maps and a wealth of useful information about this region's most famous product. The countryside surrounding Bordeaux has been producing fine wines for two thousand years, since the days when Bordeaux was a Roman city. The names of the towns and villages read like a who's who in the world of wine labels.

As might be expected in a major city, hotels run the gamut from the super plush to super sleazy. In the budget category, we like the friendly and conveniently located (behind the Bourse) HOTEL DES PYRENESS (12 rue St. Remi; Tel: [56] 81 66 58). It is large and clean; doubles run

100 to 180 Fr. Another winner in the low-price department, strategically situated in the heart of the old town, is the charming eleven-room HOTEL VIEUX BORDEAUX (22 rue du Cancera; Tel: [56] 48 07 27). For an elegant hotel in the classic nineteenth century French tradition, the GRAND HOTEL DE BORDEAUX is an excellent choice. It is in the center of town across from the Grant Theater (place de la Comedie; Tel: [56] 90 93 44). Doubles run from 400 to 800 Fr.

The youth hostel, FOYER MUNICIPAL DES JEUNES (22 cours Barbey, 33000 Bordeaux; Tel: [56] 91 59 51), is conveniently located within walking distance of the center city attractions. There are 247 beds; meals but no cooking facilities are provided.

Of the several Bordeaux area campgrounds, the most convenient is CAMPING LES GRAVIERES, located about 5 kms south of Bordeaux in Villenave-d'Ornon. A small bar serves snacks and drinks. There are stores and restaurants in the nearby village. It is open all year.

ST. ÉMILION. With its rambling stone houses in the center of a district that has been producing fine wines since before Roman times, St. Émilion is one of the most charming wine villages in the whole of France. Even if you have absolutely no interest in the fermented juice of the grape, be sure to allocate enough time to stroll through this enchanting village. Inquire at the tourist office about the interesting 45-minute tour of the town, which includes a visit to the ninth to twelfth-century **L'Église Monolithe**, built into the side of a sheer limestone cliff. Even though this is a popular tourist stop, it's refreshing to note the conspicuous absence of modern high-rise hotels and slick commercial eating establishments. In fact, such is the case for this entire region. Should you be interested in the local nectar, wine shops, many offering free tasting, abound. If you decide to spend a night or two, you can choose from a lovely campground or several comfortable hotels.

For a sampling of the elegance of rural France, treat yourself to a night at the chic HOSTELLERIE DE PLAISANCE (place du Clocher, 33330 St. Émilion; Tel: [57] 24

72 32). Each of the twelve rooms is individually furnished and the dining room is first class. Reservations are advised. Doubles run about 500 Fr. Another St. Émilion charmer with a fine view over the tile roofs of the town and a more modest tariff is the AUBERGE DE LA COMMANDERIE (rue des Cordeliers; Tel: [57] 24 70 19). For romantic dining in an intimate setting try LE RESTAURANT FRANCIS GOULLEE.

Camping is available at CAMPING LA BARBANE, 3 kms north of town on the road to Lussac (D122). It is a very nice site in a beautiful location with friendly management. There's no store or restaurant, but fresh bread is available in the morning. It is open all year.

LIBOURNE. A small attractive market town on the Dordogne, Libourne is the point from which much of the region's fine wine is shipped. Although there is not much in the city itself to interest tourists, Libourne, is on the main Paris-Bordeaux rail line and has several inexpensive hotels, which makes it a good alternate city from which to start the "Wine Country" route for those wishing to avoid the big city of Bordeaux.

Convenient and pleasant hotels near the train station include the three-star HOTEL LOUBAT (32 rue Chanzy; Tel: [57] 51 17 58) and the more modest five-room HOTEL CHANZY (16 rue Chanzy; Tel: [57] 51 05 15).

For camping, try CAMPING LE RUSTE, about 3 kms from town. Follow the signs on D243 in the direction of St. Émilion. It is a municipal site with limited facilities, open 23 March to 13 October.

BLAYE. This is a pleasant little town with a large square facing the Gironde. Perched on a hill overlooking the river is **La Citadelle**, a massive series of classical fortifications by the master French fortress builder Vauban. Within the walls of La Citadelle are a campground and a delightful small hotel. From Blaye there is regular ferry service to the Port de Lamarque in Médoc.

HOTEL LA CITADELLE is a gem of a small hotel complete with a swimming pool, romantically placed within the fortress walls.

The modern rooms, all with bath, are surprisingly reasonable: a double costs 210 Fr. The hotel restaurant is first rate. The HOTEL BELLEVUE just a few steps from the ferry dock looks out over a large park. It is not as romantic as the Citadel, but cheaper and more convenient. Doubles run 68 to 160 Fr.

CAMPING LA CITADELLE is a great location within the walls of the fortress. It is open 1 May to 15 September.

MARGAUX. Here is a tiny village that exists primarily in support of the famous **Chateau Margaux**. The chateau itself, built in the classical style in the beginning of the nineteenth century, is set among fastidiously manicured gardens. The rich-bodied red wine produced here, which rated a "grand cru" in the classification of 1855, is considered one of the finest in the world. Although on the spot visits are sometimes possible, it is best to call ahead (Tel: [56] 88 70 28).

In spite of the popularity of the Médoc, there is not the preponderance of hotels encountered in other tourist areas. There are, however, several very delightful places to stay scattered throughout the district. If you don't mind parking your bike among an assortment of Bentleys and Porsches or paying close to 1,000 Fr. per night for a double, then by all means pedal the 1.9 kms from hwy D2 to the sumptuous RELAIS DE MARGAUX. This is country elegance personified set in a fifty-five-acre estate. For reservations, contact Relais de Margaux (33460 Margaux; Tel: [56] 88 38 30). For more down-to-earth lodgings, pedal 8 kms up to the village of Lamargue and check in at the quaint little HOTEL RESTAURANT LE RELAIS DU MÉDOC, Lamargue, (33460 Margaux; Tel: [56] 58 92 27). It has six reasonably priced rooms and a wonderful restaurant featuring excellent regional fare.

There are two campgrounds within easy cycling distance of Margaux. One is at Avensan about 7 kms west of Margaux on hwy D105; the other is a small site some 8 kms north on D2 at Cussac Fort Médoc.

PAUILLAC. Yet another famous name in the annals of oenology, Pauillac is an attractive small town in a pleasant setting on the river. The main attractions located just a few kilometers outside of town are the exclusive **Chateau Mouton Rothschild** and **Chateau Lafite Rothschild**. In keeping with their exclusive reputation, there will be no gaudy free tasting or wine for sale signs at these lovely chateaux. Informative tours are conducted on an appointment basis. For details, call Chateau Lafite (Tel: [56] 59 01 74) or Chateau Mouton (Tel: [56] 59 22 22). There is no wine for sale at the chateaux.

Pauillac has several comfortable, moderately priced hotels. In spite of its lofty name, THE HOTEL YACHTING (Port de Plaisance, 33250 Pauillac; Tel: [56] 59 06 43) is a down-to-earth small hotel next to the train station, with doubles from 55 Fr. Although a bit rundown, the two-star HOTEL DE FRANCE ET D'ANGLETERRE is not without a touch of charm. It is located on the main street, but some rooms have balconies overlooking the river (Tel: [56] 59 01 20).

A good bet for a tasty, reasonably priced sampling of the local cuisine is LA COQUILLE, (18 quai Leon-Perrier). This small hotel restaurant also has eight attractive guest rooms.

HOURTIN PLAGE. A small beach settlement with no hotels, Hourtin Plage does have a good campground and a few restaurants. The beach is of fine sand in a pleasant area of dunes and pines. The nearby lake is popular with water sports fans.

It is often possible to rent rooms from local residents. Check around for signs. The HOTEL LE DAUPHIN (Tel: [56] 41 61 15) in the town of Hourtin is a small two-star hotel with doubles that start at 165 Fr.

CAMPING AIROTEL DEL LA COTE-D'ARGENT in a pine forest a short walk to the beach is a first-class site with all facilities, including rental bungelows and on site trailers. It is open 15 May to 15 September.

SOULAC-SUR-MER. This is a lovely beach resort with a number of pleasant small hotels and a gambling casino with an adjacent disco. The fine sandy beach is backed by dunes and woods and extends for some 7 kms. It is one of the few beach areas in France that is not jammed head to toe with bodies even in midsummer. Be careful when swimming on the Atlantic Coast; the currents can be tricky as the tides return with a rush.

There is not much in the way of hotels between Pauillac and Soulac. HOTEL DES PINS AT L'AMELIE, 3 kms south of town in a pine forest 100 meters from the beach, is a pleasant two-star hotel with a good restaurant (33780 Soulac-sur-Mer; Tel: [56] 09 80 01). The best budget deal in town is just a short walk from the beach: the MICHELET (1 rue Baguenard; Tel: [56] 09 84 18). There is a pleasant little seven-room hotel in St. Seurin-de-Cadourne called HOTEL DU MIDI (Tel: [56] 59 30 49).

A popular region with French campers, there are some ten campsites in and around Soulac, including campgrounds at St. Yzans, Commune de Jau Dignac et Loirac,

and Talais. CAMPING LES ARROS is conveniently located 150 meters from the beach and just a short walk from the municipal pool. It is open Easter to 15 September. CAMPING LE CORDOUAN on Route du Verdon is open all year.

For a good fresh seafood meal, try LE FIN GOURMET (10 rue Bremontier).

Rental cycles are available at the train station and from Cyclo Star (9 bis, rue F. Laffarque).

LACANAU/LACANAU OCEAN.

These are popular resorts with access to the Lac de Lacanau as well as the ocean. You'll find good beaches and plenty of activity without the mobs encountered on the Riviera.

HOTEL DE L'ETOILE-D'ARGENT (pl. de L'Europe, 33680 Lacanau Ocean; Tel: [56] 03 21 07) is close to the beach and reasonably priced with doubles from 100 to 130 Fr.

Of the many campgrounds in the area, the huge CAMPING LES GRANDS PINS at Lacanau Ocean has good access to the beach and offers a full range of facilities. It is open all year.

Dordogne

Situated in the southwest corner of the country between the Massif Central and the vineyards of Bordeaux is one of France's most delightful and fascinating regions, the Dordogne. For cyclists, the hilly nature of the region offers more of a challenge than the flat expanses of the neighboring Bordeaux wine country, but there is nothing here that the average Sunday cyclist cannot handle. Those who do venture into the Dordogne will be amply compensated for the little bit of extra effort.

As you cycle through the densely wooded countryside you will notice that the lush green of the forest is often punctuated by the appearance of a magnificent chateau set in a clearing or the ramparts of a fortress perched precipitously on a cliff overlooking a winding river. Above all, this is a region where there is a great sense of the past, and although interrupted by occasional pockets of tourism, the charm of the landscape and the ancient stone villages have not been defaced by the gaudy highrise developments seen in so many parts of Europe. Pedaling down many of the area's quiet winding lanes, one is enveloped by the prevailing sense of timelessness. The blending of the graceful chateaux, ochre-colored stone churches, and *bastides* (fortified towns) with the natural beauties of the hills and river valleys creates a seldom experienced harmony between the works of man and nature.

This part of France is sometimes referred to as "the cradle of mankind" since it contains the most incredible collection of prehistoric sites, artifacts, and cave paintings to be found anywhere. In addition to the well-known caves at Lascaux, the countryside around the tiny village of Les Eyzies is dotted with numerous examples of prehistoric art and culture. The local museum of prehistory is one of the finest of its kind in the world.

The residents of the Dordogne take great pride in their easy going life style and are gracious hosts. We have had nothing but pleasant experiences during our several recent trips through this wonderful region.

In a country where good dining is taken very seriously the cuisine of the Perigord ranks high among the wide variety of French regional cuisine. Some specialties such as truffles and *foie gras* (goose liver pâté) are enjoyed by connoisseurs of fine food far beyond the country's borders. After using the livers to make the delicious *foie gras* the rest of the goose is preserved as *confit d'oie*, another popular regional dish. Game and fresh water fish also play an important part in the cooking of the Dordogne. Although not well known outside of the country, some of the region's wines, in particular the full-bodied reds of Cahors and Bergerac, are well worth sampling.

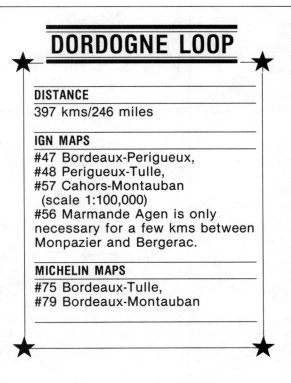

DORDOGNE LOOP

DISTANCE
397 kms/246 miles

IGN MAPS
#47 Bordeaux-Perigueux,
#48 Perigueux-Tulle,
#57 Cahors-Montauban
  (scale 1:100,000)
#56 Marmande Agen is only
necessary for a few kms between
Monpazier and Bergerac.

MICHELIN MAPS
#75 Bordeaux-Tulle,
#79 Bordeaux-Montauban

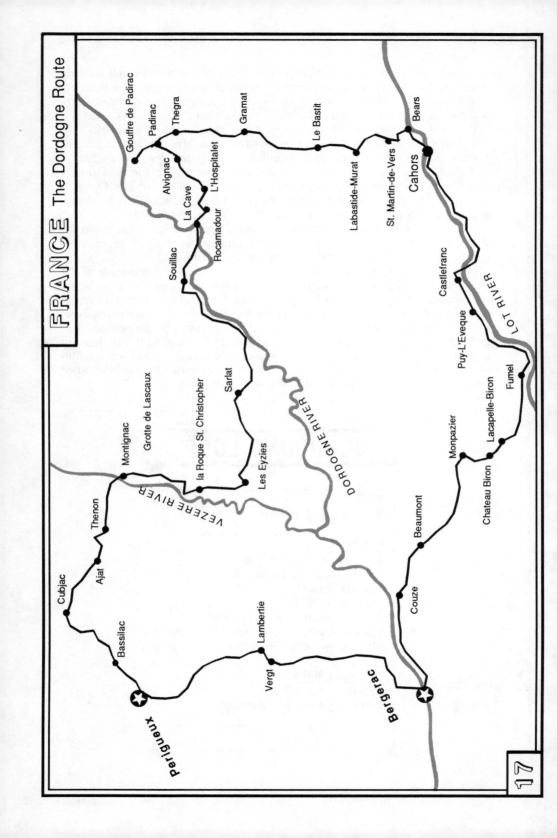

The Dordogne region is traversed by several rivers, which over eons have cut deeply into the limestone hills, exposing deep caves. Many of the caves contain fascinating paintings and relics left by our prehistoric predecessors. A number of roads in the area follow the course of these rivers along what were once primitive footpaths. Although much of the Dordogne has been cleared and is used for grazing and farming, many of the hills are covered with densely wooded tracts. The region's principal crops are strawberries, truffles, walnuts, and tobacco.

From the cyclist's viewpoint, this route offers a variety of cycling conditions: challenging hills, lengthy descents, and some pleasant meandering, flat riverside stretches. Since there is little industry in the region, the Dordogne has been spared the horrors of urbanization that have been visited upon other less fortunate parts of the country. In the area covered by this route, the largest city visited is Perigueux with a population of some 40,000. Hardly a metropolis! The route passes through an interesting assortment of stone houses set in picturesque small villages, elegant chateaux, and several well-preserved fortified towns (*bastides*).

Although this is definitely a hilly route, we have tried to lay it out in such a manner that you will be doing more coasting than climbing; however, there are some stretches that require some hard pedaling. A machine with ten or more speeds is recommended and, while olympic class conditioning is not required, you will need to be reasonably fit to be able to pedal this route and still have enough zip left to enjoy the beauties of the Dordogne. The route is laid out as a loop so it can be started at any point; but to take optimum advantage of the terrain, we suggest you travel this loop in a clockwise direction as determined when looking at the map.

Perigueux, a delightful and interesting city, is easy to reach by train and makes a good place from which to begin your exploration of the Dordogne. Cahors has good train connections to Paris as well as southern France; it is another convenient starting point. Wherever feasible we have tried to stick to the lesser traveled roads and still include the most interesting sights in the region. Bike trails are rare and in some of the valleys the roads are narrow. Generally speaking, however, cycling conditions are good and traffic is usually light.

Combining the Dordogne with the Wine Country route will give you good exposure to some of the best cycle touring that France has to offer. The Dordogne towns of Perigueux and Bergerac are both within a day's cycling of St. Émilion in the Bordeaux region. This is a good point at which to link up with the Bordeaux route. For those planning to cycle in Spain, there are direct train connections from Cahors to Barcelona. Cahors is also a good jumping off point for touring the Pyrenees and the Basque country. If the hills of the Dordogne have whet your appetite for strenuous cycling, then head into the Massif Central, a rugged mountainous region to the east of the Dordogne. Cahors and Rocamadour are gateways to this challenging cycling area.

Due to the more or less rugged nature of this region and the relative paucity of cities, the availability of accommodations is adequate but not as extensive as in the more heavily traveled areas of France. Don't be misled, however, by the use of the word rugged; all things are relative. There is certainly enough in the way of civilized amenities so that a tour of the Dordogne could hardly be considered a hardship. If you are overnighting in hotels and inns, plan your day's cycling carefully. In July and August try to phone ahead for reservations to avoid disappointment. In a pinch you can often find a bed at a farmhouse or one of the region's many rural *gites*. In high season there are also quite a few *chambres d'hote*. Campers have less of a problem as the region lends itself well to setting up a tent in a forest clearing or alongside a stream.

The climate, tempered by the Atlantic, is generally mild. In winter there is little snow, spring usually comes early, and the summers are hot. There is no clearly defined rainy season; your chances of encountering heavy, lasting rains in July, August, or September are minimal. During July and August be prepared for crowds – nothing unmanageable but reservations are advised for the main tourist spots, such as Sarlat and Rocamadour. The best times for touring the Dordogne are in June and September when the weather is often good and crowds are minimal. The region is especially beautiful in autumn with the changing colors of the leaves and the crisp air.

★ *LOOKING OUT OVER THE HANDLEBARS* ★

THE DORDOGNE LOOP

★

CITY
PERIGUEUX

ROUTE
D5 D68 N89

DISTANCE KM	TOTAL KM
35	0

ROUTE DESCRIPTION
From Perigueux, follow the signs toward the Bassilac, and continue on D5 along the Auvezere River to Cubjac. Cross the river and take D68 through the heavily wooded countryside, tiny villages, and the quaint town of Ajat, with its Romanesque church and castle. Cross the main hwy N89 to Thenon.

★

CITY
THENON

ROUTE
D67 D704

DISTANCE KM	TOTAL KM
14	35

ROUTE DESCRIPTION
Take D67 southeast out of Thenon. After a pleasant 14 kms, the road meets up with the Vézère River just north of Montignac.

CITY / ROUTE

CITY	ROUTE
MONTIGNAC	D706 D47

DISTANCE KM	TOTAL KM
25	49

ROUTE DESCRIPTION

The road follows the course of the twisting Vézère to Les Eyzies. At a number of spots along the road you can see places where the towering gray and white cliffs have been hollowed out to form caves and tunnels, which sheltered prehistoric man. At one time the river bed was 90 feet above its present level.

CITY	ROUTE
LES EYZIES	D47 D6

DISTANCE KM	TOTAL KM
22	74

ROUTE DESCRIPTION

From Les Eyzies, leave the Vézère Valley and follow D47 to Sarlat, a pleasant 22-km ride through a sparsely populated hilly region. The road, which is level for most of the way, passes the fifteenth-century to sixteenth-century Puymartin Castle (visitors welcome).

CITY	ROUTE
SARLAT	D704 D704A D703

DISTANCE KM	TOTAL KM
25	96

ROUTE DESCRIPTION

Take D704 south toward Souillac. After about 3 kms, the road forks. Follow D704A to meet up with the Dordogne River. Pick up D703 which runs along the river into Souillac.

CITY
SOUILLAC

ROUTE
D43 D247

DISTANCE KM	TOTAL KM
18	121

ROUTE DESCRIPTION

Leave Souillac in the direction of Rocamadour, and turn off just before the bridge at Port de Souillac onto the tiny D43. After crossing the narrow bridge over the Dordogne, continue to the small settlement of La Cave and take the climbing, winding D247 10 kms into Rocamadour. The nearby Belcastle Castle affords a superb view of the confluence of the Ouysse and Dordogne rivers. The turn off to D247 is easy to miss; it is a sharp right just after entering the village. After the first 2-km climb, it is an easy pedal through rolling farmlands to L'Hospitalet, which affords a magnificent view of the ancient pilgrimage village of Rocamadour.

CITY
ROCAMADOUR

ROUTE
D673 D90

DISTANCE KM	TOTAL KM
13	139

ROUTE DESCRIPTION

From L'Hospitalet, take D673 to the village of Padirac, then follow the signs to the Gouffre de Padirac, a fascinating complex of subterranean rivers and caves.

CITY
PADIRAC/GOUFFRE
DE PADIRAC

ROUTE
D14

DISTANCE KM	TOTAL KM
12	152

CITY
GRAMAT

ROUTE
D677

DISTANCE KM	TOTAL KM
22	164

CITY
LA-BASTIDE/MURAT

ROUTE
D32 D653 D49 D911

DISTANCE KM	TOTAL KM
34	186

ROUTE DESCRIPTION

Return to Padirac, then follow the signs to Thegra. From there take hwy D14 to Gramat. Take D677 across the sparsely settled limestone plateau to the tiny village of Le Bastit. Leave the village on D677. The road continues across the plateau and runs down between the sheer gray cliffs that form the valley of the Vers River. At La-Bastide take D32. Just beyond the scenic little village of St.-Martin-de-Vers, the route joins up with the main road from Figeac, D653. Follow this through the steep gorges to the Lot River. Cross over at Bears and continue on D49, which follows the south bank of the Lot. Follow the signs into Cahors. Do *not* take D49 to Les Mazuts. Stay along the river to reach Cahors.

CITY
CAHORS

ROUTE
D8 D911

DISTANCE KM	TOTAL KM
35	220

CITY
PUY-L'EVEQUE

ROUTE
D911 D710 D162 D150 D53 D2

DISTANCE KM	TOTAL KM
47	255

ROUTE DESCRIPTION

Leave Cahors on D8, which follows the south bank of the Lot as it cuts through the high plateau between Cahors and Puy-L'Eveque. Take the bridge over the Lot at Castelfranc and continue on to Puy-L'Eveque, one of the most picturesque spots in the entire valley. Stay on D911 to the industrial town of Fumel. Take D710 north. After 4 kms, the road forks; stay to left and take D162. After 7 kms, the road splits again; this time take D150 north to Lacapelle-Biron, then continue on D150 toward Chateau Biron. After a few kms, the route number changes to D53. Chateau Biron, perched on a hill and commanding a sweeping view of the surrounding countryside, is a fascinating hodgepodge of buildings and architectural styles. From the castle, continue on D53, which after several kms runs into D2 for the last 5 kms to Monpazier.

CITY

MONPAZIER

ROUTE

D660 D37

DISTANCE KM	TOTAL KM
42	302

ROUTE DESCRIPTION

From Monpazier, take D660 and pass through Beaumont, once a strongly fortified bastide. About 4 kms past Beaumont, turn down the narrow road on the left to Bannes Castle, an elegant sixteenth century fortress perched on a rocky promontory. It's worth pedaling the extra few hundred meters to have a look. D660 continues on to join up with the Dordogne at Couze. From here, take D37 along the river to Bergerac.

CITY

BERGERAC

ROUTE

N21 D21E D21 D8 N21

DISTANCE KM	TOTAL KM
53	344

CITY

PERIGUEUX

DISTANCE KM	TOTAL KM
53	397

ROUTE DESCRIPTION

Take the main hwy N21 toward Perigueux. After 7 kms the road forks. Stay to the right and follow the signs to Perigueux. The hwy numbers change several times before reaching Perigueux.

DORDOGNE SIGHTS AND ACCOMMODATIONS

PERIGUEUX. An ancient town with its origins in pre-Roman times, Perigueux, after succumbing to Caesar and his legions, flourished and became one of the finest Roman towns in Aquitaine. Although the city was sacked by the Vandals in the third century, the ruins of a vast amphitheater, a Roman villa, and the tower of Vesunna are visible remnants of the city's Roman past. In addition to the Gallo-Roman ruins in the lower part of the town, the "old town" contains the unique five-domed Byzantine-style **Cathédrale St.-Front** and the **Musée de Perigord**, which has an extensive collection of prehistoric artifacts and a fine assortment of well-preserved fifteenth-century to sixteenth-century homes.

The present-day city, pleasantly situated in the fertile Isle River Valley, is the capital of the region known as Perigord and is a popular gateway for exploring the beauties of the Dordogne.

As an important marketing and touring center for the Dordogne, Perigueux offers a good selection of reasonably priced accommodations. There is no youth hostel.

One of the most convenient and attractive low priced hotels is the small HOTEL DU MIDI (18 rue Denis-Papin, 24000 Perigueux; Tel: [53] 53 41 06) near the train station. Doubles run 70 to 120 Fr. Another good budget bet in the center of town near the bus station is the HOTEL DU LION D'OR (17 Cours Fenelon; Tel: [53] 53 49 03). The BRISTOL HOTEL (37 rue A.-Gadaud; Tel: [53] 08 75 90) is one of the town's top hotels. For a special treat, you can stay in a romantic eighteenth century chateau in Razac-sur-l'Isle, just off hwy N89, 11 kms southwest of Perigueux. It's small — just twenty-two individually appointed rooms — so reservations are advised. Rooms cost 150 to 280 Fr. If you eat at the excellent restaurant, be sure to try the duck with pepper sauce (Chateau de Lalande, 24430 Razac-sur-l'Isle; Tel: [53] 54 52 30).

Of the several campgrounds in and around Perigueux, CAMPING BARNABE PLAGE, a reasonably priced site on the river and just a few minutes walk to town, is the best choice. It is open all year.

THENON. On the main hwy N89 between Perigueux and Brive, Thenon has an inexpensive hotel (HOTEL CHEZ SERGE, Les Tournissous, 24290 Thenon; Tel: [53] 05 20 31. Rooms go from 80 Fr.) and nearby campground (CAMPING JARY CARREY is conveniently situated for an overnight stay, but it offers nothing special in the way of facilities; it is open 15 May to 15 September). About 8 kms further on N89 in the direction of Brive is **Rastignac Chateau**, an eighteenth-century mansion that bears a remarkable resemblance to the White House in Washington D.C.

MONTIGNAC. On the banks of the Vézère, with its vestiges of an ancient fortress, Montignac is well suited for an overnight stop when you visit **Lascaux Cave**, one of the most famous prehistoric sites in Europe. Unfortunately, the original cave is no longer open to the public; however, a replica known as Lascaux 2 was opened in 1983. Slide shows and a facsimile of the renowned Bull Chamber are presented. It is only 1 km from Montignac on D704.

About 5 kms south of Montignac on D706 is a turnoff to **Le Thot**. It is well worth the 1.5 kms of uphill pedaling to visit the **Centre d'Art Prehistorique** (closed Mondays). After viewing the tableau, film show, and exhibits, one is better equipped to understand the importance of this region in the study of the habits and development of early man. A few hundred meters further down D706, framed by the magnificent poplars that line the river bank, is the elegant sixteenth-century **Chateau Losse**. Guided tours are offered from 1 July to 15 September.

For the budget traveler, Mme. Guillaumard's HOTEL-RESTAURANT DE LA GROTTE (24290 Montignac) offers good value for the money; twelve rooms are available at 60 to 125 Fr. The three-star RELAIS DU SOEIL D'OR (16 rue du 4-Septembre; Tel: [53] 51 80 22) is located in a lovely wooded park and features a fine restaurant and heated pool.

If you prefer a campground to pitching a tent in the forest, check in at CAMPING LE BLEUFOND, a nice, well-shaded site alongside the river, adjacent to the municipal swimming pool. It is open 1 April to 15 October.

LES EYZIES-DE-TAYAC. A tiny village picturesquely situated in a region of steep cliffs at the joining of the Vézère and Beune rivers, Les Eyzies-de-Tayac has become a mecca for those interested in prehistory. In the mid-nineteenth century, a wealth of prehistoric dwellings, skeletons, artifacts, and cave paintings were unearthed in and around Les Eyzies, making it a virtual archaeologist's paradise. The **National Museum of Prehistory**, housed in the castle of the former Barons of Beynac, contains one of the finest collections of its kind anywhere in the world. The eleventh-century castle built into the side of a sheer cliff affords a good view of the village and the Vézère valley. Particularly interesting prehistoric cave dwellings can be found at **Roque St.-Christophe** at Peyzac-le-Mostier and **Castel-Merle** at Sergeac. Just a few hundred meters from the museum is the **Font-de-Gaume Cave**, a veritable caveman's art gallery containing some two hundred examples of prehistoric cave paintings.

Considering its size, Les Eyzies offers its numerous visitors a good range of accommodations, some of which are quite delightful.

One of the most charming places to stay in the area is the ivy covered HOTEL LES GLYCINES (24620 Les Eyzies-de-Tayac; Tel: [53] 06 97 09). Presided over by M. and Mme. Mercut, this nineteenth-century post station has been converted into a comfortable and colorful country inn. The excellent kitchen features such fine regional dishes as *Escalope de saumon aux cêpes*. A double with bath will set you back about 250 Fr. Although the name sounds a bit hokey, the HOTEL CRO-MAGNON (2460 Les Eyzies-en-Perigord; Tel: [53] 06 97 06) is a stately old ivy covered charmer that has been a hotel for more than two hundred years. The HOTEL DE FRANCE is in a traditional natural stone building around the corner from the Prehistory Museum. It offers first-class comfort at budget prices; rooms go for 62 to 150 Fr. (Tel: [53] 06 97 23).

Of the several campgrounds in the vicinity of Les Eyzies, there are two we like best. CAMPING LA RIVIERE is a nice shaded site at the river, with nearby swimming pool and tennis. It is open 1 April to 31 October. CAMPING LE MAS DE SIREUIL is a pleasant site with a pool in the hills overlooking the Beune Valley, about 7 kms from Eyzies off D47. It is open 1 June to 30 September.

SARLAT. The capital of the region known as Perigord Noir, Sarlat is a remarkably well-preserved and vibrant old town – one of the most attractive in all of France. Pick up a free walking map at the Office du Tourisme (place de la Liberté), and spend a few hours meandering through this gem of a French medieval town. In July and August the old town is host to a number of colorful open air musical and theater happenings. Take in such venerable ancient buildings as the **Cathédrale St. Sacerdos**, the **Bishop's Palace**, and the **Hotel Plamon**. And be sure to leave some room in your panniers to stock up on *foie gras* and some of the other fabulous picnic fixings temptingly displayed in the many shop windows. It's not for nothing that Sarlot has been dubbed the gastronomic capital of Perigord Noir.

This busy tourist town offers the full palate of lodging possibilities from deluxe hotels to camping.

Pampered pedalers can chain up their bikes at the HOTEL DE LA MADELIENE (1 place de la Petite Rigaudie; Tel: [53] 59 12 40). One of the Sarlat's best hotels and known for its first-class regional cuisine, it is conveniently located in the old town. The HOSTELLERIE DE MEYSSET (Lieu-Dit Argentouleau, 24200 Sarlat; Tel: [53] 59 08 29), 3 kms north of Sarlat on the road to Eyzies, is a romantic old manor house set in a wooded park. It offers outstanding vistas of the Sarlat countryside and a fine restaurant.

The youth hostel, AUBERGE DE LA JEUNESSE (15 bis ave. de Selves, 24200 Sarlat; Tel: [53] 59 47 59), is located at the north end of town. Look for the sign coming into Sarlat on D47. It is a no-frills hostel with forty-five beds. If it is full, as is often the case during July and August, try the HOTEL MARCEL just down the street (8 ave. de Selves; Tel: [53] 59 21 98). Rooms run from 58 to 135 Fr.

CAMPING LES PERIERES on D47 less than 1 km northeast of town offers all the amenities including tennis and a swimming pool. It is set in ten acres of park. If you are without a tent, they will rent you a bungalow.

SOUILLAC. At the point where the Borreze River joins the Dordogne, Souillac is the bustling center of a rich agricultural area. The town's main attraction is the ancient **abbey church** first established in the thirteenth century. Destroyed during the wars of religion, the abbey was rebuilt in the seventeenth century.

There's not much in the way of accommodations in Souillac itself; however, there are some fine places on the outskirts of this small town.

If you're in the market for a luxurious, romantic, out-of-the-way chateau hotel, then just after crossing the narrow bridge on D43 over the Dordogne, ca. 6 kms southeast of Souillac, follow the sign to CHATEAU LA TREYNE. Turn down the lane and after a few hundred meters you'll come to the fourteenth-century to seventeenth-century chateau perched on a cliff overlooking the Dordogne. It is now a luxury hotel complete with sauna and swimming pool. (For reservations: Chateau Hotel La Treyne, 46200 Souillac; Tel: [65] 32 66 66.) Another intriguing place to stay is LES GRANGES VIEILLES. Looking like something out of the Adams family, this curious mansion has eleven delightfully furnished rooms and is set in a pleasant park. Rooms cost 160 to 300 Fr. It is located 2 kms west of Souillac on D703 (Tel: [65] 37 80 92).

LE PONT DE L'OUYSEE in the little town of Lacave on the route to Rocamadour is a charming little inn – just ten rooms and a lovely terrace with a magnificent view. (For reservations: Hotel Le Pont de l'Ouysse, Lacave-46200 Souillac; Tel: [65] 37 87 04.)

There is a large campsite about 7 kms from town off D15, the road to Salignac-Eyvignes. CAMPING LA PAILLE BASSE is a first-class site with a full range of facilities including swimming pool. It is open 15 May to 15 September.

ROCAMADOUR. An important pilgrimage site since the Middle Ages, Rocamadour is one of the most dramatically situated towns in the entire country. Towered over by its fourteenth-century castle, Rocamadour is a conglomeration of buildings arranged in tiers and set into the sheer face of a 1600-foot cliff. The view of the ancient village from l'Hospitalet is breathtaking. Don your climbing shoes and scale the two hundred steps to the impressive collection of **churches at Place St.-Amadour**. From the chateau there is a spectacular panoramic view of the town and the surrounding countryside. The chateau is open for visits from 1 July to 31 August.

For a unique experience, view the flying antics of the trained eagles at **Rocher des Aigles**. From Easter through 15 October there is an outstanding sound and light spectacular. The best vantage point is from the terrace of the **Musée Roland le-Preux**.

Rocamadour is a very popular tourist destination with limited accommodations. To avoid disappointment after a hard days cycling, make reservations.

The small moderately priced HOTEL STE.-MARIE is pleasantly situated with a good terrace restaurant (place des Senhals; Tel: [65] 33 62 22). For luxury accommodations, the intimate charm of CHATEAU DE ROUMEGOUSE (Tel: [65] 33 63 81) offers a quiet respite from the busloads of tourists. There are just ten rooms in a wooded setting off D677 between Rocamadour and Gramat. HOTEL DU CHATEAU in Alvignac is a pleasant old hotel built on the foundations of an old chateau. It has been managed by the same family since 1862. (For reservations: Hotel du Chateau, Alvignac-46500 Gramat; Tel: [65] 33 60 14.)

There is a small campsite at l'Hospitalet and another municipal campground in Alvignac on the way to the Gouffre de Padirac. It is open Easter to 30 September.

PADIRAC/GOUFFRE DE PADIRAC. The Gouffre de Padirac is a huge subterreanean complex of galleries and caverns carved out of the limestone mass of the Gramat Causse by an underground river. The caverns were used as a refuge during the Hundred Years War and during the Wars of Religion. Be sure to take the 1½-hour guided tour, part of which is by boat on the vast underground lakes.

For a comfortable, inexpensive overnight stay, try the PADIRAC HOTEL (46500 Padirac; Tel: [65] 33 64 23) or the HOTEL DU QUERCY (Tel: [65] 33 64 68). There is a large well-equipped campsite at Padirac: CAMPING DES CHENES.

GRAMAT. A pleasant, out-of-the-way little town, Gramat is an important regional marketing town for sheep, nuts, and truffles. About 1 km out of town on hwy. D14 is **Gramat Safari Park**.

For such a small town, Gramat has a surprising number of hotels. The best in town is HOTEL LE LION D'OR (46500 Gramat; Tel: [65] 38 73 18). For an inexpensive room, try the LE RELAIS GOURMAND (Tel: [65] 38 83 92).

CAMPING LES SEGALIERES is a large site on the outskirts of town.

LABASTIDE-MURAT. The small village lying at the height of the Gramat Plateau is best known for one of its native sons, Joachim Murat, a hero of the French Empire during Napoleonic times.

If you plan to stay here, try the one-star AUBERGE RELAIS DU ROI DU NAPLES (46240 Labastide-Murat; Tel: [63] 31 10 02). We tried to find out why this tiny inn in the middle of France was named after the king of Naples but our French just wasn't good enough! In any case, the beds were comfortable and we slept like logs after the day's tough cycling.

There is a small municipal site – CAMPING MUNICIPAL L'ESTOMBE – which makes a convenient stopover on the tough stretch between Gramat and Cahors.

CAHORS. Located on a sharp bend in the river Lot, Cahors presents approaching visitors with an impressive array of towers, spires, and battlements. In the Middle Ages, Cahors was a prominent commercial and university town; and in the thirteenth century, it became the principal banking city in Europe. Especially worth seeing are the **Valentre Bridge**, a remarkable bridge adorned with a series of battlements and parapets constructed in the fourteenth century, and **St. Stephen's Cathedral**, an impressive three-towered structure dating back to the twelfth century.

As the largest city in the region, Cahors has quite a few hotels. At the budget end of the scale are the ten-room LES PERDREAUX (place de la Liberation; Tel: [65] 35 03 50) and HOTEL DE LA BOURSE (place Rousseau; Tel: [65] 35 17 78). The HOTEL WILSON (72 rue Wilson; Tel: [65] 35 24 50) is the town's leading hotel.

There is a small, two-star, municipal campground at the edge of town – CAMPING MUNICIPAL ST. GEORGE. It is open 15 May to 15 September.

MONPAZIER. The *bastide*, or fortified town, of Monpazier was founded in 1284 by Edward I King of England. The present-day town is one of the best-preserved examples of a fortified town in the entire region. The oblong-shaped **Place Centrale** is ringed by a covered market, arcades, and ancient houses.

The HOTEL DE FRANCE (21 rue Saint-Jacques, 24540 Monpazier; Tel: [53] 22 50 06), and HOTEL DE LONDRES (Tel: [53] 22 60 64) are both pleasant, moderately priced hotels.

There are two campsites within a few kms of the town. CAMPING MOULIN DE DAVID, on D2 3 kms from town on the road to Villereal, is a nice site with restaurant and swimming pool. It is open 1 June to 15 September. CAMPING MUNICIPAL DE VERONNE is in Marsales – about 2 kms from Monpazier, turn off D660 onto D26E. It is open 15 June to 15 September.

PUY-L'EVEQUE. With its old stone houses terraced into the cliffs above the river Lot, Puy-L'Eveque is one of the prettiest sites in the entire valley. The stone tower looking over the valley is all that remains of a thirteenth-century castle.

You can find a good room for under 200 Fr. at the HOTEL BELLEVUE (46700 Puy-L'Eveque; Tel: [65] 21 30 70) or for under 100 Fr. at the HOTEL HENRY (Tel: [65] 21 32 24).

CAMPING MUNICIPAL DE LA PLAGE is a small site pleasantly situated on the Lot River about 3 kms from town on D28. It is open 1 June to 30 September.

BERGERAC. Spread out on both sides of the Dordogne is the principal town in the southern Dordogne region and the center of an important wine and tobacco industry. Stroll through the flower-bedecked old town with its Renaissance façades and narrow winding streets, evoking memories of Cyrano de Bergerac whose statue stands on the place de la Myrpe. Also of interest is the **Tobacco Museum** housed in a seventeenth-century mansion. Just south of town is the **Monbazillac Vineyard**, producer of the region's finest wines and the ornately fortified sixteenth-century **Monbazillac Chateau**. There is a small wine museum in the chateau cellars. A tour of the chateau includes a tasting of the local wines.

CHATEAU HOTEL DU MOUNET SULLY (Route de Mussidan, 24100 Bergerac; Tel: [53] 57 04 21) has just eight cozy rooms and is romantically set in a former cloister. Rooms run from 115 to 250 Fr. (Tel: [53] 57 04 21). Another fine little hotel with an excellent kitchen that features regional classics is the HOTEL LE CYRANO (2 Boulevard Montaigne; Tel: [53] 57 02 76).

The municipal campground, CAMPING LA PELOUSE, has limited facilities but is conveniently located at the river and is open all year.

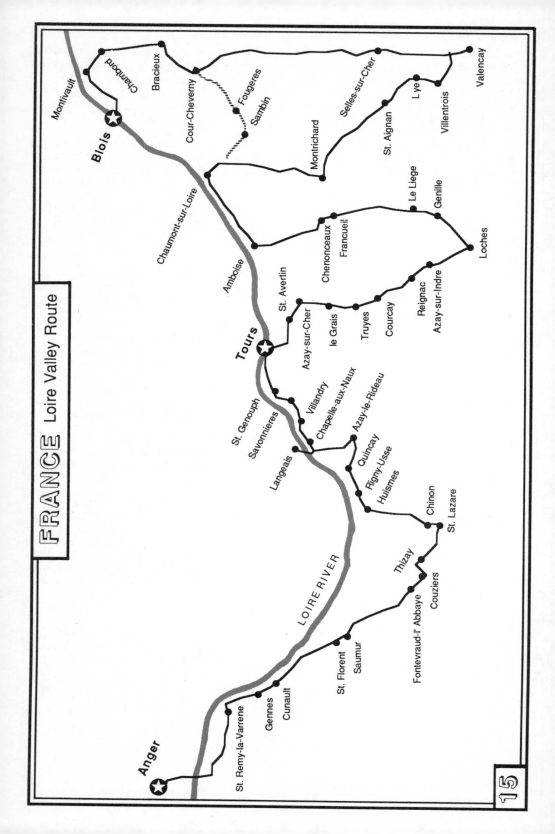

The Loire Valley

Few rivers in the world have their shores graced by the profusion of elegant architecture as is found along the course of France's romantic Loire and its tributaries. Although most of the spectacular chateaux were built during the sixteenth century Renaissance period, the region's serene beauty and mild climate, combined with its proximity to Paris, began attracting the French nobility centuries earlier. The imposing castles at Angers, Chinon, and Langeais were actually constructed during the Middle Ages.

The Loire region is often referred to as the "Garden of France" and is perhaps the most "French" of any part of the country. It is generally accepted that the French spoken here is the purest in France – a good place to practice your school French.

When you decide to pedal the Loire, you will find there are more rewards than just viewing the magnificent chateaux. In addition to the "big names," such as Chambord and Chenonceaux, there are scores of lesser-known but equally enchanting chateaux scattered throughout the countryside. In a land where things gastronomic are not taken lightly, the culinary specialties of the Loire region are considered to be among the finest that France has to offer. Particularly appealing are the locally caught freshwater fish, game dishes, and the savory minced and potted pork (*rillons* and *rillettes*). The region is also home to some superb wines, such as the whites of Vouvray, Muscadet, and Pouilly-Fumé, and the excellent red wines of Chinon and Bourgueil.

Whether you cycle up to one of the countless quaint roadside restaurants or load up your panniers at an intriguing *charcuterie* (the French version of a delicatessen) and picnic along the river or in a secluded patch of ancient forest, when you choose the Loire route you will be hard-pressed to keep from adding several kilos to your load. The region's flat character make it difficult to offset the calories ingested.

The region is easily reached from all parts of France and is readily combined with several other routes described in this book – particularly Normandy and the "Wine Country" routes. For bicyclists who are starting from Paris, the Loire region which is just over 100 kms from Paris, is a natural for a cycle tour.

THE LOIRE VALLEY ROUTE

START	FINISH	DISTANCE
BLOIS	ANGERS	406 kms/252 miles

MICHELIN MAPS	IGN MAPS
#64, Angers-Tours (scale: 1:200,000)	#25 Orléans-Tours; #25 Angers-Chinon (scale: 1:100,000)

This is essentially flat country, with occasional rolling hills especially between the Loire and Cher rivers. As you pedal along this route you will pass through a pleasant mixture of densely forested areas, placid farmland, many quaint villages, and magnificent chateaux. This is easy cycling country and ideal if you are not quite in condition to tackle any serious hills. The few hills you will encounter on this route can be easily "conquered" on a three-speed bike. Set a leisurely pace and enjoy the countryside. This is a great introduction to European cycling.

Although many guidebooks describe a tour of the Loire starting at Orléans, we have found Blois makes a much more attractive starting point. Outside of a few statues of Joan of Arc, Orléans, which was badly damaged during World War II, doesn't really have very much of interest. Blois, on the other hand, is one of the region's most delightful cities and is less than two hours by train from Paris's Austerlitz station.

In laying out this route we have taken note of the fact that there are more than one hundred chateaux that are open to the public, which is more than even the most dedicated can handle. It has been our experience, and that of most of the people we've met while biking in this region, that visiting one chateau, combined with several hours of pedaling, and taking time out for meals and rest stops makes for a very full day. Trying to cram in too much tends to overload the circuits and detract from the enjoyment of a vacation. Many of the chateaux are floodlit at night and several present enchanting son-et-lumiere (sound and light) performances on summer nights. The route we have selected follows the Loire River for part of the way but also explores some of the region's interesting inland attractions.

Note: The route as described runs from Blois to Angers. We have chosen this direction on the assumption that many cyclists will be coming from Paris, and on that basis Blois makes a convenient starting point. There is no reason not to start in Angers if you find it more convenient. Simply reverse the route directions.

SIDE TRIPS AND ADDED ATTRACTIONS

If a stopover in Paris is included in your travel plans then, time permitting, why not cycle down to Blois to start the Loire route? It is less than 200 kms and you can make interesting stopovers at the fabulous palace and gardens of Versailles just outside of Paris. Be sure to pass through Chartres and visit its magnificent cathedral. Stay off the main highways, and you'll find the cycling through the attractive, somewhat hilly countryside very enjoyable. Although it is certainly possible to continue cycling the 90 or so kilometers along the Loire from Angers to Nantes, the gateway to Brittany, the route is not nearly as interesting as the portion of the Loire described below.

May and June are excellent times to visit the region; the weather is generally good and traffic is light. Be sure to bring along raingear as showers can move in rapidly from the nearby Atlantic. September, when the weather is usually still quite good and the summer's crowds have departed, is a prime time to cycle the Loire. In July and August be prepared for heavy traffic, many tour buses, and crowded accommodations.

As in most parts of France, a dense network of campgrounds, youth hostels, small hotels, and several excellent chateau hotels are available.

THE LOIRE VALLEY

CITY
BLOIS

ROUTE
D951

DISTANCE KM	TOTAL KM
12	0

CITY
MONTIVAULT

ROUTE
D84

DISTANCE KM	TOTAL KM
7	12

CITY
CHAMBORD

ROUTE
D112 D102

DISTANCE KM	TOTAL KM
17	19

ROUTE DESCRIPTION

Leaving Blois, cross over the old stone bridge. Take the first left and follow D951 toward Orleans/Le Mans. From this side of the Loire there is a good view of Blois. Continue along the river, following the Chambord signs. Turn off on D84 to Montivault. Stay on D84 and pass through the village of Maslives into the Parc de Chambord. The road leads directly to the Chateau de Chambord. From the chateau, take D112 through the forest to Bracieux. Go through the village. At the south edge of town, pick up D102 which runs through the pleasant farm country to Cour-Cheverny.

Note: From Cheverny, our main route continues to the quaint little town of Valencay, which has an opulent castle. You can eliminate the 80-kms Valencay loop and take an alternate route to the impressive chateau at Chaumont-sur-Loire.

Alternate Route: From Cheverny, take D52 through the gentle farm country to Sambin, passing the feudal castle in Fougeres. From Sambin take C20, a meandering country lane. As you leave Sambin, you will see a sign on your right for Cande/Chaumont. Stay with this until it intersects with D114, which runs downhill into Chaumont.

CITY
COUR-CHEVERNY

ROUTE
D765

DISTANCE KM	TOTAL KM
8	46

ROUTE
D119

DISTANCE KM	TOTAL KM
20	54

ROUTE
N76

ROUTE DESCRIPTION

Continuing with the main route, from Cheverny take D765 through the Foret de Cheverny southeast toward Romarantin-Lathenay. After 8 kms, turn off onto the less heavily traveled D119. At the intersection with N76, take N76 the remaining 2 kms to Selles-sur-Cher.

CITY
SELLES-SUR-CHER

ROUTE
D956

DISTANCE KM	TOTAL KM
14	76

ROUTE DESCRIPTION

From Selles-sur-Cher, head south on D956 14 kms to Valencay. The last several kms pass through the delightful Foret de Gatine into the charming little town of Valencay.

CITY
VALENCAY

ROUTE
D956 D37

DISTANCE KM	TOTAL KM
11	90

ROUTE DESCRIPTION

Leaving Valencay to return to the Loire, take D956 north toward Selle/Cher for 1 km. Just past the edge of town, turn off to the left and follow D37 through the forest to intersect with D33 at Villentrois.

CITY
VILLENTROIS

ROUTE
D33 D17

DISTANCE KM	TOTAL KM
13	101

ROUTE DESCRIPTION

From Villentrois take D33 along the Modon River and pass through Lye. After 2.5 kms, the road runs into D17, which continues on into St. Aignan.

CITY
ST. AIGNAN

ROUTE
D17

DISTANCE KM	TOTAL KM
18	114

ROUTE DESCRIPTION

From St. Aignan, continue on D17 18 kms to Montrichard.

CITY
MONTRICHARD

ROUTE
D764 D62 D139 D114

DISTANCE KM	TOTAL KM
18	132

ROUTE DESCRIPTION

Leave Montrichard on D764, which then intersects with D62. Follow the signs to Chaumont. The route numbers change several times before reaching Chaumont on the banks of the Loire.

CITY
CHAUMONT SUR-LOIRE

ROUTE
D751

DISTANCE KM	TOTAL KM
17	150

ROUTE DESCRIPTION

From Chaumont, take D751 which follows the Loire with nice views of the river for a good portion of the 18 kms into Amboise. This section is heavily traveled.

CITY
AMBOISE

ROUTE
D115 D81 D40

DISTANCE KM	TOTAL KM
13	167

ROUTE DESCRIPTION

From the center of Amboise, take D115 toward Montrichard. After a few hundred meters, turn off onto D81 and follow the signs to Chenonceaux. The last 2 kms are on the busy D40.

CITY
CHENONCEAUX

ROUTE
D81 D764

DISTANCE KM	TOTAL KM
30	180

ROUTE DESCRIPTION

Leaving the chateau, cross the river and take D81 through Francueil and continue on this winding country road to the village of Le Liege. Go through the town and pick up D764. Continue past Genille into the Foret de Loches. At the outskirts of Loches, the road runs into the main hwy N143 to Loches.

CITY
LOCHES

ROUTE
D25 D17 D82 N76

DISTANCE KM	TOTAL KM
46	210

ROUTE DESCRIPTION

At the north edge of Loches, cross the Indre River to Corbery. Then take D25, which follows the river to Ile Thime, site of a small chateau. Cross the river again to Chambourg and stay with D17 along the river, through Azay-sur-Indre (sixteenth-century chateau) to Reignac. Once again cross the river and follow the small country lanes through La Thibaudiere, Courcay, and Truyes. At the tiny village of St. Blaise, continue north on D82 to Prieure de St. Jean de Grais, site of a twelfth-century cloister. Stay on D82 to meet up with N76 at Azay-sur-Cher. Continue along the main route N76 through St. Avertin into Tours.

CITY
TOURS

ROUTE
D88 D7

DISTANCE KM	TOTAL KM
17	256

ROUTE DESCRIPTION
From the Tours train station, take bd. Beranger to rue L. Boyer and follow this to the river. Turn left at ave. Proudhon and pedal along the levee (D88) with the Loire on your right through La Riche and St. Genouph. Then follow the signs to Savonnieres, a pleasant little town with some interesting caves. Cross the Cher at Le Port. Continue along D7 3 kms to Villandry.

CITY
VILLANDRY

ROUTE
D16

DISTANCE KM	TOTAL KM
11	273

ROUTE DESCRIPTION
Take the path opposite the Hotel du Cheval Rouge down to the river, and follow D16 toward Chapelle-aux-Naux. Cross the Loire on the old suspension bridge to Langeais, which has a powerful medieval fortress perched on a small mount overlooking the town.

CITY
LANGEAIS

ROUTE
D57

DISTANCE KM	TOTAL KM
11	284

ROUTE DESCRIPTION
From Langeais, cross back over the suspension bridge and take D57 11 kms to Azay-le-Rideau on the banks of the Indre.

CITY
AZAY-LE RIDEAU

ROUTE
D17 D7

DISTANCE KM	TOTAL KM
14	295

ROUTE DESCRIPTION
From Azay, cross the Indre and follow D17 to Quincay where it runs into D7, which continues on to Chateau d'Usse, whose towers and turrets provide an aura of mystery and intrigue.

CITY
RIGNY-USSE

ROUTE
D7 D16

DISTANCE KM	TOTAL KM
13	309

ROUTE DESCRIPTION

Take D7 toward Huisemes. About 1 km from the chateau at Le Vivier, turn left onto a small side road into Huisms. From there take D16 to Chinon and pass several interesting small chateaux along the side of the road.

CITY
CHINON

ROUTE
D749 D751

DISTANCE KM	TOTAL KM
18	322

ROUTE DESCRIPTION

From Chinon, cross the Vienne River on D749 to St. Lazare. Then continue along D751 to Thizay. About 2 kms past the village, take the small road to the left past Les Caves Blanches, through the Foret de Fontevraud, past the village of Couziers with its nearby chateau, and continue into Fontevraud-l'Abbaye.

CITY
FONTEVRAUD L'ABBAYE

ROUTE
D145

DISTANCE KM	TOTAL KM
14	340

ROUTE DESCRIPTION

Leave the abbey on D145, which winds through the forest and pleasant, hilly countryside 14 kms into Saumur.

CITY
SAUMUR

ROUTE
D751 D135 D55 N160

DISTANCE KM	TOTAL KM
52	354

CITY
ANGERS

TOTAL KM
406

ROUTE DESCRIPTION

Leaving Saumur, follow signs to the suburb of St. Florent. From there pick up D751, which runs through a pleasant wooded area along the Loire. Pass through Cunault, site of a fine eleventh-century to twelfth-century church. At the bridge by Gennes, take D132, which runs alongside the river up to St.-Remy-la-Varrene. At this point turn inland. Cycle up a few hills on D55, which joins up with D751 after 8 kms. Pass through a series of delightful small villages until the road meets up with the cloverleaf intersection of N260 and D748 just before Erigne. Take N160 over the bridge the remaining few kms into Angers.

LOIRE VALLEY SIGHTS AND ACCOMMODATIONS

BLOIS. A city that exemplifies the charm and romance of the Loire region, Blois is less than two hundred kms from Paris and is easily reached by auto or train. Whether you arrive by bike, car, or train, Blois, with its huge chateau perched on a hill overlooking the Loire, offers a good introduction to the charms of this region.

The **Blois Chateau** commands a hill above the river. This huge complex presents visitors with a startling conglomeration of architectural styles reflecting some four centuries of construction. Richly decorated, full of secret panels, and with a fascinating history of court intrigues and assassination, the Chateau of Blois is a great place to begin a visit to the fabulous French chateau country. Daily tours are offered, with a sound and light show nightly.

The combination Romanesque and Gothic-style **Eglise St. Nicholas** built in the twelfth and thirteenth centuries is one of the region's finest church buildings.

A wonderful way to enjoy the lovely countryside is to picnic in the adjacent **Foret de Blois**.

The pleasant, two-star L'HOSTELLERIE DE LA LOIRE (8 rue du Marechal de Lattre-de-Tassigny; Tel: [54] 74 26 60), right at the river overlooking the eighteenth-century arched bridge, offers comfortable rooms starting at 70 Fr. The restaurant downstairs features Loire salmon and game in season. The TOUR D'ARGENT (12 rue des Trois Clefs; Tel: [54] 78 01 73) is conveniently located in the shopping mall (look for the three giant metal keys). It has rooms for four persons from 82 to 142 Fr. Rooms at the NOVOTEL (1 rue de l'Amandin; Tel: [54] 78 33 57) run 290 Fr.

AUBERGE DE JEUNNESSE LES GRUETS (4100 Blois; Tel: [54] 78 27 21) is located on RN152, 4 kms from town in the direction of Tours. The youth hostel has forty-eight beds in a pleasant wooded setting. Another youth hostel, AUBERGE DE JEUNESSE MONTIVAULT, (41350 Vineuil, Cedex; Tel: [38] 44 61 31) is located on RN751 in the direction of Orléans, 9 kms from Blois.

For campers, the well-equipped CAMPING MUNICIPAL LA BOIRE is conveniently located just 1 km out of town on D951 in the direction of Orléans. It is open all year.

For additional information, the Office de Tourisme is just a short walk from the train station in the direction of the *centre ville*.

Rental bicycles are available at the train station and at INFO-LOISERS (12 rue du Bourg).

The TOUT CHAUD, a stand-up snack bar in the pedestrian shopping street, is a great place to indulge in tasty hot and cold munchies for only a few francs.

MONTIVAULT. As listed under Blois, there is a youth hostel here. But if you're in the mood for a quiet, delightfully furnished little country inn with a fine restaurant and views looking out onto the Loire, then pedal the extra 4 kms to the MANIOR BEL AIR (41500 St. Dye-sur-Loire; Tel: [54] 81 60 10). Rooms cost 120 to 150 Fr., all with bath.

CHAMBORD. Set in a magnificent 13,600-acre forest, the chateau at Chambord, with its 440 rooms and 365 chimneys, is the largest of the Loire chateaux. The building itself is almost devoid of furnishings, but its sheer immensity, impressive Renaissance facade, and assortment of turrets, gables, pinnacles, and vast expanse of lawns make a stop here a memorable occasion. The chateau is opened daily with a nightly sound and light show from 1 June to 30 September.

Picnic on the grounds or dine at the attractive HOTEL DU GRAND ST. MICHEL (41250 Bracieux; Tel: [54] 20 31 31), which offers a view from the terrace of the chateau. The menu starts at 80 Fr., and rooms run 95 to 310 Fr.

There is no campground in Chambord itself, but campers who discreetly pitch their tents in the adjacent forest will not be bothered usually. There are campgrounds in nearby St. Dye (5 kms). Try CAMPING LA CROIX-DU-PONT (open 1 April to 15 October) or in Bracieux, on the road to Cheverny, MUNICIPAL CAMPING DES CHATEAUX, which is located in a large park. It is open 25 March to 30 October.

COUR-CHEVERNY. The **chateau** at Cheverny was completed in 1634 in the classical style. It is richly decorated and warmly furnished and is still in the hands of the family of the original owners. As you might have guessed after pedaling through the adjacent forests, this is great hunting country, and in addition to a museum with some two thousand sets of antlers, the chateau still maintains an active pack of seventy magnificent hunting dogs. During the season, November to April, the surrounding five thousand acres of Cheverny forest are the scene of lively hunts recalling scenes from the chateau's glorious past. It is open daily, and there are sound and light shows on selected summer nights. Inquire at the local tourist office for details.

There are two charming hotels in the adjacent village of Cour-Cheverny, HOTEL SAINT HUBERT (rue nationale; Tel: [54] 79 96 60) and HOTEL TROIS-MARCHANDS (pl. de L'Eglise; Tel: [54] 79 96 44). Both have fine dining rooms.

CAMPING LES SAULES is a comfortable campground on D102, 2.5 km from town in the direction of Contres.

SELLES-SUR-CHER. A delightful little town on the Cher River, Selles-sur-Cher has a fine twelfth-century to fifteenth-century **church** and a **chateau** with a stark thirteenth-century fortress and luxurious Renaissance mansion. The chateau contains one of the largest fireplaces in France.

The one-star HOTEL LION D'OR (14 pl. de la Paix, 41130 Selles-sur-Cher; Tel: [54] 97 40 83) provides a convenient overnight stop.

CAMPING LES CHATAIGNIERS, open 1 April to 30 September, is located at the river.

VALENCAY. This quaint little town is dominated by its opulently appointed castle, still in the possession of the family of Tallyrand, that famous figure in French politics. Llamas, deer, and exotic birds roam freely through the spacious park surrounding the chateau. It is open daily from 16 March to 15 November; sound and light shows are given on Friday and Saturday evenings in July.

For first-class accommodations, try the HOTEL D'ESPAGNE (9 rue du Chateau, 36600 Valencay; Tel: [54] 00 00 02), a delightful converted coach inn. The finely appointed dining rooms feature a wide selection of appealing local specialties. Or try the more modest but attractive LION D'OR (pl. du Marche; Tel: [54] 00 00 87). Rooms run 72 to 160 Fr.

There is no campground locally, but there's a lot of forest in the vicinity in which to set up your tent!

ST. AIGNAN. This picturesque small town rises in tiers above the Cher River. Of interest are the eleventh-century and twelfth-century **church**, a **bird park**, and the **chateau** (although the interior is not open to the public).

Simple accommodations are available at the HOTEL MOULIN (2 rue Nouilliers, 41110 St. Aignan; Tel: [54] 75 15 54). Doubles go for 90 Fr. A bit fancier is the GRAND HOTEL ST. AIGNAN (7 quai J. Delorme; Tel: [54] 75 18 04), with rooms at 60 to 260 Fr. Both hotels have good restaurants.

CAMPING LES CLOCHARDS on D17 less than 1 km from town is open from 15 March to 15 October. It is a pleasant site offering a full range of conveniences.

MONTRICHARD. A quaint little town, Montrichard has a fine old bridge over the Cher and the ruins of a twelfth-century castle.

For the saddle sore cyclist with a padded wallet, there is a delightful, luxurious, fifteenth-century chateau hotel awaiting. Each of the twenty-five bedrooms has its own bath, is individually furnished, and overlooks a large wooded park. For 170 to 440 Fr., stay at the RESTAURANT DU CHATEAU DE LA MENAUDIERE (41400 Chissay en Touraine; Tel: [54] 32 02 44). Even plusher is the nearby CHATEAU DE CHISSAY (Tel: [54] 32 32 01) with luxurious accommodations from 500 to 900 Fr. for doubles.

Camping cyclists are not neglected. The municipal campground, CAMPING L'ETOURNEAU, 1 km outside of town on the road to Tours, is open 22 March to 5 October.

CHAUMONT-SUR-LOIRE. On a hill overlooking the Loire, the multi-turreted **Chateau de Chaumont**, formerly a fortress, affords a fine view of the river from the terrace. It was while living at Chaumont that, as the story goes, Catherine de'Medici, in consultation with her astrologer, was advised of the future grim fate of her three sons. In fact, all three – Francois II, Charles IX, and Henry III – died violent deaths. The one-hour tour includes the fortress, as well as the furnished apartments and stables. The chateau is open daily.

First-class accommodations in a romantic setting are available at the HOSTELERIE DU CHATEAU (rue du Marechal de Lattre de Tassigny, 41150 Chaumont; Tel: [54] 20 98 04). There are fifteen rooms which range in price from 270 to 435 Fr. A fine restaurant is located across from the chateau entrance. For something simpler, try the pleasant, somewhat dilapidated HOTEL RESTAURANT LE MOUTIER at the bridge.

The closest campground is CAMPING GROSSE GREVE at the river on N152. It is open 1 April to 30 September.

AMBOISE. One of the larger towns in the region, Amboise is a popular tourist center. Only a small portion of the original Italian Renaissance chateau remains, but it is well worth a visit even though this is not as spectacular a structure as several of the other chateaux in the region. Of interest is the fact that Leonardo da Vinci spent the last years of his life here. He is buried in the Chapelle St. Hubert. The Clos-Lucé where he lived, is now a museum containing replicas of his numerous inventions.

There are a number of good hotels, including the luxurious HOTEL CHOISEUL (36 quai Charles Guinot, 37400 Amboise; Tel: [47] 30 45 45). For seekers of accommodations more "back home" in style, there is the modern NOVOTEL (17 rue des Sablonnieres; Tel: [47] 57 42 07), where the rooms run from 270 to 320 Fr. The AUBERGE DU MAIL (32 quai de Gualle; Tel: [47] 57 60 39) has thirteen delightful rooms, as well as one of the best kitchens in town.

There is a municipal campground at the river just a few hundred meters from town: CAMPING L'ILE D'OR. It is open 1 April to 30 September.

CHENONCEAUX. A gift from Henri II to his mistress, Diane de Poiters, to celebrate his ascension to the throne in 1547, the chateau, suspended by graceful arches over the river Cher, is probably the most aesthetically pleasing of all the Loire region chateaux. The interior is magnificently furnished and the gardens are a delight to tour. It is open daily, with nightly sound and light shows from mid-June until early September.

The three-star HOTEL OTTONI right in the center of the village, a few minutes walk from the chateau, is the town's nicest (7 rue Dr. Bretonneau, 37150 Chenonceaux; Tel: [47] 23 90 02). Doubles go from 95 to 300 Fr. Another pleasant, small hotel, just down the street, is the white stone L'HOSTEL DU ROY (9 rue Dr. Bretonneau, 37150 Chenonceaux; Tel: [47] 23 90 02). Dinner in the massive beamed-ceiling dining room is truly a delight.

There is a small municipal campground, CAMPING LA FONTAINE DES PRES, just a short walk from the chateau. It is open 1 April to 30 September.

LOCHES. A gem of a medieval city in a quiet setting on the Indre, Loches is presided over by massive fortifications. Be sure to visit the chateau dungeons and walk around the impressive ramparts.

Standing in an idyllic setting in the shadow of the fortress walls is a prize of a small hotel, HOTEL RESTAURANT GEORGE SAND (39 rue Quintefol, 37600 Loches, Tel: [47] 59 39 74). Everything you've ever pictured in a romantic French hotel is here: stone, massive wooden beams, flowers, a pond, flowered wallpaper, a good restaurant, just seventeen rooms. The price: 130 to 300 Fr.

Campers can bed down at the conveniently located CAMPING MUNICIPAL, open 1 April to 30 September.

LANGEAIS. The **Chateau de Langeais** is perched on a small hill overlooking the town. Although not as spectacular as Blois and Chambord, it is nevertheless an impressive sight: a powerful medieval fortress looking down over the small town.

TOURS. The capital of Touraine lies in the heart of the Loire chateau country. One of the Loire's major cities, Tours is an active commercial and tourist center. Although Tours has no major chateau, the attractive city with its many parks, gardens, elegant shops, and quaint old town quarter is nevertheless well worth a visit. A stroll through the streets between the river and the ruins of the ancient **Basilica of St. Martin** takes one past a number of meticulously restored fifteenth century wooden houses. The area is peppered with fine restaurants and inviting outdoor cafés. In fact, Tours is considered to be the gastronomic capital of the Loire.

There are a number of hotels within the city. The Office de Tourisme across from the train station can help you find accommodations. The top luxury-class accommodations in town are found at the HOTEL MERIDIAN (292 ave. de Grammont; Tel: [47] 28 00 80). Of the several chateau hotels in the vicinity of Tours, the DOMAINE DE BEAUVOIS in Luynes, (37230 Luynes; Tel: [47] 55 50 11), just 13 km northwest of Tours, with its elegant furnishings and magnificent setting in the middle of a beautiful forest, offers some of the finest in accommodations and cuisine in the entire Loire region. A double will set you back 490 to 765 Fr. No extra charge for parking your bike! For more down-to-earth lodgings, the HOTEL BALZAC has a convenient downtown location just opposite the theater (47 rue de Scellerie; Tel: [47] 05 40 87). It will run about 200 Fr. for a double.

The youth hostel, AUBERGE DE JEUNESSE, (ave. d'Arsonval, 37200 Tours; Tel: [47] 25 14 45), has 170 beds and space for a few tents. It is somewhat inconveniently located in the Parc de Grandmont, 5 km from downtown. Meals are available but you can do better eating in town.

Of the several campgrounds around Tours, the municipal camping site in the suburb of St. Avertin, just a ten-minute bike ride to Tours center, is a large pleasant park with an adjacent swimming pool. It is open 1 March to 30 November.

For a big splurge at a restaurant, try the elegant ROTISSERIE TOURANGELLE (23 rue du Commerce) in the old town quarter. One of the region's finest, it is expensive.

Closed 14 July to 6 Aug. For a more modest sampling of the region's excellent cuisine, the L'ANTIDOTE (in spite of its offish name) is a good bet (39 rue du Grand Marche) in the old town.

VILLANDRY. One of the most original of the Loire chateaux, Villandry is best known for its acres of beautiful **gardens** which extend over three levels of terraces. The attractive Renaissance structure incorporates a medieval tower in its design. On the way, stop and visit the **Petrified Caves** at Savonnieres.

There's not much of a town here, but the HOTEL CHEVAL ROUGE (Joue Les Tours, 37510 Villandry; Tel: [47] 50 02 07), has eighteen attractive rooms from 185 to 266 Fr. and a good restaurant that features local specialties, including fresh pike from the Loire. The small municipal campground in Savonnieres is open 1 June to 30 September.

AZAY-LE-RIDEAU. The imposing **chateau** at Azay is idyllically placed in a forested setting partly surrounded by water. This is one of the region's prettiest structures. The furnished interior offers a good insight into Renaissance life. It is open daily with nightly sound and light shows.

The town's top hotel, as its name suggests, is the HOTEL LE GRAND MONARQUE (pl. de la République, 37190 Azay-Le-Rideau; Tel: [47] 45 40 08). It falls a bit short of expectations, but is a pleasant overnight stop in this heavily touristed little town. It has a good regional dining room. Rooms range from 90 to 300 Fr. The less pretentious HOTEL RESTAURANT LE COMMERCE, whose white stone facade is adorned with brightly colored blue and white awnings, has ten attractive rooms at 80 to 100 Fr. There are also a number of very pleasant and reasonably priced rooms available from local residents. Check at the tourist office for details.

CAMPING MUNICIPAL DE SABOT is open 28 March to 31 October in a pleasant, wooded setting is just a short walk from the chateau.

CHINON. This is a fortified medieval town overlooking the Vienne River. On a hill above the city are the remnants of three individual **fortresses** separated by deep moats. Little remains of the great hall in which Joan of Arc was received by the Dauphin Charles. Be sure to wander through the old quarter of Chinon, particularly Rue Voltaire.

For a pleasant diversion, take the 25-km trip in an old-fashioned steam train to the attractive seventeenth-century town of Richelieu. The trip will take 1 hour each way; a round-trip ticket costs 54 Fr.

For charming accommodations in the center of town, stop at the eighteenth-century ivy-covered HOTEL DIDEROT (4 rue Buffon, 37500 Chinon; Tel: [47] 93 18 87). Each of the twenty-two rooms is uniquely furnished; there is no restaurant, but breakfast is served in the pleasant foyer. For another fine chateau hotel, try the elegantly restored fifteenth-century CHATEAU DE MARCAY (37500 Marcay; Tel: [47] 93 03 47). It has twenty-three lovely rooms and a fine restaurant set in a wooded park 7 km south of Chinon on D116. Doubles cost 400 to 950 Fr. CAMPING ILE AUGER located at the edge of town is open 1 April to 15 October.

SAMUR. Saumur is a pleasant town on the Loire, well known for its pinnacled, **multi-colored chateau** perched on a sheer promontory above the town. This is the home of the famed cavalry group **Cadre Noir**. Riding performances are given during the last two weeks in July. Be sure to visit the museum dedicated to the history of the horse. This region is also known for its fine wines.

For a convenient in-town hotel, the pleasant HOTEL ANNE D'ANJOU is your best bet, although there is no restaurant (32-33 quai Mayaud; Tel: [41] 67 30 30).

The YOUTH HOSTEL with forty-five beds is located on an island in a park with a great view of the city (rue de Verden, Ile d'Offard, 49400 Saumur; Tel: [41] 67 45 00). It is open all year. The municipal campground next to the youth hostel and swimming pool offers a full range of facilities. It is open all year.

Chateau bikers may want to try the elegance of the CHATEAU HOTEL LE PRIEURÉ (49350 Chenehutte-les-Truffeaux; Tel: [41] 50 15 31), a fine Renaissance chateau in a huge park on D751 8 km west of Saumur on the way to Angers.

ANGERS. The former capital of Anjou sprawls over both banks of the Maine River just a few miles from its confluence with the Loire. It was in Angers that the Plantagenets, who later became kings of England, achieved power. The region is well known for its fine fruit and wines. The **Castle of Angers**, a massive structure built in the thirteenth century sits atop a hill overlooking the river. The castle houses the remarkable **Apocalypse Tapestry**. Woven in the late fourteenth century, the seventy panels that have been preserved are more than 16 feet high and extend for 551 feet. Sound and light performances are held at the castle during the summer.

Other interesting sights include the impressive **Cathédrale St.-Maurice**, which has some fine stained-glass windows, and the **Fine Arts Museum** (Logis-Barrault).

For a comfortable low-cost hotel, try the AUBERGE DE BELLE RIVE (25 bis, rue Haute de Reculee; Tel: [41] 48 18 70) at the edge of town near the hospital. The CROIX DE GUERRE (23 rue Châteaugontier; Tel: [41] 88 66 59) is a pleasant, small inn just a short walk from the center of town.

A large YOUTH HOSTEL with 184 beds is located in a recreation area just 4 kms from town (1 rue Darwin, 49000 Angers; Tel: [41] 48 14 55). Cooking facilities are available, but no meals are served.

Angers has two well-situated campgrounds. CAMPING DU PARC DE LA HAYE is conveniently located in a pleasant park just a few minutes walk from the castle. It is open 15 June to 15 September. CAMPING DU LAC DE MAINE is part of a recreation complex a few kms from the center of town; it offers a full range of facilities and is open all year.

For a good, not too expensive restaurant that features regional specialties, try the popular L'ENTR'ACTE near the theater in the center of town.

CHATEAU D'USSE. A massive structure with a proliferation of towers and turrets which evoke an aura of mystery, the **Chateau d'Usse** is said to have provided the inspiration for the classic fairy tale Sleeping Beauty. Be sure to see the famous **Aubusson Tapestry** which traces the highlights of the life of Joan of Arc.

FONTEVRAUD L'ABBAYE. Founded in 1099, the **Abbey of Fontevraud** is one of the most interesting sights in the region. It contains a fine Romanesque church, burial place of Richard the Lion-Hearted, and a magnificent kitchen with huge fireplaces and twenty chimneys.

Normandy

Although it's hard to think of Normandy without conjuring up visions of the dramatic World War II D-Day landings, there are many other reasons why this northeastern part of France is an enticing region for a cycle tour. Visit Normandy and you will encounter a wide variety of scenic, historical, and cultural attractions.

The important role of Normandy in the history of the English-speaking world stretches far back into the pages of history. It was the stream of Viking invaders from the North who gave their name to this region in the period from 300 to 400 AD. The derivation of the word "Norman" comes from "men from the north." It was from Normandy that William the Conqueror set off on his eleventh-century quest, which culminated in his victory at the Battle of Hastings in 1066 and his subsequent coronation as king of England. You will see this fascinating story unfold before your eyes when you view the incredibly well-preserved nine-hundred-year-old Bayeux Tapestry.

During the great ages of discovery, Norman explorers and navigators played an important part in the exploration of the new world. The Battle of Normandy, which started with the June 6, 1944 landing of history's largest amphibious invasion force and ended some two and a half months later, was the turning point of World War II. The price paid was high – hundreds of thousands on both sides were killed or wounded and more than 200,000 buildings were destroyed or damaged. A number of museums and monuments document this decisive struggle.

A few years ago when we cycled through the now peaceful green countryside which is lined with elegant manor houses, abbeys, chateaux, and simple, half-timbered farmhouses, it was difficult to imagine the massive death and destruction that occurred here. Buildings have been meticulously restored in the old style and whole cities have been rebuilt. The many war cemeteries remain as somber reminders of the recent past. We can remember walking the sands of Omaha Beach on a hot day summer day after having visited the American War Cemetery, which sits in a cool green wooded area overlooking the beach. It gave us an eerie feeling to see this beach filled with sun bathing vacationers, lying where so many thousands died.

On a more pleasant note, as you tour the rich agricultural and dairy lands of Normandy, you will be treated to a fine selection of tasty regional dishes in quaint country restaurants and a good variety of high-quality locally produced products in the markets. Normandy is prime dairy country, and the

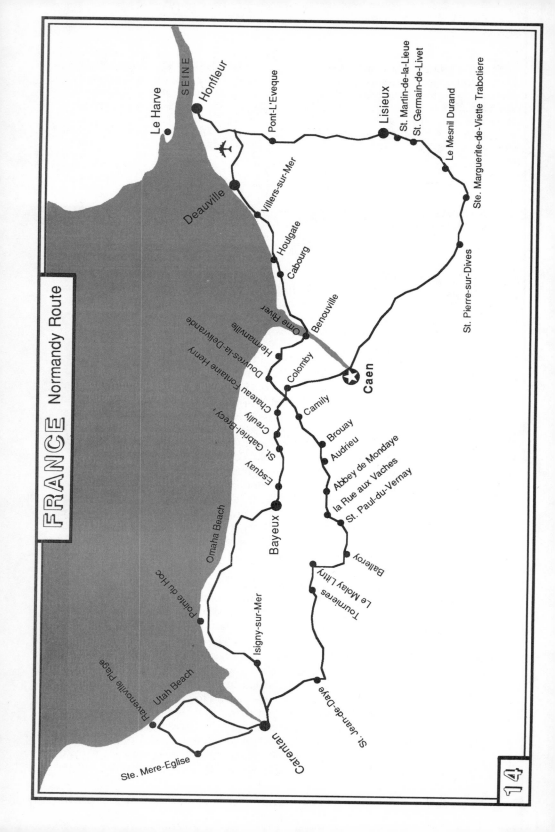

rich mellow cream that forms the mainstay of Norman cooking is widely used in the preparation of meat, fish, chicken, and vegetable dishes. The cheeses of Normandy, especially the tasty Camembert, have achieved worldwide recognition. In the course of pedaling through the Norman countryside you will be sure to encounter such tempting regional specialties as duck from Rouen, tripe from Caen, and fresh seafood from the coastal regions. This is another one of those routes where you will be hard pressed to pedal fast and hard enough to compensate for your caloric intake.

Normandy is one of the few regions of France that is not much of a wine producer. To quench your thirst, do as the Normans do and quaff the locally produced *bon bere*, a tasty fermented apple cider, which bears little or no resemblance to the apple juice we drink in the U.S. Be sure to try another local favorite – calvados, a fiery smooth applejack, the Norman equivalent of cognac. It's drunk in the middle of a copious meal and then again at the end of the meal with black coffee.

THE NORMANDY LOOP

START	FINISH
CAEN	CAEN

DISTANCE
356 kms/221 miles

IGN MAPS
6 Caen-Cherbourg,
7 Le Harve-Caen,
#18 Caen-Alencon
    (for Mount-St.-Michel),
#16 Granville-Rennes
    (scale 1:100,000)

MICHELIN MAPS
#54 Cherbourg-Rouen
    (for Mount-St.-Michel),
#59 St. Malo-Rennes

In designing this route we have tried to include a representative sampling of the wide range of attractions that Normandy presents cyclists: the invasion beaches of the Calvados Coast, the rich historical and cultural treasures of Bayeux and Caen, fashionable beach resorts such as Deauville and Cabourg, as well as the delightful interior of the region, with its many picturesque little villages. The route winds through the three major geographical divisions of Normandy: the Cotentin Peninsula, and Lower and Upper Normandy. With the exception of Caen, which has a population of about 150,000, there are no major cities along the route.

For the most part, the terrain is level, although some pretty steep hills will be encountered in the eastern half of the route, especially in the stretch from Deauville to St.-Pierre. With a good ten-speed cycle, this route can be handled by anyone in reasonably good condition. Don't pass up seeing Normandy because you're worried about the hills. They're not that bad, and if you have problems you can always dismount and push!

Even though this is a popular cycling region, you will find very few bicycle paths; however, there is an extensive network of little traveled back roads. With the exception of a few short stretches, we have managed to stay off the main highways.

Although we start our description at Caen because it is a major rail center, you can begin the route anywhere and pedal it in either direction. There are two loops which can be done separately or in combination. The western part takes in the invasion beaches, the medieval town of Bayeux, and a portion of the Normandy Bocage, a lovely area of open woodland. The eastern loop includes the seacoast resorts of Deauville and Honfleur and part of the Auge region, a little traveled favorite of ours, characterized by deep valleys, scattered half-timbered farmhouses, pastures, hedgerows, and apple orchards.

If you can manage the time, by all means make the excursion down to Mount-Saint-Michel, a fortified island crowned by a magnificent ancient abbey, which appears to rise up out of the sea. It is one of the great architectural wonders of Europe. From Mount-Saint-Michel, you are in a good position either to tour the Brittany peninsula or to link up with the Loire Valley route. It's about 130 kms from Mount-Saint-Michel to Angers. Another interesting extension of the Normandy route includes a visit to Rouen, often referred to as the "Museum Town," and site of one of the most beautiful cathedrals in France. It's just 60 kms, a day's cycling or less, from Honfleur. From Rouen, it's about 100 kms to Paris. If you plan to follow the path of William the Conquerer and invade England, there are good ferry connections from Cherbourg to Portsmouth, Weymouth, and Southampton.

When touring the Normandy region, weather is always a major consideration. While you may encounter rain at any time, October is the rainiest month of the year. July and August are the best touring months if you want to get in some beach time and don't mind sharing the roads and museums with hordes of tourists. With a little bit of luck, early September can be the ideal time for cycling. You'll have the roads and the region's many attractions virtually to yourself. If you don't mind the early morning chill and an occasional shower, late April and the month of May when the apple orchards are in bloom is a wonderful time to pedal through the Auge region and the Seine Valley. Generally speaking, the Normandy climate, which is subject to the influences of the Atlantic, is not severe. Summers are rarely very hot and winters are relatively mild.

Normandy is accustomed to receiving tourists and you will have the choice of a wide range of accommodations: from the plush hotels of Deauville to remote country inns. Official campgrounds abound and there are numerous places where you can inobtrusively pitch your tent for the night. Pedaling through the countryside you will also come across many *chambre d'hote* signs for the French equivalent of a bed and breakfast.

NORMANDY

CITY

CAEN

ROUTE

D79 D141 D22 D35 D126

DISTANCE KM	TOTAL KM
34	0

ROUTE DESCRIPTION

Leaving Caen is a bit of a hassle. From the center of town, head toward the university, which is just north of the castle, and follow the signs toward Courseulles via D79. At Colomby, after pedaling about 10 kms, take D141 to the Chateau at Fontaine Henry. Continue on D141 to the little market town of Creully (Montgomery's headquarters in June 1944). Pass through St.-Gabriel-Brecy (eleventh-century priory and a small castle). Pick up D35 on your right at the narrow road just before the church, then follow the signs to Esquay. From there continue on D126 5 kms into Bayeux.

CITY

BAYEUX

ROUTE

D6 D514 D517 N13

DISTANCE KM	TOTAL KM
55	34

ROUTE DESCRIPTION

Leave Bayeux via rue de Port en Bessin which runs into D6. Follow this to the coast and pick up D514, which hugs the famed Calvados Coast. Follow the signs reading *Circuit Debarquement*. Don't turn down the small road marked Omaha Beach; it is a dead end and a long climb back up. From the American Military Cemetery, take D517 which makes a short loop down to the actual landing site. Continue on D514 past the monument at Pointe du Hoc. The road now turns inland and passes through lush dairy country to join up with N13 in Isgny-sur-Mer. Cross the Vire and continue on N13 to Carentan. The heavily traveled N13 is wide enough at this point so that cycling is no problem.

CITY

CARENTAN

ROUTE

N13 D913 D421 D15

DISTANCE KM	TOTAL KM
33	89

ROUTE DESCRIPTION

Take N13 north 3.5 kms. Turn off onto D913 and follow the signs to Utah Beach. Along the beach front the road is called Route des Allies. At Ravenoville Plage, take D15 inland to Ste.-Mere-Eglise.

CITY
STE.-MERE-EGLISE

ROUTE
N13 N174 D8 D15 D10 D13

DISTANCE KM	TOTAL KM
48	122

ROUTE DESCRIPTION
From Ste.-Mere take N13 13 kms back to Carentan. About 3.5 km east of town turn off onto N174 and follow it down to St.-Jean-de-Daye. At the south edge of town, take D8 toward Bayeux. Continue through this gentle rolling dairy country just past the village of Tournieres. Turn off and follow the signs to Le Molay Littry.

CITY
LE MOLAY LITTRY

ROUTE
D10 D13 D99A D178 D94 D217 D83 D35

DISTANCE KM	TOTAL KM
47	170

ROUTE DESCRIPTION
Take D10 about 4 kms through the forest to the intersection with D13. Go through the town of Balleroy, past the chateau. Just past the campground, turn right and continue on D13. After about 3 kms, turn off at Les Bourgeois onto a small country lane to St.-Paul-du-Vernay.

Then pass through the quiet countryside to the settlement of la Rue aux Vaches. Follow D178 past the classical Abbey de Mondaye (the abbey library contains 30,000 volumes). From the Abbey, take D178 as it winds through the peaceful countryside to Audrieu. Then go a few kms on D94 to Brouay to pick up D217.

Note: At this point you can easily return to Caen (13 kms) to complete the western portion of the Normandy route. To continue with the rest of the route, it's more pleasant cycling the back roads to avoid the heavily industrialized parts of Caen.

ROUTE DESCRIPTION
(Continued): Continue on D217 to Camily. There the hwy number changes to D83. Follow this into Douvres-la-Delivrande (British War Cemetery). Leave town on D35 for the 5 kms into Hermanville.

CITY
HERMANVILLE-SUR-MER

ROUTE
D35 D514

DISTANCE KM	TOTAL KM
9	217

ROUTE DESCRIPTION
Take D35 to Benouville (World War II Pegasus Bridge Museum). Cross the Orne River and take D514 to the seaside resort of Cabourg.

CITY
CABOURG

ROUTE
D163 D513A D513

DISTANCE KM	TOTAL KM
18	226

ROUTE DESCRIPTION
From Cabourg, cross the river to Houlgate and take D163, a steep winding climb along the cliffs overlooking the sea. The road descends and runs into D513A a few kms before Villers-sur-Mer, which is an elegant resort with a fine beach and casino. D513 follows the coast into Deauville.

CITY
DEAUVILLE

ROUTE
D74 D288 D579

DISTANCE KM	TOTAL KM
17	244

ROUTE DESCRIPTION
Although the coast road (D513) offers some outstanding views of the ocean, the road is heavily traveled and in many places so narrow that it is dangerous for cycling. We prefer to take D74 out of Deauville toward the airport, and then cut over to the much wider D579 for about 10 kms into Honfleur. The last few kms are a straight downhill run.

CITY
HONFLEUR

ROUTE
D579

DISTANCE KM	TOTAL KM
17	261

ROUTE DESCRIPTION
From Honfleur, take D579 south to Pont-L'Eveque. It's a steep climb for the first 2 kms before the road levels out.

CITY
PONT-L'EVEQUE

ROUTE
D48

DISTANCE KM	TOTAL KM
17	278

ROUTE DESCRIPTION
Take D48 south from Pont-L'Eveque to Lisieux. The road runs through the lovely hilly pasture lands of the Auge region of Normandy. When leaving Pont-L'Eveque on D48, don't follow the big yellow sign to Lisieux; it will take you onto the busy D579.

CITY	
LISIEUX	

ROUTE	
D579 D268A D47 D273 D4	

DISTANCE KM	TOTAL KM
30	295

ROUTE DESCRIPTION

Continue south from Lisieux on D579. After 4 kms, turn off at St. Martin-de-la-Lieue to St. Germain-de-Livet. From the chateau take D268A back to the main road. At Le Mesnil Durand, turn off to the right onto D47, then immediately turn left onto D273, a narrow lane that winds through the rolling countryside. D273 joins up with the busier D4 at Ste.-Marguerite-de-Viette Trabotiere about 10 kms from St-.Pierre-sur-Dives.

CITY	
ST.-PIERRE-SUR-DIVES	

ROUTE	
D40	

DISTANCE KM	TOTAL KM
31	325

CITY	
CAEN	

TOTAL KM	
356	

ROUTE DESCRIPTION

From St.-Pierre take D40, and then N13, across the flat farmlands into the center of Caen.

NORMANDY SIGHTS AND ACCOMMODATIONS

CAEN. The capital of Lower Normandy is less than a two-hour train ride from the Paris St. Lazare station. It is an excellent place from which to begin a Normandy tour. A major, modern industrial city (Its status as a major industrial and steel producing center is attested to by the poor quality of the air.) has risen from the pile of rubble which was all that remained of the city at the close of World War II. Although Caen, which was more than 75 percent destroyed, has been restored in a modern style, the most important historical structures have been preserved and all are within a few minutes cycling distance of the central train station. The ramparts of the massive **citadel** in the center of town were erected in the eleventh century by William the Conqueror. Perhaps the most interesting attractions in Caen are the magnificent twin abbeys. Looking down from their perches on opposite sides of the city center are the **Abbaye aux Dames** and its brother abbey the fine Romanesque **Abbaye aux Hommes**. Both were constructed by William the Conqueror and his wife, Queen Matilda, as reparation offerings for the lifting of their excommunication from the church. For a good introduction to the customs and folklore of the region, be sure to visit the **Normandy Museum** located at the citadel.

Caen has a good selection of first-class and budget accommodations. For conveniently located low-cost hotel rooms, try the HOTEL MA NORMANDIE (43 bis, rue Ecuyere, 14000 Caen; Tel: [31] 86 06 01), a pleasant nine-room hotel right in the heart of the charming old town section. Rooms go for 60 to 105 Fr. Another centrally located budget hotel is the amiable HOTEL DE LA PAIX (12 rue Neuve St.-Jean; Tel: [31] 86 18 99). In the luxury category, the posh RELAIS DES GOURMETS, (15 rue de Geole; Tel: [31] 86 06 01) is at the top of the list. Doubles cost 175 to 300 Fr. Even if you don't stay at the hotel, their excellent restaurant is the place to sample the local specialty, *tripes a la mode de Caen*. The hotel is centrally located across from the citadel. Still another first-rate hotel with a gourmet restaurant (Les Quatre-Vents) is the HOTEL MODERNE (116 bd. Marechal-Leclerc; Tel: [31] 86 04 23).

The AUBERGE DE JEUNESSE (Herouville St.-Clair, 1102 quartier de la Grande Delle, 14200 Herouville St.-Clair; Tel: [31] 93 20 18) is a no-frills thirty-bed hostel at the north edge of the city, 8 kms from the Caen train station. It is open 1 April to 30 September. Cheap accommodations are also available at the university campus on the hill above the citadel during July, August, and September. Inquire directly on campus. Another place to look for inexpensive lodging is at CROUS (23 ave. de Bruxelles; Tel: [31] 94 73 37).

There is a good municipal campground, CAMPING ENTRÉE FLEURIE near the River Orne just south of the racetrack. It is open 1 June to 30 September.

FONTAINE HENRY. The imposing Renaissance **chateau** still in the possession of the family of the original owners was built in the fifteenth to sixteenth centuries on the foundations of a thirteenth-century fortress. Pleasantly situated overlooking the green Mue Valley, the richly furnished chateau is open to the public afternoons, except Tuesdays and Fridays, from 1 June to 15 September.

BAYEUX. This delightful little city is best known for the amazing tapestry which bears its name. Be certain to budget a few hours to see this remarkable chronicle of the Battle of Hastings and life in the Middle Ages. The tapestry, which is actually an embroidery, is laid out in the form of a 231-foot comic strip. It is artfully displayed in an old seminary specially converted for the purpose. Don't miss the informative film which is included in the entrance price. Just a few steps from the **Tapestry Museum** is the **Notre Dame Cathedral**, one of the most beautiful small cathedrals in France, a fine example of Norman Gothic architecture, consecrated by William the Conqueror in 1077. Jump ahead some nine hundred years in history and visit the **Battle of Normandy Museum**. This is one of the best and most informative of the many "invasion museums." A stroll through the exhibits will prepare you for touring the actual landing and battle sites. Bayeux also holds the distinction of having been the first town in France to have been liberated by the allied forces. That happy day was June 7, 1944. The Latin inscription on the memorial at the nearby British Cemetery notes that "in 1944 the British came to liberate the homeland of their former adversaries, the Normans who conquered them in 1066."

A charming one-star hotel is the twenty-six-room HOTEL AND RESTAURANT NOTRE DAME (44 rue des Cuisiniers; Tel: [31] 92 87 24), just a few steps from the cathedral. This pleasant, friendly hotel has modest prices and good food. It is capably run by M. and Mme. Christian Herbert. The attractive HOTEL LION D'OR (71 rue St.-Jean; Tel: [31] 92 06 90) has traditional Norman-style decor; it is the town's finest hotel. Their restaurant features first-class regional cooking. Rooms cost 120 to 260 Fr.

There are two small youth hostels in Bayeux: the ten-bed CENTRE D'ACCUEIL MUNICIPAL (Chemin du bois de Boulogne, 14400 Bayeux; Tel: [31] 92 08 19) and the thirty-bed FAMILY HOME (39 rue du General de Dais; Tel: [31] 92 15 22). The Family Home is a cozy hostel with great food at bargain prices. Both hostels are open all year.

For camping, the municipal site in Bayeux is one of the nicest campgrounds in Normandy. It offers a well-shaded large grassy area, adjacent to the municipal swimming pool. CAMPING MUNICIPAL is an easy five-minute walk to the Tapestry Museum. It is open 1 March to [31] October.

OMAHA BEACH. Prior to June 1944 there was no such name as Omaha Beach on maps of France. It was here that successive waves of American forces came ashore in the face of heavy German fire and suffered severe casualties before securing the beach. More than nine thousand white marble crosses in the **American Military Cemetery** set in an impressive site overlooking the beach attest to the high cost paid for these few hundred meters of sand. The communities of St.-Laurent, Colleville, and Vierville-sur-Mer have since officially adopted the name of Omaha Beach to denote the landing sites. Along with the several monuments that have been erected along the beach are the remnants of some German fortifications. There is a small but interesting **D-Day Museum** in a quonset hut at Vierville on the road to the campground.

There is a comfortable, small hotel overlooking Omaha Beach: HOTEL DU CASINO (14570 Vierville-sur-Mer; Tel: [31] 22 41 02). Another possibility in this quiet area of few hotels is one of the four rooms in a lovely country setting available from Mme. de Bellaique at LE VAUMICEL (14570 Vierville-sur-Mer; Tel: [31] 22 40 06).

CAMPING OMAHA BEACH is located in Vierville-sur-Mer on a bluff overlooking the beach near the remnants of a German gun emplacement. It is open 1 April to 30 September.

There are also several hotels and a campground a few kms further up the coast at the beach town of Grandcamp Maisy.

ISIGNY-SUR-MER. This is an attractive small town lying on an inlet of the Vire River. It is an active fishing port and has been a center for dairy products since the seventeenth century.

If you are looking for a hotel, try HOTEL DE FRANCE (rue Demagny, 14230 Isigny-sur-Mer; Tel: [31] 22 00 33). STADE MUNICIPAL (14230 Isigny-sur-Mer; Tel: [31] 22 00 03) is a small twenty-two-bed youth hostel with cooking facilities. CAMPING MUNICIPAL is a small, nicely situated municipal site with minimal facilities. It is open Easter to 30 September.

CARENTAN. Billed as the gateway to the Cotentin Peninsula, Carentan is an important cattle marketing town and a major dairy center. This small town has an impressive church, **The Notre Dame Church**, constructed in the twelfth and fifteenth centuries. The **medieval covered market** is also of interest.

Of the several small, inexpensive hotels, the best are HOTEL LE VAUBAN (7 rue Sebline, 505000 Carentan; Tel: [33] 71 00 20) and the more modest HOTEL LA RENNAISSANCE (1 rue de la 101 Airborne; Tel: [33] 42 20 05).

CAMPING MUNICIPAL LE HAUT DYCK is an open site with little shade, pleasantly situated next to the marina and adjacent to swimming pool. It is open 15 May to 15 September.

UTAH BEACH. Another of the major D-Day landing points, Utah Beach was the scene of heavy fighting. The **Invasion Museum**, housed in a converted bunker, features tanks and other original World War II military equipment, a film of the invasion, as well as models and a diorama. Along the roadside are memorial markers commemorating individual American soldiers who died in this region during the Battle of Normandy.

There are no towns or accommodations along this stretch of beach and dunes. There is a small bar and restaurant across from the Utah Beach Museum. At Ravenoville Plage about 5 kms up the coast there is a campground, CAMPING LE COMORAN, across the road from the beach. It is open 1 April to 30 September.

STE.-MERE-EGLISE. This is a quiet town in the center of the traditional Norman livestock breeding region. Early on the morning of the D-Day invasion Ste.-Mere was the object of an airborne assault by American paratroopers. Hanging from the church steeple in the town square is a lifesize replica of John Steele, an American parachutist who landed on this same steeple on June 6, 1944. Note the unusual stained glass window inside the church depicting the U.S. parachute attack. The nearby **Airborne Troops Museum** displays a number of intersting momentos from the initial days of the battle.

HOTEL LE JOHN STEELE (50480, Ste.-Mere-Eglise; Tel: [33] 41 41 16) is a quaint, ivy-covered small hotel restaurant just around the corner from the church.

There is a small well-equipped municipal camping site located next to the sports field. It is open 1 May to 30 September.

LE MOLAY LITTRY. A quiet little town with an interesting **Coal Mining Museum**, Le Molay Littry makes a convenient overnight stop if you don't want to pedal the 14 kms to Bayeux.

This small town has several good hotels. The best in town is the HOTEL CHATEAU DU MOLAY (14330 Le Molay Littry; Tel: [31] 22 90 82), a first-class establishment with thirty-eight rooms and a fine restaurant in a lovely country setting. Rooms go for 280 to 520 Fr. The one-star HOTEL DU CHEVAL BLANC (52 rue de Balleroy; Tel: [31] 22 90 72) will provide a pleasant, clean room for under 100 Fr.

CAMPING DO VAL DE SIETTE is a pleasant, but very small, site near the train station. It is open 1 June to 30 September.

CABOURG. With one of the best beaches on the Normandy coast, Cabourg has been a popular seaside resort since the days of the Second Empire. The town has managed to retain a classical turn-of-the-century elegance in contrast to many other now faded resorts. In 1066 the port of Dives-sur-Mer just across the river Dives was the embarkation point for William the Conqueror and his 50,000 men on their successful conquest of England. A column commemorates this event. There is also a interesting, well-preserved fifteenth-century to sixteenth-century **covered market** near the church. If at this point you get tired of pedaling, there is direct train service from Cabourg to Paris.

Cabourg has a wide selection of good and often expensive hotels. One of the best buys in the area is in the neighboring town of Houlgate. The FERME DU LIEU MAROT (14510 Houlgate; Tel: [31] 91 19 44) is a picture-postcard, thatched-roofed, half-timbered country inn located just a few meters from the beach. If you are looking for a room at an inn at a reasonable price in a lovely setting, this is it! The eleven rooms in this eighteenth-century *auberge* rent for 120 to 140 Fr. For a superb

dinner, try the rabbit with cider in the auberge restaurant. The AUBERGE DU PARC is a reasonably priced small hotel right in Cabourg (31 ave. General-Leclerc; Tel: [31] 91 00 82).

There are five large campgrounds in the vicinity, all within a few minutes cycling of the beach. CAMPING LE VERT PRE is a large full-facility site about 2 kms south of town on D513. It is open 1 April to 30 September. CAMPING LA PLAGE is a good site, often crowded, located at the beach.

BALLEROY. The plain little village is dominated by **Balleroy Castle**, a richly appointed seventeenth-century chateau and an unusual **Balloon Museum**. For one weekend in June, this tiny French village is transformed into the ballooning capital of the world. The International Balloon Meet sponsored by *Forbes Magazine* draws the top balloonists from all over the world for a weekend of "hot air antics" amidst a background of Renaissance splender. If you are anywhere in the area, this is an event definitely worth pedaling a few extra kilometers to get to. Check at a tourist office for the exact dates.

The HOTEL DU MARCHE (Place de Marche, 14490 Balleroy; Tel: [31] 77 50 22) in the center of town has just seven rooms. It is more like a big house than a hotel and restaurant.

CAMPING LE SAPIN is a good campground in a pleasant wooded area at the edge of town on hwy D73. It is open 15 March to 15 September.

HERMANVILLE-SUR-MER. This quiet seaside resort has a nice 2-km-long sandy beach. The portion of the coast for several kilometers on either side of Hermanville was the British and Canadian sector during the D-Day invasion. There are several war cemeteries and monuments in the area, including the famed **Pegasus Bridge**.

The small HOTEL DE LA BRECHE (14880 Hermanville-sur-Mer; Tel: [31] 97 21 40) is inexpensive for a beach town hotel. Rooms cost under 100 Fr.

There are several good campgrounds in the immediate vicinity. CAMPING LES VATTAUX is a large site with a restaurant and campstore. It is open 1 April to [31] October.

DEAUVILLE. An elegant, world-famous seaside resort literally reeking of class and money is how we describe Deauville. This is definitely not backpacker country! The boardwalk (in Deauville it's called the *Planches*) overlooking the nice sandy beach is the place for promenading – for seeing and being seen. Deauville is just that kind of place. If you stop in at one of the beach front cafés or restaurants, be prepared to shell out 30 to 50 percent more solely for the privilege of being in Deauville! We found it all a bit on the stuffy side.

If money is no object, you can park your bike and yourself at the four-star HOTEL ROYAL for 500 to 1400 Fr. It's across from the beach (bd. Cornuche, 14800 Deauville; Tel: [31] 88 16 41). If you scout around and don't insist on being directly at the beach you will be able to find an acceptable two-star hotel for 150 to 200 Fr. The HOTEL IBIS is an attractive modern hotel done in traditional Norman style. It is conveniently located just 200 meters from the town's unique train station (9 quai de la Marine; Tel: [31] 98 38 90). Rooms go for 250 to 430 Fr.

There are no campgrounds right on the beach at Deauville. There are, however, several sites within a few kilometers of the town. CAMPING DE LA VALLEE is a large, well-equipped site that includes a laundromat in St. Arnoult, 3 kms south of Deauville. It can accommodate many trailers, and has a small area for tents. The campground is open Easter to [31] October.

HONFLEUR. An ancient fishing town, Honfleur is now a favorite with excursioning Parisians. We think it is one of the most charming spots on the entire Normandy coast. During the seventeenth century Honfleur served as the base for the voyages that led to the French colonization of Canada and Louisiana. Take some time and stroll around the old town and harbor. The most interesting houses are at the **Vieux Bassin** (old harbor). One ticket will gain you admission to the **Maritime Museum** and the **Folk Art Museum**. During the summer months, the tourist office organizes an interesting two-hour walking tour of the town.

The HOSTELLERIE LECHAT (pl. Ste.-Catherine, 14600 Honfleur; Tel: [31] 89 23

85) has attractive rooms for 140 to 310 Fr. in the center of the old harbor quarter. If you are looking for a budget-priced room, try the pleasant little HOTEL FERMÉ DE LA GRANDE COUR (Cote de Grace; Tel: [31] 89 04 69). Located in an apple orchard, it has a quaint restaurant that features local specialties.

CAMPING DU PHARE is conveniently located at the edge of town near the lighthouse, but offers limited facilities. It is open 1 April to 30 September.

PONT L'EVEQUE. The town has been famous for its soft, creamy white cheese for more than seven hundred years. The town was badly damaged during World War II and only a few picturesque old houses remain.

For a comfortable, moderately priced hotel, try the HOTEL LE LION D'OR (8 pl. du Calvaire, 14130 Pont-L'Eveque; Tel: [31] 65 01 55).

There are two campgrounds in the vicinity. CAMPING LA COUR DE FRANCE is a fully equipped site (they even have a crêperie) located in a large recreation complex next to a lake. It is just off D48 south of the autoroute on the way toward Lisieux. It is open 1 March to [31] October. CAMPING MUNICIPAL is a small site on D118, the road to Beaumont-en-Auge. It is open 1 April to 30 September.

LISIEUX. An attractive city of some 30,000, Lisieux is the major business and manufacturing center of the Auge region. With the exception of the fine eleventh-century to thirteenth-century **Cathedral of St.-Pierre** and just a few other fine old buildings, Lisieux's wonderful Gothic and Renaissance houses were totally destroyed in 1944. The town is also noted for its shrine of St. Teresa.

The town has a number of good hotels, including the three-star MAPOTEL DE LA PLAGE (67 rue H-Cheron, 14100 Lisieux; Tel: [31] 31 17 44) where rooms go for 210 to 280 Fr. and the TERRASSE HOTEL (25 ave. Ste.-Therese; Tel: [31] 62 17 65).

CAMPING MUNICIPAL DE LA VALLEE is a small site in a pleasant location at the north edge of town just off D48. It is open Easter to 30 September.

ST.-GERMAIN-DE-LIVET. This is a charming and decorative fifteenth-century to sixteenth-century castle surrounded by a moat. Guided tours are available.

ST.-PIERRE-SUR-DIVES. A quiet country town, St.-Pierre-sur-Dives developed around an eleventh-century **Benedictine Abbey**. The history of the town is depicted in modern stained glass panels in the ancient church. Also worth seeing is the reconstructed **covered market**, a faithful recreation of the original eleventh-century to twelfth-century original destroyed in 1944.

Of the several hotels in town, we like the HOTEL LA RENAISSANCE (57 rue de Lisieux, 14170 St.-Pierre-sur-Dives; Tel: [31] 20 81 23).

Although there are no official campgrounds in the immediate vicinity of St.-Pierre, you should have no difficulty finding a farmer who will let you pitch a tent for the night.

❧ ══ Additional ══ ❧ Recommended Routes

I n choosing routes to describe in detail, we have tried to come up with a representative sample, combining the areas most interesting to tourists with those most suitable for cycling. Actually there is so much material we easily could have done an entire book just on France. Here are a few more cycling suggestions.

THE FRENCH ALPS

E xtending for some 250 miles from Lake Geneva to the French Riviera, the French Alps offer some of the most exciting and challenging biking to be found anywhere in Europe: mountain passes over 2,000 meters, grueling ascents, and hair-raising descents with picture-postcard alpine valleys in between. This is not beginner country. Having low, low gears (a granny wheel is recommended) and being in top condition are musts! Use Michelin maps #74, #77, #81, #84; or IGN maps #45, #53, #54, #61.

THE LOWER RHONE VALLEY

P rovence and the Camargue provide typical Mediterranean scenery, picturesque villages, and a wealth of Roman and medieval ruins. This is good, level cycling country marred only by the strong prevailing winds and heavy summer tourist traffic. The best touring times are May, June, and September. Use Michelin maps #83, #86, or #240; or IGN maps #65, #66, #72.

WEST GERMANY

POPULATION
62,000,000

RELIGION
49% Protestant; 45% Catholic

CAPITAL
Bonn

CURRENCY
Deutsche mark (DM); divided into 100 pfennigs

OFFICIAL LANGUAGE
German; English is widely spoken in tourist areas

BANKING HOURS
MTWF 0830–1230
        1400–1600
  TH 0830–1230
        1400–1730

STORE HOURS
M–F 0730 or 0830–1830
Sat 0700 or 0730–1300 or 1400
In many small towns, shops are closed from 1200–1400

EMERGENCY TELEPHONE NUMBERS
Police
Fire   Dial 110
Ambulance

TO CALL USA OR CANADA
Dial 001; area code and number

HOLIDAYS
1 Jan.; 6 Jan.; Good Friday; Easter Monday; Ascension Day; Pentecost; Corpus Christi; 25 & 26 Dec. (Some additional local holidays are observed in the predominantly Catholic south)

AMERICAN EXPRESS OFFICES
Promenadenplatz 6
MUNICH
Tel: [089] 21 990

Friedrich-Ebert-Anlange 16
HEIDELBERG
Tel: [06221] 29 001

Steinweg 5
FRANKFURT/MAIN
Tel: [0611] 21 051

ROADS

Although Germany has an extensive network of autobahns (superhighways) and one of the highest traffic densities in Europe, approximately 50 percent of all the country's roads are considered suitable for bicycling on the basis of traffic flow and physical characteristics, such as width and surface condition according to a German cycling magazine. Most motorists and truckers prefer to use the autobahns and main highways, leaving the back country roads for local traffic, tractors, cows, and cyclists. Wherever possible stay off the roads designated with the letter "B," which stands for *Bundestrasse* or federal highway. These are usually heavily utilized, especially by the truckers. Autobahns are identified by the letter "A," and their use is prohibited to bicyclists.

In many of those quaint picture-postcard old towns, cobblestone streets have been retained, and in a number of cases new cobble streets have been built. This is great for enhancing the charm and the tourist trade, but it's very difficult on the bicycles.

Except for those stretches of cobblestone, roads are maintained to a high standard.

You will be able to spend a good portion of your time in Germany on bicycle trails or lanes reserved for cyclists marked with white paint. Where such lanes are present their use is obligatory. Unless otherwise indicated, the many forest roads and hiking trails may also be used for cycling. Where hikers and bikers share a path, the hikers have the right of way.

While German drivers are a disciplined and well-trained lot, they do have a well-deserved reputation for being the fastest drivers in Europe. In general, motorists are quite considerate of cyclists; however, the German penchant for speed and their apparent reluctance to use the brakes have resulted in a few close calls for us over the years. Our advice is to always ride single file and be on the defensive. Avoid the main roads wherever possible, especially on weekends and holidays. Particularly at night and in bad weather, be sure that you can be easily seen. Ride with your lights on and wear reflective clothing. Since 1986, German law requires that bicycles be fitted with spoke reflectors on both wheels.

BIKING THROUGH EUROPE

WEST GERMANY

Although this is a land in where the automobile is revered to a degree that borders on the religious, and the country is laced with one of Europe's thickest networks of superhighways, bicycling in Germany has a long and established tradition. Das Bund Deutscher Radfahrer (The Union of German Cyclists), the country's foremost bicycling organization was founded back in 1884. In the year 1900, a Professor Schiefferdecker from Bonn wrote in his book *Bicycle Riding and Health*, "Bicycle touring, where the cyclist just glides through the countryside, is one of the best ways to travel and learn about a country and its people." In recent years, after a long slumber, interest in this activity has been rekindled and the Bund Deutscher Radfahrer currently has nearly 100,000 members in some 1,400 local clubs.

Although Germany is one of the world's most highly industrialized countries and its citizens enjoy a high standard of living, much of the "old Europe" remains there. Romantic castles perched above the Rhine, quaint Bavarian villages and elaborate castles, intact medieval towns, and such traditional rollicking spectacles as Munich's world-famous Octoberfest are just some of the many attractions that help to make Germany a favorite destination for travelers from all over the world.

Traveling through the country you will see virtually no evidence of the massive destruction that took place during the second world war. Entire cities have been reconstructed, many in a refreshing harmony of modern design and tradition, so that in spite of the incredible amount of new construction, German cities and towns have not lost touch with their rich architectural and cultural heritage. In several instances, such as the bombed-out ruins of the Kaiser Wilhelm-Gedächtniskirche in Berlin, and the infamous concentration camp at Dachau on the outskirts of Munich, things have been left as they were to serve as gripping reminders of the devastation and suffering associated with World War II.

The political and economic changes that have occurred in Germany in the little more than forty years since the end of the war have been nothing short of amazing. From the smoldering mounds of ashes and rubble of a bankrupt military dictatorship, Germany has become the dominant economic power in Europe and one of the most stable democracies on the continent by virtue of a Herculean effort on the part of its people, who have been spurred on to a great degree by substantial infusions of U.S. aid.

Germany's ties with North America are strong and reach into the heartland of the continent. A German friend of ours claims that some 30 percent of all Americans are of German heritage. While his figures might not be all that precise, it seems that wherever we go in Germany we always encounter someone with relatives in America.

Germans are often portrayed as industrious, arrogant, highly cultured, stuffy, and lacking in humor – and some indeed do fit the stereotype. But many Germans are fine, warm, sensitive people who take great delight at poking fun at their stereotypical countrymen. World War II has been over for nearly half a century – enough time for the emergence of nearly two generations of Germans with little or no association with "the War."

As citizens of one of the world's most affluent nations, Germans are among the most widely traveled peoples. It is a rare place in the world where one doesn't run into large numbers of German tourists. All of this traveling has given many Germans a broader view of the world and made an already gracious host nation even that much more gracious. You'll find that people will be courteous and helpful just about wherever you travel. As in every country, local personalities reflect regional differences. The northern German bears a striking resemblance to our taciturn New Englander, while in the southern parts of the country, especially in Bavaria, you will experience a cheerfulness and openness rarely encountered in other parts of the country. English is widely spoken in most tourist areas and large cities, especially among the younger generation.

The emergence of an active environmental movement and a heightened awareness of the health aspects of bicycling in recent years have resulted in a noticeable increase in the number of bikes on German streets. The ADFC, the country's most aggressive bike club, estimates that approximately 15 million of their countrymen take to the streets astride bicycles on a more or less regular basis. It is not unusual to encounter a colorfully costumed Bavarian pedaling down the road on the way to a local festival or a farmer balancing a scythe on his shoulder propelling a rickety old bike to work in the fields.

Recently there has been an increase in the construction of separate cycling paths, as well as in designating and signposting interesting bike touring routes throughout the country. Many large cities have also undertaken programs to encourage the use of bicycles. For example, Munich has laid out a network of some 1,100 kms of marked bicycle ways in and around the city. While the popularity of biking has not yet approached that of such "cycle crazy" countries as France, Denmark, or Holland, cycling in Germany is definitely on the upsurge.

Germany offers an incredible variety of attractions and cycling conditions guaranteed to keep even the most demanding cycle tourer from becoming bored. The northern part of the country encompassing Schleswig Holstein is pretty flat. Bordered on the north by the Danish peninsula of Jutland and facing both the North Sea and the Baltic, this rich dairy and agricultural country interspersed with some lovely lakes and fine beaches offers easy cycling. The countryside is quite pleasant and provides the only beach access in Germany. Hamburg and Bremen, both interesting cities to visit, are the country's major seaports.

As you head south the country becomes increasingly mountainous, culminating in the rugged alpine peaks that dominate the southeastern corner of Bavaria in the vicinity of Garmisch-Partenkirchen and Berchtesgaden – a region of spectacular natural beauty.

The Harz Mountains near the border with East Germany offer plenty of challenging cycling with a number of interesting attractions, including Gosler, one of the country's most delightful medieval towns. The valleys of the Rhine, Neckar, and Moselle rivers give you the opportunity to visit scores of romantic castles and pedal through some of Europe's finest wine-producing districts.

MAPS

There are a number of good maps available for planning purposes. **Michelin map #987, Germany, Austria, Benelux** (scale: 1:1,000,000) is one of the best for this. **Michelin map #413 Bavaria-Baden Würtemberg** (scale 1:400,000) is also useful for planning routes in southern Germany.

A free map showing some suggested long-distance tours (scale 1:1,500,000; 1 cm = 15 kms) is available from the **Bund Deutscher Radfahrer** (Otto-Fleck-Schneise 4, 6000 Frankfurt 71).

For actual cycling purposes there is a large selection of detailed maps available. The best that we have come across are those issued by the ADFC. In addition to showing actual bicycle paths, roads most suitable for cycling based on studies of traffic density are indicated. Roads marked in red indicate an average daily usage of less than 1,000 vehicles. These are considered to be the most suitable for cycling. Roads that handle between 1,000 and 3,000 vehicles daily are shown in orange; those that handle 3,000 to 10,000 vehicles daily are shown in dark yellow; and "unsuitable" roads handling over 10,000 vehicles daily are marked light yellow. Steep grades are indicated by arrows – one arrow for grades between 3 and 7 percent and two arrows for grades steeper than 7 percent. This series covers the entire country in thirty-five separate maps (scale

1:100,000; 1 cm = 1 km). Each map details an area of 100 by 100 kms. They are available at bookstores throughout Germany at a cost of about 10 DM. Look for a green folder with ADFC and the word "Radtourenkarte" on the cover.

Another good series of maps is the **die Generalkarte** published by Mair, which covers Germany in twenty-six maps (scale 1:200,000; 1 cm = 2 kms). These are good quality detailed maps; however, there are no special markings for cyclists. They are available at bookstores all over Germany and cost about 7 DM each.

For those of you who read German, the **BDR** (Bund Deutscher Radfahrer) publishes an extensive series of books describing regional cycling tours. These are particularly useful if you plan to stay in one area and do a lot of local touring. They cost 20 to 25 DM each. Contact the BDR for details.

BICYCLE SHOPS AND RENTALS

Just about every town has at least one cycle shop. The routes we have detailed are in regions that are popular with cyclists; should you encounter difficulties, you will have no trouble finding a shop. The magic words in German are "*Wo ist die nähste Fahrrad Werkstadt?*" Where is the nearest cycle repair shop? Germany is on the metric system. If your bike requires nonmetric tools and tires bring them along.

The **Deutsche Bundesbahn** (German Federal Railroad) is the country's largest cycle renter. Rental bikes are available at some 270 train stations between 1 April and 31 October and at some stations during the entire year. If you have a railroad ticket, you will pay a daily charge of 5 DM. Without a ticket, you pay 10 DM. Cycles can be returned at any participating train station. As you might imagine, 5 DM per day is not going to get you a super Peugeot touring bike. These are solid, heavy-duty machines best suited for local touring in flat terrain. The participating train stations are chosen for their accessibility to interesting cycling country. Brochures listing participating stations and showing a reference map are available at all Bundesbahn ticket counters. Advance reservations are accepted.

Most popular resort areas also have rental bikes available; these often are of better quality. For detailed information, check with local tourist offices or in the classified section of the phone book under *Fahrradverleih*.

TRANSPORTATION WITHIN THE COUNTRY

The **DB** or **Deutsche Bundesbahn**, as the national railroad system is called, is one of the most efficient and reliable rail systems in Europe.

All trains with baggage cars, with the exception of Inter-City and TEE trains, will transport bicycles. The timetables posted in the train stations indicate which trains have baggage cars with a symbol that looks like a suitcase. If you are traveling on the same train, it is necessary to purchase a separate ticket called a *Fahrradkarte* for your bike. The cost for the *Fahrradkarte* which is valid for accompanied transport anywhere in Germany, is 6.50 DM. You are responsible for loading and unloading the bike yourself, even when you transfer trains.

If you are not traveling on the same train, it is necessary to ship the bike as baggage, or *gepäck* in German. Rates are based on the distance traveled. Be sure to allow plenty of time. The Bundesbahn will guarantee arrival within two days anywhere in Germany and requires four days for European destinations outside the country. In many of the larger cities such as Munich, bicycles may be carried on the commuter trains (S-Bahn) and the subways (U-Bahn) except on weekends and during the weekday rush hour periods.

As matter of policy, bikes will not be transported on intercity buses. In individual cases, a sympathetic driver will occasionally bend the rules, but don't count on it. Several large cities, including Wiesbaden, Bonn, Bremen, and Wuppertal, have added a *Fahradbus* (bicycle bus) to their transportation service.

Germany's scenic river valleys – the Rhine, Moselle, and Neckar – are wonderful for cycling touring. One of the best ways to enjoy this romantic region is to cycle one way along the river and return on one of the many excursion boats that ply these rivers. They will always find a place for your bike on board. The same holds true for the numerous ferries that cross the major rivers. In most cases no charge is made for the bicycle.

ACCOMMODATIONS

Hotels in Germany range from romantic old *Schloss* or castle hotels to sleek chrome and glass high-rise business hotels. One thing that nearly all German hotels have in common is the great attention paid to neatness and cleanliness. We've never stayed in a German hotel that's been anything but sparkling clean.

While hotels are generally the most expensive type of accommodation, there are many pleasant money-saving alternatives. When touring Germany you will never be very far away from a pension or *gasthaus*. In many instances, rooms are available in private homes; in fact, many pensions are little more than private homes where the owners rent out a few rooms to supplement their income. These are great places to stay – warm, friendly, and wonderful places where you can swap travel yarns over breakfast with your host or the other guests. In practically *every* case, breakfast is included in the price. A typical German breakfast (*Frühstück*) consists of fresh rolls (*Brötchen*), butter, jam, coffee, and occasionally a soft-boiled egg. When searching for an inexpensive room, the words to look for are *Fremdenzimmer, Pension, Frühstückspension, Gasthaus,* and *Zimmer Frei.*

Local tourist offices will provide lists of available accommodations. For a small charge they will also make reservations for you. If your travel plans include being near any of the major festivals or tourist events, such as Munich's Octoberfest or the Oberammergau Passion Play, be sure to book your accommodations well in advance.

The youth hostel movement was founded in Germany just after the turn of the century. In this land of hikers and active travelers, the movement has grown into the largest in Europe. There are more than five hundred *Jugendherberge*, the German word for youth hostel, spread throughout the country. Although the densest concentration is in the Black Forest region, most other areas in which you will be touring have hostels spaced within a day's cycling distance.

The philosophy concerning management and regulations is similar to that encountered at many campgrounds – tight control and strict observance of the rules. However, German hostels are usually spotlessly clean with excellent facilities. Most hostels are closed for at least several hours during the day. Often hostels are literally taken over by youth groups, which is why it is a good idea to reserve in advance. Throughout the country preference is given to travelers under 27; in Bavaria, the maximum age for staying in a hostel is 27.

There are more than two thousand officially registered campgrounds in Germany. Even though the greatest number of these sites are concentrated in the major tourist areas, there is a sufficient distribution of campgrounds to allow you to include a nightly campground stop for most of the tours you will be planning. In our route descriptions we list campgrounds at intervals easily reached in a day's pedaling.

Although a Camping Carnet is not required, many sites, particularly those affiliated with the DCC (Deutsche Camping Club) will grant a 10 percent discount to holders of the card. Since German campgrounds are relatively expensive, this card will easily pay for itself if you spend any appreciable amount of time in Germany.

Rules and regulations at German campgrounds are taken very seriously by the staff and fellow campers. Among the many regulations is the phenomenon known as the *Mittags Pause*. The campground is simply shut down between 1 and 3 in the afternoon: no checking in, no checking out, no bike riding, no vehicles – a total shut down! Campgrounds are well maintained and kept scrupulously clean, with many offering cooking facilities and washing machines.

FOOD AND DRINK

Mention Germany to many people and visions of overflowing beer steins, crisp sausages, and plump dumplings instantly appear in their heads. While these are definitely a part of the food scene, the variety and quality of food you will be exposed to while touring Germany are overwhelming, starting with the basics: bread – "the staff of life." German bakeries (*Bäckerei*) turn out some forty varieties of bread, in addition to an incredible assortment of delectable cakes and pastries.

In the larger cities, American-style supermarkets have become a part of the landscape, though not to the exclusion of the many individual food shops. When stocking up for a picnic, be sure to stop in at a *Metzgerei* or butcher shop where you will see a mind-boggling assortment of cold cuts, sausages (*wurst*), and delicious prepared salads of meats and vegetables. In recent years, a number of health food stores (*Reformhaus*) have opened.

Traditional dishes still account for a good portion of the restaurant food consumed, however, an ever-increasing awareness of the health aspects of food has led to the development of a much lighter health-oriented "nouvelle German cuisine." The large increase in the number of foreigners living in the country coupled with a heightened awareness of other types of foods generated by increased travel has led to the appearance of Chinese, Yugoslavian, Italian, Greek, and even Mexican restaurants all over the country. Also, there is hardly a town of any consequence that doesn't have a McDonalds or Burger King.

If you are looking for the traditional, in Bavaria try the tasty *Schweinshaxen* (roast pork shanks) served with *Knödel* (dumplings) and gravy and washed down with a stein of great Bavarian beer. Game dishes are also a Bavarian favorite. Especially good is *Hirsch Ragout* (venison stew). In the north of the country the emphasis is more on seafood. Restaurant menus feature a variety of fish, herring, and eel dishes. *Forelle* (fresh lake trout) is popular throughout the country as is the ubiquitous *Schnitzel*, a thinly sliced steak, usually of veal or pork. *Weinerschnitzel*, a tasty breaded veal steak, is the most popular of the many ways Schnitzel is prepared.

Traditionally the main meal is eaten at noon. Dinner or *Abendbrot* usually consists of cold cuts or cheese and bread. The best bargain at most restaurants is the *Tagesmenu* (menu of the day). Although tax and service are included in the bill, it is customary to round off to the nearest mark or two if the service has been satisfactory. For an inexpensive meal, try a *Schnell Imbiss*, the German version of a fast food place, or a department store cafeteria. A *Gastätte* is a less expensive, informal restaurant.

When it comes to quenching your thirst, the choices are many. In Bavaria, the world's beer drinking capital, the favorite suds is a tasty light brew. When ordering it, ask for "*ein Helles Bitte.*" *Weiss Bier*, fermented from wheat, is another Bavarian favorite. *Pilsner* is more commonly drunk in the central and northern parts of the country. German wines, especially the whites from the Rhine and Moselle valleys, are excellent and are very popular throughout the world. For a balanced thirst-quencher after a tough mountainous stretch, try *Isostar*, the German version of Gatorade. It is available at supermarkets and sporting goods stores.

Americans traveling in Germany often run into a problem when ordering water. According to an old German saying, "*Wasser ist nur für waschen und Zähne putzen*" (water is only for washing and tooth brushing). When they do drink water, most Germans drink mineral water, which in restaurants is often more expensive than beer. If you want tap water, ask for *Leitungswasser*.

SOURCES OF ADDITIONAL INFORMATION

Local tourist offices are well organized and can provide you with more on-the-spot information than you can stuff into your panniers. Just about every town with something of interest (and in Germany that's just about every town) has a local **Fremdenverkehrsamt** or **Verkehrsverein**, the German words for tourist office. Many of these offices have put together material describing interesting cycling possibilities in their regions.

Bund Deutscher Radfahrer (Otto-Fleck-Schneise 4, 6000 Frankfurt am Main 71; Tel: [0611] 67 89 222) is Germany's largest cycling organization, an important national organization with many local affiliates. It is involved in the publication of many regional cycling guidebooks.

Allgemeiner Deutscher Fahrrad Club (ADFC) (postfach 107744, 2800 Bremen 1; Tel: [0421] 74 052) not to be confused with the ADAC, the German automobile club, is a very active national organization working to improve German cycling conditions. It publishes an excellent series of maps and the bimonthly magazine, *Radfahrer*.

Bavaria

When it comes to scenic beauty and attractions, few places in the country can compete with *Bayern*, as Bavaria, the largest of the country's eleven federal states, is known in German. The capital city of Munich with its fine museums and boisterous Octoberfest, the spectacular alpine vistas of Garmisch-Partenkirchen, the wonderful painted houses and intricate wood carvings of Oberammergau, the ornate castles built by the eccentric King Ludwig, idyllic villages, crystal clear lakes, charming fräulein in colorful dirndl, brass oom-pah bands, Lederhosen, and beer, beer, and more beer are just a small part of what awaits when you cycle through this inviting part of Germany.

Bavaria, which borders on Czechoslovakia and Austria, is a rich fertile land of lush rolling hills dotted with delightful villages whose onion-domed churches and decoratively painted houses grace the fronts of countless picture postcards and scenic calendars. Southern Bavaria is Germany's gateway to the alps, and there the scenery is nothing short of breathtaking as the rolling hills give way to the rugged wall of mountains that form a major portion of the border with Austria.

Nowhere in Germany will you find a prouder, more fiercely independent, but, at the same time friendlier or more hospitable, group of people than those of the "Free State of Bavaria," as the Bavarians refer to their part of the Federal Republic of Germany. The Bavarians speak a form of German that bears little resemblance to German spoken in the north of the country.

There is no better place to start a tour of Bavaria than in its lively capital, Munich. Many scheduled and charter airlines fly into Munich directly from the States. This is a great place to begin your European cycling tour. Munich is easily reached by train from other parts of Europe. The route we have laid out covers many of Bavaria's most interesting sights and attractions and combines well with several other routes in this book. From Munich, it's just a day's cycling along a bike trail by way of Fürstenfeldbruck to Augsburg, where you can continue up or down "The Castle and Romantic Roads Route" as described further into this chapter.

BAVARIAN HIGHLIGHTS TOUR

START	FINISH	DISTANCE
MUNICH	MUNICH	421 kms/262 miles

DIE GENERALKARTE MAPS	ADFC MAPS
#22, #23, #25, #26 (scale: 1:200,000)	#35, Münich-Salzburg; #34, Allgau-Lechfeld (scale 1:100,000)

We've described this loop starting and ending in Munich cycling in a counterclockwise direction – heading south from Munich to Füssen and King Ludwig's castles via Starnberg and Weilheim. The route can just as easily be done in the opposite direction by heading out toward Wasserburg, although this will have you going the "wrong way" on some of the hilly sections – in particular the 7-km climb up from Oberau near Garmisch to the Ettal Monastery.

The terrain is moderately difficult with many short hilly sections and a few long steep grades. A ten-speed bike is advised and a "granny sprocket" will be a big asset in helping you propel a heavily loaded touring bike up some of the steeper grades. But the scenery you will encounter is nothing short of magnificent, well worth the extra effort required to cover the route as described. There are numerous hiking trails and forest service roads in this region, particularly in the southern stretch between Füssen and Bad Tölz, which are ideal for a mountain bike. Local tourist offices can be a big help in suggesting off road routes for local touring.

SIDE TRIPS AND ADDED ATTRACTIONS

If you cycle this route in a clockwise direction (that is starting from Munich and heading first toward Chiemsee), then at the Wies Church, instead of returning to Munich via Weilheim, you can continue with "The Castle and Romantic Roads Route" all the way up to Heidelberg. From Füssen it's not very difficult to link up with the "Lake Constance Route." From Garmisch-Partenkirchen it's only about 45 kms into Innsbruck, part of it down the very steep Zirler Berg road. At Innsbruck you can link up with the Austrian route, "Mountains to Mozart." Salzburg and the mountains of Berchtesgaden are readily accessible by continuing east from Chiemsee. The possibilities for expanding this route in many interesting directions are limited only by your own energy and time available. Bavaria and its surroundings are so rich in interesting touring and sightseeing opportunities that you could easily spend several seasons of cycling here and still not see it all.

In general, Bavaria has some of the nicest weather in Germany. When it is cold and rainy in Hamburg and Frankfurt, the sun may be favoring Bavaria with its warming rays. We have spent some magnificent days cycling around Garmisch-Partenkirchen in late September and well into October when the leaves had turned the landscape into a bright montage of autumn colors. But then there was the autumn of '81 when we had several inches of snow in mid-October. Your best bet for this region is to tour in September when the weather usually is still warm, although mornings and evenings are often brisk, and the number of tourists on the roads and at major tourist attractions has somewhat diminished. The famous Munich Octoberfest is held annually during the two weeks preceding the first Sunday in October.

One of the compensations for putting up with the crowds everywhere in high season is the opportunity for impromptu swimming in Bavaria's many fine lakes. There is nothing like a refreshing dip in a cool clear lake to wash off accumulated road dust and caked auto exhaust. When touring in July and August, be aware that the weather often changes very quickly and sudden summer thunderstorms are a frequent occurrence. Fortunately they usually don't last very long.

Late spring can be a wonderful time to cycle Bavaria, although you may still run into an occasional snow flurry or two.

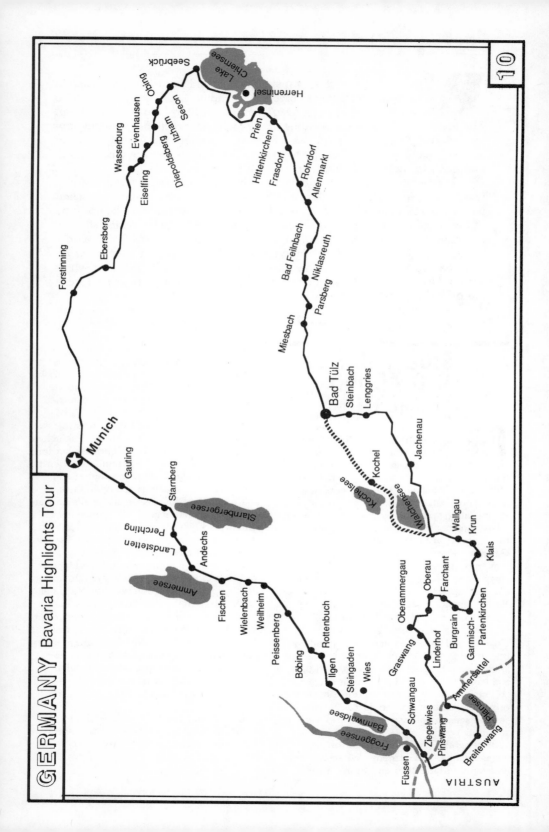

BAVARIAN HIGHLIGHTS TOUR

CITY
MUNICH

DISTANCE KM	TOTAL KM
58	0

ROUTE DESCRIPTION

From the Hauptbahnhof, head west on the Landsbergerstrasse toward München Passing and continue on Bodenseestr. to Unterpfaffenhofen. At the south edge of town, pick up a little-traveled road that runs under the autobahn and continues through the forest to Gauting. From Gauting, follow the signs into the popular resort town of Starnberg at the head of the lake of the same name. In 10 kms you will gain gain about 60 meters in altitude. Take a dip in the lake (weather permitting), then head across the rolling hills to the monastery at Andechs by way of Perchting and Landstetten. Conclude your tour of the monastery by sampling the fine dark beer. Take the road out of Andechs to Fischen am Ammersee. Just outside of town there is a great view of Ammersee, one of several large glacial lakes in the area. Continue into Weilheim via Wielenbach.

CITY
WEILHEIM

ROUTE
B2 B17 (The Romantic Road)

DISTANCE KM	TOTAL KM
28	58

ROUTE DESCRIPTION

From Weilheim, take B2 into the pleasant little town of Peissenberg at the foot of the 1,000-meter-high Hohenpeissenberg. Then take the road to Bobing, which crosses the Ammer River and climbs gradually, rising some 150 meters over about 10 kms. Continue on the same road, crossing the Ammer again into Rottenbuch, a quiet town in a beautiful setting ringed by high mountains in the distance. From Rottenbach, stay on the same road another 8 kms to intersect with B17 at Ilgen.

CITY
ILGEN

ROUTE
B17 (The Romantic Road)

DISTANCE KM	TOTAL KM
38	86

ROUTE DESCRIPTION

From Ilgen it is just 3 kms on B17 to Steingaden. At Steingaden, follow the signs 6 kms to the Wies Kirche for an interesting side trip. This is probably Europe's finest rococo church. Return to Steingaden and follow B17 in Schwangau to Füssen, the southern terminus of the Romantic Road.

CITY
FÜSSEN

ROUTE
S14

DISTANCE KM	TOTAL KM
42	124

ROUTE DESCRIPTION

After visiting Ludwig's castles, leave Füssen/Schwangau, following the signs to the Austrian border at Ziegelwies. Take the alternate road to Reutte by way of Pinswang (and avoid the heavily traveled 314). Bypass Reutte on S14 and turn off at Breitenwang to follow the signs to Plansee. The scenic road climbs steeply to this mountain lake. Continue climbing to the border, crossing back into Germany at Ammersattel. About 8 kms past the border, turn off to the left to Linderhof, one of King Ludwig's most enchanting castles. From the castle, take the forest road to Graswang. Don't be surprised if you see a lot of American GI's running around there. This is a U.S. adventure training area. From Graswang, it's another 5 kms to Oberammergau, one of Bavaria's loveliest and most popular towns.

CITY
OBERAMMERGAU

ROUTE
B23 E533

DISTANCE KM	TOTAL KM
23	166

ROUTE DESCRIPTION

After a stop to visit the monastery at Ettal, take the steep, winding 7-km descent to Oberau. Avoid the traffic on E533 by taking the path that parallels this busy hwy. To pick up the path, cross the Loisach River by the Oberau Bahnhof and take the path through the fields to Farchant, past the swimming pool, to the bridge at Burgrain and pick up B23 into Garmisch-Partenkirchen.

CITY
GARMISCH-PARTENKIRCHEN

ROUTE
B2 B11

DISTANCE K	TOTAL KM
21	189

ROUTE DESCRIPTION

Take hwy B2 out of Garmisch, following the signs toward Mittenwald. The road, part of the German Alpine Hwy, climbs for the first few kms out of Garmisch. The jagged peaks in the background are part of the Karwendel group. At Klais, follow the road to Krün. From there, take B11 to Wallgau.

CITY
WALLGAU

DISTANCE KM	TOTAL KM
35	210

ROUTE DESCRIPTION

A short steep hill leads out of Wallgau to Walchensee, one of the loveliest lakes in the region. At the lake, turn right and follow the signs to Jachenau.

For part of the way the road hugs the lake and then climbs and winds through a pleasant forested area along the Jachen River, coming out into the open at the quiet little town of Jachenau. Follow the Jachenaur Strasse into Lenggries. At Lenggries, cross the bridge over the Isar River and take the back road into Bäd Tolz by way of Steinbach.

Note: For a more challenging route, continue at Walchensee on B11 over the Kesselberg. The winding 6-km mountain stretch has superb vistas as a reward for the climb. At the bottom, follow the signs to Bad Tölz by way of Kochel. In Kochel, be sure to stop at the SCHMIED VOM KOCHEL, a delightful small hotel with one of the best restaurants in the region. One of our favorites!

CITY
BAD TÖLZ

ROUTE
B472

DISTANCE KM	TOTAL KM
61	245

ROUTE DESCRIPTION
Leave Bad Tölz on B472 just past the U.S. Army Special Forces Base, following the signs to Miesbach. In Miesbach, leave B472 and take the road to Bad Feilnbach, passing through Parsberg, then continuing up a steep grade to Niklasreuth. From Bad Feilnbach, the road winds through several small villages before crossing the Inn River at Altenmarkt. From Altenmarkt, follow the signs to Rohrdorf. Then pick up the cycle path that runs along the autobahn most of the way into Frasdorf.

CITY
FRASDORF

DISTANCE KM	TOTAL KM
11	306

ROUTE DESCRIPTION
From Frasdorf the road climbs for a short distance to Hittenkirchen. Catch your breath there and enjoy the fine view of Lake Chiemsee before coasting down to the lakeside resort of Prien.

CITY
PRIEN

DISTANCE KM	TOTAL KM
19	317

ROUTE DESCRIPTION
Follow the road along the shore to Seebrück at the northern end of the lake. The larger of the two offshore islands that you see along the way is the Herreninsel, site of one of King Ludwig's castles.

CITY
SEEBRÜCK

DISTANCE KM	TOTAL KM
32	336

ROUTE DESCRIPTION
From Seebrück, take the road through the marshlands to Seeon on the beautiful little Kloster See. Continue on to Obing. From Obing, avoid the busy hwy B304 to Wasserburg and instead follow the sparsely traveled road that runs through the pleasant little towns of Ilzham, Diepoldsberg, Evenhausen, and Eiselfing.

CITY	
WASSERBURG	

ROUTE	
B304	

DISTANCE KM	TOTAL KM
53	368

ROUTE DESCRIPTION

Just outside of Wasserburg at the intersection of B15 and B304, pick up B304 and follow it into Ebersberg. From there, continue on to Forstinning through the Ebersberg Forest. Follow the signs into Munich, which will lead you into the city past the airport.

CITY	
MUNICH	

DISTANCE KM	TOTAL KM
0	421

BAVARIAN SIGHTS AND ACCOMMODATIONS

MUNICH. Probably more than any other city, Munich personifies the West Germany on the verge of the twenty-first century – vibrant, exciting, a place where hi-tech industry, urban renewal, rapid transit, minority difficulties and massive traffic problems are all part of the scene. However, none of this has been allowed to obscure the city's fine old architecture and rich traditions, or the people's flair for life, which seems to exude from every corner of this wonderful Bavarian capital. When you see a pretty *fräulein* in a colorful dirndl or a proud Bayer clad in lederhosen enjoying Bavaria's favorite brew in one of Munich's many beer gardens, you can be sure that the sight is not being staged for the benefit of the passing tourists. Müncheners, as the city's residents are called, are a proud, friendly folk who thoroughly enjoy their city and its many traditions.

Bicycles provide an important means of getting around in Munich, and much has been done to meet the needs of the city's many cyclists. Check in at the tourist office information counter in the train station or at the airport and pick up a copy of their excellent brochure, *Munich for Cyclists*. Although it's only available in German, the many maps are great for navigating the city by bike.

Rental bicycles are available from FAHRRADVERLEIGH BORUCKI (Hans-Sachs-Str. 7; Tel: [089] 26 65 06) and from FAHRRADVERLEIH BUSS in the English Gardens.

Try to time your visit to the **Marienplatz**, the busy hub of Munich's bustling outdoor street life, to catch the playing of the **glockenspiel**, one of Germany's finest, atop the colorful **Rathaus** (City Hall) daily at 11 AM and 5 PM. Adjacent to the neo-Gothic Rathaus are two of the city's oldest churches: **Peterskirche** and the **Frauenkirche**, whose twin onion-domed spires are a Munich landmark. The pedestrian zone radiating out from the Marienplatz is a lively potpourri of outdoor cafés, kitschy souvenir shops, elegant boutiques, and street performers of all kinds: musicians, jugglers and pantomimists. Be sure to walk over to the **Viktualienmarkt**, Munich's deliciously colorful open air market just a few blocks south of the Marienplatz. Its a great place to stock your panniers with Bavarian treats for a picnic or for eating right on the spot!

No visit to Munich would be complete without having at least one beer at the world-famous **Hofbräuhaus am Plätzl**, only a "wurst's length" from the Marienplatz. Sure it's touristy, but it's also authentic. They've been serving that fine Munich beer since 1589, long before the first cheap charter flight or tour bus!

An expansive blending of baroque and rococo styles make **Nymphenburg Palace**, the former residence of the Bavarian kings set in a beautiful five-hundred-acre park at the west edge of the city, one of Germany's finest royal palaces. The **Residenz**, a large complex in the center of the city which also encompasses the National Theater, was the city residence of the Wittelsbachs, Bavaria's royal family. Not much to look at from the outside, the interior is chock full of rich furnishings and art treasures.

Of Munich's many fine museums, one of the most unusual and intriguing is the **Deutsches Museum**, an outstanding collection of technical and scientific exhibits innovatively displayed. It is literally a science textbook come to life. Other museums worth visiting include the **Alte Pinakothek**, which has a fine collection of Reubens; the **Neue Pinakothek**, a collection primarily of nineteenth-century works housed in an inviting modern building; and the **Staatsgalerie Moderner Kunst**, one of Europe's best modern art museums.

On a much more somber plane is the **Dachau Concentration Camp Memorial Museum**. Located on the northwest edge of the city, this memorial is on the site of the infamous concentration camp where so many thousands were killed during World War II. It documents with models, exhibits, and films the events of that horrible era.

Munich's nighttime activities and café life are centered mainly in the district of **Schwabing**. The area is best described as a composite of Paris's Latin quarter, London's Soho, and New York's Greenwich Village, topped off with a unique German flair.

If you are anywhere near Munich during the two weeks preceding the first Sunday in October, be sure to make a beeline for that grandaddy of all folkfests, the **Octoberfest**. Brass bands, huge beer tents packed with singing fest-goers, thrilling rides, mountains of food, and over a million gallons of beer to be consumed make a visit to the Munich Octoberfest an unforgettable experience.

With nearly 30,000 hotel beds plus several youth hostels and campgrounds available, the choice of accommodations is enormous. The tourist office has a room-finding service for which they charge a fee of 3 DM.

If after some vigorous pedaling you would like to wash off the accumulated road dust and grime in the most luxurious circumstances the city has to offer, check in and enjoy the quiet elegance of the HOTEL BAYERISCHER HOF (Promenadeplatz 2-6; Tel: [089] 21 200). For a quiet moderately priced hotel, try the HOTEL BIEDERSTEIN (Keferstr. 18; Tel: [089] 39 50 72) located near the English Gardens, playground of the city's nudist set. Of the Munich's numerous inexpensive pensions, we like the comfortable PENSION AM KAISERPLATZ (Kaiserplatz 12; Tel: [089] 34 91 90), PENSION THERESIA (Luisenstr. 51; Tel: [089] 52 12 50), with its convenient Schwabing location, as well as the friendly PENSION ISABELLA (Isabellastr. 35; Tel: [089] 27 13 503).

There are three youth hostels in the Munich area. In addition to these official hostels, there are several "youth hotels," which offer similar accommodations at budget prices without the restrictions in place at most youth hostels. The DJH JUGENDHERBERGE (Wendl-Dietrich Str. 20, 8 Munich 19; Tel: [089] 13 11 560) is a huge, bustling place with more than 500 beds. Meals are available. The DHJ JUGENDGASTHAUS (Thalkirchen, Miesingstr. 4; Tel: [089] 72 36 550) is a modern hostel with 346 beds in a dormitory near the Thalkirchen campground. The popular DJH JUGENDHERBERGE BURG SCHWANECK (Burgweg 4-6, 8023 Pullach; Tel: [089] 79 30 643) is about 12 kms from center of town near the S-bahn station. It is a neat old converted castle with 131 beds. There is no age limit and no Youth Hostel card is required to stay at the HAUS INTERNATIONAL YOUTH HOTEL (Elisabethstr. 87; Tel: [089] 18 50 81). This convenient youth hotel has 480 beds, as well as a disco and swimming pool. The SLEEPING TENT AM KAPUZINERHÖLZL, a unique Munich experience, has 400 sleeping places in a huge tent set up by the city's youth department. Showers, toilet facilities, and blankets are provided for 5 DM per night. Stays are limited to three nights.

Of the several regular Munich area campgrounds, the most lively is CAMPING MÜNCHEN-THALKIRCHEN, set in a wooded area on the Isar River near the zoo. The full range of facilities include a laundromat. It is open 15 March to 30 October. Other convenient Munich campgrounds include CAMPINGPLATZ MÜNCHEN-OBERMENZING, open 15 March to 5 November, and CAMPING NORDWEST, open all year.

WEILHEIM. A pleasant little market town, Weilheim is set in the midst of southern Bavaria's beautiful countryside and is within a few hours cycling distance of Munich; Oberammergau; the monasteries at Ettal, Andechs, Steingaden, and Benedictbeuern; and the Ammersee, Starnberger See, and Staffelsee, to name just a few of the region's most popular lakes. The town of Weilheim itself dates back to 1238, and the old town section, now a pedestrian zone, has a number of well-preserved medieval and baroque buildings.

The town's top hotel is the HOTEL BRAUWÄSTL (Schmiedstr. 15, 8120 Weilheim; Tel: [0881] 7471) located in the center of the old town. (Brauwästl is also the name of the very fine local beer.) The GASTHOF ALLGAUER HOF (Marienplatz 17; Tel: [0881] 2086) is a modestly priced little inn with a good local restaurant.

The tourist office located in the Reisebüro Stolzle & Simader (Am Marienplatz; Tel: [0881] 3090) will locate an inexpensive room for you in a private home.

There is no campground directly in Weilheim. CAMPINGPLATZ AMMERTAL on the Wörther See just outside of Peissenberg is about a forty-minute cycle ride from Weilheim. The facilities include a washing machine, camp store, and snack bar. It is open all year.

FUSSEN / SCHWANGAU. See "The Castle and Romantic Roads" Sights and Accommodations.

OBERAMMERGAU. To many travelers Oberammergau is synonymous with the world-famous passion play held just once every ten years. The next performance will be in 1990. Oberammergau is a delightful town in a magnificent high alpine valley setting, with a wealth of beautifully painted house facades. The name means the region of the upper Ammer River. It is also one of Germany's most famous wood-carving centers. Should you be in the market for a wood carving to send home as a souvenir, this is the place where you should look. Strolling through the quiet streets it's hard to imagine that some 500,000 persons attended performances of the 1980 passion play.

On the way to Oberammergau from Füssen, be sure to stop and see the **Linderhof Castle**. The turn-off is just 8 kms from the Austrian border crossing. This "modest-sized" rococo castle with its famous underground grotto and lake was King Ludwig's favorite residence. Leaving Oberammergau on the way to Garmisch-Partenkirchen, you will see the graceful lines of the imposing **Benedictine Monastery at Ettal** framed against a magnificent alpine background.

The HOTEL ALOIS LANG (St. Lukasstr. 15) is a small but well-appointed first-class traditional hotel. For more moderately priced lodgings, try the HOTEL WOLF (Dorfstr. 1).

The IYHF JUGENDHERBERGE OBER-AMMERGAU (Malensteinweg 10; Tel: [08822] 4114) has meals available and is open all year, except December.

The closest campground is CAMPING OBERAMMERGAU AM SPORTPLATZ, just off of the main road next to the soccer field – a two-minute cycle ride into town. The facilities are nothing much; in fact, they border on the primitive. But they are adequate and the location is convenient. The campground is open 1 May to 15 October.

GARMISCH-PARTENKIRCHEN. The villages of Garmisch and Partenkirchen were united to form a single town in 1935 prior to their hosting the 1936 Winter Olympics. Favored by a wonderful location in the broad Loisach Valley just 100 kms from Munich and surrounded by an impressive chain of mountains that includes the **Zugspitze**, Germany's highest peak, Garmisch-Partenkirchen has developed into a world-class all-year resort while still retaining much of its village character. Try to spend a few days hiking and biking in the local mountains. The 7-km path around the Eibsee at the foot of the towering Zugspitze offers a superb panorama combined with some idyllic picnic and swimming opportunities. On a clear day you can see forever! That is, if you take the funky cog train up to the top of the Zugspitze.

If you wonder why there appear to be so many Americans everywhere that you go in Garmisch, it's because Garmisch has been the major recreation center for the U.S. Armed Forces in Europe since shortly after World War II.

For a special treat, take a day off from cycling and spend a few hours at the **Alpspitz Wellenbad**, a super complex of indoor and outdoor swimming pools with a magnificent view of the surrounding mountains.

The town's most romantic first-class hotel is CLAUSINGS POST HOTEL (Marienplatz 12; Tel: [08821] 58 071) in a picture-postcard setting right in the center of Garmisch. It offers comfortable rooms and an excellent restaurant as well as a *gemütlich Bier Stube* and a sidewalk café that serves delicious pastries. Partenkirchen's popular GASTHAUS FRAUENDORFER (Ludwigstr. 24; Tel: [08821] 2176) is a traditional favorite with comfortable

inexpensive rooms and a restaurant that features Bavarian specialties with folk entertainment. It is a great place for an inexpensive evening. A favorite budget-category pension is the GASTHOF KORN-MÜLLER (Höllentalstr 36, Garmisch; Tel: [08821] 3557).

For help in finding a room in this often fully booked Bavarian gem, stop in at the tourist office a few meters down the street on your left as you walk out of the train station.

IYHF JUGENDHERBERGE GARMISCH (Jochstr. 10, 8100 Garmisch-Partenkirchen; Tel: [08821] 2980) is located in Burgrain about 4 kms from the Garmisch train station in the direction of Munich.

Garmisch's only campground, CAMPING ZUGSPITZE, sits just at the edge of town on the road to Grainau. It is a pleasant grassy site between the road and the Loisach River with some nice views of the mountains and is open all year.

WALLGAU. Wallgau is an attractive little village on the road to the Walchensee, picturesquely placed at the foot of the Karwendel Range. If you tire of pedaling or want to spend a little time in this beautiful countryside at the foot of the alps, stop in at the delightful **WALLGAU POST HOTEL** located on Wallgau's main street. Even if you don't stay there, sample their restaurant for some of the finest cooking and most abundant portions anywhere around.

Campers can stop at the CAMPING TENNSEE just a few kms down the road between Klais and Krün. Recently remodeled and boasting a full range of facilities, this is considered to be one of the most modern campgrounds in Germany. It is expensive! The campground is open all year, except from 3 November to 14 December.

If you decide to save money and free camp around the Walchensee, be sure to keep your tent well out of view. The area is well patrolled and overnight camping prohibited.

BAD TÖLZ. A gem of a health spa spanning both sides of the Isar River, Bad Tölz in the alpine foothills south of Munich is a popular destination for many Germans who go there to avail themselves of the healing waters. The **Iodine Springs** are especially well known. Outside of Germany the charms of this pleasant spa in its idyllic setting are a well-kept secret. There is nothing spectacular there in the way of cathedrals or famous museums, although the town does have a few picturesque churches and a small **Heimat Museum** (Hometown Museum). On the right bank of the Isar lies the **Old Town** with a traffic-free Market Street flanked by fine old houses decorated in traditional old Bavarian style. The spa portion of Bad Tölz has lovely parks and gardens; it lies on the Isar's left bank.

This is great cycling country – there are some 500 kms of marked bike paths to allow you to pedal through the lush countryside against a backdrop of the Bavarian alps. The **Städtische Kurverwaltung** (tourist office) (Ludwigstrasse 11, 8170 Bad Tölz; Tel: [08041] 4149) has put together an attractive seven-day cycling package in and around Bad Tölz. Contact them directly for details.

In addition to the many health-oriented sanatorium-type hotels, there are plenty of charming conventional hotels and pensions. One of the most convenient and reasonably priced is the POST HOTEL KOLBERBRAU (Marktstrasse 29, 8170 Bad Tölz; Tel: [08041] 9158) located in an historic old coaching inn right on the main street in the heart of the pedestrian zone. The top hotel in town offering a full range of health spa facilities is the fashionable HOTEL JOD-QUELLENHOF ALPARMARE (Ludwig-strasse 15; Tel: [08041] 5091). Even if you don't stay at the hotel, spend a few hours enjoying the impressive complex of swimming pools, some with wave-making machines, and the various medicinal baths. HAUS CHARLOTTE (Buchner Strasse 24; Tel: [08041] 3348) is a comfortable inexpensive rustic pension.

There are two campgrounds in the immediate vicinity of the town. CAMPING-PLATZ STALLAUER WEIHER is about 4 kms west of town off hwy B472 in a beautiful setting on a small lake. It has nothing fancy in the way of facilities, but it is very adequate and is open all year. There is a cycle path from the campground to town. CAMPING ARZBACH, 5 kms south of Bad Tölz in Arzbach, is in a lovely scenic setting next to a good restaurant. It is crowded in the summer and open all year.

FRASDORF. A quiet village nestled in the rolling hills with the alps as a backdrop, Frasdorf is the first town you will approach in the Chiemsee region as you come from Bad Tölz. Chiemsee, the largest of the Bavarian lakes, is a popular center for sailing and other water sports. The lake's largest island, Herreninsel, contains yet another of King Ludwig's castles. **Schloss Herrenchiemsee** is, on a more modest but nevertheless impressive scale, a Bavarian version of the French Versailles, complete with a sumptuous hall of mirrors. During the summer months, candlelight chamber music concerts are held in the Schloss. There is also a luxury hotel on the island.

GASTHOF HOCHRIES (Hauptstrasse 2-3, 8201 Frasdorf; Tel: [08052] 1473), is a comfortable, twenty-six-room, moderately priced gasthaus in a pleasant rural setting. GASTHOF OBHOLZER (Hauptstrasse 28; Tel: [08052] 1002) is a small inexpensive family-run guest house.

The closest campground is in nearby Aschau (4 kms). It is called CAMPING AM MOOR and is a small site in a wooded area. The facilities include a camp store and snack bar. The campground is open all year.

WASSERBURG. In German, Wasser-burg means water fortress and Wasserburg on the Inn River is just that. A medieval fortress town built on a peninsula jutting into the river, Wasserburg's history goes back to the twelfth century. Restored and renovated many times over but always with an eye toward preserving the town's traditional character and beauty, this is one of Bavaria's most attractive and unusual towns. Access to the old town from the south is over a modern bridge built in the old style which passes through a gate in the fifteenth-century watchtower.

Of particular interest are the **Old Fortress**, the **St. Michael Kapelle**, the **Museum Wasserburg**, and the fifteenth-century **Rathaus**.

The HOTEL GASTHOF PAULANER STUBEN (8090 Wasserburg am Inn; Tel: [08071] 3903) is located in the historic old Kernhaus am Marienplatz in the center of the old town. It is a comfortable old hotel with lots of charm and moderate prices. It has a good restaurant and cozy *Bier Stube*.

The HOTEL FLETZINGER (Fletzinger-gasse 3; Tel: [08071] 8010) is another cozy hotel restaurant combination.

The tourist office located in the historic old Rathaus (Tel: [08071] 1050) can help you find a reasonably priced room in a private home.

The closest campground is at Soyen See about 6 kms northwest of Wasserburg off hwy 15. CAMPING AM SOYEN SEE is a small nicely situated site on the lake with a snack bar and camp store. It is open 1 April to 31 October.

PRIEN. Prien is the principal resort town on the lake and the center for excursions on the lake.

The HOTEL BAYERISCHER HOF (Bernauer Strasse 3, 8210 Prien; Tel: [08051] 1095) is a nice moderately priced hotel with a good restaurant. For a comfortable inexpensive room in a nicely situated quiet pension, try GASTHAUS ALPENBLICK (Ringstrasse 3; Tel: [08051] 61 764).

CAMPING HARRAS is a large pleasant site with a small beach on the lake. It is open 1 May to 10 October.

SEEBRÜCK. Seebrück is a popular little resort town with a large boat harbor at the north end of the lake.

The LANDESGASTHAUS LAMBACH-HOF (Lambach 10, 8221 Seebrück; Tel: [08667] 427) is a pleasant resort hotel with a private swimming pool on the lake. GASTHAUS STETTEN (Stetten 12; Tel: [08056] 454) is a modest little two-room pension.

CAMPING KUPFERSCHMIEDE is on a large meadow with access to the lake. It is located about 2 kms south of Seebrück at the turnoff to Trostberg. The facilities include a washing machine, camp store, and restaurant. It is open 1 April to 30 September.

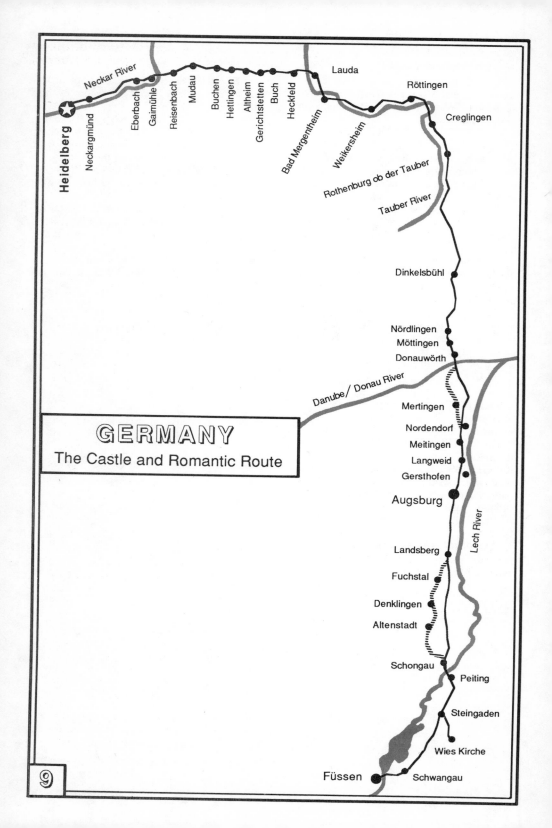

GERMANY
The Castle and Romantic Route

Heidelberg

Neckargmünd

Neckar River

Eberbach

Gaimühle

Reisenbach

Mudau

Buchen

Hettingen

Altheim

Gerichtstetten

Buch

Heckfeld

Bad Mergentheim

Lauda

Weikersheim

Röttingen

Creglingen

Rothenburg ob der Tauber

Tauber River

Dinkelsbühl

Nördlingen

Möttingen

Donauwörth

Danube / Donau River

Mertingen

Nordendorf

Meitingen

Langweid

Gersthofen

Augsburg

Lech River

Landsberg

Fuchstal

Denklingen

Altenstadt

Schongau

Peiting

Steingaden

Wies Kirche

Füssen

Schwangau

9

The Castle and Romantic Roads

Shortly before we completed the manuscript for this book, some friends asked for help in laying out an itinerary for a short European cycling vacation. It was in response to their request that we set up this route, which they followed all the way down the line. They had a wonderful time.

In designing this route, we've incorporated a potpourri of some the best in the way of attractions, scenery, and charm that Germany has to offer. Starting off in the romantic old university town of Heidelberg, the route follows a portion of the famed Castle Road along the valley of the Neckar River. One of several named or theme roads in Germany, the Castle Road is actually made up of a series of roads extending some 300 kms between Mannheim and Nürnberg and includes more than thirty fortified castles and palaces. At the delightful spa resort of Eberbach on the Neckar, our route leaves the Neckar Valley and climbs up into the Odenwald, one of central Germany's finest forest areas. This is hill country interspersed with some remarkable medieval towns. The highest peak is the 626-meter-high Katzenbuckel near Eberbach. After traversing a good portion of the Oldenwald, the route crosses the Tauber River to meet up with the Romantic Road, the oldest and most famous of Germany's scenic roads.

Starting in the beautiful baroque city of Würzburg and winding through a succession of varied landscapes, including the beautiful Tauber Valley, the Romantic Road passes through some of the best-preserved and most delightful medieval towns in Germany before concluding some 350 kms later in the pleasant Bavarian city of Füssen, site of two of King Ludwig's most famous castles: Neuschwanstein and Hohenschwangau.

For aficionados of European art and architecture, this route offers a wide variety of interesting structures, including the imposing ruins of Heidelberg Castle, the enchanting medieval town of Rothenburg ob der Tauber, the creative designs of Balthasar Neumann, the incredible intricate wood carvings of Tilman Riemenschneider, and the breathtaking beauty of the rococo Wies Church in southern Bavaria. By the time you arrive at the Füssen at the end of this route, you will have had an opportunity to sample all of the important European styles: Romanesque, Gothic, Renaissance, baroque, and rococo.

This route can be done by starting either at Heidelberg or Füssen. We found that it seemed to flow better when we pedaled from north to south and have set up our description that way. The hills seemed less ominous when we were heading south.

Heidelberg, an important crossroad lying on a major rail line, is readily accessible from all over the country. From Frankfurt it's about 80 kms down to Heidelberg. If you are cycling and are not intimidated by some pretty steep hills, follow the western edge of the Odenwald and pass through the delightful old towns of Bensheim and Heppenheim. If time is a problem, or if you are shy of hills, there are frequent trains between Frankfurt and Heidelberg.

THE CASTLE AND ROMANTIC ROADS ROUTE

START	FINISH
HEIDELBERG	FÜSSEN

DISTANCE
414 kms/257 miles

ADFC MAPS
#23, Rund um Mannheim;
#24, Würzburg-Heilbronn,
#25, Rund um Nürnberg;
#29, Donau-Lech/Augsburg;
#34, Allgau/Lechfeld
  (scale: 1:100,000)

DIE GENERALKARTE MAPS
#16, #19, #22, #25
  (scale 1:200,000)

The section from Heidelberg along the Neckar River is level and easy cycling. For most of the way, bicycle paths run right alongside the river. The section of the route across the Odenwald from Eberbach to the Romantic Road is pretty hilly and is definitely terrain for a ten-speed and a cyclist in good condition. However, there is a simple way to bypass the Oldenwald stretch. Instead of turning off at Eberbach, continue along the Castle Road, which follows the Neckar as it winds down to Heilbronn. From there, take the train to Lauda and continue on with the rest of the route.

The ride down the Romantic Road to its terminus at Füssen is a piece of cake. The cycling is easy and the landscape inspiring. Most of the northern part of the route is along marked cycle ways. From Nördlingen south to Füssen there are intermittent bike paths along the actual Romantic Road. This route often has heavy traffic especially during the summer. If you get tired of breathing exhaust fumes, there are several less heavily traveled roads that more or less parallel the Romantic Road.

With just a bit of a favorable nod from the weatherman, September is the ideal time to do this route. Since many of Germany's principal attractions are included, count on meeting up with a lot of fellow travelers if you decide to tour this region in July or August. By September you will be able to enjoy the attractions with a bit more peace and quiet. By the time October rolls around, the chances of hitting a cold, rainy spell increase, but if you are lucky you can pedal through the Odenwald and in the rolling hills of southern Bavaria to a backdrop of brilliant autumn colors and enjoy an unforgettable experience. Or you may be tempted to try to catch the blossoming of the fruit orchards in April and May, but combining that with warm sunshine is a pretty chancy business. Remember those April showers? They also have them in Germany! June can be a great month to travel this route as most European kids are still in school, and the weather is often perfect for cycling.

This is a great route for campers. Not only are there plenty of official campgrounds, but you will have all sorts of opportunities to pitch your tent in the forests and fields along the way. Maintain a low profile and keep your tent out of sight and you'll have no problems.

For those of you who feel the need for a soft feather bed at the end of the day's cycling, the route is lined with a profusion of accommodations ranging from modest mom and pop pensions to stately castle hotels.

Side Trips and Added Attractions

If you are coming south from Frankfurt, you can get in a good portion of the Odenwald and the Bergstrasse Nature Park on the way to Heidelberg. The best cycling starts just south of Darmstadt. This whole region is laced with hiking trails, dirt tracks, and forest service roads, which are ideal for getting the most out of your all-terrain bike.

If you have a little extra time and want to cycle the Romantic Road in its entirety, then after leaving the Neckar at Eberbach, follow the route as described to Mudau. From there head north, following the signs to Amorbach, Weilbach, and Miltenberg. From Miltenberg there is a bike path that runs along the Main River most of the way into Würzburg. At Bettingen on the Main, head east. Go under the autobahn and follow the signs to Würzburg, the starting point for the Romantic Road. The least heavily traveled route from Bettingen on the Main River into Würzburg will take you through Dertingen, Heimstadt, Waldbrunn, and Eisingen. You can pick up signs for the Romantic Road out of Würzburg by the Marienburg Fortress. If you miss these, head out of town in the direction of the zoo.

Another interesting side trip is to follow the continuation of the Castle Road past the intersection with the Romantic Road at Rothenberg ob der Tauber into Nürnberg with its fine old town section.

From Füssen at the end of this route you can continue with the "Bavarian Highlights Tour," as discussed earlier.

If you are bored with level stuff and want to test your gears and legs on some real mountains, take the following series of roads to link up with the "Lake Constance Route." From Füssen, take E532 to Nesselwang, turn off to Wertach and continue on to Immenstadt. Then pick up the German Alpine Highway (B308) and take it to Oberstaufen. From Oberstaufen, turn off toward Steinebach, Krebs, and the Austrian border. Continue on to Krumbach, then follow the road down into Bregenz on Lake Constance by way of Zwing, Kirchdorf, and Langen.

THE CASTLE AND ROMANTIC ROADS ROUTE

CITY
HEIDELBERG

ROUTE
B37 (Romantic Road)

DISTANCE KM	TOTAL KM
32	0

ROUTE DESCRIPTION
Leave Heidelberg by crossing the Neckar on the Alte Brücke. Follow the Heidelberger Strasse, which runs along the river bank, to the quaint medieval town of Neckargemünd. At this point the road merges with hwy B37. This is part of the famous Castle Road. There are intermittent stretches of bike paths between Heidelberg and Eberbach. This is delightful cycling country with great views of the river and castles perched on the surrounding hills.

CITY
EBERBACH

ROUTE
12311

DISTANCE KM	TOTAL KM
34	32

ROUTE DESCRIPTION
From the Eberbach tourist office, take Oldenwaldstrasse to the Friedrichsdorfer Landstrasse, following the sign to Gaimühle. After a short way the Friedrichsdorger Landstrasse becomes hwy 12311. (Don't follow the signs to Mudau unless you want to pedal 7 kms up an 8 percent grade). The road winds through the dense forest past a small lake into Gaimühle. Cross the stream and pick up the road to Mudau. There is a steep but short climb into Reisenbach. Then it's downhill all the way into Buchen by way of Mudau. Beyond Mudau the landscape changes from forest to rolling farmlands.

CITY
BUCHEN

ROUTE
B290 (Romantic Road)

DISTANCE KM	TOTAL KM
50	66

ROUTE DESCRIPTION
From Buchen, take the road to Hettingen and continue on through the hilly farm country past quiet villages with pointed church steeples. A series of little-traveled country roads will take you to Lauda on the Tauber River by way of

the tiny villages of Altheim, Gericht-stetten, Buch, and Heckfeld. Leaving Heckfeld, take the road toward Tauber Bischofsheim; after 1 km, turn off to the right to Lauda. After crossing the bridge over the Tauber you will intersect with hwy B290. Take the bike path that follows the road into Bad Mergentheim. This section of the route is marked with green and yellow signs.

CITY
BAD MERGENTHEIM

ROUTE
B19 (Romantic Road)

DISTANCE KM	TOTAL KM
49	116

ROUTE DESCRIPTION
Continue on to Rothenburg on the cycle path that follows the Romantic Road (B19) along the idyllic Tauber through the delightful ancient towns of Weiker-sheim, Röttingen, and Creglingen.

CITY
ROTHENBURG OB DER TAUBER

ROUTE
B25 (Romantic Road)

DISTANCE KM	TOTAL KM
40	165

ROUTE DESCRIPTION
From Rothenburg, continue on the good cycle path that follows the Romantic Road across the Frankenhöhe and along the Wornitz Valley into the historic town of Dinkelsbühl.

CITY
DINKELSBÜHL

ROUTE
B25 (Romantic Road)

DISTANCE KM	TOTAL KM
31	205

ROUTE DESCRIPTION
From Dinkelsbühl it's an easy 31 kms of bike path cycling along B25 to Nördlingen, which is set in the fertile Ries depression.

CITY
NÖRDLINGEN

ROUTE
B25 (Romantic Road)

DISTANCE KM	TOTAL KM
29	236

ROUTE DESCRIPTION
Take hwy B25 out of Nördlingen to Mottingen and then into Donauwörth. The cycle path ends at Mottingen although there are plans to continue it.

CITY
DONAUWÖRTH

ROUTE
B2 (Romantic Road)

DISTANCE KM	TOTAL KM
36	265

ROUTE DESCRIPTION

Leave Donauwörth crossing the Danube.
Then follow the signs to the suburb of
Nördheim and continue on the Romantic
Road (B2), which runs the entire way
into Augsburg. There is no cycle path
along this busy stretch at present. If
traffic is heavy, turn off B2 to Mertingen
and take the less congested side roads
via Nordendorf, Meitingen, Langweid,
and Gersthofen. At Gersthofen, pick up
the cycle path that will take you through
Augsburg.

CITY
AUGSBURG

ROUTE
B17 (Romantic Road)

DISTANCE KM	TOTAL KM
38	301

ROUTE DESCRIPTION

Head south out of Augsburg on B17,
which parallels the Lech River, and
continue to the fine old walled city of
Landsberg.

CITY
LANDSBERG AM LECH

ROUTE
B17 (Romantic Road)

DISTANCE KM	TOTAL KM
30	339

ROUTE DESCRIPTION

Leave Landsberg on the cycle path that
runs for several kms along B17 toward
Schongau. If you encounter heavy
traffic, you can escape on the much
less congested side roads through
Fuchstal, Denklingen, and Altenstadt
into Schongau.

CITY
SCHONGAU

ROUTE
B17 (Romantic Road)

DISTANCE KM	TOTAL KM
45	369

ROUTE DESCRIPTION

From the center of town, take the cycle
path across the Lech into Peiting and
follow B17 through the idyllic region
known as the Pfaffenwinkel. At
Steingaden, follow the signs 6 kms to
the Wies Kirche for an interesting side
trip. Return to Steingaden and follow
B17 against the striking backdrop of the
steeply rising alps into Schwangau/
Füssen, the southern terminus of the
Romantic Road.

CITY
FÜSSEN

DISTANCE KM	TOTAL KM
0	414

THE CASTLE AND ROMANTIC ROADS SIGHTS AND ACCOMMODATIONS

HEIDELBURG. Romantically situated among densely forested hills and overlooking the Neckar River, Heidelberg is home to Germany's oldest university and is high on the list of "must see places" for most Americans visiting Europe. A good part of the city's popularity can be attributed to composer Sigmund Romberg, who in 1924 set a popular play called *Old Heidelberg* to music. The result was the immortal operetta, *The Student Prince*, which has brought the romance of the ancient city to millions throughout the world. In spite of being the headquarters of the U.S. Army in Europe and being invaded every summer by armies of tourists, there is still much to recommend a visit to the city of the Student Prince.

The ruins of the ancient **Heidelberg Castle** loom above the city and afford a unusual perspective of the intricate maze of constricted alleys and rambling rooftops of the historic **Old Town**. Although the castle itself was destroyed by the French during the Thirty Years War in 1622, the ruins contain a number of interesting attractions, including **Das Grosse Fass**, the world's largest wine barrel – it holds 50,000 gallons – and the **Deutsches Apotheken Museum**, a unique apothecary museum. For more about the history of Heidelberg and to view the interior of the castle, be sure to take the interesting guided tour which is offered in English regularly during the summer. For a spectacular view of the castle and the city from across the river, hike up the **Philosophenweg** (Philosopher's Lane) and then climb the tower of the thirteenth-century **St. Stephan's Kloster**. The castle is magnificently illuminated at night and is the scene of a colorful **fireworks display** on the first Saturday nights of June, July, and August.

The university is the oldest in Germany and is the cultural and intellectual center of the city. It celebrated its six hundredth anniversary in 1986. Except for late summer when school is out, the students' presence is felt throughout the town.

Other interesting Heidelberg sights include the **Old Students' Jail**, the **Karl-Theodor Bridge**, and the town's principal museum, the **Kurpfälzisches Museum**, which contains a cast of the jaw of the Heidelberg man (50,000 BC). Heidelberg is one of the few important German cities to emerge unscathed from World War II, and a stroll among the original medieval buildings clustered around the picturesque Karl-Theodor Bridge is a rewarding experience.

As befits such a popular town, Heidelberg offers a wide range of accommodations. During the summer it's often tough to get a room. The tourist office located just outside of train station will help you find a room for a small fee.

The **Roter Ochsen** (Hauptstrasse 217) has been a favorite student hangout since 1703. If you drop in when school is in session you might actually encounter some real students among the tourists.

One of the best bargains and most convenient student hotels located at the edge of the old town under the shadow of the castle is the HOTEL JESKE (Mittelbadgasse 2; Tel: [06221] 23 733). Figure on paying about 35 DM for a pretty Spartan double without a bath or breakfast. The HOTEL REGINA (Luisenstrasse 6; Tel: [06221] 26 465) is a pleasant, convenient, and moderately priced hotel. All rooms come with a bath. The top luxury hotel in town is the DER EUROPÄISCHER HOF (Friedrich-Ebert-Anlage 1; Tel: [06221] 27 101), a venerable old establishment with an excellent restaurant. The rooms and meals are expensive.

The HEIDELBERG YOUTH HOSTEL (Tiergartenstrasse; Tel: [06221] 41 20 66) is a modern but often crowded hostel located next to the zoo across the river from the main part of town in Heidelberg Neuenheim. It is about a ten-minute bike ride from the train station.

Of the several campgrounds in the vicinity of Heidelberg, the most convenient to town is CAMPING NECKARTAL located right at the river in Schlierbach about 7 kms from the center of Heidelberg. It has a washing machine, small store, and is open 1 May to 15 October.

EBERBACH. One of those towns that few Americans have ever heard of, Eberbach is a gem of a small German resort town with a modern health spa and medicinal springs. Beautifully situated facing the quiet Neckar River and surrounded by the Oldenwald hills, the town contains a number of well-preserved old houses. Some, such as **Das Thalheim'sche Haus**, date back to the fourteenth century.

The enterprising local tourist office organizes week-long bicycle tours through the Neckar Valley using Eberbach as a base. The price per person for seven days half pension (room, breakfast, and either dinner or lunch), using your own bike, and including a guide is 230 DM. For details, contact **Kurverwaltung Eberbach** (Kellereistrasse 32-34, 6930 Eberbach am Neckar; Tel: [06271] 4899).

In addition to several good hotels there are a number of pleasant rooms available in private homes. For details, check in at the tourist office. For an absolutely charming small hotel, try the ALTES BADHAUS (am Lindenplatz, 6930 Eberbach; Tel: [06271] 5616). The seven delightful rooms are done in the old half-timbered style with all modern comforts. The restaurant is one of the region's finest. It will cost 100 DM for a double. A pleasant double without a bath can be had for about 60 DM at the GAST-HOF GRÜNER BAUM (Neckarstrasse 51; Tel: [06271] 2444).

The JUGENDHERBERGE EBERBACH (Richard-Schirrmann Strasse 6, 6930 Eberbach; Tel: [06271] 2593) is a pleasant hostel next to the campground run by Herr and Frau Bittner.

CAMPINGPARK EBERBACH is a pleasant grassy site directly at the river. The facilities include a camp store and washing machine. It is open 1 April to 30 September.

BUCHEN. Nestled in the forested hills of the Odenwald, Buchen is a delightful 1,200-year-old small town of leaning half-timbered houses and a well-preserved medieval old town center. Today Buchen is popular with vacationers from other parts of Germany who come to enjoy hiking in the surrounding Odenwald.

The HOTEL PRINZ CARL (Hochstadtstrasse 1, 6967 Buchen; Tel: [06281] 1877) is an attractive old hotel with a traditional wine *Stube*. The GASTHAUS ZUM

RIESEN (Marktstrasse 33; Tel: [06281] 3434) features modern reasonably priced rooms in an attractive half-timbered building located in the historic market square. The on-premises café features excellent local dishes.

The closest campground is in Eichenbuhl on the Erfa River about 20 kms to the north. With all of the woods in the area there is no reason to pedal all that way just to pitch a tent for the night.

BAD MERGENTHEIM. A well-known health spa, Bad Mergentheim is an attractive town with many fine medieval houses situated in the delightful Tauber Valley. The powerful Order of Teutonic Knights founded during the Crusades was headquartered in the imposing **Renaissance Mergentheim Palace** from 1525 until they were dislodged during the Napoleonic Wars. The Palace, which was redesigned by Balthasar Neumann in the eighteenth century, houses a museum on the Teutonic Order as well as an interesting local history museum. This picturesque ancient town also boasts of an interesting **automobile museum**.

Several Tauber Valley hotels participate in a scheme in which for a small fee they will transport your baggage to the next hotel along the way. For details, contact the tourist office, **Städtisches Verkehrsamt** (Marktplatz 3, 6990 Bad Mergentheim; Tel: [07931] 57 232).

The GASTHAUS RUMMLER (6990 Bad Mergentheim; Tel [07931] 2693) is a pleasant little ten-room gasthaus and restaurant in the Neunkirchen section of town. The BOCKSBEUTELSTEUBEN (Schlossgartenstrasse 23; Tel: [07931] 2339) is a small family-run hotel with a *gemütlich wein stube* and café in the center of town. For more luxurious accommodations, check in at the stately old KURHOTEL VICTORIA (Poststrasse 2-4; Tel: [07931] 5930).

The JUGENDHERBERGE IGERSHEIM (Erlenbachtalstrasse 44, 6990 Bad Mergentheim; Tel: [07931] 6373) is a first-class hostel with 150 beds. Meals are available and it is open all year.

CAMPING WILLINGER TAL, located about 2 kms south of town on the road to Wachbach, is a good well-equipped site with a washing machine, camp store, and restaurant. It is open all year.

ROTHENBURG OB DER TAUBER.

If ever there was a town worthy of being called a "living museum," Rothenburg ob der Tauber must surely lay claim to that title. Blot out the automobiles, tour buses, and camera-toting tourists and you are back in sixteenth-century Germany, albeit with modern conveniences. There is no single spectacular "must see" attraction, rather the appeal of this medieval jewel lies in the overall impressions you glean from wandering the narrow cobblestone streets, prowling the town's historic walls and bastions, and just soaking up the atmosphere. Give yourself some time there. Explore the town in the early morning hours or late in the evening when the tour buses have departed.

Throughout the year, Rothenburg is the scene of a variety of colorful events from costumed historical festivals to enchanting puppet shows. A full schedule of events is posted outside the tourist office in the Market Square.

While in Rothenburg, visit the impressive half-Gothic half-Renaissance **Town Hall** and climb up to the top of the sixty-meter-high tower for a bird's-eye view of the town and its fortifications. The twin-steepled **St. James Church** started in 1300 and completed in 1490 houses one of the finest examples of the wood-carver's art to found anywhere. The incredibly detailed figures of Tilman Riemenschneider's **Heiligen Blut Altar** seem to come to life under your gaze. Another outstanding example of the work of this inspired wood-carver is the famous **Crucifixon Altar** in the village church in neighboring Detwang. The **Medieval Criminal Museum**, the only one of its kind in Europe, has four floors of exhibits dealing with crime collected over the past seven centuries.

In this sixteenth-century Disneyland, one hotel seems to outcharm the other. If you stay in town, expect to pay a premium. One of our favorites in the big splurge category is the HOTEL EISENHUT (Herrngasse 3-5, 8803 Rothenburg o.d. Tauber; Tel: [09861] 2041), an amalgamation of several fine medieval patrician houses joined to make a truly delightful hotel. The rooms have period furnishings and inspiring vistas, while the excellent dining room overlooks the Tauber River. Although there are no great bargains to be had in Roth-

enburg, you can get a clean reasonably priced room in one of the town's many pensions. We like the ZUM SCHWARZEN LAMM (Detwang 21; Tel: [09861] 6727) located in neighboring Detwang and the GASTHOF KLINGENTOR (Mergentheimerstrasse 14; Tel: [09861] 3468), where a pleasant double will cost about 50 DM – about a quarter of the price of a room at the Eisenhut.

The JUGENDHERBERGE ROSSMÜHLE (Mühlacker 1, 8803 Rothenburg o.d. Tauber; Tel: [09861] 4510) is about a ten-minute walk from the tourist office in the direction of the old hospital. Housed in an old mill, the hostel offers a friendly atmosphere and a truly international crowd. Overflow accommodations in this busy town are provided at the JUGENDHERBERGE SPITALHOF (Tel: [09861] 7889) just next door.

The most convenient campground is CAMPING TAUBER IDYLL, located at the north edge of town in Detwang. The bike path from Bad Mergentheim passes right by. It is a nicely situated site, popular with campers from all over. The full facilities include a washing machine, camp store, and restaurant. CAMPING TAUBER-ROMANTIK in Detwang is a nice new campground, a welcome addition to relieve the often-crowded Camping Tauber Idyll. Both sites are open from Easter to 31 October.

DINKELSBÜHL. Every bit as attractive as Rothenburg, Dinkelsbühl, while not exactly void of tourists, is on the whole a lot more sedate. This is another great town for strolling and letting one's fantasies run free. The cobblestone streets are lined with enchanting fifteenth-century and sixteenth-century houses. One of the most elaborate is the **Deutsches Haus**, a fifteenth-century half-timbered historic inn. **Saint George's Cathedral** in the town center, while not actually a cathedral, is nonetheless a most impressive fifteenth-century ecclesiastical structure housing yet another of Tilman Riemenschneider's carved masterpieces.

The town is particularly lively and colorful during the **Kinderzeche**, a children's festival held in mid-July to commemorate the town's salvation in the Thirty Years War. There is also a colorful open air drama festival in July and August. You can get details from Tourist Information (Marktplatz, 8804 Dinkelsbühl; Tel: [09851] 3013.

The number one hotel choice of most people headed for Dinkelsbühl is the ornate fifteenth-century DEUTSCHES HOUSE (Weinmarkt 3, 8804 Dinkelsbühl; Tel: [09851] 2346) just across the Marktplatz. It is a great place and not all that expensive – but there are only thirteen rooms! It is best to reserve well in advance. If you don't get in, don't despair; there are several other charming spots to spend the night. In any case, treat yourself to a fine meal and soak up the atmosphere at their cozy restaurant. The last time we pedaled by this way, we had an enjoyable stay at the comfortable old HOTEL GOLDENE ROSE (Marktplatz 4; Tel: [09851] 831).

There is no better way to get in the spirit of this medieval town than to stay in an early seventeenth-century building. The IYHF Hostel, JUGENDHERBERGE DINKELSBÜHL (Köppinggasse 10, 8804 Dinkelsbühl; Tel: [09851] 509), is housed in a great old building that dates back to 1609.

DCC CAMPINGPARK ROMANTISCHE STRASSE just outside of town off B25 in the direction of Feuchtwangen is a large first-class site with a full range of facilities, including a washing machine, restaurant, and camp store. There is a good view of the town across a small lake. It is open all year.

NÖRDLINGEN. A delightful town where the local inhabitants still dress in traditional costumes on market day and observe many of the ancient medieval customs, Nördlingen is billed as the "living medieval city." A fine example of a fortified town, the city is completely ringed by massive walls topped by roofed parapet walkways ideal for observing the town's beautiful setting in the bowl of the Ries Depression, one of the world's largest meteor craters. The **"Daniel,"** as the tower of the fifteenth-century Gothic **Saint George's Church** is called, is a perfect place from which study the layout and fortifications of this classic medieval town. Every three years in September a colorful **Historical City Wall Festival** is held in the old town. The next dates are 1987 and 1990.

Prices are a bit more reasonable in Nördlingen than at some of the more heavily visited Romantic Road cities, such as Rothenburg. For a charming old world inn with modern comforts, try the five-hundred-year-old HOTEL SONNE (Marktplatz 3, 8860 Nördlingen; Tel: [09081] 5067), where a double will set you back about 100 DM. In the budget category, try the GASTHOF DREI MOHREN (Reimlinger Strasse 18; Tel: [09081] 3113).

Considering the availability of much more pleasant accommodations for only a few additional marks, there's not a whole lot of incentive to stay at the local military-type youth hostel. JUGENDHERBERGE NÖRDLINGEN, (Kaiserwiese 2; Tel: [09081] 84 100) is located at the edge of town near the Baldinger Tor.

The nearest campground is about 5 kms southwest of town in Utzmemmingen. CAMPING GASTHOF TIESBLICKE has limited facilities and an adjacent restaurant. It is open all year.

DONAUWÖRTH. Until the seventeenth century, Donauwörth was known by the name of Werd. It is a quiet market town lying at the confluence of the Danube and Wornitz rivers. In imperial times, the town was an important way station on the trade route between Augsburg and Nüremberg. Of interest to visitors are the **Reichstrasse** with the Town Hall, the **parish church**, the **House of the Knights of the Teutonic Order** and **Leitheim Castle**.

Somewhat off the beaten tourist path, Donauwörth has several good moderately priced hotels and *gasthauses*. For a pleasant hotel with a good restaurant, try the HOTEL DONAUWÖRTHER HOF (Teutonenweg 16, 8850 Donauwörth; Tel: [0906] 5950). A double at the tiny PENSION GRAF (Zirgesheimer Strasse 5; Tel: [0906] 5117) will run about 50 DM.

The closest campground is about 7 kms to the south just off the main road to Augsburg near the train station in Mertingen. CAMPING ZUM ZUGLE is a small site with limited facilities. It is good for an overnight stay and is open all year.

AUGSBURG. From the time of its founding in 15 BC by the Roman emperor Augustus whose name it bears, Augsburg has been an important crossroads in the development of European trade and commerce. The oldest city on the Romantic Road, Augsburg was a Roman provincial capital for more than four centuries and a free imperial city for five hundred years before becoming part of the kingdom of Bavaria in the early nineteenth century. The city's Golden Age took place during the Renaissance when it blossomed culturally and economically under the auspices of two powerful banking families, the Fuggers and Welsers. It was the Fuggers, at one time Europe's wealthiest family, who in addition to generously endowing the arts were responsible for establishing the world's first social housing project. Founded in 1519 and called the **Fuggerei**, it is still in operation and may be seen just east of the town center.

In addition to the Fuggerei, the old town section contains some other interesting reminders of its glorious past. The modern parts of the city are of little interest. Maximillianstrasse, the town's main street is dotted with lovely Renaissance mansions. At the foot of Maximillanstrasse are a pair of particularly attractive fifteenth-century churches, one Catholic and the other Protestant, both called **Saint Ulrich**. The imposing **cathedral** (dom) at the north end of town dates back to the tenth century. In the summer months, Mozart concerts are held in the court behind the cathedral.

Augsburg boasts of a number of prominent native sons, including Jakob Fugger, Hans Holbein, Leopold Mozart, Rudolf Diesel, Bertold Brecht, and Willy Messerschmidt.

The tourist office (Bahnhofstrasse 7) near the train station can give brochures and information about local cycle tours in the nearby Nature Park Augsburg Westliche Wälder. For dining with fine food and loads of atmosphere, try the **Fuggerkeller** in the cellars of the former Fugger residence.

The HOTEL DREI MOHREN (Maximillianstrasse 40, 8900 Augsburg, Tel: [0821] 51 00 31) has been an Augsburg institution since 1723, attracting such guests as Goethe and Mozart. Destroyed during World War II, the hotel has been restored in a blending of contemporary and traditional decor. It is conveniently located near the center of the old town and rooms are expensive. A more modest but pleasant hotel is the DOM HOTEL (Frauentorstrasse 8; Tel: [08021] 15 30 31), just a few blocks north of the cathedral. At the budget end of the accommodations spectrum are a number of pensions. PENSION VIOLA (Herrenbachstrasse 19; Tel: [0821] 55 54 59) at the east end of town near the Lech River is one of the town's best bargains with doubles without a bath going for 50 DM.

The GROSSJUGENDHERBERGE (Beim Pfaffenkeller 3, 8900 Augsburg; Tel: [0821] 33 909) is a large, modern, 170-bed hostel conveniently located just a few minutes walk east of the cathedral.

There are two campsites in the immediate vicinity of the city. The most convenient is CAMPINGPLATZ AUGUSTA, a large site located on a lake just off the Munich-Augsburg autobahn at the northeast edge of the city about 4 kms from the town center. The campground's full facilities include a washing machine, restaurant, and camp store. It is open all year.

LANDSBERG AM LECH. Beautifully situated in a lovely wooded area above the Lech River and almost completely encircled by a well-preserved medieval wall complete with turrets and towers, Landsberg has served as an important cultural link between Schwabia and Bavaria for centuries. The attractive old town is the scene of the well-known **Ruethenfest**. Every four years the colorfully costumed children of Landsberg present a parade illustrating important happenings from the town's rich history. Check with the tourist office (*Verkehrsamt*) (Hauptplätz 1 8910; Tel: [08191] 12 82 46) in Landsberg for details on this and the many other colorful pageants held in the busy little medieval town.

The tourist office will also provide you with itineraries for several interesting cycle tours in the beautiful surrounding countryside, including accommodations, breakfast, luggage transportation from hotel to hotel, and the use of a three-speed bike. The price for these six-day tours runs about 350 DM per person. You ride at your own pace, without a guide, on well-marked cycle trails.

The town's architectural pride is the Gothic **Bayertor**, one of the most impressive gateways in southern Germany.

The HOTEL GÖGGL (Herkomerstrasse 19-20, 8910 Landsberg am Lech; Tel: [08191] 2081) is a conveniently located, comfortable, middle-class hotel. Inexpensive rooms are also available in private homes. The tourist office will provide you with a list and help in making arrangements. For a clean, comfy room in a quiet neighborhood, try HAUS ANNA KRAMER (Alpenstrasse 8; Tel: [08191] 50 465).

The DCC CAMPINGPARK ROMANTIK AM LECH is a particularly attractive site with superb views of the surrounding countryside. It is just a few minutes cycling from town. The campground's modern facilities include a laundromat, camp store, and restaurant. It is open all year.

STEINGADEN. Located about midway between Schongau and Füssen, Steingaden is the closest town of any size to the **Wies Kirche**, built between 1746 and 1754 by Dominikus Zimmermann. *Wies* means meadow in the local Bavarian dialect and the church is located in one. With spectacular alpine vistas in the background, this pilgrimage shrine is considered to be the finest example of a rococo church in all of Europe.

SCHONGAU. Schongau is another one of those delightful little German towns that few people outside of Germany have ever heard of. The town, still surrounded by nearly intact medieval walls, was founded toward the end of the eleventh century. Picturesquely situated on a hill overlooking the Lech River, Schongau was for centuries an important station on the Via Claudia, the old Roman trade route between Augsburg and Verona, Italy. Worth taking a look at in this well-preserved medieval town are the Gothic **Ballenhaus** and the **Church of the Assumption**.

The town has several good small hotels, including the comfortable HOTEL ALTE POST (Marienplatz 19, 8920 Schongau; Tel: [08861] 8058), which has a good restaurant with a first-class *patisserie* on the premises. Doubles go for about 90 DM. A room for two will cost you about 60 DM at the GASTHOF ZUR SONNE (Lindenplatz 13; Tel [08861] 7275).

There is no official campground in Schongau; however, you should have no problem finding a place in the local forests or getting permission to pitch a tent for the night from a local farmer.

FÜSSEN / SCHWANGAU. In a magnificent setting at the base of the Algau alps at an elevation of some 800 meters, Füssen and the neighboring town of Schwangau are the terminus of the Romantic Road and the gateway to the Austrian alps. Although the towns with their medieval stone buildings are in themselves a most interesting destination, most people who pass through here are mainly interested in seeing "the Disneyland Castle." What they are referring to is one of King Ludwig of Bavaria's extravagant creations, **Neuschwanstein**, one of the most impressive castles in Germany. Referred to as the Disneyland castle because it was used as the model for the castle at Disneyland, with its conglomeration of pinnacles, turrets, towers, and ornate furnishings, Neuschwanstein is not to be missed. King Ludwig lived in his dream castle for less than a year before he drowned mysteriously in the nearby Starnberg Lake. **Hohenschwangau** just up the hill from Neuschwanstein is a much more conventional castle. It was here that Ludwig grew up. Both castles are perched in magnificent settings in the hills just a few minutes ride from Schwangau.

The HOTEL SONNE (Reichenstrasse 37, 8958 Füssen; Tel: (08362) 6061) is a popular, rustic, moderately priced hotel in the center of Füssen. For an inexpensive pension, try PENSION ROGG (Gernspitzstrasse 10; Tel: (08362) 7235). The comfortable PENSION HEIM (Landweg 3; Tel: (08362) 7507) is a delightful house in a lovely garden setting in Füssen-Bad Faulenbach, just a few minutes from the center of town – a real gem.

The often very crowded youth hostel, JUGENDHERBERGE FÜSSEN (Mariahilfer Weg 5, Tel: [083621] 7754), is located just a few minutes from the train station.

The INTERNATIONALER CAMPINGPLATZ HOPFENSEE, located right on the shores of nearby Hopfensee is one the best-equipped campsites in southern Germany. It is located about 6 kms from the castles and is open all year except 1 November to 15 December.

The Rhine and Moselle Valleys

Old castles, some little more than ruins, and well-preserved medieval fortresses positioned like vigilant sentinels dot the steep vineyard-covered inclines that rise up on both sides of the Rhine, one of the world's great rivers. Beginning as a mere trickle at its source in the glaciers of the Swiss Alps, the Rhine increases in size and momentum along its more than eight-hundred-mile journey through Switzerland, France, Germany, and Holland before emptying into the North Sea. The stretch we cover in our cycling route, running from Wiesbaden to Cologne, a distance of some 150 kms, is without a doubt the most fascinating portion of this magnificent river. Although reports of pollution and overdevelopment in recent years have tarnished its reputation, there is still plenty to recommend seeing the Rhine Valley from the saddle of your bicycle. After all you don't have to drink the water!

No other stretch of river in the world offers such a conglomeration of castles of all sizes and shapes. But it's not just the castles, romantic tales, and ancient legends of Rhine maidens and heroic knights that make the Rhine Valley so fascinating. Pedaling along the river as it cuts its way through scenic gorges, you will pass through a picture-postcard landscape of enchanting villages and vineyard-clad hills. In the days before motorized transport, the Rhine was one of Europe's principal thoroughfares; in fact, many of the castles along this route, including the unique Die Pfalz near Kaub, were built to aid the local lords and robber barons (who were often one in the same) in the collection of tolls. The Rhine still plays an important role in the transport of goods. As you follow the river, you'll be treated to a steady procession of colorful barges chugging up stream against the strong current and cruising downstream toward the North Sea. Whenever we're in the vicinity we always have problems accepting the fact that the water really is flowing in the right direction. It seems like it should flow down to Basel rather than "uphill" into the North Sea! The river is suitable for commercial traffic all the way to the Swiss port of Basel.

This area includes some of the world's finest white wine producing regions. Connoisseurs claim that the best grapes are grown in the Rheingau, which lies along the river between Wiesbaden and Koblenz. The last portion of this route, which follows the tortuous course of the Moselle as it winds its way to meet up with the Rhine at Koblenz, will take you through another delightful wine-producing region with fine castles at Cochem and Eltz.

In between the Rhine and the Moselle, our route will take you through a part of Germany not usually visited by American tourists. It's called the "Eifel," an area of great natural beauty characterized by low mountains and a unique series of crater lakes known in German as *maars*. The border city of Aachen, with its famous imperial cathedral, and the ancient Roman city of Trier, are convenient gateways to the Eifel region.

In addition to sampling the profusion of fine wines produced along this route, you will have ample opportunity to sample some tasty local dishes, including *sauerbraten*, a pot roast that is marinated in red wine and spices for several days. Another local favorite is *himmel und erde*, which literally means heaven and earth. This dish will give you enough of a carbohydrate load to propel you up the steepest of mountain roads. It's a casserole made of potatoes, apples, sugar, bacon, onions, and blood sausage.

The Rhinelanders are known throughout Germany for their friendliness and fun-loving ways. Around harvest time, the clinking of glasses from the many boisterous wine festivals can be heard up and down the valley.

For those of you arriving in Frankfurt, this route is an excellent introduction to European cycling. From Frankfurt, it's about 40 kms of cycling to reach Mainz, following the Main as it runs down to the Rhine a good part of the way through a heavily industrialized area. Otherwise hop on a train and head toward Mainz or Rüdesheim where the most interesting part of the river begins.

THE RHINE AND MOSELLE VALLEYS TOUR

START	FINISH	DISTANCE
MAINZ	BINGEN/RÜDESHEIM	646 kms/402 miles

DIE GENERALKARTE MAPS	ADFC MAPS
#10, #12, #15 (scale 1:200,000)	#18, Westerwald-Taunus; #17, Eifel-Mosel/Ahrtal; #14, Köln-Aachen/Rhurgebiet (scale 1:100,000)

The view over the handlebars is everchanging: castles, vineyards, heavily laden river barges, often with the captain's wash fluttering in the breeze, sleek sightseeing boats, and everywhere, inviting riverside towns with their steeply roofed, half-timbered houses and colorful riverfront cafés and restaurants.

The sections of the route that run along the Rhine and Moselle banks offer easy cycling and provide excellent opportunities for watching the busy and colorful river traffic. Although this is a popular area, it is possible to avoid the swarms of autos and tour buses by sticking to the marked cycle paths that follow the course of these two important rivers. As is usually the case when riding next to a river, the terrain is basically level; however, in many places the rivers are flanked by deep gorges and steep vine-covered hills. As soon as you venture away from either river, the pedaling gets tough.

For this route we have chosen to follow both rivers in a downstream direction. It has to be psychological, but it always seems to be easier to follow a river downstream than to pedal against the current.

The portion of the route through the Eifel, especially between Aachen and Trier, contains some pretty challenging terrain. There are few cycle paths; however, the region is not heavily infested with motorized traffic and there are enough secondary roads to keep you out of the way of exhaust fumes. The grades encountered are generally steep but short, and most peaks are 500 to 600 meters high. The highest point in the Eifel is the 750-meter-high Hohe Acht near Adenau. The hills are densely forested and are cut by numerous meandering rivers and streams. The pleasant landscape is frequently punctuated by charming little towns and idyllic villages. Throughout your tour of the Eifel, you will encounter examples of the region's most characteristic natural features: numerous crater lakes or *maaren* crown the eroded tops of the Eifel's many extinct volcanoes.

If you just stick to the river valley portions of the route and take the train from either Cologne or Aachen to Trier, the route can be pedaled by even the most timid cyclist. A multispeed bike is not an absolute necessity for the river stretches; however, a good ten-speed or more should be used to tackle the Eifel.

This part of Germany, particularly the Rhine region, has been catering to foreign guests for well over a hundred years. During this time an extensive and efficient infrastructure has been developed so that you can choose between treating yourself to the luxury of overnighting in romantic castle hotels or pitching your tent at a campground along the river and watching the barges and excursion boats glide by. In all categories, from modest pensions to posh hotels, you will find the standards of service and cleanliness to be beyond reproach.

Cycling along this route can be very pleasant any time from late April to mid-October, unless you encounter a spell of cold, rainy weather. The possibilities of hitting such a spell of unpleasant weather in central Germany between April and October are pretty high; however, you can minimize this risk by touring during July and August when your main concern will be threading your way between the throngs of tourists who invade the Rhine Valley every summer. The Moselle and Eifel regions, while not exactly deserted, are a lot less crowded. The entire region is particularly attractive in late April and May when the orchards are in blossom. During late September and early October, the towns along the Rhine and Moselle are hosts to a series of colorful wine festivals. Details are available from local tourist offices or from the **German National Tourist Office**.

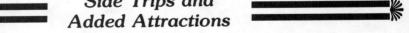

Side Trips and Added Attractions

This route easily links up with the "Castle and Romantic Roads Tour." It is about 80 kms from Mainz to Heidelberg.

Once you get to Aachen you will be within a short cycling distance of Holland and Belgium. From Trier, it's a simple matter to cycle in Germany, Luxembourg, and France all in the same day.

One of the most pleasant ways to enjoy the Rhine or Moselle is on board a sightseeing boat. It's a great way to take a break from pedaling and still keep moving. The possibilities are many, ranging from short hops of less than a hour to luxury cruises lasting several days. Ticket and information stands are situated all along the river. There is no extra charge for transporting your bike.

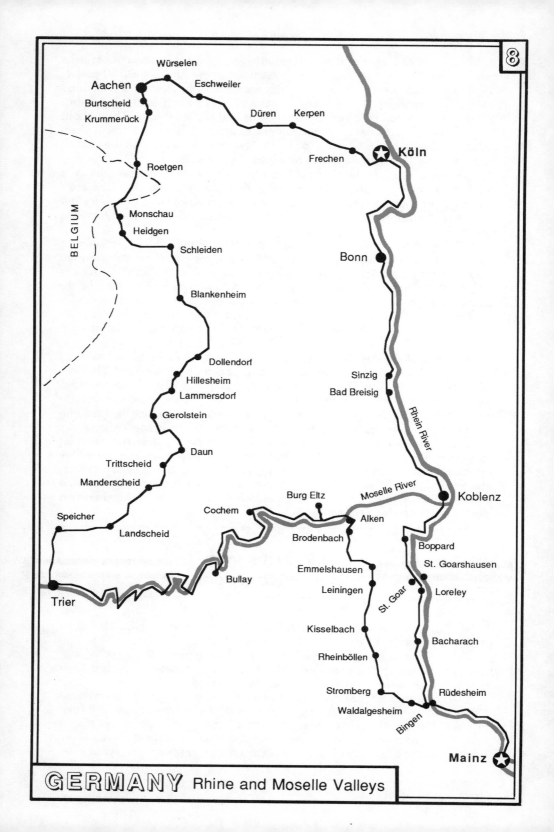

GERMANY Rhine and Moselle Valleys

THE RHINE AND MOSELLE VALLEYS

CITY
MAINZ

ROUTE
B42

DISTANCE KM	TOTAL KM
35	0

ROUTE DESCRIPTION
From the center of Mainz, take the bridge over the Rhine and follow B42 along the right bank of the river into Rüdesheim. There are bike paths for just a short part of this stretch. Traffic during July and August is apt to be pretty heavy. After leaving the Mainz region you will notice that the steep right bank of the river is lined with vineyards. Called the Rheingau, this is one of Germany's prime wine-producing areas.

CITY	ROUTE
RÜDESHEIM	B9

DISTANCE KM	TOTAL KM
28	35

ROUTE DESCRIPTION
Take the ferry across the Rhine from Rüdesheim to Bingen. Pick up B9 to Bonn which runs along the left bank for two good reasons: The scenery is better and there is a cycle path for most of the way. Although the route itself is quite level, the hills on both banks of the river rise rather steeply. Allow some time for a stop at Bacharach, one of the most attractive towns along the river. Be sure to see the Loreley rock on your right just before St. Goar.

CITY
ST. GOAR/ST. GOARSHAUSEN

ROUTE
B9

DISTANCE KM	TOTAL KM
39	63

ROUTE DESCRIPTION
From St. Goar there is an almost continuous cycle path that parallels B9 and follows the Rhine on its serpentine course down to Koblenz, where it is joined by the Moselle. Just beyond the pleasant little town of Boppard, the steep gorges end and the surrounding countryside flattens out.

CITY
KOBLENZ

ROUTE
B9

DISTANCE KM	TOTAL KM
60	102

ROUTE DESCRIPTION
A cycle path follows the river and parallels B9 most of the way to Bonn. At Bad Breisig, it's necessary to cut inland along B9 to Sinzig. From Sinzig, the path returns to the Rhine for the rest of the way into Bonn.

CITY
BONN

DISTANCE KM	TOTAL KM
25	162

ROUTE DESCRIPTION
Continue along the river about 25 kms into Köln (Cologne).

CITY
KÖLN (COLOGNE)

ROUTE
B264 B57

DISTANCE KM	TOTAL KM
60	187

ROUTE DESCRIPTION
Making your way through the maze of Cologne traffic, head west for Kerpen, a pleasant little village on an artificial lake about 15 kms from the center of Cologne. Your best bet for getting out of the city is to pick up B264 which goes to Frechen and then Kerpen. There is a bike path most of the way. From Kerpen take B264 to Düren. Continue on B264 out of Düren to Eschweiler along the border of the German-Belgian nature reserve. From Eschweiler follow the bike path along B264 to Würselen. In Würselen, connect with the bike path that follows B57 into Aachen.

CITY	ROUTE
AACHEN	B258

DISTANCE KM	TOTAL KM
25	247

ROUTE DESCRIPTION
From the center of Aachen, take B258 out of the city, through the suburbs of Burtscheid and Krummerück, and on to Roetgen. Most of the way you will travel on a cycle path. Climb the hill out of Roetgen and stay with B258, cutting across a corner of Belgium to reach Monschau.

CITY
MONSCHAU

ROUTE
B258

DISTANCE KM	TOTAL KM
77	272

ROUTE DESCRIPTION
Take the road to Heidgen, then pick up B258 which runs through the forest down into Schleiden. From Schleiden, B258 climbs up through a wooded hilly area before reaching Blankenheim. Follow B258 along the Ahr River to the junction with the road to Dollendorf. Leave the Ahr and follow the stream up to the village of Dollendorf. From there, continue to Hillesheim. Leave Hillesheim on the road to Gerolstein by way of Lammersdorf.

CITY
GEROLSTEIN

DISTANCE KM	TOTAL KM
42	349

ROUTE DESCRIPTION
From Gerolstein, the road to Daun climbs sharply. Take the road out of Daun to Trittscheid, then continue on, following the signs to Manderscheid.

CITY
MANDERSCHEID

DISTANCE KM	TOTAL KM
47	391

ROUTE DESCRIPTION

From Manderscheid it's mostly downhill all the way to Landscheid. Leaving Landscheid, follow the signs to Speicher. From there take the road down to the Kyll River. Follow the river partly on a forest road and partly on a lightly traveled highway as it winds its way down to the Moselle at Trier.

CITY	ROUTE
TRIER	B53

DISTANCE KM	TOTAL KM
51	438

ROUTE DESCRIPTION

From Trier, follow the tortuous course of the Moselle as it flows toward the Rhine. For most of the way you have the choice of bike trails on either side of the river. Some of Germany's finest wines are produced in this hilly region and as you pedal along the river there will be ample tasting opportunities.

CITY
BERNKASTEL-KUES

ROUTE
B53 B49

DISTANCE KM	TOTAL KM
82	489

ROUTE DESCRIPTION

From Bernkastel, continue along the bike path adjacent to B53, which follows the Moselle. At Bullay, the highway changes to B49. The cycle path continues most of the way into Cochem.

Note: To avoid the following stretch, which is lovely but rather hilly riding through a little visited part of the Rhineland, continue from Cochem along the Moselle about 30 kms to rejoin the Rhine at Koblenz. From Koblenz, either follow the Rhine back to Bingen or take the train from Koblenz to Heidelberg to connect with the "Castle and Romantic Roads Tour."

CITY	ROUTE
COCHEM	B49 B416

DISTANCE KM	TOTAL KM
75	571

ROUTE DESCRIPTION

Follow the cycle path from Cochem down the river to Burg Eltz. Cross the river at Alken and head back 2.5 kms to Brodenbach on the cycle path adjacent to B49. From Brodenbach, take the road to Emmelshausen and continue on to Rheinböllen, passing through Leiningen and Kisselbach. The road then follows the Guldenbach River into Stromberg. From Stromberg, follow the signs to rejoin the Rhine at Bingen, passing under the autobahn and through Waldalgesheim.

CITY
BINGEN

DISTANCE KM	TOTAL KM
0	646

RHINE AND MOSELLE VALLEYS SIGHTS AND ACCOMMODATIONS

MAINZ. A two-thousand-year-old city at the point where the Main flows into the Rhine, Mainz is perhaps best known for its native son, Johannnes Gutenberg, who invented movable type in the You can see the **original Gutenberg Bible** and a replica of this innovative printer's press at the **Gutenberg Museum** on the Liebfrauenplatz. The **Mainz Cathedral** is of interest for its fine art treasures, otherwise the city doesn't offer a whole lot. The really interesting parts of the Rhine start down river from here.

If you arrive in Mainz on the train, you'll find the HOTEL HAMMER (Bahnhofplatz 6, 6500 Mainz; Tel: [06131] 61 10 61) just across from the train station – a clean, modern, moderately priced hotel. In the budget category, try the GASTHOF GOLDENE ENTE (Oppenheimer Str. 2, Tel: [06131] 86 116).

The IYHF JUGENDHERBERGE (am Fort Weisenau, 6500 Mainz; Tel: [06131] 85 332) is at the river near the Weisenau train station. There are 220 beds and breakfast is available. There is also a hostel across the river in Wiesbaden: JUNGENDHERBERGE WIESBADEN (Blucherstr. 66; Tel: [06121] 48 657).

There are several conveniently located campgrounds on the river between Mainz and Wiesbaden. CAMPING MAINZ-WIES-BADED MAARAUE is a large site right at the junction of the Main and Rhine. From Mainz, cross the Rhine bridge and turn right. The site is well marked. It has a washing machine and camp store and a restaurant is nearby. The campground is open 1 April to 30 September.

RUDESHEIM. One of the principal wine towns on the Rhine, Rüdesheim is also one of the most popular with tour operators. The town always seems to be packed with tourists. The main attraction, the **Drosselgasse**, is a narrow alley packed with wine bars, restaurants, and souvenir shops. There are several wineries that offer tours, including the firm of Asbach-Uralt. Details can be obtained from the busy but helpful tourist office (Rhein Str. 16) on the river between the train station and boat docks. One of the region's best wine museums is housed in the nearly one-thousand-year-old **Bromserburg** at the west end of town. For a bird's-eye view of the Rhine without pedaling up the steep hills rising above the river bank, take the chairlift to Niederwald. On an island in the middle of the river is the famous **Mouse Tower**. The **Mouse Castle** is farther downriver. In August Rüdesheim is the scene of a boisterous wine festival. Check with the tourist office for exact dates.

The WALDHOTEL JAGDSCHLOSS NIEDERWALD (Auf dem Niederwald, 6220 Rüdesheim; Tel: [06722] 1004) is an authentic Rhine castle turned hotel. This was once the hunting lodge of the Archbishop of Mainz. Stash your bike at the train station and take the cable car or pedal about 3 kms up the hill to the hotel. It is closed in the winter. For more down-to-earth lodgings both in price and altitude, try the GASTOF WINZERSCHANKE (Markt Str. 27; Tel: [06722] 2733).

The RÜDESHEIM JUNGENDHER-BERGE (am Drachenfels, 6220 Rüdesheim; Tel: [06722] 2711) is in the hills overlooking the town.

The CAMPINGPLATZ AM RHEIN is nicely situated on the river just 600 meters from town. It has good facilities, which include a washing machine, camp store, and restaurant. The campground is open 1 May to 30 September.

ST. GOAR/ST. GOARSHAUSEN.

Attractive twin towns perched on opposite sides of the Rhine, St. Goar and St. Goarshausen command one of the most romantic stretches of this fabled river. The towns are connected by regular ferry service across this placid portion of the Rhine. Only a few kms upstream on the St. Goarshausen side sits one Europe's most written and sung about hunks of rock: the legendary **Loreley**. The days of such sirens are long past and the modern Rhine sailors now glide smugly by in huge barges equipped with the latest radar devices to ward off any eventual return to those treacherous days of the Rhine sagas. Nevertheless the Loreley has a permanently established honored place in German folklore.

Burg Rheinfels is an expansive fortress that has been watching over this portion of the Rhine from a solid perch in the hills above St. Goar for over seven hundred years. Visiting all of the castles along this stretch would probably consume most, if not all, of the time allotted for your trip. However, there are a few more worth stopping to explore, including **Burg Katz** at the southern edge of St. Goarshausen and **Burg Maus** about 2 kms downstream. Another famous landmark is **Die Pfalz**, an impressive looking multiturreted fortress-like medieval toll station sitting on a tiny island in the middle of the river just a short distance upstream from St. Goar. The castle perched on the hill above Kaub is **Burg Gutenfels**.

Built into the ruins of the ancient Rheinfels Castle and looking out across the Rhine is one of the more romantically situated Rhineland hotels with a first-class terrace restaurant: SCHLOSSHOTEL RHEINFELS (Schlossberg 47, 5401 St. Goar; Tel: [06741] 2071). Figure on paying about 110 to 140 DM for a double. For a pleasant, more modest hotel, try the HOTEL WINZERHAUS LORELEY (An der Loreley 49, Tel: [06741] 334). On the other side of the river in St. Goarshausen, we like the cozy little HOTEL LORELEY SCHLÖSSCHEN (Rhein Str. 60; Tel: [06771] 463). At HAUS ZIMMERMAN (Loreley Plateau; Tel: [06771] 489), a modest pension, you can get a double for about 40 DM.

Each of the twin towns has a youth hostel (Bismarck Weg 17, 5401 St. Goar; Tel: [06741] 388 and AUF DER LORELEY, 5422 St. Goarshausen; Tel: [06771] 619).

Like the towns themselves, there are twin campgrounds that face each other across the river. In St. Goar, it's CAMPING LORELEYBLICK, a large site on the river just south of town with a wonderful view of the Loreley Cliff and Burg Katz. It has a camp store and restaurant and is open all year. Across the river is CAMPING LORELEYSTADT, on the riverbank at the south end of St. Goarshausen. The castle that you see when you look up is Burg Rheinfels. The campground is open 15 March to 31 October.

KOBLENZ.

Koblenz can trace its history back to its founding by the Romans. Located at the confluence of the Rhine and Moselle rivers, it is little wonder that Koblenz has developed into an important tourist center. The exact meeting point of these two rivers is at a narrow sliver of land dubbed **Deutsches Eck**, or German Corner. **Ehrenbreitstein Fortress**, one of the city's landmarks, is a massive early nineteenth-century structure. Looking down upon the city from its perch across the river, the fortress affords a magnificent view of the joining of the Rhine and Moselle. Located within its walls is a youth hostel. The fortress can be reached either by road or by way of a chairlift that rises up from the city. The history of Koblenz and that of the surrounding area is well presented at the **Middle Rhine Museum**.

HOTEL TRIERER HOF (Dienhardplatz 1, 5400 Koblenz; Tel: [0261] 31060) is a good moderately priced hotel well located near the town's center. PENSION MACKLER (Helffenstein Str. 63, Tel: [0261] 73725) on the fortress side of the river offers rooms for under 50 DM.

The two-hundred-room JUGENDHERBERGE KOBLENZ (Ehrenbreitstein Fortress; Tel: [0261] 73737) is located in one of the region's most impressive sites.

CAMPINGPLATZ RHEIN-MOSEL is a large site across from the Deutsches Eck at the Rhine-Moselle confluence. It has good views of the fortress and Deutsches Eck and a washing machine on site. There are stores within 1 km. It is open Easter to 15 October.

BONN/BAD GODESBERG. The capital of western Europe's most powerful industrial nation is a provincial town on the Rhine. Bonn is definitely not in the "major leagues" of capital cities. What Bonn does have to offer is the attraction of a quiet town with the international flair that is part and parcel of being the capital of such an important nation. Of sightseeing interest are **Beethoven's Birthplace** and the twelfth-century Romanesque church, the **Münster**. A stroll through the shopping district in adjoining Bad Godesberg where most of the diplomats live is a bit like visiting the United Nations. The streets and shops are full of Africans, Arabs, and Orientals often dressed in their colorful native dress. An unusual sight for small town Germany!

As in most places where there is a large diplomatic presence, hotel rooms are expensive. The appropriately named HOTEL BEETHOVEN (Rheingasse 26, 5300 Bonn; Tel: [0228] 63 14 11) is a modern moderately priced hotel well located by the river. Another good moderately priced bet is the centrally located HOTEL BERGISCHER HOF (Münsterplatz 23; Tel: [0228] 63 34 41). One of the few inexpensive pensions in the area is PENSION ZECK (Rheinallee 29, Tel: [0228] 36 31 03).

JUGENDHERBERGE BONN (Venusberg, Haager Weg, 5300 Bonn; Tel: [0228] 28 12 00) is a clean pleasant hostel in a wooded area in the hills halfway between Bonn and Bad Godesberg. There is another hostel in Bad Godesberg: JUGENDHER-BERGE BAD GODESBERG (Horion Str. 60, Tel: [0228] 31 75 16).

CAMPINGPLATZ GENIENAUE in Mehlem is a lovely spot right on the river with bike path into the city. It is open all year.

KÖLN (Cologne). It's pretty difficult to visit Cologne and not be impressed by the **Dom**, the magnificent Gothic cathedral that dominates the city's skyline. Although some 90 percent of Cologne was destroyed by bombing during World War II, this twin-spired masterpiece of Gothic architecture set in its own square overlooking the Rhine escaped practically unscathed. The cathedral's construction was a long term project. Started in 1248, it was finally completed in 1880 after numerous interruptions. In addition to its inspiring exterior, the Dom contains a multitude of art treasures, including some excellent fourteenth-century stained glass windows. If your legs are not too tired after pedaling into Cologne, climb the five hundred steps to the top of one of the spires for a bird's-eye view of the city.

Of Cologne's several fine museums there is one that definitely should not be missed: the **Wallraf-Richartz Museum**. A unique museum just a few steps from the cathedral, it houses one of Europe's finest and most varied art collections. Other museums of interest, all within a few minutes walking distance of each other, include the **Römisch-Germanisches Museum** and the **Schnutgen Museum**.

The ALSTADT HOTEL (Salzgasse 7, 5000 Köln; Tel: [0221] 23 41 87) is a pleasant moderately priced small hotel in the old town near the river. Doubles without bath cost about 80 DM. The EXCELSIOR HOTEL ERNST (Domplatz; Tel: [0221] 2701), a fine old-world hotel between the cathedral and the train station is first class in every way. In the budget category, we like the convenience of the PENSION FRIEDRICHE (Dom Str. 23; Tel: [0221] 12 33 03).

Of the city's two youth hostels, the most conveniently located one is just across the river from the Dom: IYHF KÖLN (Siegstrasse 21, 5000 Köln; Tel: [0221] 81 47 11). If this is full, try the other one farther down the river (Konrad Adenauer Ufer 1; Tel: [0221] 73 17 20).

Of the city's several campgrounds, we prefer the municipal site, CAMPINGPLATZ POLLER FISCHERHAUS, on the right bank of the river just under the autobahn bridge. Facilities include a washing machine and camp store. There is a restaurant nearby. The campground is open 1 May to 15 October. CAMPING WALDBAD is an all-year site about 10 kms from the city center in the Dunnwald section of Cologne.

AACHEN. It was from Aachen, this ancient city where Germany, the Nether-lands, and Belgium meet, that Charlemagne (to the Germans he's known as Karl der Grosse) ruled over the Holy Roman Empire in the early ninth century. The main attraction in this rather somber city is the impressive **Dom**, the oldest parts of which are built in the Byzantine style. Inside the Dom you will find the simple marble throne from which the greater part of Central Europe was once ruled. The Dom's treasure chamber (Domschatz) contains a gold bust of Charlemagne. The **Sürmondt Museum** contains a fine collection of medieval sculpture.

The city's top hotel, an elegant grand old dowager complete with its own thermal spa, is the PARKHOTEL QUELLENHOF (Monheimsallee 52, 5100 Aachen; Tel: [0241] 15 20 81). For pampered luxury and an old-world spa to treat your saddle sores, this is the place – for around 300 DM per night for a double. On a more modest note for the same price, you can spend a whole week at the small GASTHOF GÖBEL (Trierer Str. 546; Tel: [0241] 52 32 44). In the middle price range, we like the comfortable HOTEL DREILÄNDERECK (Dreiländerweg 105; Tel: [0241] 82 300).

Aachen also has a good youth hostel, IYHF JUGENDHERBERGE AACHEN (Am Colyushof, 5100 Aachen; Tel: [0241] 71 101).

CAMPINGPLATZ PASSSTRASSE is a small site near the city park and spa. Its facilities include a washing machine, camp store, and restaurant. It is open 1 May to 30 September.

MONSCHAU. A picturesque little town nestled in the narrow rocky cliffs of the Rur Valley is one of the main gateways to the Eifel and the German-Belgian Nature Park. It's not much more than a stone's throw from Monschau to the Belgian border.

You can get a double at the pleasant BURGHOTEL (Laufenstr. 1, 5108 Monschau; Tel: [02472] 2332) from 60 DM. For a quiet inexpensive pension on the same street, try HAUS KRIEGER (Laufenstr. 104; Tel: [02472] 697).

This small town also has two youth hostels, one right in the center of town and the other at Hagard just outside of town.

Of the two campgrounds in the immediate vicinity, we like CAMPING PERLENAU the best. It is located about 2 kms south of town: Follow the signs from B399 to a nice site in a wooded area. It is open from Easter to 30 September.

GEROLSTEIN. A small resort town on the Kyll River, Gerolstein draws guests mainly from other parts of Germany. The surrounding hills are rich in prehistoric caves.

For a fine mountain hotel with a sauna and swimming pool to nurse your tired muscles, check in for a day or two at the comfortable WALDHOTEL ROSE (Zur Buschkapelle, 5530 Gerolstein; Tel: [06591] 643). HAUS BECHTOLD (Zum Sandborn 37; Tel: [06591] 3639) is not as plush, but you'll sleep just as comfortably in their feather beds.

There is a youth hostel right at the edge of town and a campground about 15 kms farther down the road at Daun: LUBA FREIZEIT PARK. The campground is part of a large recreation complex with a full range of facilities, including a washing machine. It is open all year.

MANDERSCHEID. An attractive and popular resort town, Manderscheid is at the center of a region rich in crater lakes.

For a comfortable middle-class hotel, try the HOTEL FISCHERHEID (Kurfurstnerstr. 31, 5562 Manderscheid; Tel: [06572] 701). The town has a large number of inexpensive pensions and *gasthauses*. For atmosphere at reasonable prices, try the ALT MANDERSCHEID (Markt 4; Tel: [06572] 2395).

In addition to the JUGENDHERBERGE MANDERSCHEID near the town center, there is also a large, well-equipped campground: CAMPING MORITZ. To get there, follow the signs in town. It is open 1 April to 30 October.

TRIER. On the banks of the Moselle not far from the confluence of the German, French, and Luxembourg borders, Trier has the distinction of being Germany's oldest city. In Roman times, Trier was one of the most important in Rome's far-flung network of foreign outposts. No fewer than six Roman emperors established their northern headquarters there. The city retained its importance long after the fall of the Roman Empire and remained a power to be reckoned with throughout the Middle Ages and well into the Renaissance. Today the essentially modern city constructed after the devastating World War II bombings is an important center for the fine wines grown along the Moselle.

Amidst this modern city are some significant reminders of Trier's long and flourishing history. The **Porta Nigra**, a magnificent gateway, was once a part of the huge sandstone fortress, built in 115 AD, which formed an important part of the city's defenses. Housed within the Porta Nigra is the **Städtisches Museum**, which has some fine examples of medieval art. Other remnants of Trier's glorious Roman past include the ruins of the **amphitheater** and the **Kaisertherman** (Emperor's Baths).

The **Trier Dom**, reflecting a conglomeration of architectural styles dating back to the fourth century, is believed to be Germany's oldest Christian church.

The birthplace of Trier's most famous native son is now a museum containing exhibits, documents, and excerpts from his writings. For an unusual and informative experience, visit **Karl Marx Haus** (Brückenstrasse 10).

Two conveniently situated inexpensive pensions are ZUR ROMERBRÜCKE (Karl Marx Str. 78, 5500 Trier; Tel: [0651] 73 407) and GASTHAUS GERICHTSKLAUSE (Dietrich Str. 36; Tel: [0651] 73 430). In the moderate price category, try HOTEL KLOSTERSCHENKE (Kloster Str. 10; Tel: [0651] 6089).

The IYHF JUGENDHERBERGE TRIER (Maar Str. 156, 5500 Trier; Tel: [0651] 41 092) is a large modern hostel near the river. The JUGENDHOTEL KÖLPING-HAUS (Dietrich Str. 42, Tel: [0651] 75 131). is a centrally located budget price youth hotel, part of the Hotel Warsberger Hof.

The CAMPINGPARK TRIER CITY is located at a large meadow fronting the Moselle between the Römerbrucke and the Adenauerbrücke. Its full facilities include a washing machine, restaurant, and camp store. It is open 15 March to 31 October.

CAMPING MONAISE is a large site on the grounds of an eighteenth-century palace. It is located on the Moselle about 5 kms upriver in the direction of Zewen. It is open 1 April to 31 October.

BERNKASTEL-KUES. With half-timbered houses, wine bars, and souvenir shops following the narrow winding streets up from the river, Bernkastel-Kues is one of the most popular and picturesque of the Moselle wine towns.

For a comfortable modern hotel, try the ALPHA HOTELPARK (5550 Bernkastel-Kues; Tel: [06531] 2011).

The IYHF YOUTH HOSTEL BERN-KASTEL (Tel: [06531] 2395) is located in the hills above the town not far from the ruins of Burg Landshut.

CAMPINGPLATZ KUESER WERTH is located at the river near the boat harbor in the direction of Lieser. There is an on-site washing machine, camp store, and restaurant. It is open 15 April to 30 September.

COCHEM. A pleasant town built into the hills above the Moselle, Cochem's main attraction is the imposing **Burg Cochem**. Dating back to the eleventh century, the fortress was destroyed by the French in 1689 and later rebuilt in the manner of a fantasy castle by its nineteenth-century restorers. **Burg Eltz**, about 20 kms downriver from Cochem, is a fascinating conglomeration of architectural styles. One of the few castles in Germany that has escaped fire, capture, and bombing – a must for castle enthusiasts!

Cochem has a number of inexpensive small hotels and pensions. The **Informationszentrum** (Tel: [02671] 3971) near the bridge will furnish details and book you a room for a fee of 2 DM.

The IYHF JUGENDHERBERGE COCHEM (Klottenstrasse in nearby Cond; Tel: [02671] 8633) is about a ten-minute pedal across the bridge from the train station.

CAMPINGPLATZ AM STADION is in a pleasant location on the right side of the Moselle. Follow the signs toward Wellenbad. It has a camp store and restaurant nearby and is open Easter to 31 October.

THE BLACK FOREST

DER SCHWARZWALD, more commonly known to English-speaking travelers as the Black Forest, is an enchanting area of cuckoo clocks, heavily forested mountains, and rich, verdant valleys. Tucked in the southwestern corner of the country, bordered by France and Switzerland, and covering an area roughly 100 kms from north to south and 50 kms wide, the Black Forest is a vacationer's delight. But, this not the place for the weak of leg or short of breath. While nothing extraordinary by alpine standards (the highest peak is the Feldberg at just short of 1,500 meters), the mountains do provide some pretty stimulating cycling. There are few level roads and those few are heavily trafficked. If you follow the lightly traveled but often torturous secondary roads that wind their way up and over the numerous flat-topped mountains, your efforts will be well rewarded. In spite of the region's popularity, many rich green valleys with traditional farmhouses and quaint villages have retained an idyllic feeling. The many hiking trails and logging roads make this excellent country for a mountain bike. A particular treat and fine example of the area's long standing as a wood-carving center are the many intricately carved road markers and direction signs. There's no problem with accommodations: Campgrounds, youth hostels, cozy old farmhouses, and delightful country inns abound.

The traditional gateway to the Black Forest is the ancient city of **Freiburg**. When planning a Black Forest tour, be sure to include the **Monastery of St. Peter** in the town of the same name just a few kms east of Freiburg, the chic international resort of **Titisee**, and the delightful **Munstertal Valley** with its many typical Black Forest farms.

A Black Forest tour can be extended easily to link up with the "Lake Constance Route" or to make a good combination tour with the Alsace region of France just across the Rhine. There is an enjoyable series of bike trails that follow the Rhine north from Freiburg up to Heidelberg.

The best maps for touring are the ADFC #27, Schwarzwald-Nord and #32, Schwarzwald-Sud.

SCHLESWIG HOLSTEIN

Way up at the northern end of this many faceted country lies the pastoral expanses of Schleswig Holstein. Seldom visited by Americans, this region counts a number of fine sandy beaches among its numerous attractions. In marked contrast to southern Germany, this tranquil dairy land is flat cycling country. The only hindrance to effortless cycling are the often strong winds. The winds on the eastern portion coming off the Baltic are relatively light in comparison to the usually strong prevailing North Sea winds. The eastern side of the peninsula is also the more interesting. Of particular interest are the old Hanseatic trading city of **Lübeck** and the **lake district** around Plön, which is known as **"Little Switzerland."**

Just to the south on the Elbe River is **Hamburg**, Germany's major port and one of northern Europe's most attractive and sophisticated cities. There is a ferry every other day from Hamburg to the English East Anglian port of Harwich. Extending south from Hamburg is the vast expanse of the **Lüneberger Heide**, a very pleasant cycling area especially from late August through October, when the heather is in blossom.

Pick up ADFC maps #3, Holsteinische Schweiz/Ostsee and #6, Hamburg/Lübeck for detailed touring information on Schleswig Holstein and Hamburg.

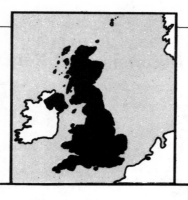

GREAT BRITAIN

POPULATION
56,000,000

RELIGION
Predominantly Church of England

CURRENCY
Pound Sterling (£); divided into 100 pence

CURRENCY RESTRICTIONS
None

OFFICIAL LANGUAGE
English; Welsh spoken widely in Wales, Gaelic in Scotland

EMERGENCY PHONES
Ambulance, Police 999 (no coin required)

TO CALL USA AND CANADA
Dial 0101, area code, and number
(Note: there will be high surcharges if you make your calls from a hotel.)

BANKING HOURS
M–F 0930–1530

STORE HOURS
M–S 0900–1730
Stores in the rural areas usually close Wednesday or Saturday afternoons

U.S.A. CONSULATE/EMBASSY
1 Grosvenor Square
LONDON W1A 1AE
Tel: (01) 499-9000
Telex: 26677

Queens House 14 Queen St.
BELFAST BT1 6EQ
Tel: (021) 228-239
Telex: 747512

3 Regent Terrace
EDINBURGH EJ7 5BW
Tel: (031) 556-8315
Telex: 727303

CANADIAN CONSULATE/EMBASSY
Canadian High Commission
1 Grosvenor Square
LONDON W1X OAB
Tel: (01) 629-9492

AMERICAN EXPRESS OFFICES

Abbott Travel
25 Sidney St.
CAMBRIDGE
Tel: (0223) 51636

Powell Duffryn Travel
41 The Buttermarket
IPSWICH, Suffolk
Tel: (0473) 210-821

American Express Europe
6 Haymarket
LONDON
Tel: (01) 930-4411

American Express Europe
52 Cannon St.
LONDON
Tel: (01) 248-2671

Keith Bailey Travel
Cowley Centre
OXFORD
37–39 Upper Barr
Tel: (0865) 770-841

James Bird Travel
4 Yield Hall Palace
READING, Berkshire
Tel: (0734) 580-456

B&C Travel
54 Chapel St.
STRATFORD-UPON-AVON
Tel: (0789) 293-582

HOLIDAYS

1 Jan., New Year's; 2 Jan., public holiday in Scotland only; 17 Mar., St. Patrick's Day in Northern Ireland only; Good Friday, movable; Easter Monday, public holiday except in Scotland; 6 May, May Day; 12 July, Northern Ireland only; 5 Aug., public holiday in Scotland only; 26 Aug., summer bank holiday except in Scotland; 25 Dec., Christmas; 26 Dec., Boxing Day. Note: Scotland does not observe Easter Monday or Boxing Day.

TRANSPORTATION WITHIN THE COUNTRY

BR, which stands for British Rail, is generally a bicycle friendly organization. On most of the 14,000 trains operated daily, bicycles may be carried on at no extra charge. All you do is wheel your cycle up to the baggage car, load it yourself, and unload it when you arrive at your destination. If you change trains, the transfer is your responsibility. When placing your bike in the baggage car, be sure to fasten it securely to prevent damage. While it is unlikely that someone will be lurking about to rip off your bike, it is still not a bad idea to remove your bags and lock the bike to the side of the baggage car.

Intercity 125 trains are express trains operating on long-distance routes. These trains have limited luggage space; however, it is normally possible to make arrangements to have your cycle carried in the guard's car. There is no charge on weekends, but a small charge is made on weekdays. Cycle tickets can be purchased at main-line rail stations, and where necessary reservations can be made. Regular (non-IC 125) trains also operate on IC 125 routes; so should you have trouble getting on an intercity train, you can always take your cycle on a slower train on the same route.

There is a charge made for cycles carried on the trains that connect with the Channel ferries; however, cycles are carried free on the train that connects Harwich (ferries from Holland, Denmark, and Germany) with London.

In London itself, cycles may be taken only on commuter trains traveling against the peak travel flow. There are no restrictions on weekends. Due to lack of access, bicycles may not be taken on the following London transport underground subway lines: Victoria, Central, Northern, Bakerloo, Jubilee, and Piccadilly.

The long distance buses, the National Express coaches, do not carry bicycles.

Most airlines flying in and out of London will transport a bicycle as part of your baggage allowance. Be prepared to remove the pedals and front wheel. Check with the airline for details when you buy your ticket.

BIKING THROUGH EUROPE

GREAT BRITAIN

Even though it's rather a small country – when measured in square miles it's not quite as large as the state of Wisconsin – England offers an array of historical, cultural, and scenic attractions worthy of a much larger nation. Its compactness translates into an ideal situation for cycle touring. In the space of a single biking vacation, or "holiday" as the English say, you will be able to experience a wonderful variety of pleasures and attractions, without having to spend many hours and lots of money traveling between touring areas. The picturesque rugged Cornish coastline, the ancient castles and ruins of Northumbria, the lonely moors to the north of York (where riding on a foggy autumn afternoon, we were sure we heard the hounds of the Baskervilles howling across the moors), the Cotswolds, or heart of England – home of Shakespeare and a region of quiet, little travel-poster villages and inviting pubs – as well as the craggy mountains and lake-dotted valleys of Cumbria and the Lake District are just some of the regions ideally suited to the pace and mood of a cycle tour.

Another pleasant aspect of England's compactness – compared with such spread-out destinations as Spain or the Scandinavian countries – is the reassurance you get from knowing that you are seldom more than a short cycling distance from a cozy B&B (bed and breakfast) or inviting country inn.

The museums and galleries of England's towns and cities offer a richness and variety of treasures far out of proportion to the country's size. They contain reminders of those days not so long ago when "the sun never set on the British Empire."

One of the nicest aspects of the English and of touring in England is the language. Even though there is a great deal of truth in the often-quoted saying that "the Americans and the British are two peoples separated by a common language," it is nevertheless very nice to be able to stop anyone, anywhere, and ask for directions without having to stumble along trying to find the appropriate phrase in a pocket dictionary. No matter how complete they seem in a bookstore back home, these instant language guides never seem to have just quite the right words for the occasion.

Yet another pleasant aspect of touring in Great Britain is the fact that the metric system hasn't made much more progress there than in the U.S. This is the only place in Europe where you can navigate in miles and order your beer by the pint.

As for the British themselves, you will find them to be subdued and polite, with a dry humor that has a quality all its own. The one endearing quality that does come through is the genuine hospitality of the British, often in the face of and in spite of the brashness of their colonial cousins from across the Atlantic. Cycle touring is a very popular British pastime and as a cyclist you will find a warm welcome wherever you go.

MAPS

For such a small country it is amazing what a large variety of maps is available. The **BTA** (British Tourist Authority) issues a map that is good for getting an overall perspective of the country. The flip side has a map of the greater London area and a lot of useful information for tourists. The scale is 1:1,175,000. The cost is just 50 pence.

The **Bartholomew Map of the British Isles** (scale 1:1,000,000) is the best overall planning map. Somewhat more detailed, but not really suitable for on-the-road use, is the Michelin series, which covers all of the United Kingdom plus Ireland in five separate sheets (scale 1:400,000 or 1 cm = 4 kms). These are great maps for driving but are not quite detailed enough to use for cycling.

The **Ordnance Survey Routemaster** or **Bartholomew GT Series** of maps (scale 1:250,000 or 1 cm = 2.5 kms) cover all of Britain in nine sheets. This is the minimum scale that is practical for touring purposes if you want to get off the main roads. Contours, hill shading, small villages, and most minor roads are shown.

The best and most practical maps for cycle touring are the **Bartholomew National Series**, which show all of Britain in sixty-two excellent maps, each covering an area of 100 kms by 60 kms (scale 1:100,000; 1 cm = 1 km). All villages, all paved roads, some unsurfaced tracks, and even such helpful navigational aids as windmills are indicated. The cost is 2.50 pounds each.

Those who insist on following each bend in the road and checking off every ruin and church should consider using the **Ordnance Survey Maps** (scale 1:50,000; 1 cm = 0.5 kms). These are extremely accurate maps with contour lines showing height and indicating such items as ruins, churches, and even orchards. Britain is covered in two hundred individual sheets. If you plan to cover any distance at all, you will find using these just too cumbersome and expensive. For the cost of purchasing even half of the series, you can buy a decent bike!

If you find yourself getting bogged down with maps, you can save a bit of space and weight by cutting off the covers. Changes are constantly being made and maps revised, so always try to obtain up-to-date maps.

The Bartholomew Maps can be ordered directly from the company (John Bartholomew & Son Ltd, Duncan Street, Edinburgh EH9 1TA, Scotland; Tel: [031] 667-9341) or from the Cyclist's Touring Club.

Most bookstores just carry maps for their local regions, although some of the big city stores, such as London's Hatchards (187 Piccadilly) or the book department at Harrods (87-135 Brompton Road, Knightsbridge) carry the entire range. Another good London source is Edward Stanford Ltd. (12-14 Long Acre, London WC2E 9LP; Tel: [01] 836-1321).

BICYCLE SHOPS AND RENTALS

Most of the larger towns have repair shops, and mechanics will usually go out of their way to help a stranded tourist. Since Britain is not on the metric system, many British parts can be used on American bikes, which means that you will not be stranded for long.

The cycles available for rental throughout Britain range from old clunkers to good quality ten-speeds; in some places, even mountain bikes can be rented. The best rental bikes and the widest selection are usually found in the major centers, such as London and Cambridge. The **Cyclist's Touring Club** issues a list of all rental firms in Britain for its members. Also check with the local tourist information offices or look in the yellow pages.

In London, daily rental rates (1986 prices) for a basic "no speed" machine are about 2.50 pounds; 40 to 50 pounds for the weekly rental of a decent ten-speed. In London, contact DIAL-A-BIKE (18 Gillingham St.; Tel: [01] 828-4040) and RENT-A-BIKE (Kensington Student Centre, Kensington, Church Street, London, W8). In Oxford, check out BEELINE BIKES (14 Worcester St.) and in Cambridge, CAMBRIDGE CYCLE HIRE (118 Milton Rd.) In Ireland, there is a chain of some one hundred Raleigh Rent-a-Bike dealers. For details, contact TI IRISH RALEIGH LTD. (Broomhill Road, County Tallaght, Dublin, Ireland). For mountain bike rentals in the southeast of England, contact MOUNTABIKE (Gillingham, Kent ME7 2BR; Tel: [0634] 31080).

As an alternative to renting, consider purchasing a bike in Britain. Depending on the exchange rate, this could prove to be a money-saving proposition. In London, the following shops have good selections: THE LONDON BICYCLE COMPANY (41-42 Floral St., Covent Garden, London WC2 and 55 Pimlico Road, Victoria, London SW1 8NE) and F.W. EVANS (77-79 The Cut, London SE1).

ROADS

One of the most appealing aspects of cycling in Britain is the vast network of back roads and country lanes. Almost as if designed just for the cyclist, these infrequently traveled lanes meander through some of the most delightful parts of the country. Even during the peak summer months, it is possible to pedal for hours and hardly encounter an automobile. In the organizational scheme of things, these country lanes are considered unclassified roads, and many are shown only on detailed maps – those with a scale of 1:100,000 or better.

Roads marked with the letter "M" are motorways, the English designation for freeway. Bicycles are not permitted on these roads. "A" roads are the main highways, usually connecting major cities. Frequently these are heavily traveled, especially in the summer, and should be avoided whenever possible. "A" roads with more than two numbers usually have less traffic than the one-number and two-number "A" roads. "B" roads generally connect towns and are less heavily traveled than the "A" roads and provide a good compromise when you want to get directly from town to town. If you cycle the unclassified lanes, be careful when navigating by road signs that you don't get lured onto the busy "A" or "B" roads. Many of these country roads are not numbered; they just indicate the name of the town that they go to.

In addition to the large network of unclassified paved lanes, there are numerous unsurfaced bridle paths open to cyclists. Remember that you will be sharing these with horses. Most of these are shown only on Ordnance Survey maps with a scale of 1:50,000. The bridle paths are ideally suited for touring with an ATB (all-terrain bike). Other inviting terrain for a rugged touring bike or, better yet, a mountain bike is provided by the many Forestry Commission roads and the towpaths that run alongside the canals and navigable rivers. One surprising thing about cycling in England is the relative scarcity of actual bicycle trails.

Great Britain and Ireland are the only countries you will encounter in Europe where they drive on the left side of the road. Don't avoid England out of fear of the "wrong way traffic." It just takes a little more concentration, especially on the roundabouts (traffic circles). Be especially on guard when you are tired and your reflexes are still attuned to riding on the right-hand side of the road.

ACCOMMODATIONS

For the tired cyclist looking for a place to rest aching muscles after a tough day's pedaling, Britain is a veritable paradise. Whether you are traveling on a shoestring or enjoying a luxury tour, you will never be very far away from suitable accommodations. Although Britain has its fair share of conventional hotels, a great part of the fun of traveling in a country like Britain comes from spending a night or two in a ramshackle, half-timbered, thatched-roof country inn or friendly little bed and breakfast.

Although there is no official rating system (as in France), hotels, inns, and guest houses with four or more rooms for rent are required to post their minimum and maximum prices. In nearly all cases, a full English breakfast is included in the rate. Practically every town you will visit has a local tourist information office that will help you to find a room. The charges range from 50 pence to 1 pound.

At the luxury end of the accommodations scale are the **castle hotels**. These are authentic old family castles and country manor houses, often of significant historic importance, which have been converted to hotels. For more details, obtain the BTA booklet entitled *Castle and Country*.

B&Bs, as the British call them, are places where you get a bed and breakfast. The typical B&B is a small family-run establishment geared to provide low-cost accommodations in a friendly family setting. Often it may just be a farmhouse or a private home that has a spare bedroom or two. Although the usual arrangement is for a bed and breakfast, often arrangements can be made for taking dinner if you are staying for a few nights. This is a great way to experience British hospitality and meet the local people. B&Bs usually run about 8 pounds per person per night. It may be difficult to find singles in high season.

If you plan to do a lot of cycling in Britain it would be worthwhile to get a copy of the *Ramblers' & Cyclists' Bed & Breakfast Guide*, which lists more than 2,300 countryside addresses. It costs 1.75 pounds at most bookstores in Britain. For an informative brochure with information on making reservations, contact **Bed & Breakfast** (PO Box 66, Henley-on-Thames, Oxon RG9 1XS; Tel: [0491] 578-803). The BTA also publishes an interesting brochure called *Stay at an Inn*, which lists a selection of historic inns all over Britain.

At the budget end of the accommodations scale, Britain has some four hundred **IYHF Youth Hostels**, which provide clean, inexpensive lodging, often in historic surroundings. All provide cooking facilities and some have meals available. A sheet and sleeping sack is required at all hostels. These may be purchased or rented locally at the hostel or purchased from the American Youth Hostel Council.

The BTA issues a free brochure, *Youth Accommodation*, which contains much useful information, including a listing of some hostels that do not require a membership card.

If you do not have a card when you arrive in England, you can purchase an **International Guest Card** from the Youth Hostel Association (14 Southampton Street, Covent Garden, London WC2) or at your first hostel.

Many of the country's official campsites are primarily set up for trailers (caravans) and campers; these can be a bit intimidating to cyclists with their small tents. Unless you are in need of the amenities that the official sites offer (hot showers, swimming pools, laundromats, and the like), it is generally more pleasant to just pitch your tent in a convenient field or farm yard. Remember that *every* piece of land belongs to somebody! Get permission wherever you can and don't spoil things for those who will follow in your tracks. Many youth hostels also have camping facilities which are available to members only, who pay one-half of the "indoor rate." For information on campsites that cater to cycle campers, contact the **Association of Lightweight Campers**.

FOOD AND DRINK

Wtook our first English cycling tour after having become accustomed to the rather skimpy continental breakfast of rolls and coffee commonly served on the mainland. Imagine our delight when at our first breakfast at a B&B we were served orange juice, cereal, eggs, sausage (called bangers in England), bacon, grilled tomatoes, mushrooms, toast, butter, marmalade, and all the tea or coffee we wanted.

From there our experiences with English cuisine went downhill. Not that typical British fare is terrible; on the contrary, there are some bright spots on the culinary horizon. It's just that when compared to the food in France, Italy, Belgium, or Germany, Britain comes up a poor second. In fact, the best restaurant food in most English towns is usually found in the "foreign" restaurants. Chinese, Indian, and Italian eating places abound. One notable exception to this, and one of the best sources of good, reasonably priced non-ethnic food, is that venerable old English institution, the public house, better known as the pub. For a good lunch, "pub grub" as the locals refer to it is nothing fancy but can be quite tasty, featuring such traditional dishes as steak and kidney pie, Cornish pastie (potatoes, meat, and vegetables in a pastry shell), and toad-in-the-hole (sausages in a blanket of baked batter).

Even more important than being a source of hearty inexpensive food is the pub's role as a social institution. Hours upon hours are whiled away on darts, pool, and even video games. The standard pub drink is beer, which is usually dispensed by the pint. The British Imperial pint has 20 ounces as compared with the American 16-ounce

version. Pub hours, which vary somewhat from place to place, take a bit of getting used to. Most are open from 11 A.M. to 3 P.M. and from 5:30 to 11 P.M.

In most restaurants, a 15 percent service charge is added to the bill. If the service has been good, it is common practice to leave a few extra pence on the table.

In the course of pedaling through the countryside, you will often come across open-air markets, which are great places to stock up on picnic fixings. The best of the English cheeses, in addition to the popular Cheddar and Stilton, include Walton, an interesting blend of Cheddar and Stilton.

SOURCES OF ADDITIONAL INFORMATION

Within Britain there are more than seven hundred regional and local tourist offices which can provide a wealth of material and services ranging from booking a room to providing local cycling itineraries. The **British Tourist Authority** has offices in the U.S. and Canada:

John Hancock Center
Suite 3320
875 Michigan Ave.
Chicago, IL 60611
Tel: [312] 787-0490

Plaza of the Americas
750 North Tower
Dallas, TX 75201
Tel: [214] 720-4040

612 South Flower St.
Los Angeles, CA 90017
Tel: [213] 623-8196

West 57th St.
New York, NY 10019
Tel: [212] 581-4700

94 Cumberland St.
Suite 600
Toronto, Ont. M5R 3N3
Tel: [416] 925-6326

The **British Cycling Federation** (16 Upper Woburn Pl, London WC1) does offer a touring service for members, although it is primarily concerned with racing.

The **Association of Lightweight Campers** (11 Lower Grosvenor Place, London, SW1W OEY, Tel: [01] 660-7294) is the division of the Camping and Caravanning Club dedicated to "lightweight" (cycle) campers. Temporary membership is available at a cost of 6 pounds for three months. Association members are "people who like camping in small tents, usually on quiet sites."

The **Cyclists' Touring Club** (69 Meadrow, Godalming, Surrey GU7 3HS; Tel: [04868] 7217) is Britain's largest and most active national cycling organization. Yearly membership is 13 pounds and includes cycle insurance, third-party insurance, the club magazine, *Cycletouring*, a map locating service, organized tours, and information for cyclists traveling on their own.

London and the Romantic Heartland of England

With its lack of bike paths and horrendous traffic, London is not exactly a cyclist's paradise. But it is pretty difficult to imagine visiting England without spending at least a few days seeing this great city. Then it's an easy pedal away from the hustle and clamor of the big city to the serene beauty and romance of the English countryside which over the centuries has inspired some of the finest poets and writers of the English language. Along this route we have included a number of attractions that are practically synonymous with England. Not many of us would think of England without giving at least a passing thought to Oxford, seat of one of the world's great universities, or to Stratford-upon-Avon, Shakespeare's birthplace, which has managed to retain a good deal of its appeal in spite of the concessions made to mass tourism. Wandering just a bit off of that proverbial well-trodden tourist path, our route meanders through quiet villages little touched by the stream of hit-and-run tourists rushing by on the "A" roads.

A region of rolling hills that gradually rise up from the grasslands of the upper Thames, the Cotswolds are dotted with idyllic little settlements of houses made from warm honey-colored stone. They are the embodiment of the perfect English village. During the Middle Ages, the wool merchants in this region ranked high among the country's most prosperous classes and enriched their villages with fine churches and houses. It is a delightful experience to come upon one of these little gems of a village after a few hours of fighting the ridges that make up the western portion of this region and then to rest in the cozy comfort of a country inn or local pub and enjoy afternoon tea, perhaps accompanied by a piece of fresh apple pie smothered with rich country cream.

In addition to traveling through some of Britain's loveliest countryside, our route includes a sampling of fine castles and stately manors, including the royal castle at Windsor and Winston Churchill's impressive birthplace, Blenheim Palace, near Oxford. While pedaling the southern portion of the route, you will have a chance to see the fine cathedrals at Salisbury and Winchester, as well as the mystifying stone formations at Stonehenge.

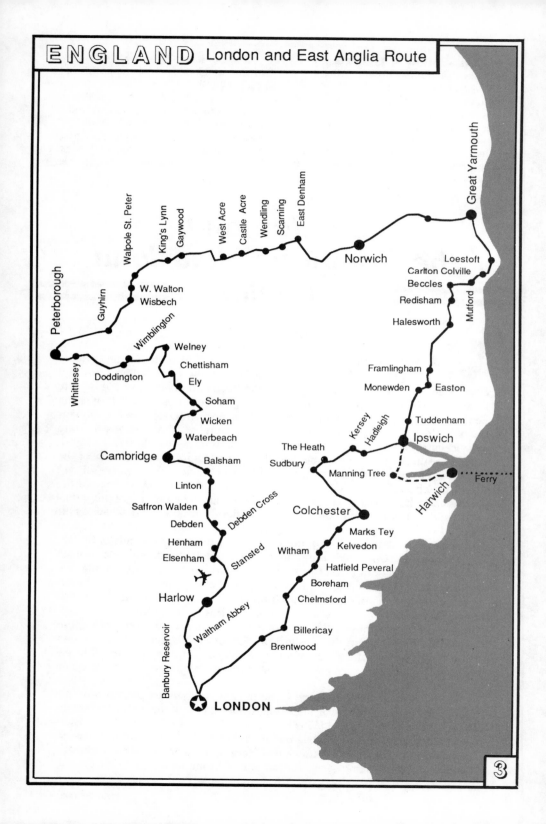

Great Yarmouth

Walpole St. Peter
King's Lynn
Gaywood
West Acre
Castle Acre
Wendling
Scarning
East Denham

Loestoft
Carlton Colville
Beccles
Redisham
Halesworth

Norwich

Mutford

Peterborough

Guyhirn

W. Walton
Wisbech

Wimblington

Welney

Framlingham
Monewden
Easton

Chettisham

Whittlesey

Doddington

Ely

Soham

Wicken

Waterbeach

Tuddenham

Kersey
Hadleigh

Ipswich

The Heath

Cambridge

Balsham

Sudbury

Manning Tree

Linton

Debden Cross

Colchester

Harwich

Ferry

Saffron Walden

Marks Tey
Kelvedon

Debden

Stansted

Witham

Hatfield Peveral

Henham

Boreham

Elsenham

Chelmsford

Harlow

Waltham Abbey

Billericay

Banbury Reservoir

Brentwood

★ LONDON

3

THROUGH THE HEART OF ENGLAND LOOP

START	FINISH	DISTANCE KM
LONDON	LONDON	724 kms/450 miles

MICHELIN MAPS
For a good overview, #404, South East, Midlands, East Anglia (scale 1:400,000)

BARTHOLOMEW GT SERIES
Also good for navigating, #2, South Coast; #4, Midlands (scale 1:250,000)

BARTHOLOMEW NATIONAL SERIES MAPS
To navigate, #7, Briston and No. Somerset; #8, Reading and Salisbury Plain; #13, Hereford and Gloucester; #14, Oxford; #18, Vale of Severn and Radnor Forest (scale 1:100,000)

This route encompasses many attractions and covers a variety of terrain. The northern portion of the route, stretching from Oxford across the Cotswolds and touching on the Shropshire Hills near Shrewsbury, contains some sections of tough pedaling. There are plenty of steep hills. These are not mountains in the alpine sense, but you do need low gears and should be in reasonably good condition to enjoy this portion of the route. But the scenery looks just as pretty whether you are riding or pushing your bike up a hill. Cycling along the Avon and Severn rivers is easy going with a backdrop of fruit orchards and lush meadows, as is cycling the stretch that takes you over the broad Salisbury Plain. The fact that this route is not all that easy going and is packed with a lot of interesting places to visit should give you cause to plan to take a little longer to do this route than you would normally take to cover the same distance. Including a few days in London, three weeks would give you time to really enjoy this part of England.

If you are coming directly from the States or Canada, chances are that you will be flying into London. So the route as we have described it starts and ends in London; however, you can easily begin at any place and pedal it in either direction.

From Winchester, it is just a short ride to Portsmouth, where you can catch the ferry to Cherbourg and continue with the Normandy route. Hereford, at the western edge of the loop, is a good jumping off point for exploring the beauties of Wales. Should you wish to avoid a hilly stretch or move on to another part of the country at some point along the way, there are a number of towns on the route with good rail connections. These include Oxford, Stratford-upon-Avon, Worcester, Shrewsbury, Hereford, Bath, and Salisbury.

The British weather has been the butt of many a joke and, unfortunately, most of them have been based on fact. If you plan to cycle in Britain for a two-week or three-week period at any time of the year, you better be prepared for rain. How much is a matter of luck. The reason the lush, green English countryside looks as it does even in August and not like the interior of Spain is simply a matter of rainfall. As a general rule, the farther north and west you go from the center of the country, the greater the chances of encountering rain. One saving grace is the fact that British showers are often short-lived and the weather can quickly change.

Places such as London, Stratford, and Oxford are very crowded during July and August, often making it difficult to find a room. If you travel in high season, try to call ahead and make a reservation, or at least plan to roll into a town early enough in the afternoon to give yourself a chance to make the rounds. Note that many tourist offices, your best bet for finding accommodations, close at 5 P.M.

As this route covers a number of England's most popular tourist areas, you will find a good selection of accommodations of every sort. Even during peak periods the local tourist offices will make every effort to find you a room.

★ *LOOKING OUT OVER THE HANDLEBARS* ★

LONDON AND THE HEART OF ENGLAND LOOP

CITY	CITY
LONDON	WINDSOR

ROUTE	ROUTE
B376 B470	B3024 A329 B4016 A415

DISTANCE KM	TOTAL KM	DISTANCE KM	TOTAL KM
35	0	65	35

ROUTE DESCRIPTION

The best way to start this route is to take the train out of London to Windsor from either Waterloo or Paddington stations. It is a forty-minute trip. If you fly into Heathrow and are anxious to get on the road and save London for last, then unpack your cycle and head for Windsor by way of Datchet on B376 and B470, which runs right by the castle.

ROUTE DESCRIPTION

Leave Windsor on B3024 and head west to Twyford, crossing over the M4 motorway just before Waltham St. Lawrence. From Twyford, follow the signs to the rather drab industrial city of Reading by way of Whistley Green. Cross over the A329 motorway and take hwy A329 into Reading. Head out of town on A329, which runs through a pleasant wooded area along the Thames. When the road forks after 10 kms, stay with A329 to just before Blewbury. Turn off onto B4016 toward Didcot and continue past the nuclear power plant (a bit of a contradiction in this beautiful countryside of grazing horses and quiet farmlands). Go through Appleford. Then take A415 into Abingdon — a jewel of an English town right on the Thames. Continue the last few kms into Oxford along the back lane which winds through Radley and Kennington before picking up the cycle path into Oxford.

CITY
OXFORD

ROUTE
A34 B4437 B4450

DISTANCE KM	TOTAL KM
43	100

ROUTE DESCRIPTION
Leave Oxford and pick up A34 and follow the signs toward Stratford. There is a cycle path most of the way to Blenheim Palace and the adjacent village of Woodstock, a picture-postcard collection of ancient stone buildings, inviting pubs, and antique shops. Just past Woodstock, turn left onto B4437 and continue through a succession of delightful little quiet villages: Charlbury, Ascott-under-Wychwood, and Shipton-under-Wychwood. This is great back road cycling: pretty villages, rolling hills, and hardly a car. Continue on to Idbury and then Bledington. From there it's up a steep hill to Stow-on-the-Wold via B4450.

CITY
STOW-ON-THE-WOLD

ROUTE
A436 A4019

DISTANCE KM	TOTAL KM
38	143

ROUTE DESCRIPTION
Fron Stow, it is a steep downhill run to Bourton-on-the-Water, one of the loveliest of the Cotswolds villages, set on both sides of the Windrush River. Plan at least a short stopover in Bourton. Continue on A436 toward Cheltenham. Just before the road intersects with A40, turn off onto the country lane going to Whittington. From the top of Ham Hill, it's an exhilarating descent into Cheltenham, an elegant spa resort with a number of fine Regency buildings. (If you are interested in castles, take the alternate route from Cheltenham up Cleeve Hill to Sudley Castle just south of Winchcombe. Then continue on to Tewkesbury.) Take A4019 out of Cheltenham a few kms to Uckington; turn off and follow the winding country lane to Tewkesbury, crossing the motorway several times and passing by Hardwicke, Tredington, and Walton Cardiff.

CITY
TEWKESBURY

ROUTE
A438 A435 B4510 A46

DISTANCE KM	TOTAL KM
45	181

ROUTE DESCRIPTION

From Tewkesbury, take A438, cross the motorway, and continue to the intersection with A435. Take A435 toward Stratford. About halfway to Stratford, you will pass through Evesham at the edge of the Cotswolds. Enclosed on three sides by the river Avon, Evesham is a marketing center for the region's fruit and vegetable crops. Just outside of town at the traffic circle by Bengeworth, turn off onto B4510. Follow this along the Avon to Welford. Cut over to A46 which runs into Stratford.

CITY
STRATFORD-UPON-AVON

ROUTE
A422

DISTANCE KM	TOTAL KM
35	226

ROUTE DESCRIPTION

Take A422 out of Stratford 35 kms to Worcester.

CITY
WORCESTER

ROUTE
B4204 B4197 B4202 B4363 B4373 B4380 A5

DISTANCE KM	TOTAL KM
75	261

ROUTE DESCRIPTION

From Worcester, take B4204 to intersect with B4197 at the village of Martley. Take this as far as Great Witley. From there, pick up B4202 to Cleobury Mortimer, which has a church with a massive Norman tower. Take B4363 from Cleobury to Bridgnorth. Then take B4373 to Ironbridge, a small town of pretty cottages set on the banks of a gorge. The world's first iron bridge spans the Severn River at this point. B4380 will take you from Ironbridge to A5, the main road between Birmingham and Shrewsbury. Take A5 for the last few kms into town.

CITY
SHREWSBURY

ROUTE
A49 B4368 B4367 B4385 A4113 A4110

DISTANCE KM	TOTAL KM
76	336

ROUTE DESCRIPTION

Leave Shrewsbury on the road to Ratlinghope and follow it for about 20 kms. Then turn off to Church Stetton, a popular resort beautifully set in the green Shropshire Hills. Be prepared for some climbing on this stretch. From Church Stetton, take A49 to Craven Arms. Then continue on B4368 for 2 kms to the intersection with B4367. Turn left and follow B4367 to B4385. Make another left and continue on B4385 for 2 kms to A4113. Follow this toward Knighton for about 1 km. Then turn off onto A4110, which runs through Wigmore and Mortimers Cross into Hereford.

CITY
HEREFORD

ROUTE
B4224 B4221 B4215 A40

DISTANCE KM	TOTAL KM
35	412

ROUTE DESCRIPTION
Take B4224 out of Hereford, passing through Fownhope, a pleasant village of half-timbered houses. Continue on B4224, roughly paralleling the Wye River and cross A449 into Crow Hill. Take B4221 over the M50 motorway and follow B4215 to intersect with A40 just before Gloucester.

CITY
GLOUCESTER

ROUTE
A419

DISTANCE KM	TOTAL KM
34	447

ROUTE DESCRIPTION
From Gloucester, follow the signs to Stroud, for centuries the center of the West England wool trade. In a lovely setting at the meeting of five deep valleys, it is surrounded by rolling hill country. From Stroud, take A419 into Cirencester.

CITY
CIRENCESTER

ROUTE
B4040 B4039

DISTANCE KM	TOTAL KM
67	481

ROUTE DESCRIPTION
Take the road to Somerford Keynes and Minety out of Cirencester. From Minety, take B4040 to Malmesbury, site of a fine Norman abbey and interesting old town quarter. Stay on B4040 to Sherston. Then take the narrow path out of town to the villages of Sopworth and Little and Great Badminton. At Acton Turville, take the road over the M4 motorway and continue on B4039 to Castle Combe, a delightful aggregation of traditional stone houses. Take the winding country lane from Castle Combe by way of Mountain Bower to Marshfield, once a stop on the stagecoach route to Bath. From Marshfield, follow the road to Saint Catherine and then into Bath.

CITY
BATH

ROUTE
A36 A363 A50 A36 B390

DISTANCE KM	TOTAL KM
62	548

ROUTE DESCRIPTION
Follow the busy A36 along the Avon River valley to the turn off to Winsley and Bradford-on-Avon, a pleasant town with an eighth-century church. From Bradford, take A363 to Westbury. Then take A50 for just a short stretch to Warminster. From there, pick up A36 to

the village of Heytesbury. Then take B390 along the border of the military reservation into Shrewton. From Shrewton, it's just a short distance to Stonehenge on the outskirts of Amesbury. Take the narrow road that parallels the busier A345 into Salisbury, passing Wilsford and Woodford.

CITY
SALISBURY

ROUTE
A36 A3090

DISTANCE KM	TOTAL KM
44	610

ROUTE DESCRIPTION

Leave Salisbury on A36. Turn off at Alderbury and follow the road along the railroad through W. Grimsted, W. Dean, and Mottisfont. Cross A3057 and continue into Winchester on A3090 for the last few kms.

Note: There is not a whole lot of interest between Winchester and London. At this point you can easily board a train and return to London or pedal down to Portsmouth and hop on the ferry to Cherbourg to continue on the Normandy route.

CITY
WINCHESTER

ROUTE
B3047 A31

DISTANCE KM	TOTAL KM
45	654

ROUTE DESCRIPTION

Head north out of Winchester to the suburb of Kings Worthy. From there, take B3047 to New Alresford. Continue by way of Bighton and Medstead to Alton. At Alton take A31 into Farnham

CITY
FARNHAM

ROUTE
A321 A3095

DISTANCE KM	TOTAL KM
25	699

ROUTE DESCRIPTION

Take A321 to Sandhurst, the British equivalent of West Point. Then take A3095 to Windsor. From there, return to London by train or pedal about 10 kms to Heathrow Airport if you have a plane to catch.

CITY
LONDON/WINDSOR

DISTANCE KM	TOTAL KM
0	724

LONDON AND THE HEARTLAND OF ENGLAND: SIGHTS AND ACCOMMODATIONS

LONDON. Very few people we know are neutral about London, one of the great cities of the world. They either love it or detest it. Even if you are not a fan of huge cities, and we certainly aren't, London should not be missed.

Approached strictly from a statistical perspective, Greater London, an amalgamation of many individual villages, covers an area of 620 square miles and is home to nearly 7 million people of all races and religious beliefs. The one-mile-square historic and commerical heart of this megalopolis is Central London, one of the many villages that make up the whole of Greater London. There is nothing villagelike about "the City," which is what Central London is commonly called. Covering the area that was the original Roman London, the City contains the major sights and attractions and is where the action is.

Although we do see cyclists on the streets of London, and we have pedaled past Big Ben and the Tower of London ourselves, it is not really that much fun. Heavy traffic — in the wrong direction at that — and the lack of any real network of cycle paths make cycling in London, at least for our tastes, too much of a hassle. For more on this subject, check out *On Your Bike! A Guide to Cycling in London* by the London Cycling Campaign and Friends of the Earth available from **London Cycling Campaign** (Colombo Street Centre, London SE1) and the *Bartholomew/CTC Guide to Cycling in and Around London*, which is available at most London bookshops.

For parking your bicycle, there is a supervised **Cycle Park** available in Central London at the Poland Street Garage, off Oxford Street. It is open Monday to Saturday from 6:00 A.M. to midnight. Lockers are provided for the storage of luggage and accessories.

Everyone has his own way of approaching London, and the wonderful thing is that this amazing city seems to be able to accommodate an infinite variety of its visitors' needs. We like to think of the city from two perspectives. The first is to see the traditional London of **double-decker buses**, dome-hatted **bobbies, Westminster Abbey, Big Ben,** the **Tower of London**, and **Buckingham Palace**. The other face is that of a modern metropolis struggling to come to grips with massive traffic congestion, urban renewal, purple-haired punkers, and a flood of immigrants from all corners of the former empire. Our suggestion for visiting London in the several days that you will probably allocate for that purpose is forget about trying to see it all. It will exhaust you and leave you with just a blur of recollections. Take one of the two-hour sight-seeing tours offered by London Transport and then go back and concentrate on a few of the attractions that you think will interest you.

Be sure to leave some time for just strolling about. London is a great city for walking. You will probably want to see some of the highlights. **Westminster Abbey** has been the traditional coronation, marriage, and final resting place for English monarchs ever since the coronation of William the Conqueror was held there in 1066. **Buckingham Palace**, unfortunately closed to the public, is nevertheless an important traditional part of the London visit because of the colorful **changing of the guards ceremony**, held at 11:30 A.M. daily (only on even numbered days in winter) in the forecourt of the palace. Still watched over by the impressively clad **Beefeater Guards**, the **Tower of London** with exhibits of the **Crown Jewels** and menacing **torture implements** is one of London's favorite tourist attractions. At the **House of Parliament** on the Thames by **Westminster Bridge**, the world's most famous clock, **Big Ben**, still sonorously tolls off the hours to the delight of the passing tourists. Practically within shouting distance of the Parliament buildings is yet another famous address, **Number 10 Downing Street**, the official residence of the prime minister. **St. Paul's Cathedral**, London's largest church and one of the city's landmarks, is a masterpiece of Renaissance architecture. Designed by Sir Christopher Wren, it contains the tombs of two of England's greatest military heroes: Admiral Nelson and Lord Wellington.

Within a small area, London has concentrated some of the world's most outstanding museums, filled with treasures gathered during the heyday of British imperialism. The **British Museum** in the elegant **Bloomsbury District** across from London University exhibits the famous **Elgin Marbles** (from the Parthenon in Athens), the **Rosetta Stone**, and the original **Magna Carta** as part of its enormous permanent collection. The **Tate Gallery** and the **Victoria and Albert Museum** house impressive collections of both fine and applied art. The **National Gallery** on busy **Trafalgar Square** displays one of the world's finest collections of great masters. The grandmere of all wax museums, **Madame Tussaud's**, has been a London institution since 1802.

In spite of its size, London is an easy city to negotiate. If you plan to use the excellent public transportation system extensively, you can save money by purchasing a "London Explorer Ticket," good for unlimited use of the buses and trains for one, three, four, or seven days, or the weekly "Travel Card" (passport photo necessary).

Obtaining tourist information in London is no problem. In fact, there is so much available that it is sometimes difficult and time consuming to sort it all out. Some of the best places for finding information include the **British Travel Centre** (Lower Regent St., London W1), **Tourist Information Centre** (Victoria Station), and **City of London Information Centre** (St. Paul's Churchyard and at the Tower of London).

For recorded information on the day's happenings call [01] 246-8041. Calling [01] 246-8007 will get you a recording on events of interest to children. Bookstores and newsstands are full of guidebooks, maps, and magazines with entertainment listings.

When changing money, stick to the banks; many change bureaus charge as much as a 5 percent commission.

Information on pubs all over Britain is available from **The Pub Information Centre** (93 Buckingham Palace Rd.; Tel: [01] 222-3232).

Accommodations in London are often in short supply and almost always expensive. Don't expect to find much of the fabled English charm and quaintness here unless you are willing to pay through the nose for it. Although the traditional B&B is a great place to stay throughout Britain, that is not the case in London. Functional, expensive, and devoid of charm would best describe the typical London B&B. In a pinch and for a fee, the **National Tourist Information Centre** at Victoria Station will find you a room. Whatever choice you make, be sure to clarify whether the 15 percent VAT (value-added tax) is included and whether you are getting an English or continental breakfast. Here are some of our best bets for spending a few nights in London.

If money is no object, and you have traded your Porsche for a Motobecane just to get the exercise, then the swank DORCHESTER (Park Lane; Tel: [01] 629-8888) overlooking Hyde Park is just for you. More in line with what most cyclists are looking for is a collection of decent bargain accommodations in the pleasant **Bloomsbury District**. For a nice budget hotel, try the pleasant and clean GRESHAM HOTEL (36 Bloomsbury; Tel: [01] 636-4888). If it's convenience you are seeking at the price of ambience, then head for the area around Victoria Station, particularly Belgrave Road and St. George's Drive. Try the BEVERLY TOWERS (106–108 Belgrave Rd.; Tel: [01] 828-6767).

There are five official youth hostels in London, all located away from Central London. The required membership card can be purchased at any of the five hostels. Two of the more accessible ones are located near the Earl's Court Tube Station (38 Bolton Gardens, SW5; Tel: [01] 373-7083) and near the St. Paul's Tube Station (36 Carter Lane, EC4; Tel: [01] 236-4965).

There are a number of campgrounds in the greater London vicinity; however, none are really conveniently located with respect to central London. Although London has several very lovely conveniently located parks, we advise against setting up a tent unless you want to have an unpleasant encounter with the otherwise very helpful London bobbies. One of the closest of the official sites is the EASTWAY CYCLE CIRCUIT, part of the Lee Valley Park (Temple Mills Lane) near Leyton Station on the Central Line. It is open 1 April to 31 October.

WINDSOR. On the outskirts of London not far from Heathrow Airport, the little town of Windsor sits picturesquely on the Thames, surrounded by 4,800 acres of park land. The main attraction here is **Windsor Castle**, the Queen's official residence and the largest occupied castle in the world. Erected in 1066 by William the Conqueror following his victory at the Battle of Hastings, this huge storybook castle dominates the surroundings. The elegantly furnished **state apartments** may be visited when not in use. Just across the river is the equally delightful town of Eton, site of one of Britain's most venerable and exclusive boy's school.

For a quiet, inexpensive B&B in Windsor, see MRS. MARTIN (34 Dedworth Road, Windsor SL4 3HF; Tel: [07535] 60876). The WINDSOR YOUTH HOSTEL (Edgeworth House, Mill Lane, Windsor, Berkshire SL4 5JE; Tel: (07535) 61710) is open March through November and offers dormitory accommodations.

Although there is a large campground 3 kms west of Windsor, WILLOWS RIVERSIDE PARK, they generally do not accept tent campers. With 4,800 acres of park land surrounding Windsor, you should have no problem finding a place to hide a tent for the night.

OXFORD. Site of Britain's oldest university, Oxford is the quintessential college town, even though it must now share the stage with such twentieth-century intrusions as a major automobile manufacturing plant in adjacent Cowley. There is no single Oxford University building, but rather some thirty-five separate colleges, each more or less an entity within itself, containing living quarters, dining halls, and libraries.

To visit Oxford is to visit the individual colleges, most of which are within easy walking distance of **Carafax**, the intersection of the town's four main thoroughfares. Among the colleges worth visiting are **Christ Church**, which has the largest quad and most prestigious reputation; **Magdalen College**, perhaps the most attractive of them all; and **St. Catherine's**, the most impressive of the women's colleges. Be sure to include the **Ashmolean Museum**, Britain's first public museum, in your intinerary.

Oxford takes a little time to get to know; try to stay a bit longer than the busloads of day-trippers who dash up from London for a few hours to "do" Oxford. Wander the streets, do some pub crawling (TURF TAVERN at 4 Bath pl. is an inviting cozy retreat nestled in a sprawling thirteenth-century building), and take a punt on the Thames to get the feel of the town. A good way to get acquainted is to take a guided walking tour. Cost for these pleasant and informative two-hour strolls is 1.50 pounds.

Blenheim Palace, just a short cycling distance north of Oxford and adjoining the delightful village of **Woodstock**, is England's largest private home and birthplace of Winston Churchill. Set in a huge park, the grandly furnished palace is open to visitors.

The place to stay in Oxford, which is short on formal hotel beds, is at a B&B. The town is full of them although most are a few kms from the center of town. COURTFIELD (367 Iffley Rd.; Tel: [0865] 242-991) is a good place to try first. If Mrs. Tong, the owner, doesn't have a free room, she will do her best to see that you find one. Another pleasant B&B in a quiet neighborhood at the far end of town toward Headington is PICKWICKS GUEST HOUSE (17 London Rd., Headington; Tel: [0865] 750-487). It is often free when others are full. The OLD BLACK HORSE (102 St. Clements; Tel: [0865] 244-691) is a cozy old traditional inn.

If you are looking for a youth hostel, check in at the YHA HOSTEL (Jack Straw's Lane, Headington; Tel: [0865] 62997). It offers 112 beds and meals are available.

A pleasant enough place, but a few kms cycling from the center of town, OXFORD CAMPING INTERNATIONAL (426 Abington Rd.) at the south end of town is a level, grassy campsite with a washing machine and camp store. It is open all year.

STOW-ON-THE-WOLD. Perched on a hill lying along the **Fosse Way**, one of the major Roman roads that traverses southern England, Stow-on-the-Wold has been the marketing center for this important sheep-raising and wool-producing region since medieval times. The market square contains a number of fine old Cotswolds houses.

The entire region is dotted with some absolutely delightful villages. Along the route, a short detour will lead you through two "gems": **Upper** and **Lower Slaughter**, whose names belie the tranquillity of these villages.

Bourton-on-the-Water, just down the hill from Stow, although often besieged with tourists, is worth a short visit. The town which exhibits a number of lovely honey-colored houses of Cotswolds stone, spans both sides of the Windrush River, which is crossed by a series of small graceful bridges. The **Birdland Zoo Gardens** at the edge of town is a large preserve with many rare species of birds.

THE KING'S ARMS (Market Square, Stow-on-the Wold, Cheltenham, Glos. GL54 1AU; Tel: [0451] 30364) is a delightful country inn that has been offering simple, inexpensive lodgings to passing horsemen and cyclists for some five hundred years! The GRAPEVINE HOTEL (Sheep Street, Stow-on-the-Wold; Tel: (0451] 30344) is another delightful country hotel, featuring modern comforts and lots of local stone, exposed beams, and a good dining room. For an especially pleasant and friendly B&B in nearby Bourton-on-the-Water, we recommend COOMBE HOUSE (Rissington Rd., Bourton-on-the-Water, Glos. GL54 2DT; Tel: [0451] 21966).

Campers should look for a small campground just off A436, 1 km past the junction with A429 in the direction of Cheltenham. There is also a campground, CAMPING LONGWILLOWS, about 5 kms out of Cheltenham off A435 going toward Evesham, near the railroad bridge by Bishops Cleeve. It is open 1 March to 31 October.

TEWKESBURY. Once an important crossroad at the junction of the Avon and Severn rivers, Tewkesbury has retained its medieval charm and character and yet remains somewhat aloof from the tourism that influenced so many of her sister cities. The pride of the town is the twelfth-century **Tewkesbury Abbey**. The small **Tewkesbury Museum** next to the tourist office is also worth a visit.

TOLSEY HOUSE (Tolsey Lane, Tewkesbury, Glos. GL20 5RT; Tel: [0684] 296512), a ramshackle old house creaking with atmosphere, was mentioned in the *Domesday Book*, a book that registered the holding of land during the twelfth-century reign of William the Conqueror. It is a pleasant B&B with a friendly hostess: Mrs. Sayers. In the luxury class, we like the ROYAL HOP POLE CREST HOTEL (Church Street; Tel: [0684] 293-293), a half-timbered old house with a fine cozy restaurant. The hotel was immortalized by Dickens in the *Pickwick Papers*. The rooms are expensive.

Campers can set up a tent for the night at MRS. EYRE'S SUNSET VIEW (Church End Lane, Twyning), about 5 kms north of Tewkesbury on A38 or at a local farmer's. The Mill Avon Campground is only for trailers and motorhomes!

STRATFORD-UPON-AVON. In spite of the blatant exploitation of its famous native son and the busloads of tourists who make the pilgrimage to anything and anyplace even remotely associated with the much celebrated "Bard of Avon," Stratford has much to recommend a visit. It is especially attractive early in the morning and in the early evening hours before and after the arrival and departure of the hordes of tourists.

There are five principal sites associated with Shakespeare: The **Birthplace** on Henely St., with an adjacent museum, The **New Place**, the foundations and gardens of what was once Shakespeare's house; **Hall's Croft**, a well-kept house where Shakespeare's daughter Susanna lived; **Anne Hathaway's Cottage**, a lovely thatched-roof cottage on the outskirts of town, and **Mary Arden's House**, the farmhouse where Shakespeare's mother lived before her marriage. If you can manage the tickets, attending a performance of the Royal Shakespeare Company on their home ground is a rare treat. Shakespeare was baptized and buried at the **Holy Trinity Church** on the River Avon.

If you would like to stay awhile and explore the local area by bike using Stratford as a base, the very busy but friendly folks at the **Tourist Information Centre** (1 High St.) can book a room for you and provide suggestions for local cycling itineraries.

Although the town is full of charming and some not so charming B&Bs, it is still difficult in the summer to get a room. If you can, try to make advance reservations. BROOK LODGE (192 Alcester Rd., Stratford-on-Avon, CV37 6AU; Tel: [0789] 295-988) is a pleasant B&B (small rooms, big breakfasts) just a few minutes cycling from the center of town. For a touch of authentic Elizabethan luxury, the SHAKESPEARE HOTEL (Chapel St.; Tel: [0789] 294-771), a sixteenth-century gabled Stratford landmark, is hard to beat. Doubles go from 65 pounds. Vegetarians can indulge to their hearts' content at Mrs. Pettitt's MAYFIELD HOUSE (7 Mayfield Ave.; Tel: [0789] 66214), a "vegetarian B&B" which offers evening meals.

The youth hostel, HEMMINGFORD HOUSE (Wellesbourne Rd., Alverton, CV37 7RG; Tel: [0789] 297-093), is about 3 kms from Stratford on B4086. It is a large attractive facility with dormitories and two family rooms.

There are several good campsites in the vicinity of Stratford, including DODWELL PARK on A439, about 3 kms from town in the direction of Evesham. Its full facilities include a washing machine and camp store. It is open all year.

WORCESTER. A quiet town on the River Severn somewhat away from the mainstream of tourism, Worcester is best known for its fine **cathedral**, which encompasses nine hundred years of English history. King John was buried there in 1216, and in 1652, during the Civil War, King Charles II perched in the tower and watched the defeat of his forces by those of Oliver Cromwell. Not far from the cathedral is the manufacturer of some of England's best china: the **Worcester Porcelain Company**. There is a shop on the premises and tours of the factory are given. The **Commandery** located in a fifteenth-century inn now houses a **Civil War Museum**.

The LOCH RYAN HOTEL (119 Sidbury, Worcester WR5 2DH; Tel: [0905] 351-143) is a reasonably priced historic hotel located next to the porcelain factory. An inexpensive Worcester hotel is the HILLEND HOUSE (Church Hill Lane, Whittington; Tel: [0905] 355-545), a large old Victorian house with antique furnishings, on the outskirts of town.

There is a conveniently located campground at the local racetrack in Pitchcroft: CAMPING WORCESTER RACECOURSE. It doesn't have much in the way of facilities, but is open 1 April to 31 October.

SHREWSBURY. One of the best-preserved medieval and Tudor towns in all of England, Shrewsbury is the historic capital of Shropshire. Attractively situated on a horseshoe bend in the River Severn, Shrewsbury is often referred to as the "town of flowers" and has retained its rural character. The narrow streets of the old town are lined with many well-preserved "black and white" half-timbered houses.

The top hotel in town is the traditionally styled but modernly outfitted PRINCE RUPERT HOTEL (Butcher Row, Shrewsbury SY1 1UQ; Tel: [0743] 52461). The WHITE HOUSE HOTEL (Hanwood, Shrewsbury; Tel: [0743] 53107) is a charming half-timbered, inexpensive, five-room hotel that dates back to the sixteenth century. Another Shrewsbury institution, with parts of the house dating back to the fifteenth century, and which has hosted such personages as Dickens and Disraeli, is THE LION (Wyle Cop, Shrewsbury; Tel: [0743] 53107). MRS. COLLEY'S GUEST HOUSE (3 Coton Crescent, SY1 2NY; Tel: [0743] 54712) is a pleasant, inexpensive B&B.

HEREFORD. Located on the River Wye close to the border with Wales, Hereford is an attractive town of traditional houses in a lush rural setting. The imposing eleventh-century **Hereford Cathedral** contains a number of treasures, including the **Mappa Mundi**, a rare, early fourteenth-century map showing that the world is flat. The **City Museum** houses a fine collection of Roman finds, as well as an unusual assortment of odds and ends. Hereford is also an important cattle and cider marketing center. The famous Hereford cattle come from this region. The **Museum of Cider** at the edge of town documents the history of cider making.

THE GREEN DRAGON HOTEL (Broad St., Hereford, HR4 9BG; Tel: [0432] 272-506), once a coaching inn, is now an impressive hotel. It is located near the cathedral and doubles run from 40 pounds. THE LONGWORTH HALL HOTEL (Lugwardine, Hereford; Tel: [0432] 850223) is a small comfortable hotel located in a Georgian mansion overlooking the Wye River. Mrs. Carr's CEDAR TREE GUEST HOUSE (123 Whitecross Rd., Hereford; Tel: [0432] 267-235) is your best bet for low-cost accommodations in Hereford. Evening meals and packed lunches are available.

The HEREFORD RACECOURSE CAMPGROUND is about 2 kms north of town near the racetrack. It is a large site with many amenities, including a camp store. It is open 19 April to 22 September.

GLOUCESTER. An ancient cathedral city on the River Severn, Gloucester still displays remnants of its Roman past in the center of town and in sections of the old city wall. The unique nineteenth-century **Victorian docks** are becoming popular as a tourist attraction. Gloucester is also home to an interesting **Folk Museum**.

THE TARA HOTEL (Upton Hill, Upton St. Leonards, Gloucester GL4 8DE; Tel: [0452] 617412) is a small, comfortable hotel in a seventeenth-century Cotswolds stone house in a park-like setting 5 kms from the city center. It offers panoramic views of the Severn Valley and Malvern Hills. The NEW COUNTY HOTEL (44 Southgate St., Gloucester GL1 2DU; Tel: [0452] 24977), once a coaching inn, is now a good moderately priced hotel, conveniently located in the center of Gloucester. For an inexpensive B&B, try Mrs. Pepler's friendly WESTVILLE GUEST HOUSE (225 Stroud Rd., GL1 5JZ; Tel: [0452] 31228).

HIGHNAM COURT (Highnam Court, Gloucester, GL2 8DP; Tel: [0452] 22703) is a youth hostel (no membership card required) with singles, doubles, and dormitory accommodations.

The RAC (Royal Automobile Club) has a campground at the RED LION INN, about 6 kms north of Gloucester. From A38, turn off at sign for Wainlode Hill. It is a large site with a store and restaurant and it is open all year.

CIRENCESTER. Scattered throughout the Cotswolds are some of the best remaining examples of the Roman presence in Britain. Of these, Cirencester, established at the point where the Fosse Way met five other major roads, is considered to be one of the finest. In Roman times named Corinium Dobunnorum, Cirencester was surpassed in size only by London. The **amphitheater** is the only building left standing; however, the **Corinium Museum** contains a number of fine Roman artifacts. The **Church of St. John the Baptist**, one of the largest in the country, contains some excellent examples of medieval stained glass.

THE FLEECE HOTEL (Market Place, Cirencester, Glos. GL7 4NZ; Tel: [0285] 68507) is an old Tudor coaching inn that has been recently restored. It offers rustic country decor, open fireplaces, and four-poster beds, as well as a fine restaurant and moderate prices. For budget-priced rooms, we like the friendly and helpful attitude found at the WITS END (50 Ashcroft Rd.; Tel: [0285] 68926), conveniently located in the center of town.

Campers can check in at the RAC site, COTSWOLDS CARAVAN PARK, 7 kms southeast of town on A419. Follow the signs toward Cotswolds Water Park. It is a large site with full facilities and is open Easter to 31 October.

BATH. As its name implies, Bath is a city where "taking the waters" is a major pastime. In fact, people have been doing just that since Roman times when the city was known as Aquae Sulis. In Georgian times, Bath was acknowledged to be England's second social capital as throngs of aristocrats flocked there for the waters and accompanying activities. Badly bombed during World War II, Bath has been carefully restored, and even though its population is now approaching the 100,000 mark and industrial development is beginning to appear on the scene, the city is still well known as a spa and health resort. Be sure to visit the practically intact remains of the original **Roman Baths** and the adjoining museum. There are guided walking tours of the old portion of the city. You can get details from the Tourist Information Office at the Abbey Church Yard in the center of town.

Bath gets very crowded in the summer so try to make advance reservations. As in most popular tourist centers, prices tend to be higher than in many other regions. If you are in the market for a luxury-class hotel, you will have quite a good assortment to choose from. At the top of the list is the very elegant HOTEL ROYAL CRESCENT (15-16 Royal Crescent, Bath, Avon; Tel: [0225] 319-090). Even if you don't want to shell out the 100 pounds or more to stay there for the night, do at least have a look. This historic Georgian hotel is one of Bath's finest buildings. On a more modest level, we like the unassuming and inexpensive HOTEL COUNTY (18-19 Pulteney Rd.; Tel: [0225] 25003). The town is full of pleasant inexpensive B&Bs. We especially like MRS. ROWE'S (7 Widcombe Crescent, Widcombe Hill; Tel: [0225] 22726) – a first-class B&B in every respect.

There is an IYHF YOUTH HOSTEL (Bathwick Hill; Tel: [0225] 65674) in a pleasant old mansion overlooking the city. It offers dormitory accommodations.

NEWTON MILL TOURING CENTER, a large grassy site on the outskirts of town just south of the junction of A4 and A39, offers camping facilities. It has a washing machine and camp store and is open all year.

SALISBURY. Salisbury is best known for its fine thirteenth-century cathedral which rises up some four hundred feet above the flat Salisbury Plain. Next to that of the Dom in Cologne, it has the world's highest church spire. The area around the cathedral contains some wonderful old homes, including the **Mompesson House**, which with its fine plaster work is the best-preserved of the several old houses in the area. The **Salisbury Wiltshire Museum** has a series of exhibits that follow the development of Salisbury, as well as some interesting material about nearby **Stonehenge**, that mystifying collection of 4,000-year-old stones. Stonehenge is located 16 kms north of Salisbury near the village of Amesbury.

THE ROSE AND CROWN HOTEL (Harnham Rd., Harnham; Tel: [0722] 27908) on the banks of the Avon at the south edge of Salisbury is a pleasant mixture of a half-medieval and half-modern hotel. For a B&B, try MRS. WHITMARSH'S HOUSE (3 The Crescent, Salisbury; Tel: [0722] 334-046), a pleasant home away from home.

The IYHF YOUTH HOSTEL MILFORD HILL HOUSE (Milford Hill; Tel: [0722] 27572) is a quaint old house in a garden setting with space for tents.

For a regular campground, check in at the SALISBURY CAMPING CLUB HUDSON FIELD SITE on Castle Road, a large grassy field with minimal amenities. To get there, take A345 toward Old Sarum and follow the signs. It is about 3 kms from Salisbury. It is open 1 April to 30 September. There is also a full-facility all-year site at Race Plain, COOMBE NURSERIES TOURING CARAVAN PARK. It is near the race track in Netherhampton about 3 kms west of the city off A3094.

FARNHAM. A pleasant old market town on the River Wye, Farnham has kept many of its lovely eighteenth-century and nineteenth-century buildings and houses. **Farnham Castle**, of Norman origin, is open to visitors.

WISHANGER STUD (Frensham Lane, Churt, Surrey GU10 2QQ; Tel: [025125] 4170) is a comfortable hunting lodge on a country estate in the heart of the Surrey countryside, 4 kms from Farnham on A287 in the direction of Haslemere.

WINCHESTER. Until it was eclipsed in the thirteenth century by London, Winchester was England's number one city. Dominating the center of the city and its main attraction is the massive **Winchester Cathedral**, which dates back to the eleventh century. Inside the **Great Hall**, all that remains of William the Conqueror's twelfth-century castle, is a fourteenth-century replica of the legendary King Arthur's Round Table.

Of the many Winchester B&Bs, we like two best. ANN & TONY FARRELL'S (5 Ranelagh Rd., Winchester, Hants SO23 9TA; Tel: [0962] 69555) is a delightful old Victorian house just a few minutes from the center of town, and MRS. HENNESSY'S AQUARIUS (31 Hyde St.; Tel: [0962] 54729) is another convenient Victorian B&B.

The IYHF YOUTH HOSTEL (1 Water Lane; Tel: [0962] 53723) offers rather spartan facilities in a converted eighteenth-century water mill.

The WINCHESTER RECREATION CENTRE provides a field suitable for tenting next to the city recreation center. To get there just follow the signs.

East Anglia

While it wouldn't really be fair to say that East Anglia is well off the beaten track, it is an area where you often can cycle for hours along meandering rural lanes and enjoy the gentle undulating countryside totally undisturbed. When you do encounter other tourists along the way, they somehow seem to be of a different nature than the day-trippers who pour out of the buses and invade such "must see" places as Stratford-upon-Avon and Oxford every summer. For some reason, the pace of things in East Anglia appears to be a bit slower. Although this region prospered during medieval times, the industrial revolution which transformed so much of the country essentially passed by East Anglia, leaving a peaceful rural backwater. More often than not the tourists you do meet are fellow cyclists. It is no secret that this part of England offers easy touring along with scenic beauty and interesting attractions.

Shaped somewhat in the form of an overstuffed peninsula pushing out into the North Sea and bordered by the broad yawning mouth of the Thames in the south and in the north by a wide inlet simply known as The Wash, East Anglia has had a long and intimate relationship with the sea. In fact, a good portion of the present peninsula, the flat marshy region in the northwest known as "the Fens," was covered by sea water for centuries. When the English talk about "the Broads," they are not referring to the female half of the species but rather to that expanse of meandering waterways, bogs, and bird preserves between Norwich and the sea known as the Norfolk Broads. This is prime bird-watching country, so bring along your favorite bird-watcher's guide and a pair of binoculars. The East Anglian coast is dotted with seaside resorts, although there are far better places in Europe for catching rays than England.

Included on this route are visits to the lovely university town of Cambridge and the massive seventh-century cathedral at Ely. The time spent in London can serve to add a cultural dimension to this tour.

EAST ANGLIA ROUTE

START	FINISH	BARTHOLOMEW NATIONAL SERIES
LONDON	LONDON	For navigation, use #15, Herts and Bucks; #16, Essex; #20, Cambridge; #21, Suffolk; #25, Fenland; #26, Norfolk (scale 1:100,000)

DISTANCE KM
501 kms/311 miles

MICHELIN MAPS
For an overall perspective, use Michelin #404, South East, Midlands, East Anglia
(scale 1:400,000)

BARTHOLOMEW GT SERIES
#5, East Anglia (scale 1:250,000)

If you are intimidated by the hilly sections of the "Heart of England Loop," this is the ideal route for you. Natural beauty, culture, and old English tradition are all laid out on a route where what would be considered not much more than a bump on the road in the Cotswolds is looked at by the East Anglians as a veritable mountain. Flat and easy is the name of the game. That is not to say that the countryside is boring. There are some gently undulating hills through the rich farmlands and occasional wooded area. Although you can cycle the entire route on a conventional one-speed bike, we like having the flexibility that a multi-speed bicycle offers, especially when encountering strong head winds, a frequent occurrence in "the Broads." The prevailing winds in the East Anglia region are from the southwest. The winds coming from the north and northeast often portend cold and nasty weather.

We start this route in London and follow it clockwise up to Cambridge and the cathedral city of Peterborough. At this point you can easily diverge from the route and tour Lincolnshire and the East Midlands. There are also good train connections from Peterborough to York and other parts of northern England and Scotland. The east coast port of Harwich is the terminal for ferries to Holland, Germany, and Denmark.

Although the route can be pedaled in either direction starting from any point along the way, the prevailing winds generally favor the clockwise approach.

This is ideal country for high season cycle touring. We have traveled through East Anglia in July and August and found the roads relatively free of auto traffic and the cities, with the exception of the beach resorts and such popular attractions as Cambridge, surprisingly uncrowded. It is well-known that it can rain anywhere and at any time in England; however, generally speaking, the East Anglian region is one of the drier areas of the country. The weather is often at its best in June and July.

This is not the area for huge vacation complexes or ultra-luxury hotels, but rather a region of quiet country inns and friendly B&Bs. Most of the major cities have youth hostels, and although there is a sprinkling of campgrounds in the interior, the greatest concentration is found along the coastline.

ENGLAND Through the Heart of England Loop

★ Shrewsbury

Ratlinghope
Ironbridge
Church Setton
Craven Arms
Bridgnorth
Wigmore
Mortimers Cross
Cleobury Mortimer
Great Witley
Martley
★ Worcester
Hereford
Fownhope
Evesham
Tewkesbury
Walton Cardiff
Crow Hill
Tredington
Welford
Bengeworth
★ Stratford
Hardwicke
Winchcombe
Gloucester ★
Uckington
Bourton
Stow
Stroud
Cheltenham
Sledington
Wittington
Idbury
Shipton
Charlbury
Cirencester
Ascott
Woodstock
Somerford Keynes
Blenheim
Sherston
Minety
Sopworth
Badminton
Malmesbury
Castle Combe
Kennington
★ Oxford
Marshfield
Acton Turville
Radley
Abingdon
Bath ★
Mountain Bower
Didcot
Appleford
Winsley
Blewbury
Westbury
Warminster
Whisley Green
Twyford
Heytesbury
Waltham
Windsor
Shrewton
Stonehenge
Reading
Datchet
Amesbury
Wilsford
Woodford
Sandhurst
Salisbury
Bighton
Medstead
Alton
Alderbury
Kings Worthy
London
Winchester ★
New Alresford
Farnham
Portsmouth

4

★ *LOOKING OUT OVER THE HANDLEBARS* ★

LONDON AND ONCE AROUND EAST ANGLIA

CITY
LONDON

ROUTE
A112 B194 B183

DISTANCE KM	TOTAL KM
58	0

ROUTE DESCRIPTION
Rather than fight your way out of London traffic, take the train from Liverpool St. Station to Harlow and start cycling from there. Otherwise, from the Liverpool Station, work your way out to Epping Forest, picking up A112 at Banbury Reservoir and taking that to Waltham Abbey. From there, follow B194 into Harlow. From Harlow, take B183 to the junction with A120. Continue north on B183 past Stansted Airport to the little village of Elsenham. Follow the signs to Henham and then to Debden Cross (not much more than a couple of houses and a barn). Take the road to the village of Debden and continue on into Saffron Walden.

CITY	ROUTE
SAFFRON WALDEN	B1052

DISTANCE KM	TOTAL KM
24	58

ROUTE DESCRIPTION
Leave Saffron on B1052 to Linton. Go through the town and continue through the pleasant rolling farmlands to Balsham. Then follow the signs to Cambridge.

CITY
CAMBRIDGE

ROUTE
A1309 A1123 A142

DISTANCE KM	TOTAL KM
29	82

ROUTE DESCRIPTION
From Cambridge, head toward Ely on Milton St. (A1309), the small road to Waterbeach which parallels the busy A10. From Waterbeach, head across the Fens to intersect with A1123. Turn right. After 3 kms, you will come to Wicken Fen (the oldest nature reserve in the country). Continue to A142 which runs through Soham and into Ely.

CITY
ELY

ROUTE
B1411 A1101 B1093 A605

DISTANCE KM	TOTAL KM
55	111

ROUTE DESCRIPTION
Leave Ely on B1411, and travel first to Chettisham, then to the intersection with A1101. Take A1101 to Delphi Bridge in the village of Welney. Continue 3 kms to B1093, turn left, and follow B1093 through Wimblington and Doddington to intersect with A605 just before Whittlesey. From Whittlesey it is only about 8 kms into Peterborough.

CITY
PETERBOROUGH

ROUTE
A47 B1141 A17

DISTANCE KM	TOTAL KM
48	166

ROUTE DESCRIPTION
Take A47 from Peterborough to Guyhirn. From there, follow B1441 to Wisbech. From Wisbech, take the road through West Walton and Walpole St. Peter to intersect with A17, which runs the last few kms into King's Lynn.

CITY
KING'S LYNN

ROUTE
B1145 B1153 A47 B1135 B1108

DISTANCE KM	TOTAL KM
65	214

ROUTE DESCRIPTION
From King's Lynn station, go out to Gaywood. Then pick up B1145 and follow it until the intersection with B1153. Turn right and follow B1153 through the rolling hill country to West Acre and then Castle Acre, continuing across A1065 to A47. Take A47 for 2 kms, then turn off in Wendling and continue through Scarning into East Denham. Take B1135 out of East Denham and stay with it until the juction with B1108. Take B1108 into Norwich.

CITY
NORWICH

ROUTE
B1140 A47

DISTANCE KM	TOTAL KM
33	279

ROUTE DESCRIPTION
Leave Norwich on B1140 across the Broads toward Great Yarmouth. After 18 kms, the road joins A47 at Acle and runs to the coast and the beach resort of Great Yarmouth.

Note: There is a ferry from Great Yarmouth to Scheveningen, Holland.

CITY
GREAT YARMOUTH

ROUTE
B1127

DISTANCE KM	TOTAL KM
25	312

ROUTE DESCRIPTION
Cross over the Yar and hug the coast down to the seaside resort and fishing port of Lowestoft. At the south edge of town past the golf course, take the road to Carlton Colville. Then continue to Beccles by way of Mutford and B1127.

CITY
BECCLES

ROUTE
B1117 B1120

DISTANCE KM	TOTAL KM
55	337

ROUTE DESCRIPTION

Take the road to Redisham. Then follow the signs to Halesworth. Pick up B1117 and continue on this until it meets up with B1120. Stay on B1120 past the castle at Framlingham. Then follow the back country lanes into Ipswich, passing through a series of tiny villages including Easton, Monewden, and Tuddenham.

CITY
IPSWICH

ROUTE
A1071 A1141 B1508

DISTANCE KM	TOTAL KM
56	392

ROUTE DESCRIPTION

Take A1071 to Hadleigh. Continue on A1141 toward Lavenham. After 2 kms, follow the signs to Kersey. From Kersey, follow the road to Sudbury, passing through The Heath. This is beautiful lush country with some actual hilly stretches. Take B1508 out of Sudbury about 20 kms to Colchester.

Note: If you are catching the ferry from Harwich, take A137 from Ipswich. Turn off at Manning Tree and take B1352 into Harwich. The ferry docks are well marked.

CITY
COLCHESTER

ROUTE
A604 B1024 A12 B1389 B1137 A12

DISTANCE KM	TOTAL KM
35	448

ROUTE DESCRIPTION

From Colchester, take A604 to where it runs into B1408 (traffic circle). Just past Marks Tey, pick up the cycle path, which ends on B1024 beyond the intersection with A12. Stay on B1024 through Kelvedon. Then take A12 to Witham. Continue on B1389 through Witham. Then take B1137 through Hatfield Peveral to rejoin A12 just past Boreham and continue on to Chelmsford.

CITY
CHELMSFORD

ROUTE
B1007 A129 A12

DISTANCE KM	TOTAL KM
18	483

ROUTE DESCRIPTION

Take B1007 out of Chelmsford to Billericay. Then take A129 to Brentwood. At this point, to avoid the heavy London traffic, we advise taking the train for the few kms into downtown London. If you stay on A12, it will take you into the center of London (about 30 kms), but it is tough and dangerous cycling.

CITY
LONDON/BRENTWOOD

DISTANCE KM	TOTAL KM
0	501

LONDON AND EAST ANGLIA: SIGHTS AND ACCOMMODATIONS

LONDON. See discussion under "Through The Heart of England Loop."

SAFFRON WALDEN. With one of the finest collections of medieval buildings in all of East Anglia, and possibly all of England, the market town of Saffron Walden dates back to the time of the Saxon invasions. Be sure to have a look at the **Sun Inn**, a fifteenth-century house with fine examples of seventeenth-century **pargetting** (an East Anglian tradition of carving in plaster). The inn was used as Cromwell's headquarters during the English Civil War. Also of interest are a local **museum** and the ruins of a **twelfth-century castle**. On the way up to Cambridge, stop in the village of Hadstock for a look at the lovely local church.

Thaxted, just a few kilometers from Debden Cross on the road from Harlow, is yet another jewel of an English country village. Spend a night at ARMIGERS (Thaxted CM6 2NN; Tel: [0371] 830-618), a sixteenth-century farmhouse inn, which has plenty of open beams and stone hearth fireplaces and is located in a beautiful garden setting.

The IYHF YOUTH HOSTEL (1 Myddylton Place, Saffron Walden CB10 1BB; Tel: [0799] 23117) is located in a fifteenth-century building at the north end of town.

CAMBRIDGE. If we could turn back the clock and do it all over again, then we would both choose Cambridge as the place to go to college. The stately college buildings which dominate the scene are set picturesquely amidst plenty of lawn and ivy along the Cam River. Although the centuries-old battle between Oxford and Cambridge over academic supremacy still rages, it's no contest when it comes to which town is the prettiest. With its sweeping lawns and parks, Cambridge wins hands down!

With the most important colleges all located within a short walking distance of one another, Cambridge is an ideal city to explore on foot or by bicycle. The town is jammed with cyclists; sometimes it seems as if the poor motorists don't have a chance.

Even if your visit is a short one, there are a few colleges that should be seen to capture the spirit of Cambridge. **Trinity College** founded in 1546, Cambridge's largest and most ostentatious college, boasts an impressive list of alumni that includes Francis Bacon, Issac Newton, and Lord Tennyson. The **Great Court** of Trinity college is the largest court in Cambridge. **King's College** (founded in 1441) is the site of the magnificent Gothic chapel begun in 1446 by Henry VII. Completed ninety years later, this is acclaimed by many as one of England's finest buildings. **Queen's College**, perhaps the most picturesque of them all, was founded in 1448 by Margaret of Anjou, the wife of Henry VI, and Elizabeth Woodville, wife of Edward IV.

The Fitzwilliam Museum, one of the country's oldest public museums, houses an interesting collection of Egyptian and Chinese antiquities and a diverse selection of paintings. Located in a beautifully landscaped setting on the Madingley Road some 7 kms outside of town is the **American Military Cemetery**, which contains the graves of thousands of American servicemen who died in World War II fighting from bases in Britain. The East Anglian region contained many U.S. Air Force bases.

Besides pub-crawling and cycling, another favorite Cambridge activity is **punting** (propelling a flat bottomed boat with a pole) on the Cam.

In this town of many pubs, where each one has more atmosphere than the other, the EAGLE, in a seventeenth-century coaching inn, is our favorite.

For a fine, traditional, old-style luxury hotel, check in at the UNIVERSITY ARMS HOTEL (Regent St., Cambridge CB4 3AN; Tel: [0223] 351-241) the edge of Parkers Piece opposite Emmanual College.

Cambridge has a large number of good B&Bs; however, they fill up fast, especially the singles, in the summer. One of the better ones is Mrs. Northrup's BON

ACCORD HOUSE (20 St. Margaret's Sq., Cherry Hinton Rd., Cambridge CB1 4AP; Tel: [0223] 246-568) just 3 kms from the center of town.

The CAMBRIDGE YOUTH HOSTEL, (97 Tenison Rd.; Tel: [0223] 344-601) is a large pleasant hostel with 125 beds, a few minutes walk from the train station.

Campers have the choice of several sites in the Cambridge area. The most conveniently located is HIGHFIELD FARM CAMPING SITE in Comberton, about 5 kms west of town off A603. It is a large grassy site with camp store, open 1 April to 31 October.

ELY. The outline of Ely's imposing **cathedral** can be seen from far across the level Fens, which surround this ancient little market town. Until the Fens were drained, the town stood on an island. Much larger than would normally be associated with a city the size of Ely, the cathedral was founded in 673. When Ely was conquered during the Norman invasion, the cathedral underwent substantial changes over a three-hundred-year period. In its present form it represents one of the country's finest examples of medieval architecture. Inside the cathedral is an interesting **stained glass museum**. Many of the adjoining old **monastic buildings** are still intact. Nearby is **Cromwell House**, the cottage in which Oliver Cromwell lived from 1636 to 1647.

The CASTLE LODGE HOTEL (50 New Barnes Rd., Ely CB7 4PW; Tel: [0353] 2276) is a comfortable eight-room family-run hotel in a quiet residential neighborhood just a five-minute walk from the cathedral. It offers home-cooked meals. NYTON GUEST HOUSE (7 Barton Rd.; Tel: (0353) 2459) is a nice little B&B.

The IYHF YOUTH HOSTEL BEDFORD HOUSE (28 St. Mary's St.; no phone) offers the basics with a minimum of comforts in a choice location in the center of town.

Campers can make arrangements to set up at BRAHAM FARM about 2 kms south of town near the golf course.

PETERBOROUGH. Although the city of Peterborough has little of interest for tourists, the **Peterborough Cathedral** is another story. From all aspects, this is a fine example of Norman architecture. The elaborate thirteenth-century painted ceiling is of particular interest. Stop by the **City Museum and Art Gallery** and view the archaeological exhibit.

The BULL HOTEL (Westgate, Peterborough PE1 1RB; Tel: [0733] 61364) is a fine eighteenth-century establishment with all the modern conveniences. It is located in the heart of the city. For a B&B, try MILTON GUEST HOUSE (156 High St.; Tel: [0733] 66870) only a few minutes by bicycle from the center of town.

KING'S LYNN. Set on both sides of the River Ouse, (pronounced ooze), the town of King's Lynn was one of England's principal ports in the early seventeenth century. During the heyday of the Hanseatic League, the city was an important link to north German and Scandinavian trading centers, and much of the dockside architecture reflects this close relationship. There are some particularly interesting buildings among the narrow riverside streets. The fifteenth century **Guildhall of St. George** has the distinction of being known as the only remaining building in England in which Shakespeare appeared in one of his own plays. This region has a centuries-old established tradition as a glass blowing center. For a better appreciation of this fascinating process, visit the **Wedgewood Crystal Factory**.

The STUART HOUSE HOTEL (35 Goodwins Rd., King's Lynn PE30 5QX; Tel: [0553] 772-169) is a quiet, moderately priced hotel near the center of town. For an inexpensive B&B, try Mrs. Bastone's MARANATHA GUEST HOUSE (115 Gaywood Rd.; Tel: [0553] 774-596).

The YOUTH HOSTEL (Thorsbey College, College Lane; Tel: [0553] 772-461) is conveniently located across from the tourist office.

WOODLAKE CARAVAN AND CAMPING PARK is a large open site with plenty of room for tents. It is located in South Runcton about 6 kms south of King's Lynn off A10 and is open 1 April to 31 October.

NORWICH. The cultural center of this corner of East Anglia and gateway to the maze of waterways that make up the **Norfolk Broads**, Norwich has been an important trading center since the Middle Ages, when it was second only to London. **Norwich Castle**, a massive stone structure atop a grassy hill set right in the center of town, was built by the Normans in 1130. The castle battlements afford superb views of the city and the surrounding flatlands. Another monumental vestige of Norman times is the twelfth-century **Norwich Cathedral**. To get a better appreciation of the bike you are riding, stop in at the **Bridewell Museum** and take a look at the old tricycle collection. A daily open-air market is held in the shadow of the Guildhall.

Norwich makes a good starting point for your exploration of the **Norfolk Broads**. Formed by the flooding of medieval peat bogs, this region of nature reserves is a favorite for bird-watchers. For further information, contact the **Broads Tours Information Centre** in nearby Wroxham (Tel: [0603] 610-734).

The CASTLE HOTEL (Castle Meadow, Norwich NR1 3PZ; Tel: [0603] 611-511) is a traditional old hotel located opposite the Norman Castle. For an inexpensive family-run hotel close to the center of town, try the ANNESLEY HOTEL (6-8 Newmarket Rd.; Tel: [0603] 624-533). Our Norwich B&B favorite is MRS. GREENSLADE'S HOUSE (24 Eaton Rd.; Tel: [0603] 57115) which is about a ten-minute bike ride from the center of town.

The NORWICH YOUTH HOSTEL (112 Turner Rd.; Tel: [0603] 627-647) is a pleasant facility about 1 km from the castle. Meals are available.

There is camping at KIRBY BEDON, about 5 km southeast of town off A146. There is an RAC campsite, CLIPPESBY HOLIDAYS, at Acle on the road to Great Yarmouth. It is a large shaded site with a camp store, open 19 May to 29 September.

GREAT YARMOUTH. With some fifteen miles of sandy beaches and a host of recreational facilities, Great Yarmouth is one of Britain's largest and most popular seaside resorts. The region's great maritime heritage is reflected in the exhibits on display at the **East Anglian Maritime Museum**. Vestiges of the old city wall remain.

The STAR HOTEL (24 Hall Quay, Great Yarmouth NR30 1HG; Tel: [0493] 842-294) is located in a sixteenth-century building and has good access to the Broads. For a friendly B&B, Mrs. Albone's BEAUMONT HOUSE (52 Wellesley Rd.; Tel: [0493] 843-957) is hard to beat.

The YOUTH HOSTEL is located at 2 Sandown Road (Tel: [0493] 843-991).

Of the several campgrounds in the area, we like the BURGH CASTLE CARAVAN HARBOUR & MARINA, near the Burgh Castle Marina about 5 km west of town. It is open all year.

BECCLES. A popular market town, Beccles is located on the south bank of the Waveney River, at the edge of the Broads. Virtually destroyed by a fire in the sixteenth century, Beccles contains more relatively new buildings than old.

THE SHIP GUEST HOUSE & RESTAURANT (Bridge St., Beccles NR34 9BA; Tel: [0502] 717-463) is a restored, one-time riverside inn with four-poster beds and good home-cooking.

There is a campground on the road from Great Yarmouth at Carlton Coleville: HEDLEY HOUSE PARK HOTEL CARAVAN SITE. It is a large grassy site with full facilities, open 1 April to 31 October.

IPSWICH. Standing on the site of an early Anglo-Saxon settlement at the head of an estuary of the River Orwell, Ipswich is Suffolk's principal industrial and commercial center. Ipswich has been one of England's most prosperous ports since medieval times. The nineteenth-century **Customs House** dominates the old part of the harbor. The **Christchurch Mansion** houses a fine collection of paintings by Constable and Gainsborough.

The portion of the route from Ipswich to Colchester passes through some of the prettiest and most interesting parts of East Anglia, including the busy market town of **Hadleigh**, whose High Street contains a remarkable variety of Suffolk architecture. The tiny village of **Kersey**, with its steep main street lined with ancient timbered houses, is a wonderful place to stop for a pleasant lunch or afternoon tea break. **Sudbury** was the birthplace of the famous English painter, Gainsborough, whose house is open to visitors. The landscape of this entire region is reminiscent of the paintings of John Constable, who spent a great deal of time capturing its beauty on canvas.

The BELSTEAD BROOK HOTEL (Belstead Rd., Ipswich IP2 9HB; Tel: [0473] 684-241) offers sixteenth-century Tudor atmosphere with twentieth-century comforts. For a cozy Ipswich B&B, try RIVERINA (6 Anglesea Rd.; Tel: [0473] 56417).

Campers can pitch their tents at PRIORY PARK, a large grassy site with full facilities, including a washing machine and camp store. It is located at the junction of A45 and A12, only a few kms southeast of the city center. The campground is open 1 May to 30 September.

COLCHESTER. Laying claim to being the oldest recorded town in England, Colchester's history goes back to the Iron Age. Captured by the Romans in 43 AD, it became the first Roman city in Britain. The **Norman Keep**, constructed on the ruins of a Roman temple, is the largest in Europe and houses a fine museum with exhibits from Colchester's Roman past. **The Bourne Mill** built in the sixteenth century as a fishing lodge still has functioning machinery. Colchester has been well known for its delicious oysters for centuries.

The ROSE AND CROWN HOTEL (East Gates, Colchester CO1 2TZ; Tel: [0206] 867-676), fully equipped with modern conveniences, is the oldest inn in this ancient town. For a well-located B&B, try GIL NICHOLSON (14 Roman Road; Tel: [0206] 577-905). It has comfortable rooms in a pleasant family atmosphere.

The Colchester YOUTH HOSTEL is in East Bay House (18 East Bay; Tel: [0206] 867-982). Meals are available.

There is a fully equipped campground, COLCHESTER CAMPING AND CARAVANNING PARK, on A604 at the junction with A12. It is open 1 April to 31 October.

CHELMSFORD. An important marketing center on the outskirts of London, Chelmsford was known in Roman times by the name of Caesaromagus. The history of the city is depicted in the **Chelmsford and Essex Museum**.

For a comfortable place to stay before heading back to London, check in at the PONTLANDS PARK COUNTRY HOTEL (West Hanningfield Rd., Great Baddow, Chelmsford CM2 8HR; Tel: [0245] 76444). It is an old Victorian mansion that has been converted into a small country hotel. For a good inexpensive hotel, try the TANUDA HOTEL (217-219 New London Rd.; Tel: [0245] 354-295).

Additional Recommended Routes

There is enough interesting cycle touring in Britain and Ireland to easily fill an entire book. Here are just some of the highlights of a few other favorite regions.

CUMBRIA AND THE LAKE DISTRICT

On the map the area looks a bit like a small bump on the west coast of England between the Scottish border on the north and the city of Lancaster in the south. Seen up close, Cumbria and the Lake District is one of England's most enchanting regions. Long a favorite with hikers, the lake district is rugged mountainous country with placid lakes and quiet villages. If you cycle here, plan to do some heavy-duty climbing – not quite alpine in difficulty, but not for the out-of-shape beginner either. When you look at a map of the region you will see that the major lakes radiate out from Grasmere at the center of the district. Although it's really a matter of taste, the most beautiful lake is probably Derwentwater near Keswick.

This region is best toured in September when the heavy summer tourist traffic is gone, and the roads are more suitable for cycling. For more information, contact the **British Tourist Authority** or the **Cumbria Tourist Board** (Holly Road, Ashleigh, Windermere, Cumbria LA23 2AQ; Tel: [09662] 4444).

Cyclorama Holidays (The Grange Hotel, Grange-over-Sands, LA11 6ET; Tel: [04484] 3666) offers complete cycling vacations in the Lake District.

WALES

With its dramatic coastline, an interior of rolling hills, isolated farms, impressive castles, and quiet valleys, Wales offers some of Britain's most beautiful landscapes. Cycling on the deserted back roads and trails is not as strenuous as cycling in the Lake District or the Scottish Highlands, but it still requires a good low-geared bike and a bit of stamina. Highlights include Pembroke, with its fine old castle; Betws-y-Coed, one of the loveliest villages in Wales; and the cathedral city of Hereford on the Wye River. For further information, contact the **Wales Tourist Board** (2/3 Maddox Street, London W1R 9PN).

THE SCOTTISH HIGHLANDS

An enchanting region of challenging cycling, the Scottish Highlands provide cyclists with an inspiring backdrop of rugged mountains and deep fjord-like lochs. Some of the region's highlights include Stirling – "Gateway to the Highlands" – Glencoe, and Inverness and the nearby Loch Ness. For further information, write or call the **Scottish Tourist Board** (23 Ravelston Terrace, Edinburgh EH4 3EU; Tel: [031] 332-2433).

IRELAND

Ireland's deserted country lanes, refreshing landscapes, and wonderful hospitality combine to make it a nearly perfect cycling destination. It is reached via regular ferry service from Fishguard in Wales to Rosslare in southern Ireland or from Holyhead to Dun Laoghaire near Dublin. The crossing time is about 3½ hours.

Connecting With Mainland Europe

Although Britain is an island, it is most definitely a very accessible one. Assuming that you fly into London and wish to continue your cycling on the continent, you will have a number of interesting routes to chose from. On most of the ferries that link Britain with mainland Europe, you will pay the so-called "foot-passenger" rate. In some cases, a nominal charge for your cycle will be made. Of the numerous ferry routes, the crossings between Dover, Felixstowe, and Folkstone in England and Calais, Boulogne, and Dunkerque in France are the shortest and most frequent. Crossing time is about 1½ hours. To connect with Normandy, take the ferry from Portsmouth/Weymouth to Cherbourg. The Dover-Ostend crossing will take you directly to Belgium in about 4½ hours. The East Anglian port of Harwich is the jumping off point for ferries to the Hoek of Holland as well as to the northern European ports of Hamburg, Germany and Esbjerg, Denmark.

THE NETHERLANDS

POPULATION
14,275,000

RELIGION
40% Roman Catholic;
33% Protestant

CAPITAL
Amsterdam
(The Hague: seat of government)

CURRENCY
Dutch gulden or guilder or florin
(Fl.); divided into 100 cents

OFFICIAL LANGUAGE
Dutch; English widely spoken

BANKING HOURS
M–F 0900–1600

STORE HOURS
M   1300–1800
T–S 0830 or 0900–1730 or 1800

EMERGENCY TELEPHONE NUMBERS
There is no one emergency
number; check directory

TO CALL USA OR CANADA
Dial 091; area code and number

HOLIDAYS
1 Jan.; Good Friday; Easter
Monday; 30 April; Ascension
Day; Pentecost; 25 and 26 Dec.

USA CONSULATES
Lange Voorhout 102
THE HAGUE
Tel: [070] 62 49 11
Museumplein 19
AMSTERDAM
Tel: [020] 79 03 21

CANADIAN CONSULATE
Sophialaan 7
THE HAGUE
Tel: [070] 61 41 11

TRANSPORTATION WITHIN THE COUNTRY

In a country as small as the Netherlands, there is not much cause to ship your bike from one part of the country to another. However, if you should be in a hurry or get caught up in a spell of bad weather, it's reassuring to know that you can hop on a train along with your bike at more than three hundred stations throughout the country. **NS** in Holland stands for **Nederlandse Spoorwegen**, the spotlessly clean and efficient national railroad system. Their excellent booklet, *Fiets en Spoor*, available at train stations and VVV offices, explains in detail all you need to know about traveling with a bicycle on the Dutch railways. Unfortunately, this booklet is only printed in Dutch.

Basically, you can take your bike along any place and at any time except between 0700 and 0900 and between 1630 and 1800 from Monday to Friday. You are required to remove bags and luggage from the bike and to load and unload the bike yourself. On some trains it is necessary to push a button to open the automatic doors on the baggage car. In addition to your own train ticket, you will also be required to buy a special ticket for the bike. The price depends on the distance traveled and varies from about 8 Fl. to 16 Fl.

During July and August it is possible to send your bike ahead. It will be shipped in a special bicycle car at a cost of 8 Fl. This service is available from sixty main train stations, and approximately two working days are required to reach destinations within the country.

Bicycles may not be transported on buses. Most Dutch ferries will let you take your bike along at no extra charge.

MAPS

With customary Dutch efficiency, this small country has been mapped to an extraordinary degree. For cycling purposes, the excellent series of maps on a scale of 1:100,000 published by **ANWB** (the Dutch Automobile Club) is hard to beat. The entire country is covered by fourteen maps which show the smallest of villages as well as cycle paths and the smallest country roads and lanes. The red dotted lines marked *Fietspad* denote cycle paths, and the dotted black lines marked *Brom-fietspad* refer to paths where mopeds are also allowed. Each map costs about 9 Fl.

For planning purposes and a good overall view of the country, use the ANWB map called *Overzichtskaart Brom/Fietsroutes in Nederland* (scale 1:500,000). This shows the principal bike routes in the Netherlands. ANWB maps can be purchased by mail from the ANWB head office and in person from branch offices, as well as in many book stores and VVV Tourist Information Offices in the larger cities.

The **Michelin Map #408, Netherlands** (scale: 1:400,000) is also good for an overview of the country; however, bike paths are not shown. VVV offices often have very detailed maps along with cycling suggestions for their immediate areas. If you have the ANWB series, these are usually superfluous.

When looking for place names on maps or road signs you will notice that within the Benelux countries (the Netherlands, Belgium, and Luxembourg) some cities have more than one name. For example, The Hague is known in Holland as *Den Haag* and *'s-Gravenhage*.

BIKING THROUGH EUROPE

THE NETHERLANDS

The country is not very big: a motorist can zoom from one end of the Netherlands to the other in just a few hours. In fact, the entire country could fit inside the state of West Virginia with plenty of space left over. Holland has one of the world's highest population densities and land is very much at a premium – some 20 percent of the land surface has been reclaimed from the sea and actually lies below sea level.

From a bicyclist's perspective, this compactness offers many advantages. The Netherlands is one of the world's most "bicycle friendly" countries, and it offers a wide range of excellent touring opportunities. An extensive 10,000-kilometer network of cycle lanes and trails passes through a variety of appealing landscapes – from the sandy dunes of the windswept North Sea beaches, through fertile farmlands and tidy villages, to the wooded hills in the "three country corner" at the southeastern edge of the country where Holland meets Germany and Belgium.

Although we use the terms Holland and the Netherlands interchangeably, there is, as a Dutch friend recently reminded us, a slight difference. The term Holland used in its strictest sense refers to the provinces of North and South Holland which make up the fen region, the economic and cultural heartland, lying in the northwest part of the country. He assured us, however, that no one in either the Netherlands or Holland would be upset if we continue to interchange these two terms.

Despite the fact that the Dutch watch *Dallas* on their Japanese tv's and munch on Big Macs while punching programs into their Apple PC's, a large portion of what we consider the traditional Holland remains essentially unaltered. Even though they have long since become obsolete, and some have been converted into museums, as you cycle through the flat countryside you will still encounter a good number of picturesque windmills silhouetted against the flat Dutch landscape. Dutch flowers continue to set the standard for the world, and one of the joys of a cycle tour through Holland in the spring is pedaling through the acres and acres of fields ablaze with blossoming flowers.

The famed Dutch tulips, hyacinths, and crocuses are in bloom from the end of March to mid-May. Amsterdam, as it has been for centuries, is still a teeming melting pot of various cultures and races. The country's great museums continue to pay homage to such monumental artists as Rembrandt, Franz Hals, and Van Gogh.

The Dutch pride themselves on being among the world's most hospitable people. As you tour this tiny constitutional monarchy where more than three quarters of the population ride bicycles, you will have many opportunities to sample and enjoy this warm hospitality. Don't worry about communicating with your hosts. English has been mandatory in the schools for years. While you will occasionally run into some older people who speak no English – especially in the more remote regions (there's not many in this densely populated little country) – most people have at least a working knowledge of English.

With the exception of the rather hilly province of Limburg (which is wedged between Belgium and Germany) and the few hills in the Veluwe region, the Netherlands is very flat, which makes this an ideal starting point for a first European cycling tour.

The country's highest point, **Dreilandenpunt** (Three country point) at the joining of the Dutch, German, and French borders is all of 321 meters (1,046 feet) high! Get your legs in shape here before moving on to tackle some of the more challenging terrain in Germany, Austria, Switzerland, and France. Amsterdam's Schiphol Airport is one of Europe's major gateways.

Even though the routes we have laid out pass through mainly flat country, the often strong winds make the use of a multispeed bike more of a necessity than a luxury. In the face of a strong North Sea wind, a low gear can be a good friend; and when pushed by a friendly tailwind, it's nice to get extra speed by pedaling effectively with the wind.

ROADS

Special lanes and paths for cyclists are literally everywhere. Some 10,000 miles of pathways are identified by a round blue sign with a white bicycle in the middle. This means you can crisscross this tiny country for most of your tour and not have to put up with fighting traffic or worrying about getting clipped by a passing auto. Even the cities and towns are well covered. The words "Fietspad" and "Rijwielpad" refer to so-called optional cycling lanes. Marked by small rectangular black signs, these often provide some of the country's most enjoyable cycling, well away from roads and automobiles. Mopeds may not be operated on these lanes with their motors on.

But while you can cycle virtually anywhere in the Netherlands without giving much concern to auto traffic, you do have to be very concerned with your fellow cyclists. Pedaling along some bike lanes, which are shared with bromfiets (motor bikes), is a bit like being on a cyclist's Hollywood freeway with bikes zooming about in all directions. Around the major cities some of these paths are four lanes wide and packed with two-wheelers of all sorts – noisy mopeds, sleek racers, and heavily laden touring bikes. There are even special traffic lights for cycles along some paths. This is one of the few countries in which we've cycled where we don't feel like second-class citizens.

Where marked cycle paths or lanes are present, the law requires that they be used. Because of the large number of cycles in use, it is necessary that a few special traffic rules applying to bicycles and mopeds be observed:

1. **Keep to the right and pass on the left.**
2. **Fast moving bikes have the right-of-way over slower moving traffic.**
3. **Traffic turning left or right must yield to oncoming traffic.**
4. **Cycles are not permitted on freeways and autobahns.**
5. **Turns must be indicated by clearly extending the left or right arm.**
6. **"Effective" lighting must be used between thirty minutes before sunset and thirty minutes after sunrise.**

All pretty much common sense, but observing these few basics will make your stay in the Netherlands a safer and more enjoyable one. The Dutch have a penchant for using bells; whenever you hear a clinking behind you – or for that matter the whine of a moped engine – it means move over or be run over. A bell is required equipment on all bikes operated in the country. On the rare occasions where you find yourself exposed to Dutch motor traffic, you will find that drivers are courteous and respectful with regard to bicyclists.

Wherever you go, whether along cycle paths or on the surfaced streets, you will find an excellent system of signposts with distances marked in kms. The many road signs will also have an additional white sign with red lettering and a red bicycle. These indicate roads with low traffic densities that are particularly well suited for cycling. Many small country roads and cycle paths are marked with low concrete globs, which because of their shape are often called mushrooms. Each of these concrete mushrooms has a number that is marked on the ANWB maps (scale 1:100,000).

Those of you who choose to tour Holland with a finely tuned lightweight skinny-tired racer will soon come to envy your colleagues mounted on sturdy fat-tired cycles. They are not much to look at, but great for absorbing cobblestones, ruts, and potholes, which are frequently encountered.

BICYCLE SHOPS AND RENTALS

As you might well imagine in such a bicycle happy country, you are never very far away from a repair shop. There are more than five thousand such shops scattered throughout the country; very few towns or large villages are without some sort of bicycle repair facility. Since Holland is on the metric system, it is difficult to get nonmetric spare parts.

There are probably more opportunities for renting bicycles in Holland than in any other country in Europe. Most of these are basic, heavy-duty, one-speed or three-speed machines.

In addition to the some one hundred railroad stations that rent cycles, there are also a number of private firms that specialize in bicycle rentals. One outfit called **Rent a Bike** has a plan that allows you to rent a bike at one place and return it to any of the fifty participating firms. Lists of rental firms are available from local VVV offices and **Stichting Fiets**, the organization that represents the Dutch bicycle industry. It sells a list with the names and address of more than one thousand rental firms. You can rent a basic machine for as little as 6 Fl. per day.

Here are just a few rental firms: In Amsterdam, contact RENT A BIKE (Stationsplein 6) next to the Central Station, HEJA (Bestevaerstraat 39), or FIETS-O-FIETS (Amsterdamse Bos).

Parking bicycles can often be a problem. More than one hundred railroad stations offer "parking facilities" for bicycles, and many towns have private cycle storage depots called *Rijwielstallingen*. Ask at the local VVV offices for details.

Bicycle theft is a major problem in Holland's big cities. Amsterdam is particularly notorious, so be sure to securely lock your bike even if you are leaving it just for a few minutes.

The Dutch make some very fine bicycles and if the purchase of a new bike is in your plans, you might want to consider purchasing one there.

ACCOMMODATIONS

The Dutch have perfected the art and science of providing comfortable accommodations for their many guests. Whether a luxury hotel, modest inn, youth hostel, or campground, you can count on it being immaculately clean. In fact, the whole country, with perhaps the exception of parts of Amsterdam, gives a tidy, clean, orderly appearance.

Hotels are classified by two systems. The system where a "plain but comfortable hotel" receives one star and a luxury hotel receives five stars is being replaced by the Benelux Hotel Classification system, also in effect in Belgium and Luxembourg. It is compulsory for all establishments offering accommodations. Category 1 denotes the minimum in facilities and category 5 the highest level.

Prices for a single with breakfast in a modest hotel run from 45 Fl. upwards, while the minimum price for the same in a luxury hotel is 200 Fl. Breakfast is normally included in the room price.

In addition to regular hotels, there are many small guest houses and private homes with rooms available. For details, check at the local VVV offices, which also offer a room finding service.

The National Reservations Center (Postbus 404, 2260 AK Leidschendam; Tel: [070] 20 25 00; Telex: 33755) is a booking service offered by the Dutch hotel trade. Reservations can be made by telephone, telex, or by mail. Be sure to clearly state your requirements – arrival and departure dates, desired price range, number of people, and whether a private bath is required. There is no charge for this service, and you will receive written confirmation of your reservation.

At the budget end of the accommodations, there are more than fifty youth hostels. Although there is a heavy concentration of hostels along the North Sea coast, distances throughout the country are such that it is possible to cycle between hostels in a day. Meals are available at all hostels but only a few provide kitchen facilities. Membership is no longer required, but members qualify for reduced rates. For

further information about youth hostels, contact **Stichting Nederlandse Jeugderberg Centrale (NJHC)** (Prof. Tulpplein 4, 1018 GX Amsterdam; Tel: [020] 26 44 33). In addition to the youth hostels, there are also a number of inexpensive youth hotels and sleep-ins. For details, write to the NBT for their booklet, *Holland, A Young and Lively Country*.

Campers have their choice of 2,500 official campgrounds, one of the highest concentrations in Europe. To promote and encourage cycle-camping, some ninety campgrounds, located at intervals of from 20 to 50 kms have banded together. For details, contact **Stichting Gastvrije Fietscampings** (Postbox 27, 4493 ZG, Kamperland Holland). Free camping is prohibited, and since just about every square meter of land in Holland seems to be accounted for, it's a good idea to ask permission before putting up your tent.

FOOD AND DRINK

One word comes to mind when we think of Dutch food, and that is hearty. Perhaps it's something that has evolved over the years to provide the fuel to ward off the bone-chilling cold North Sea winds that sweep across the country in winter and occasionally in summer. Should you encounter such a spell of weather, park your bike at the nearest restaurant and load up on a heaping bowl of hot, thick Dutch split-pea soup (*erwtensoep*) and a glass of *jenever*, the native gin. It's the best cure for the cold.

For a quick snack along the way, stop at a *broodjeswinkel* (sandwich shop) where you can get delicious rolls with an incredible variety of fillings. A favorite Dutch institution is the *bruine kroeg* (brown cafés). These are cozy, simply furnished cafés, full of atmosphere and great for meeting people.

If you are doing your own shopping and picnicking along the way or doing some light cooking in campgrounds or hostels, you will find a wide variety of food products in Dutch markets. The bakeries are nothing short of outstanding, featuring all sorts of tasty breads and rolls which, when combined with any one of the many fine Dutch cheeses, make for a tasty and inexpensive lunch. Fruits and vegetables are first-class, and produce stands and open-air markets abound.

Holland's close association with the sea is mirrored in its cuisine. Fresh fish, mussels, and oysters are widely eaten, particularly in the province of Zeeland. Herring prepared in a variety of ways and served with all sorts of sauces is the most popular form of seafood. The *haringkar* or herring cart is found in towns and villages throughout the country.

A traditional meal and one that will probably keep you cycling for a week could consist of *hutspot*, or hodgepodge, a stew with potatoes and boiled beef, sauerkraut with all the trimmings, thick pea soup, and cabbage with sausages, with all of this washed down by a liter or so of a good Dutch beer, such as Heineken or Amstel.

Throughout the country some 250 restaurants display a sign reading *Neerlands Dis* and feature moderately priced, traditional meals in atmospheric surroundings. For budget-priced meals, look for restaurants featuring the three-course Tourist Menu for a fixed price of just under 20 Fl.

One of the enduring benefits of the Dutch colonial period, the days when this tiny nation of seafarers controlled vast interests in the Far East, is the influence on the cuisine in The Netherlands. Dutch markets are full of food products from all over Asia, and oriental restaurants – especially those serving Indonesian food – are some of the best in Europe.

SOURCES OF ADDITIONAL INFORMATION

Through its offices in the U.S. and Canada, **The Netherlands Board of Tourism (NCT)** can provide general information, including a useful booklet called *Cycling in Holland*, which also lists a number of package cycle tours. Within the country there are more than 400 local **VVV Tourist Information Offices** (Vereniging Voor Vreemdelingen Veerker is Dutch for organization for Tourism). They are denoted by blue triangular VVV signs. These offices can provide information on everything from rooms in private homes to cycle rentals and regional touring suggestions. Since VVV offices receive no financial support from the government, there is a charge for most of the material they provide.

Netherlands Board of Tourism (NBT)
355 N. Lexington Ave.
New York, NY 10017
Tel: [212] 223-8141

605 Market St. Room 401
San Francisco, Ca. 94105
Tel: [415] 543-6772
25 Adelaide St. East, Suite 710
Toronto, Ont. M5C 1YC
Tel: [416] 363-1577

Stichting Fiets (Europaplein 2, 1078 GZ Amsterdam; Tel: [020] 42 55 50), the organization of the Dutch cycling industry, can provide a list of cycle rental firms, as well as a general information sheet in English called *Cycling in the Netherlands*. They also publish a number of booklets (in Dutch only) that describe various cycle touring routes.

Koninklijke Nederlandse Toeristenbond (ANWB) (Wassenaarsweg 220, 2509 BA The Hague; Tel: [070] 26 44 26), the Royal Dutch Automobile Club, has offices throughout the country. They publish an excellent series of cycling maps and route suggestions (in Dutch).

Nederlandse Rijwiel Toer Unie (NRTU) (Postbus 326, 3900 AH Veenendaal; Tel: [08385] 21 421) is the Dutch National Cycle Touring Club. In addition to their touring magazine, they also have a listing of some 350 cycling routes.

The Historic Heart of Holland

Although Amsterdam is the country's capital, the actual seat of the government is located in the stately old city of Den Hague, some sixty kilometers removed. The western portion of the country, the location of both capitals, also contains most of Holland's other important cities, including the largely modern city of Rotterdam, with its busy harbor, and the provincial capital of Utrecht, a unique combination of state-of-the-art urban planning and well-preserved historical buildings. Within the loop formed by connecting these major cities lies Holland's greatest concentration of industrial resources and nearly half of its population. Also concentrated within this circle of cities known as the Randstad are some of Europe's finest museums and cultural treasures. All of these cities – even busy Amsterdam – have excellent networks of cycle paths that make visiting a pleasure for cyclists.

Even though this is the most densely populated portion of the Netherlands, the stretches between the major cities are oases of tranquillity, providing a pleasant contrast to the bustle and activity of big city life. This is the region of the classic Dutch landscape that has intrigued artists over the centuries. Pedaling through this delightful flat countryside, we were amazed at just how much of the charm and beauty of "Old Holland" is still intact – lush green pastures, the intricate maze of canals spanned by quaint chain bridges, picturesque little villages, and even a surprising number of old-fashioned windmills.

The North Sea coast, which extends from Den Hague to Den Helder is a region of broad sandy beaches with huge sand dunes and fashionable seaside resorts. The province of North Holland contains the famous cheese towns of Alkmaar and Edam. Beyond Den Helder, the naval base at the tip of the peninsula, ferries can take you to the quiet beaches of Texel, the southernmost of the series of Wadden Islands which lie just off the Dutch coast. Our route returns to Amsterdam along the shore of the Ijsselmeer, the former Zuiderzee, now the object of an extensive reclamation project.

HOLLAND Amsterdam and the Historic Heart of Holland

TEXEL

De Koog
Den Burg
Den Helder — Ferry
Den Oever
Amstelmeer
Wieringerwerf
IJSSELMEER
Medemblik
Andijk
Wevershoof
Enkhuizen
Hoorn
MARKERMEER
Alkmaar
Bergen aan Zee
Boekel
Ankersloot
Alkmaarder Meer
Beverwijk
Edam
Marken
Volendam
Velsen Noord
Monnickendam
Ijmuiden
Noordzee Kanaal
Oosterpoel
Bloemendaal aan Zee
Amsterdam
Uitdam
NORTH SEA
Haarlem
Durgerdam
Schiphol Airport
Veluwe meer
Zandvoort
Rijnkanaal
Keukenhof
Amstel River
Loenen
Ruigenhoek
Lisse
Breukelen
Katwijk
Maarssen
Leiden
De Meern
Utrech
Wassenaar
Woerden
Scheveningen
Den Haag
Ijssel
Oudewater
Hoek van Holland
Gouda
Schie River
Stolwijkersluis
Stolwijk
Delft
Lek River
Hollandse
Krimpen
Rotterdam
Kinderdijk

5

AMSTERDAM AND THE HISTORIC HEART OF HOLLAND

START	FINISH	ANWB TOERISTENKAARTEN MAPS
AMSTERDAM	AMSTERDAM	#5, Randstad noord en 't Gooi, #6, Randstad midden en Zuid; #1, Noord-Holland noord (scale 1:100,000)

DISTANCE	
481 kms/299 miles	

On a scale of one to ten, with ten being the most difficult, we would have to grade this route with a number one. This is level easy-going cycling. If you can pedal your bike to the corner grocery store and back without having to take supplementary oxygen, you will have no difficulty doing this route. The only possible cause for huffing and puffing would be if you encounter some strong headwinds. Although there is no guarantee that the winds will follow our recommendations, the normal pattern of prevailing winds in this part of the country gives you the best chance of having tailwinds rather than headwinds if you follow this route in a clockwise direction.

The route as described starts in Amsterdam, which is readily accessible by train from all over Europe, and whose Schiphol Airport is one of the continent's most convenient gateways. Drawn out on the map, the route looks like a figure eight; it can be picked up at any point along the way. For example, if you are coming from England, the ferry from Harwich will deposit you at the Hook of Holland, just south of the Hague, while the boat from the East Anglian port of Great Yarmouth will take you to the beach resort of Scheveningen. If you have budgeted only a short time for your tour of Holland, you can do just one of the loops of the figure eight and then catch a train in Amsterdam for your next country. Conversely, should you want to see more of the Netherlands after completing this route, you can follow the directions for the loop through the Veluwe region.

For maximum enjoyment of the famous Dutch tulip fields and flower gardens of De Keukenhof, the ideal time to come is during April and May when the polders are transformed into a carpet of brightly colored blossoms stretching as far as the eye can see. The North Sea coast is at its best during July and August, although in good weather, the sun-starved natives who haven't abandoned their homeland for the beaches of southern Europe jam the local beaches. Any time you travel in this part of Europe, you should be prepared for rain. Fortunately, there are plenty of cozy bars and cafés along the route should you need to seek refuge from the elements.

Since this route passes through some of the most heavily populated and most popular portions of the country, accommodations of all types are plentiful, although reservations are advised at the beach resorts and during high season.

AMSTERDAM AND THE HISTORIC HEART OF HOLLAND

CITY	ROUTE
AMSTERDAM	S108 A9

DISTANCE KM	TOTAL KM
28	0

ROUTE DESCRIPTION

From the Central Station, follow S108 through the Amsterdamse Bos. At the autobahn A9, pick up the cycle route that runs alongside the autobahn past Schiphol Airport into Haarlem.

CITY
HAARLEM

DISTANCE KM	TOTAL KM
36	28

ROUTE DESCRIPTION

Head out from the Haarlem Central Station along the pleasant bike path that runs through the woods and dunes, following the main road to the beach at Bloemendaal aan Zee. Continue north along the coast through the Nationaal-park De Kennemer to the port town of Ijmuiden at the mouth of the Noordzee Kanaal. Follow the signs to Velsen Zuid, cross the canal into Velsen Noord, and continue through the town of Beverwijk. At Beverwijk/Meerstein, join up with the cycle path that runs through the small town of Ankersloot on the Alkmaarder Meer, and then continue for 2 kms along the Noord Hollands Kanaal. At Boekel, meet up with the bike trail that leads into the center of Alkmaar.

CITY
ALKMAAR

DISTANCE KM	TOTAL KM
47	64

ROUTE DESCRIPTION

Follow the cycle path from the center of Alkmaar to the seaside resort of Bergen aan Zee. From there the cycle path extends practically uninterrupted through the dunes and along the rugged North Sea coast 35 kms to the port city of Den Helder, passing some of the country's finest beaches along the way.

CITY
DEN HELDER

DISTANCE KM	TOTAL KM
45	111

ROUTE DESCRIPTION

Pedal down to the harbor and take the 20-minute ferry ride over to the island of Texel. Upon leaving the ferry, follow the cycle path to Den Burg, the principal town on the island. From there the path passes through De Koog at the beach, where there are several good campsites. Continue along the path, paralleling the beach, and return to Den Burg through the rich farmland that makes up most of the interior of the island.

CITY
TEXEL

DISTANCE KM	TOTAL KM
46	156

ROUTE DESCRIPTION

After returning to Den Helder, pedal about 23 kms through the rich polder land to the small port of Den Oever at the beginning of the 30-km-long dike that connects the provinces of North Holland and Friesland. This remarkable feat of engineering was built in 1927-32 and turned the former Zuiderzee into an inland lake, the Ijssermeer. A cycle path parallels the road across the dike. From Den Oever, a good cycle path follows the road to the small coastal town of Medemblik, first passing through the village of Wieringerwerf, center of the Wieringermeer Polder, which until the 1930s was completely under water.

CITY
MEDEMBLIK

DISTANCE KM	TOTAL KM
19	202

ROUTE DESCRIPTION

From Medemblik, continue along the coast road through Wevershoof to Andijk. Then head south along the bike path through the tulip fields into the port town of Enkhuizen.

CITY
ENKHUIZEN

DISTANCE KM	TOTAL KM
19	221

ROUTE DESCRIPTION

The 19 kms from Enkhuizen to Hoorn are best covered on the path that runs alongside the main road between these two port towns. The road passes through one of the country's most prosperous rural regions.

CITY
HOORN

DISTANCE KM	TOTAL KM
15	240

ROUTE DESCRIPTION

From Hoorn, follow the narrow road along the dike to Edam. Although there is no cycle path, traffic is generally light. Stop occasionally to climb to the top of the dike for views of the sea.

CITY
EDAM

DISTANCE KM	TOTAL KM
30	255

ROUTE DESCRIPTION

The most pleasant way to return to Amsterdam to continue with this route or to take the "Amsterdam and the Veluwe Region Route" is to follow the road alongside the dike, passing through the quaint villages of Monnickendam and Uitdam. Called Waterland, this region is a delightful expanse of rich pasture land interspersed with numerous small lakes and waterways. For an interesting side trip, at Oosterpoel just south of Monnickendam, take the causeway leading to the former island of Marken, a popular tourist spot.

The local inhabitants often don traditional costumes for the enjoyment of the tourists. From Marken continue toward Durgerdam, and from there follow the signs to Nieuwendam. Then continue to the IJ ferry, which docks just behind Amsterdam's Central Station.

Note: To continue with the "Veluwe Region Route," from Durgerdam, follow hwy N10 across the bridge and continue on N10 until it intersects with S113. Follow S113 through Diemen and continue with Veluwe route.

CITY
AMSTERDAM

DISTANCE KM	TOTAL KM
38	285

ROUTE DESCRIPTION
From the center of Amsterdam, follow the Amstel River out of the city to Amstel Park. At the park, pick up a bike trail that follows autobahn A2 toward Utrecht. At the intersection with N201, turn off toward Hilversum. After crossing the bridge over the Amsterdam Rijnkanaal, pick up the cycle trail to Loenen. From Loenen take the small road along the canal to Breukelen and continue on to Maarssen. In Maarssen, pick up the bike path that runs along the canal and continues into the center of Utrecht.

CITY
UTRECHT

DISTANCE KM	TOTAL KM
30	323

ROUTE DESCRIPTION
From the Utrecht Central Station, follow the road toward Woerden, crossing the Merwede Kanaal and then the Amsterdam Rijnkanaal. In the village of De Meern, pick up the cycle path that runs alongside the road to Gouda. This picturesque route follows the Hollandse Ijssel as it winds its way through the lush green farmlands. The marketplace in the little village of Oudewater, 18 kms from Utrecht, displays some fine examples of seventeenth-century gabled architecture.

CITY
GOUDA

ROUTE
N207

DISTANCE KM	TOTAL KM
29	353

ROUTE DESCRIPTION
From Stolwijkersluis on the river at the south edge of Gouda, take N207 for about 1 km toward Stolwijk. Turn right onto the road (no autos allowed) which after about 4 kms runs into a bike path that winds its way into Krimpen A/D Lek. Cross over the Lek River at this point to visit Kinderdijk, the country's largest concentration of windmills. Head back over the river to Krimpen and follow the signs into Rotterdam centrum.

CITY
ROTTERDAM

DISTANCE KM	TOTAL KM
10	382

ROUTE DESCRIPTION
From the Rotterdam Kleiweg Station, take the cycle path east just past the airport. Cross over the Schie River and follow the path 7 kms up to Delft.

CITY
DELFT

DISTANCE KM	TOTAL KM
8	392

ROUTE DESCRIPTION
From Delft, a good cycle path runs 8 kms into the center of Den Haag.

CITY
DEN HAAG/SCHEVENINGEN

DISTANCE KM	TOTAL KM
28	400

ROUTE DESCRIPTION
From Scheveningen, a good cycle path runs through a vast area of dunes, small lakes, and beaches to the resort town of Katwijk. About 8 km north of Scheveningen, a bike route turns off into Wassenaar, site of one of Holland's major amusement parks, Duinrell. Leaving Katwijk, the bike path follows the main road 5 kms into the center of Leiden.

CITY	ROUTE
LEIDEN	N208

DISTANCE KM	TOTAL KM
25	428

ROUTE DESCRIPTION
From Leiden, take N208 north in the direction of Haarlem. This region south of Haarlem is the heart of the world-famous Dutch tulip industry. At Lisse, turn off to Keukenhof, where in the gardens of a medieval castle the world's largest flower show is held. From Keukenhof, continue west where after crossing hwy N206 at Ruigenhoek you can pick up the cycle path that runs through the dunes to the beach. An excellent cycle path then runs north 8 kms through a rugged area of dunes, high grass, and sandy beaches to the seaside resort of Zandvoort. Continue north past the Grand Prix Race Track. At Bloemendaal aan Zee, take the bike trail that runs along the main road into Haarlem.

CITY
HAARLEM

ROUTE
A9

DISTANCE KM	TOTAL KM
28	453

ROUTE DESCRIPTION
From Haarlem, the bike path follows autobahn A9 past Schiphol Airport into the Amsterdamse Bos to the Olympic Stadium and from there into the center city.

CITY
AMSTERDAM

DISTANCE KM	TOTAL KM
0	481

THE HISTORIC HEART OF HOLLAND SIGHTS AND ACCOMMODATIONS

AMSTERDAM. Amsterdam is one of those great European cities where no matter what it is that you want to do or what you are looking for, there is a good chance that you'll find it. Founded in the last quarter of the thirteenth century, the city is rich in tradition. Amsterdam boasts of having the largest historical inner city in Europe, with nearly seven thousand buildings under protection as historical landmarks, the majority of which were constructed in the seventeenth and eighteenth centuries. This is a city that lives with its past; classic old buildings are not torn down and replaced with steel and glass towers, but rather carefully restored to be functioning components of the other Amsterdam that is a progressive, forward-moving, twentieth-century European capital. It is not unusual, for example, to find a computer store with the latest model PCs on display in a meticulously restored seventeenth-century town house – or for that matter, an assortment of young and some not-so-young ladies also in display windows in the heart of Amsterdam's outrageous red-light district. It's all a part of Amsterdam, a city of many moods and faces – sometimes cultured and refined, sometimes brash and vulgar!

Some of the great museums of the world are located in Amsterdam. Most famous of the city's more than forty museums is the **Rijksmuseum**, which has an outstanding collection of Dutch masters, including Rembrandt's monumental *Night Watch*. Just down the street is the **Van Gogh Museum**, which houses an impressive collection of the works of this famous Dutch artist. To round out this trio of big three museums clustered around the **Museumplein**, visit the **Stedelijk Museum**, one of the world's great modern art museums.

Besides the great museums, there are a few other highlights that should not be missed: **Anne Frank's House** (Prinsengracht 263) is the house where the Frank family hid from the Nazis for two years and where Anne Frank wrote her famous diary. No one who visits here remains unmoved by this tender and tragic story. In the heart of the Jewish quarter in the eastern part of the city is the **Rembrandt House** (Jodenbreetstraat 4), the faithfully restored house where the artist lived from 1639 to 1658. Yet another part of a visit to Amsterdam, which has been a diamond cutting center for some four hundred years, is a visit to a **diamond cutting and polishing factory**. Be sure to also cruise by the **Albert Cuyp Market** near the Museumplein. This is Amsterdam's largest and most colorful open market. You name it, they have it!

Amsterdam is also well represented in the world of classical music by the fine **Amsterdam Concertgebouw Orchestra**. Don't hesitate to attend a concert just because you don't have the "right clothes" in your panniers. In Amsterdam, jeans and dinner jackets mix without any difficulty – it's that kind of place. In fact, Amsterdam is a city well known for its remarkable tolerance. Drugs are sold openly, prostitutes brazenly solicit from street corners and storefront windows, and a sex museum does a thriving business on the Damrak, one of the city's main streets.

A good part of the city's swinging nightlife is concentrated on **Leidesplein** and **Rembrandtsplein**. Restaurant-goers have their pick of an incredible variety of both local and exotic establishments, in particular, the many Chinese and Indonesian restaurants.

In its physical layout, Amsterdam is unique; the heart of the city is located in an area ringed by a series of concentric and intersecting canals. More than one hundred kilometers of canals are spanned by one thousand bridges. Unlike Rome or Paris, Amsterdam is not a city of spectacular monuments; it is city that takes a little time to get to know. Stroll the streets along the canals lined with colorful houseboats. Explore the **Jordaan**, an area of blue-collar workers, and "dropouts" that is filled with cozy cafés, bars, and antique shops.

If you decide to explore Amsterdam on your bicycle, you won't be alone: Nearly three-fourths of the city's residents own bicycles, and the streets are jammed with people scurrying about on their bikes. It is a great city for riding. There are marked bike lanes all over, and motorists are very alert to cyclists.

For finding out what's going on in this busy capital, check at one of the city's three VVV offices located at Central Station (Stationsplein 10), Leidestraat 106, and Rijksweg A2 at the entrance to the city coming from Utrecht. Get a free copy of their publication, *Amsterdam This Week*, or *Use It*, a multilingual paper aimed at students. The informative English language monthlies, *Holland Life* and *Holland Herald*, are sold at most newsstands. Movies are shown in their original language.

There are a lot of different ways to spend the night in Amsterdam depending on your inclinations and budget. They range from sleeping in Vondel Park (very illegal) to a comfortable room at the Grand Hotel Krasnapolsky (very expensive). There are, of course, a number of less extreme solutions. Should you find yourself in a bind, join the crowd lined up at the Central Station VVV office, and the friendly overworked staff will help you out.

If you are after a first-class hotel and money is no object, stay at the GRAND HOTEL KRASNAPOLSKY (Dam 9, 1012 Amsterdam; Tel: [020] 55 46 048), better known as the "Kras." It is conveniently located right on the Dam. For a comfortable, traditional hotel conveniently located facing the Amstel River, try the EDEN HOTEL (Amstel 144; Tel: [020] 26 62 43) and plan to spend about 150 Fl. for a double. The HOTEL DE MOOR (Prinsengracht 1015-1017; Tel: [020] 23 16 66) is a friendly, modestly priced hotel within walking distance of the major art museums. In the inexpensive hotel category, we like the homey atmosphere and the quiet neighborhood of the HOTEL VAN OSTADE (Van Ostadestraat 123, Tel: [020] 79 34 52).

In addition to the two official youth hostels, Amsterdam also has a number of cheap student hotels and sleep-ins. The IYHF YOUTH HOSTEL VONDELPARK (Zandpad 5, 1054 GA Amsterdam; Tel: [020] 83 17 44) is nicely located overlooking Vondel Park. It is open from 1 March to 31 October. The IYHF STADSDOELEN (Kloveniersburgwal 97; Tel: [020] 24 68 32) is conveniently situated in the city and is open all year. Of the several inexpensive youth hotels, we like the Spartan, but clean, HANS BRINKER STUTEL (Kerkstraat 136-138; Tel: [020] 22 06 87). The location of the sleep-ins can change from year to year, so check with the VVV for the latest information. The last time we were in Amsterdam, there was a five-hundred-bed sleep-in costing 10 Fl. per night at SLEEP IN MAURITSKADE ('s-Gravzandestraat 1; Tel: [020] 94 74 44).

Campers in Amsterdam have their choice of several good, but often crowded, sites. The two most convenient, both within easy cycling distance of downtown, are CAMPING AMSTERDAMSE IJSCLUB near the Olympic Stadium (open 15 March to 1 October) and CAMPING HET AMSTERDAMSE BOS at the south edge of the city near Amstelveen (open 1 April to 1 November).

HAARLEM. Practically a suburb of Amsterdam, Haarlem has one of Holland's best-preserved old town centers and is a major attraction in its own right. It is from there that the flower bulbs grown in the surrounding region are shipped throughout the world. In addition to the fine medieval square, **Grote Markt**, which is encircled by a number of well-preserved classic buildings, the **Church of St. Bavo** and the excellent collection at the **Frans Hals Museum** are well worth seeing. In the summer candlelight concerts are held in the museum.

The nearby beach resort of **Zandvoort** is itself nothing special, consisting mostly of modern charmless buildings and a wind-blown beach. There are, however, several good campsites in the dunes just north of town. The sea promenade is lined with stands serving delicious fried fish. For an unusual taste treat, be sure to try the deep-fried mussels served with a tempting variety of sauces.

Haarlem's top hotel is the GOLDEN TULIP HOTEL LION D'OR, (Kruisweg 34-36, 2011 LC Haarlem; Tel: [023] 32 17 50). The best low-priced rooms in town are at the HOTEL CARILON (Grote Markt 27; Tel: [023] 31 05 91) and PENSION STADSCAFE (Zijlstraat 56; Tel: [023] 32 52 02).

The YOUTH HOSTEL JAN GIJZEN (Jan Gijzenpad 3; Tel: [023] 37 37 93) has 108 beds and is conveniently located close to the train station. The DE ZANDERIJ (Korte Zijllweg 9; Tel: [023] 32 65 99) has eighty-six beds in the suburb of Overveen, just 2 kms west of the central station.

The most conveniently located campground is CAMPING DE LIEDE (Liewegje 17). This small site is open all year.

ALKMAAR. Founded in the tenth century, Alkmaar is a delightful old town best known for its colorful **cheese market**, which is held Friday mornings from 10 to 12 on the **Waagplein** (weighing square) in the center of the old town. There is also an interesting **Beer Museum** at Houttil 1.

Alkmaar doesn't offer a whole lot in the way of accommodations. The neighboring resort town of Bergen has a much bigger selection. In Alkmaar, the comfortable ten-bed PENSION 'T KOMBIUS (Lombardsteeg 7, 1811 LA, Alkmaar; Tel: [072] 11 68 25) offers cozy quarters at reasonable prices.

For campers, CAMPING ALKMAAR is conveniently situated at the west edge of town on the road to Bergen. It is open 30 March to 15 October.

The HOTEL CAFE DE ZILVERSPAR (Breelaan 21, 1861 GC Bergen; Tel: [02208] 96 009) in Bergen is a quaint, moderately priced, old family-run hotel and restaurant. At Schoorl just north of Bergen aan Zee is the 110-bed YOUTH HOSTEL TEUN DE JAGER (Duinweg 14, 1865 AB, Bergen aan Zee; Tel: [02209] 1448).

DEN HELDER. Located at the tip of the province of North Holland, Den Helder is the country's largest naval port and center of a large bulb growing region. There is an interesting small naval museum adjacent to the navy base.

The town's best hotel is the BEATRIX-HOTEL (Badhuisstr. 2-10, 1783 Den Helder; Tel: [02233] 14 800). There are also several good inexpensive pensions in Den Helder, including the WAPEN VAN DEN HELDER (Spoorgracht 43-44, 1781 CD, Den Helder; Tel: [02230] 22 240) and PENSION REINA (Zuidstraat 23; Tel: [02230] 13 608).

The closest youth hostel, JEUGDHERBERG NIEUWLAND(Gemenelandsweg 116, 1779 GD Den Over; Tel: [902271] 1272), is on the route after returning from the island of Texel.

Of the numerous campgrounds nestled in the dunes between Bergen aan Zee and Den Helder, one of the nicest is the large six-acre campsite at Donkere Duinen just south of Den Helder called CAMPING DE DONKERE DUINEN. It is open 1 April to 1 October.

The DE TROUBADOUR (Beatrixstraat 62) is a quaint, pleasant, moderately priced restaurant.

TEXEL. Texel, the largest and most easily accessible of the Wadden Islands, is just a twenty-minute ferry ride from Den Helder. Largely agricultural in nature, the island has some excellent beaches and number of good camping spots. If you are there on a Wednesday afternoon, be sure to take in the colorful demonstration of Dutch handicrafts by traditionally clad locals.

If you are not camping, there is a good moderately priced hotel in Den Burg, HOTEL BOS EN DUIN (Bakkenweg 16, 1799 AA Den Burg; Tel: [902220] 2569), as well as several in De Koog, including the pleasantly situated HOTEL DE STRAND-PLEVIER (Dorpsstraat 39, 1796 BA De Koog; Tel: [02228] 348).

Both of the island's youth hostels are in Den Burg: JEUGDHERBERG PANORAMA (Schansweg 7; Tel [02220] 2197) and JEUGDHERBERG DE EYERCOOGH (Pontweg 106; Tel: [02220] 2907).

For campers the island is ideal. There are some twenty campgrounds and a number of farms where camping is possible – not to mention all of the free camping possibilities the island affords. One of the best of the official campsites is CAMPING DE KRIM in De Cocksdorp near the northern tip of the island. This is a huge sixty-acre site with plenty of space to tuck your tent in the dunes. The full facilities include a washing machine, snack bar, and camp store. It is open 1 April to 31 October.

MEDEMBLIK. A small old harbor town on the Ijsselmeer, Medemblik is surrounded by a region of polders containing some of Holland's richest farm and pasture land. Of interest in this pleasant little town are the **Church of St. Bonifatius** and the thirteenth-century **Kasteel Radboud**.

The comfortable little HOTEL WAPEN VAN MEDEMBLIK (Oosterhaven 1, 1671 AA Medemblik; Tel: [02274] 3844) makes a convenient stopover in this sparsely populated region.

There is also a good-sized campground, CAMPING ZUIDERZEE, at the Oosterdijk. It is open 1 April to 15 October.

ENKHUIZEN. A small seaport with ferry connections to the province of Friesland, Enkhuizen is known for its well-preserved old buildings and picturesque canals. It is one of the country's most attractive small towns – popular with both locals and tourists. Be sure to visit the **Zuiderzee Museum** (Wierdijk 18), which documents the fascinating development of this region bordering on what was once the famous Zuiderzee. An inhabited reconstructed village of more than one hundred homes and shops is a part of this most interesting regional museum.

The HOTEL HET WAPEN VAN ENKHUIZEN (Breedstraat 59, 1601 KB Enkhuizen; Tel: [02280] 13 434) is a good middle-class hotel. For a cozy resting place in this attractive town, try the small ten-bed DIE PORT VAN CLEVE (Dijk 74-76, Tel: [02280] 12 510), a pleasant family-run

budget hotel with a good restaurant in a quaint old building overlooking the harbor.

Campers can pitch their tents at CAMPING ENKHUIZER ZAND, a large site at the beach in the north end of town just 1 km from the Zuiderzee Museum. It is open 1 April to 1 October.

The RESTAURANT DU PASSAGE (Parktuinen 6-8) is a good choice for traditional Dutch cuisine.

HOORN. Although it has declined in importance since its heyday in the sixteenth century when it was the most important port on the Zuiderzee, Hoorn has managed to preserve a great deal of its old flavor and charm. The seventeenth-century **Town Hall** and the **West Friesian Museum** are of particular interest.

For pleasant, reasonably priced accommodations, try the HOTEL DE MAGNEET (Kleine Oost 5-7, 1621 GR Hoorn; Tel: [02290] 15 021) or the HOTEL DE POSTHOORN (Breed 27; Tel: [02290] 14 057).

CAMPING WESTERKOGGE at the southern edge of town is a full facility campground, open 1 April to 30 September.

For dining in the traditional style, try the RESTAURANT DE WAAG (Rode Steen 8) in a well-preserved seventeenth-century building right in the heart of the old town.

EDAM. Edam is a pleasant little market town known throughout the world for its fine cheese. The seventeenth-century town square is quite attractive.

Volendam, a popular tourist town 5 kms south of Edam, has a picturesque harbor and is well known for its colorful folk costumes.

For a cozy, quaint, small town hotel in Edam, try the DAMHOTEL (Keizergracht 1, 1135 EZ Edam; Tel: [02993] 71766). In Vollendam, try the HOTEL VAN DEN HOGEN (Havn 106, 1131 EV Volendam; Tel: [02993] 63775).

Edam has a good campground with access to swimming in the sea. CAMPING STRANDBAD is located right off the dike road toward Hoorn and is open 1 April to 30 September.

UTRECHT. Holland's fourth largest city, Utrecht was founded by the Romans in 47 AD. Although the city has fallen prey to a good deal of urban renewal, the medieval city center, ringed by an ancient moat called the **Singel**, still contains a number of interesting old buildings. The **Cathedral of St. Micheal** (on Domplein) in the center of the old town is one of the country's finest pieces of ecclesiastical architecture. For the mechanically minded, the **Dutch Railway Museum (Nederlands Spoorwegmuseum)** located in a converted train station (Johan van Oldenbarneveltlaan 6) offers an intriguing glimpse into rail transportation in this efficient little country. **Hoog Catharijne** located between the central station and the old town center is the largest covered shopping complex in western Europe.

At the village of **Haarzuilens**, 5 kms northwest of the city, is the formidable **De Haar Castle**. In a lovely setting surrounded by water, the castle's grounds are patterned after Versailles.

For a good, moderately priced hotel, try the small HOTEL DE BARONIE (Biltstraat 29-31, 3572 AC, Utrecht; Tel: [030] 32 14 15). Since Utrecht is not especially known for its inexpensive hotels, your best bet for cheap lodging is the 130-bed youth hostel in Bunnik, 6 kms east of Utrecht: YOUTH HOSTEL FRIJNAUWEN, (Rijnauwenselaan 14; Tel: [03405] 1277).

For campers, CAMPING DE BEREKUIL (Arienslaan 5) is open from 1 March to 15 October. It is conveniently located in an attractive setting at the east edge of the city.

The VVV Vredenburg 90 (in the Music Center) can help you (for a fee) find a bed in a sleep-in or boarding house.

Of the many restaurants on the Oude Gracht, the EATHUIS HET DRAECKJE (Kelders Oude Gracht 114-116) is a local favorite for traditional Dutch dishes.

GOUDA. Set in the rich polder area of the province of South Holland, Gouda is a typical old Dutch market town known worldwide for its fine cheeses. The **St. Janskerk** just south of the marketplace is the largest church in the Netherlands and has a number of fine stained glass windows. The **Municipal Museum** has a number of interesting exhibits, including an ancient pharmacy, antique medical instruments, and a torture chamber. A **cheese market** is held Thursday mornings (10 to 12) and a colorful **cheese and wine festival** takes place at the end of August. There are several traditional windmills along the river at the edge of town.

Kinderdijk, just south of Krimpen on the route to Rotterdam, has the country's largest collection of windmills. Every Saturday afternoon in July and August all nineteen of these giants are unleashed, which presents quite a spectacle.

For an inexpensive room in town, try the small HOTEL HET BLAUWE KRUIS (Westhaven 4, 2801 PH Gouda; Tel: [01820] 12 677).

There is a small pleasant campground located on the lake just 1 km north of town. CAMPING DE ELZENHOF is open 1 April to 1 October.

ROTTERDAM. It was from Rotterdam's harbor, **Delfshaven**, that the Pilgrims set sail for America in 1620. Although this historic section of the city survived massive bombing raids during World War II and has been carefully preserved, the rest of Rotterdam was just about totally leveled. Holland's second largest city has been rebuilt in a bold modern style and offers little of historical interest with the exception of the **Delfshaven Quarter**. Be sure to visit the **Pilgrim Father's Church**, built in 1416. This is where the Pilgrims prayed prior to setting out for the New World. The **Stolk Atlas** housed in the old Delfshaven town hall has one of the best-known collections of ancient maps and sea charts. For an interesting view of the working of a large modern harbor, take a boat cruise around the huge **Europort** complex. It is also possible to take tours from there to visit the **Delta Project**, the world's largest flood control project.

In contrast to the many sterile business-men's hotels, we like the inexpensive, offbeat HOTEL HET WAPEN VAN CHARLOIS (Doklaan 59, 3082 RC Rotterdam; Tel: [010] 296921).

The 160-bed youth hostel, DE WINDROOS (Rochussenstraat 107-109, Tel: [010] 365763), is open all year.

CAMPING ROTTERDAM, located near the airport, is a first-class site in a park setting. Its facilities include a washing machine, camp store, and restaurant, and it is open 1 April to 1 October.

DELFT. Delft is a picturesque old Dutch town surrounded by canals. The delicate blue and white porcelains produced here have been world famous since the seventeenth century. Guided tours are given at **Royal Delftware de Porceleyne Fles** (Rotterdamseweg 196), the small factory where Delft pieces are still hand-painted.

Delft as the traditional burial place for the royal family has great historical significance for the Dutch. It was here that William the Silent of Orange, the nation's founder, was assassinated in 1584. The **Het Prinsenhof**, housed in a fifteenth-century convent, one-time home of William of Orange, is a fine museum with exhibits that chronicle the country's long struggle for independence from Spain.

There are several medium-priced hotels in town, including the conveniently located HOTEL DE ARK (Koornmarkt 59-65, 2611 EC Delft; Tel: [015] 14 05 52). Inexpensive accommodations are available in student housing from 15 June to 31 August. Try STUDENT-FLATS KRAKEELHOF (9 Jacob van Bieranlaan; Tel: [015] 13 59 53). The PENSION DE VOS (Breestraat 5a; Tel: [015] 12 32 58) near the train station has clean inexpensive rooms.

There is a small pleasant campground located adjacent to a deer park at the northeast edge of town just across the autobahn. MUNICIPAL CAMPING DELFT is open 1 May to 15 September.

The SPIJSHUIS DE DIS (Beestenmarkt 26-34) is a popular restaurant that features regional specialties. Also worth trying are the delicious Dutch pancakes (*pannekoeken*) at any of the several restaurants on Oude Delft.

THE HAGUE (Den Haag/'S-Gravenhage). By whatever name you choose to call it, the seat of the government of the Netherlands is an old dowager of a city, stately and elegant. Its collection of pleasant parks and wooded areas has earned it the distinction of being known as Holland's greenest city.

Although it has an interesting assortment of royal palaces and fine museums, the attraction that seems to draw the greatest number of visitors is **Madurodam**, a delightful replica in miniature of a typical Dutch town. The two-mile-long visitors' route is a fun trip on a Lilliputian scale through the wonders and attractions of Holland. Madurodam was built by the parents of George Maduro as a living memorial to their son who died in the Dachau concentration camp. The park is open from 1 April to the third Sunday in October.

Of the city's many museums, the **Mauritshuis Museum** in a seventeenth-century palace, which houses an outstanding collection of the works of the Dutch masters, and the **Gemeente Museum**, which has a fine collection of modern paintings and rare musical instruments, are the most interesting. Also of interest is the **Binnenhof**, a stately group of brick buildings whose facades are reflected in the waters of the Hofvijver. This is where both houses of the Dutch Parliament, as well as a number of government ministries, are located. The thirteenth-century **Ridderzaal** (Knight's Hall) contains some splendid tapestries and stained glass windows.

Scheveningen, once a simple fishing village, is the seaside extension of this elegant city. Even though somewhat faded, Scheveningen is the country's most famous beach resort and center of The Hague's nightlife. Although there is a good sandy beach, strong westerly winds often detract from its enjoyment. The newly renovated **Kurhaus Hotel**, which contains the most elegant of Holland's three gambling casinos, has helped to restore a bit of this resort's former luster.

If you would like to sample the best in luxurious accommodations that the Netherlands has to offer and don't mind spending 300-350 Fl. for your night of luxury, then head for Scheveningen's KURHAUS HOTEL (Gevers Deynootplein 30, 2586 CK, Den Haag; Tel: [070] 52 00 52). On a more down-to-earth level in the same neighborhood but at a fraction of the price is the modest HOTEL ALBION (Gevers Deynootweg 120; Tel: [070] 55 79 87).

For budget accommodations, there are several youth hostels within easy cycling distance, including the large, three-hundred-bed OCKENBURGH HOSTEL (Monsterseweg 4; Tel: [070] 97 00 11) located in a rambling old house just down the coast in Kijkduin. The YOUTH HOSTEL T'SEE-HUYS (Zeekant 45; Tel: [070] 55 95 85) is located in Scheveningen.

Campers have their choice of two good campgrounds, one out by the youth hostel in Kijkduin. CAMPING OCKENBURGH is a very large well-equipped municipal site right at the beach, open 31 March to 30 September. CAMPING DUINRELL is located in Wassenaar about 8 kms northeast of Den Haag. This very popular site is located on the grounds of one of Holland's busiest amusement parks. A separate "wilderness" section has been set up for camping in the dunes. It is open all year. CAMPING DE NOORDUINEN at the north edge of Katwijk is also a good place for pitching a tent in the dunes. The beach is about 500 meters away.

LEIDEN (Leyden). Site of a major university and one of Holland's most important cultural centers, Leiden is also one of the country's oldest and most picturesque towns. Of the city's eleven museums, the **Rijksmuseum voor Volken Kunde** (National Museum of Ethnology), with its wealth of fine material from the former Dutch colonies in the Far East, should not be missed. No trip to Holland would be complete without a visit to a windmill and the **Molenmuseum "De Valk"** at the edge of the old town is one of the most interesting. Built in 1743, this impressive mill was in actual use until 1945. The **Pilgrim Fathers Documents Center** (Boisokade 2a) has some interesting exhibits relating to America's early settlers.

In addition to the modern and expensive Holiday Inn, there are a number of guest houses and inexpensive small hotels. Best bets are HOTEL DE CEDER (Rijnsburgerweg 80, 2330 AD, Leiden; Tel: [071] 17 59 03) and HOTEL HAAS (Marienpoelstraat 1-A; Tel: [071] 17 47 87). PENSION WITTE, (Witte Singel 80; Tel: [071] 12 45 92) is one of the town's best small guest houses.

There is a youth hostel DE TREK-SCHUIT (Julianalaan 19; Tel: (02524) 4297) in nearby De Kaag about 5 kms northeast of Leiden.

The all-year campground, CAMPING DUINRELL, in Wassenar is only about 5 kms away.

Amsterdam and
the Veluwe Region

Beyond Amsterdam, this route leads off into a part of the Netherlands that is a bit away from the main tourist circuit. The country's really well-known attractions and those most frequently visited by first-time travelers to Holland are in the western part and make up the major part of our other route. If you can spare the time, this route, which covers much of the central and eastern parts of the country, can be easily combined with the "Amsterdam and the Historic Heart of Holland" route.

This route runs through Flevoland, the newest part of the Netherlands. The Dutch have taken a unique path toward solving some of the problems inherent in having so many people living in such a small area. As you cycle across Flevoland, you will be pedaling through a region that up to a few years ago was some fifteen feet below sea level under what was once the Zuiderzee. In recent years several hundred thousand acres have been reclaimed and cultivated. Obviously this is not a region where you will encounter quaint medieval buildings and narrow cobblestone streets. What this portion of the route does offer is the opportunity to see a bit into the future. Starting so to speak from scratch, Dutch designers and urban planners have had the chance to create entire new communities and put many theoretical concepts to practical use.

Besides the new polders of Flevoland, the route visits the old Hanseatic towns of Kampen and Zwolle. Although tiny Holland hardly can be compared to such countries as neighboring Germany when it comes to tracts of dense forests, or to Spain when speaking of wide open spaces, nevertheless, the conservation-minded Dutch have set aside a portion of their small country as a national park. The National Park de Hoge Veluwe is a part of the larger Veluwe region, a vast region of sand dunes interspersed with heather, woods, and even a few hills. This is very pleasant cycling – sparsely populated roads with very little traffic. Within the park itself is a game reserve and the very fine Kröller-Müller art museum.

AMSTERDAM AND THE VELUWE REGION ROUTE

START	FINISH	ANWB TOERISTENKAARTEN MAPS
AMSTERDAM	AMSTERDAM	#5, Randstad noord en 't Gooi;
		#6, Randstad midden en zuid;
DISTANCE		#7, Veluwe (scale 1:100,000)
308 kms/191 miles		

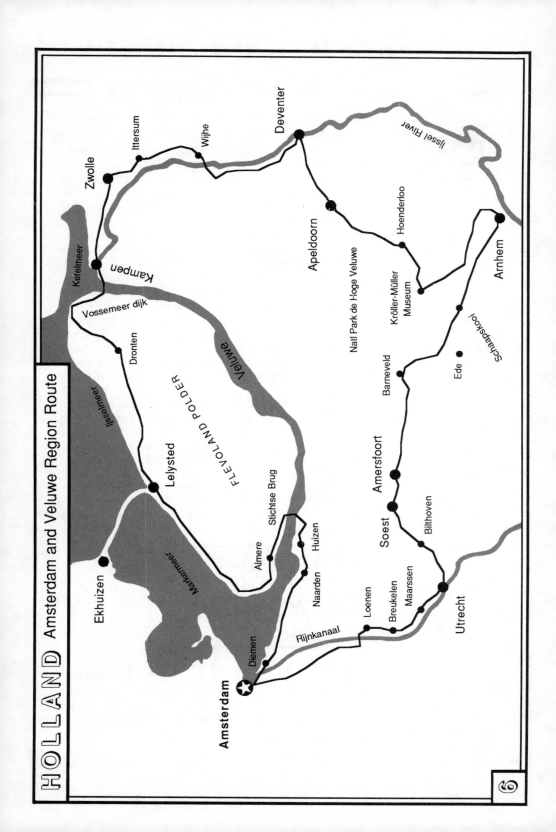

HOLLAND Amsterdam and Veluwe Region Route

Amsterdam

Zwolle

Ittersum

Wijhe

Deventer

Ijssel River

Apeldoorn

Hoenderloo

Arnhem

Natl Park de Hoge Veluwe

Kröller-Müller Museum

Schaapskooi

Ede

Barneveld

Amersfoort

Soest

Bilthoven

Veluwe

Kampen

Kefelmeer

Vossemeer dijk

Dronten

Ijsselmeer

FLEVOLAND POLDER

Lelysted

Stichtse Brug

Almere

Huizen

Naarden

Ekhuizen

Markermeer

Maarssen

Breukelen

Loenen

Diemen

Rijnkanaal

Utrecht

With the exception of a few low hills in the Veluwe region, this route is easy pedaling and can be handled without difficulty by just about anyone on just about any kind of bike. Time permitting, the route lends itself well to several interesting side trips. From Zwolle, its just a short distance up to the province of Drenthe, a quiet region of lush meadows, tiny lakes, and idyllic villages. Laced with a tight network of cycle paths, Drenthe is prime biking country.

★ *LOOKING OUT OVER THE HANDLEBARS* ★

AMSTERDAM AND THE VELUWE REGION ROUTE

CITY
AMSTERDAM

ROUTE
A1 N27

DISTANCE KM	TOTAL KM
70	0

ROUTE DESCRIPTION

Leave Amsterdam by cycling along the Amstel, continuing until you pick up the small road that runs alongside the Amsterdam-Hilversum Autobahn A1, which goes to Hilversum. You will pass through Diemen and Naarden. From Narden, continue on to Huizen. From there take the road that runs alongside the main hwy N27, across the Stichtse Brug (bridge) onto the Flevoland Polder. The route then follows the Flevoland shoreline past the Hollandse Brug and the new town of Almere. Stay along the shore to Lelysted, the administrative center of the Flevoland Polders.

CITY
LELYSTED

ROUTE
N50

DISTANCE KM	TOTAL KM
52	70

ROUTE DESCRIPTION

Head east from Lelysted, following the road across the polder to Dronten, a small market town built in the old style. Follow the road north 5 kms to the Ketelmeer coast. Stop and visit the small Ketelhavn Archaeological Maritime Museum. Then follow the Vossemeerdijk to intersect with the road into Kampen. From Kampen, cross the Ijssel River and take the cycle path along hwy N50 to Zwolle.

CITY
ZWOLLE

DISTANCE KM	TOTAL KM
35	122

ROUTE DESCRIPTION
From the center of Zwolle, head south to the suburb of Ittersum. Continue on the cycle trail that runs alongside the main road to Deventer. After 11 kms, at Wijhe, cross the river and take the road along the dike into Deventer. There are some nice views of the river and a few old windmills along the way.

CITY
DEVENTER

ROUTE
N344

DISTANCE KM	TOTAL KM
15	157

ROUTE DESCRIPTION
From Deventer there is a well-marked cycle path alongside N344 to Apeldoorn.

CITY
APELDOORN

DISTANCE KM	TOTAL KM
30	172

ROUTE DESCRIPTION
From Apeldoorn, follow the signs toward Ede, which lies about 25 kms to the southwest. After a short stretch alongside the main highway, the bike path winds through forests and dunes to the village of Hoenderloo at the eastern edge of the National Park de Hoge Veluwe. From Hoenderloo, continue on the bike trail through the lovely park to the Museum Kröller-Müller. Take the path leading from the museum 10 kms to Arnhem.

CITY
ARNHEM

ROUTE
N224

DISTANCE KM	TOTAL KM
43	202

ROUTE DESCRIPTION
From the Arnhem train station, pick up N224 the main road to Ede. After a few hundred meters, a bike path accompanies this road, crossing autobahn A50 and then A12. About 4 kms before Ede at Schaapskooi, take the path north to Barneveld, passing through the middle point of Holland. From Barneveld, follow the signs 13 kms to Amersfoort. The route passes through level wooded regions interspersed with areas of moors and farmlands.

CITY
AMERSFOORT

ROUTE
N221

DISTANCE KM	TOTAL KM
25	245

ROUTE DESCRIPTION

Take N221 out of Amersfoort to Soest. From the Royal Palace at Soestdijk on the north edge of Soest there is a good cycle trail that runs through the woods into Utrecht by way of Bilthoven.

CITY
UTRECHT

ROUTE
N201

DISTANCE KM	TOTAL KM
38	270

ROUTE DESCRIPTION

From Utrecht, take the bike path along the Amsterdam Rijnkanaal to Maarssen. From Maarssen, follow the small road to Loenen, passing through Breukelen along the way. At Loenen, pick up the cycle path toward Amsterdam. At the intersection with N201, turn toward Haarlem. Cross the bridge over the canal and at the autobahn intersection, pick up the bike path that runs along the autobahn for most of the way into Amsterdam. The stretch into the center of Amsterdam is well marked.

CITY
AMSTERDAM

DISTANCE KM	TOTAL KM
0	308

AMSTERDAM AND THE VELUWE REGION SIGHTS AND ACCOMMODATIONS

AMSTERDAM. See discussion under "Amsterdam and the Historic Heart of Holland" route.

LELYSTED. The administrative center for the Flevoland Polders, Lelysted has only been in existence since 1967 and already has a population in excess of 20,000. Not everyone's idea of what a Dutch city should be, Lelysted has been the subject of much controversy. While we far prefer the quaint charm of "old world" Holland, this is also a part of the Netherlands and it deserves to be seen. The settlement of **Almere**, separated from Lelysted by a large nature reserve, is targeted to reach a population of 200,000 by the turn of the century.

There are several hotels in this new town, including the comfortable HOTEL LELYSTED (Agoraweg 11, 8224 Lelysted; Tel: [03200] 42 444).

There are a few good campgrounds at the eastern edge of the polder near Biddinghuizen and the Flavohof Recreation Area, including RIVERIA CAMPING, a huge, full facility site. It is open 1 April to 15 September.

ZWOLLE. An ancient Hanseatic town whose origins date back to 1040, Zwolle is the capital of the province of Overijssel and is an important marketing center. The town contains a number of fine old buildings, including the fifteenth-century **St. Michaelskerk**, and is surrounded by several beautiful parks. Nearby **Kampen**, with a picturesque old town, was also a member of the Hanseatic Trading League.

The town's nicest hotel is the HOTEL WIENTJES (Stationsweg 7, 8011 CZ Zwolle; Tel: [038] 21 12 00). For a low-cost place to spend the night, try the SLAAPHUIS SLEEP IN (Rode Torenplein 4; Tel: [038] 22 74 84) or the CAMP-GROUND VECHTERSTRANDE, at the north edge of town by the Overijsselse Vecht River.

DEVENTER. Deventer is essentially a modern industrial town and an important bicycle producing center.

For a good small hotel, try the HOTEL ROYAL BRINK (Brink 94, 7411 BZ Deventer; Tel: [05700] 11 880). The hotel also has a good restaurant that features local specialties.

There is a simple campground across the river at De Hoven. It is open 15 April to 15 September.

APELDOORN. A fashionable park-lined residential town, Apeldoorn serves as a good jumping-off point for visiting the 13,343-acre **National Park de Hoge Veluwe**. The park, a vast unpopulated expanse of forest and sandy dunes, is a geological remnant of the Ice Ages. While in Apeldoorn, visit the museum at **Het Loo Palace**, formerly a royal residence in Koninklijk Park at the northwest edge of town. To see how the well-to-do Dutch live, pedal through the beautiful suburb of Berg en Bos in the western part of the city.

The HOTEL PENSION BERG EN BOS (Aquamarijnstraat 58, 7314 HZ Apeldoorn; Tel: [055] 55 23 52) is a comfortable seventeen-room inn situated in a quiet neighborhood. Doubles with a bath run from 75 Fl.

In addition to a number of boarding houses, there is also a 136-bed youth hostel, DE GROTE BEER (Asselsestraat 330, 7312 TS Apeldoorn; Tel: [055] 55 31 18).

A huge camping and vacation complex is located just south of Apeldoorn in Hoenderloo. It's called AEGON VAKANTIEVERBLIJF and has full facilities, including a swimming pool and washing machine. It is open 1 March to 31 October.

ARNHEM. Arnhem is a large modern city rebuilt after having suffered nearly complete destruction during World War II. It was here that the disastrous battle depicted in the film *A Bridge Too Far* took place in 1944. Significant mementos of that campaign can be seen at the **Airborne Cemetery** in nearby **Oosterbeek** and at the **Airborne Museum**. A much more pleasant place to visit is the one-hundred-acre **Openlucht** (Open Air Museum) just north of town. Traditional houses, windmills, and farms have been faithfully reconstructed to give a detailed picture of Dutch country life. For a quick change of scenery, shift to the African Veld and take the exciting train ride through the **Safari Park** just to the west of the Open Air Museum.

Just 10 kilometers to the north in a magnificent wooded setting in the heart of the National Park de Hoge Veluwe is the **Museum Kröller-Müller**. This is one of Europe's finest art museums with a large number of outstanding paintings by Vincent Van Gogh. Be sure to see the excellent sculpture garden.

In addition to a number of boarding houses, there are several moderately priced hotels and pensions in the Arnhem vicinity. A good budget bet is the HOTEL REMBRANDT (Paterstraat 1-3, 6828 AG Arnhem; Tel: [085] 42 01 53). For a taste of Dutch country luxury, enjoy the forested setting of the stately GROOT WARNSBORN (Bakenbergseweg 277; Tel: [085] 45 57 51). Located about 6 kms northwest of Arnhem center, this is a lovely old manor house with twenty-nine pleasantly furnished rooms and an excellent French restaurant.

For a manor house of a different sort, try the first-class two-hundred-bed Arnhem youth hostel, ALTEVEER (Diepenbrocklaan 27; Tel: [085] 42 01 14).

Campers can pitch their tents at any one of a number of good sites in the region, including the grassy meadows at CAMPING WARNSBORN (Bakenbergseweg 257) just down the road from the Groot Warnsborn. It is open 1 April to 15 September. As an alternative, the huge, seventy-acre KAMPEERCENTRUM ARNHEM in a pleasant meadow surrounded by woods is a great place to pitch your tent while exploring the region. It is open 1 March to 1 November.

AMERSFOORT. Amersfoort is a lively town in a very pleasant wooded setting at the confluence of several rivers. The attractive old town core contains some fine medieval buildings and is ringed by a double row of canals. The city, which was chartered in 1259, was an early member of the Hanseatic Trading League.

On the way into Utrecht, be sure to take the path through **Soest** to see the **Royal Palace at Soestdijk**, a magnificent hunting lodge in a beautiful park at the north edge of town.

For a comfortable, moderately priced hotel, try the HOTEL DE WITTE (Utrechtseweg 2, 3811 NB Amersfoort; Tel: [033] 14 142).

Amersfoort also has a good youth hostel: the 130-bed DE GRASHEUVEL (De Genestetlaan 9; Tel: [033] 14 271). It is open from 22 March until the end of October.

There is a conveniently located campsite in Birkhaven, a pleasant wooded area at the southwest edge of town just across from hwy N221. It is called CAMPING KINGS HOME and is open 1 April to 31 October.

For fine dining in the traditional Dutch style, try the quaint LAMME GOETSACK (Lieve Vrouwestraat 8) located in a fine old sixteenth-century house in the center of the old town. The more modest STATION-SPLEIN 4, near the train station is also highly recommended.

UTRECHT. See the discussion in "Amsterdam and the Historic Heart of Holland" route.

Additional Recommended Routes

Although the two detailed routes we have chosen for the Netherlands cover the best-known and most popular parts of the country, there are several additional interesting touring possibilities.

NORTHEASTERN PROVINCES

The northeastern part of the Netherlands, consisting of the provinces of **Friesland**, **Groningen**, and **Drenthe**, offers some lovely back-country cycling in the most rural part of the country. Drenthe offers a dense network of cycle paths running through lovely villages where tradition is preserved in open-air museums and folklore markets. It is one of the most enjoyable parts of the country for cycle touring. The region is largely unspoiled by tourism and is also known for its prehistoric megaliths.

ZEELAND

The province of Zeeland, the delta of the Netherlands, is an interesting region of islands, inland seas, and medieval harbor towns. Worth riding out to take a look at is the enormous **Delta Project**, one of the world's most ambitious engineering projects, designed to protect Zeeland from incursions of the North Sea.

LIMBURG

When you tire of pedaling the flatlands and are ready to "head for the hills," turn to the province of Limburg – a high plateau region intersected by the Maas (Meuse) River in the southeastern corner of the country. This is pleasant hilly country with rolling farmlands and fruit orchards – nothing heroic, just some nice hills for variety. The town of **Maastricht**, one of the oldest towns in the Netherlands, has many interesting buildings. It is the region's cultural and economic center. The little town of **Valkenburg** in the center of the province has a large monastery and the ruins of a thirteenth-century castle. It is a popular vacation center.

This is one of the few parts of the country where there are not a lot of bike trails. From anywhere in this region it's a simple matter to pedal over to Aachen and pick up the "Rhine and Moselle Valleys" route described in the chapter on West Germany.

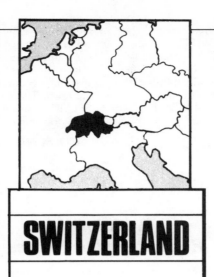

SWITZERLAND

POPULATION
6,366,000

RELIGION
49% Roman Catholic;
48% Protestant

CAPITAL
Bern

CURRENCY
Swiss Franc (SFr.); divided into
100 centimes (French) or 100
rappen (German)

OFFICIAL LANGUAGE
German: 75%; French: 20%;
Italian: 4%; Romansh: 1%;
English widely spoken in tourist
areas.

TO CALL USA OR CANADA
Dial 001; area code and number

BANKING HOURS
MTWF 0800–1200
       1330–1630
Th   0800–1200
       1330–1830
Exchange offices at major
railroad stations and airports
are open Sat. & Sun.
(0800–2000).

STORE HOURS
M   1330–1830
T–F 0800–1200
     1330–1830
Sat. 0800–1600
Large stores normally do not
close at noon.

EMERGENCY TELEPHONE NUMBERS
Police	117
Fire	140
Ambulance	118

HOLIDAYS

1 Jan.; 2 Jan.; Good Friday; Easter Monday; Ascension Day; Pentecost; 1 Aug., Independence Day; 25 & 26 Dec. (In addition to these national holidays, individual cantons observe various religious holidays.)

USA CONSULATES

Jubiläums Str. 93
3005 BERN
Tel: [031] 43 70 11

11 Route de Pergny
1290 CHAMBESY (near Geneva)
Tel: [022] 99 02 11

Zφliker Str. 141
8008 ZÜRICH
Tel: [01] 55 25 66 or 55 25 57

CANADIAN CONSULATES

Permanent Mission of Canada to the Office of the United Nations, Consular Section
10A ave. de Bude
1202 GENEVA
Tel: [022] 33 90 00

Kirchenfield Str. 88
BERN
Tel: [031] 44 63 81

AMERICAN EXPRESS OFFICES

Marktgasse 37
BERN
Tel: [031] 22 94 01

7 rue du Mont Blanc
GENEVA
Tel: [022] 31 76 00

14 ave. Mon-Repos
LAUSANNE
Tel: [021] 20 74 25

Bahnhofstrasse 20
ZÜRICH
Tel: [01] 21 18 370

ROADS

In recent years there has been an extensive campaign to develop a network of marked cycle paths, part of an increased overall interest in cycling. However, at this point, there are still many places, especially in the narrow valleys and in the mountains, where there are no cycle trails. Where cycle paths are present their use is mandatory.

When it comes to enforcing rules and regulations, the Swiss can be nitpickers. Exhausted after a long day's drive we once pulled our camper into a campground in Basel only to be welcomed by the screaming manager who had lost his Swiss composure all because we were a foot beyond the white line denoting the entrance to the campground! It's not that they shoot jaywalkers in Switzerland (actually the death penalty was abolished years ago), but it is a good idea to follow their rules.

As is the case with everything in the country, you will find that roads are well maintained and that, with the exception of some small villages, few cobblestone streets remain. In the narrow valleys and in the mountains, there are few secondary roads and traffic during July and August as well as on holidays can be quite heavy. Over the last few years the Swiss have greatly expanded their network of autobahns, which has relieved the congestion on many highways. When planning a tour, look for roads that parallel an autobahn.

Swiss drivers seem to be used to sharing the road with cyclists but are often impatient. Stay as far to the right as possible. When riding in the mountains you should be aware of the fact that the yellow post buses have the right of way and are not shy about exercising it.

Many roads through the mountains go through poorly lit tunnels, so be sure that your front and rear lights are working. Some, cut through sheer rock, are cold and wet even on hot sunny days. To avoid getting chilled, take a jacket or sweater along.

When looking for flat places to ride, follow river valleys and lake shores wherever possible.

For road conditions in the language of the region you are in, dial 163.

BIKING THROUGH EUROPE

SWITZERLAND

Switzerland is somewhat of an oddball among European nations, being the only central European nation that has managed to avoid an active role in both world wars. The much-vaunted Swiss neutrality is not the only thing that holds this tiny landlocked nation apart from its often envious neighbors. For one thing, the Swiss have somehow managed their affairs so that the country has experienced virtually no inflation or unemployment. How this has been achieved in this country of six million inhabitants who are officially divided into four separate language groups could easily be the subject of a thesis in economics and would certainly be out of place in a cycling book. What this all does mean for visitors to Switzerland is that the country is the epitome of efficiency. Everything works! And more than that – it works well. The trains and buses are on time; there is fast, efficient service in restaurants, hotels, and stores; and an infrastructure goes about the business of handling tourism with the precision that has made the Swiss watch industry the standard of the world.

The only drawback is that all of this efficient service comes at a price. Expect to pay premium prices for what is highly publicized in the country as *Schweizer Qualität* (Swiss quality). One of the best ways to take maximum advantage of the wealth of attractions that, in spite of the cost, make Switzerland one of Europe's top drawing cards is to provide your own transportation and bring your shelter along or take advantage of the country's nearly one hundred youth hostels and many inexpensive pensions and guest houses.

There is plenty to see here; in fact, you can easily make a visit to Switzerland seem like a three-country excursion without ever crossing a border. The three principal official languages – German, French, and Italian (the fourth language, Romansh, is spoken by less than 1 percent of the population) – correspond to the three main ethnic divisions of the country. The Italian part of Switzerland, the canton of Ticino, is like a miniature Italy, the only difference being that everything functions perfectly and is spotlessly clean. A visit to the French-speaking region, which roughly corresponds to the area west of a line running from Basel to Zermatt, is akin to visiting neighboring France.

The signs, food, and even the temperaments have a decided French flair. The German-speaking region, which accounts for some 70 percent of the population, mirrors the Teutonic influence of Switzerland's two northern neighbors, Germany and Austria.

Although there are some fine museums and interesting churches, Switzerland's main attractions are scenic – idyllic alpine villages reminiscent of scenes from *Heidi*, quiet mountain lakes, and the grandeur of Grindelwald's famous big three peaks: Eiger, Monch, and Jungfrau. Switzerland has some of the most magnificent scenery anywhere, at altitudes ranging from 196 meters above sea level at the Mediterranean-like Lago Maggiore in the Italian section, to 4,634 meters, the country's highest point, at the Dufour summit in the Monte Rosa massif. And all of this in a country no bigger than the state of West Virginia!

Tidiness and cleanliness are two traits that, although not exclusively Swiss, are nevertheless practiced with such dedication that they have become something close to national obsessions. The contrast with some other parts of Europe or the U.S. for that matter is nothing short of striking! After you have done some cycling through the cities and countryside, you'll see what we mean.

The Swiss are friendly enough, but very stiff, proper, and hard to get to know. As a cyclist quietly making your way through the countryside, you have a better chance than most of breaking through this barrier of formality. Most young Swiss speak English and are often anxious to practice what they've learned in school.

The Swiss are very active and outdoor oriented, using their small country's wonderful resources to full advantage. Cycling is a popular pastime and both colorfully costumed road racers and heavily ladened cycle tourers are common sights. Just as flat Holland is the ideal country for effortless touring, Switzerland is the place to test your mountain legs and low, low gears. Although Switzerland's magnificent landscape contains many diverse elements, the mountains are the dominant feature. It is possible, however, with careful planning and judicious use of the excellent Swiss National Railway to see a good portion of the country's beauty without having to have legs and lungs of steel – more about that later.

FOOD AND DRINK

The Swiss take great pride in the quality of their food products and for good reason. Whether you shop for picnic supplies at an open-air stall or at a modern supermarket, the quality will be first-class. Breads and other bakery products are excellent. Swiss cheeses enjoyed throughout the world taste even better when eaten in the country. The cheese known as Swiss in the States is called *Emmentaler* there and is but one of a large and tasty variety of locally produced cheeses. Just about every town of any size has a cheese store where you can sample these delicious products. The beer is very good, and Swiss wines, while rarely found outside of the country, are delicious.

Your best bet for cutting down on the high cost of food is to shop at either of the country's two major food store chains, **Migro** or **Coop**. The Migro stores also carry high-energy food and drink products designed for high-performance sports – ideal for those tough mountain passes. Many of their stores also have cafeteria restaurants that serve lots of good food at reasonable prices, a great way to beat the high cost of Swiss restaurants.

MAPS

For overall planning, we like **Michelin map #427** (scale 1:400,000; 1 cm = 4 kms), which shows scenic roads and some contour shading. If you would like a more detailed planning map, get the **Kümmerly and Frey** official Auto Club (ACS) map of Switzerland (scale 1:250,000; 1 cm = 2.5 kms). The large somewhat unwieldy sheet also has tourist information in German, French, and English on the back. Michelin also prints a series (#216, #217, #218, #219) that covers the entire country in four maps (scale 1:200,000; 1 cm = 2 kms). These more detailed maps are adequate for cycling but may require frequent stopping to ask for directions. Scenic roads are marked in green and steep grades indicated with arrows.

The ultimate in Swiss cycling maps are those issued by **Kümmerly and Frey** in conjunction with the **Swiss Traffic Club** (VCS). These maps show the country in incredible detail. The scale is 1:50,000 (1 cm = 0.5 kms), and the roads most suitable for cycling, as well as detailed contour lines, are shown. At present there are fifteen maps in the series. Although they are the most detailed maps available for cycle touring, we have several problems with them. First, they are so detailed that we often find ourselves with heads buried in the maps watching the country go by on paper rather than enjoying it live! Another problem is that at a scale of only 0.5 kilometers per centimeter it doesn't take very long before you've cycled clear off of the map even in this tiny country. And finally at a cost of up to 25 SFr. per map, touring can become pretty expensive. These maps can be purchased at most Swiss bookstores or by mail from the VCS (Postfach, 3360 Herzogenbuchsee; Switzerland).

BICYCLE SHOPS AND RENTALS

As cycling has become more popular over the last few years, there has been a corresponding increase in the number of cycle shops. There are currently more than 2 million bikes registered in this country and about two thousand repair shops. But don't expect to find a bike shop in every village as is the case in Holland or France. Most repair shops are located in the larger towns.

Since Switzerland is on the metric scale, nonmetric parts are rarely available. One place we know of that has a selection of nonmetric parts is **Jelmoli** (Uraniastrasse 31, **Zürich**, Tel: [01] 22 04 411).

If you are considering the purchase of a bike, don't plan to buy one in Switzerland. Prices there are considerably higher than in neighboring France.

Bicycles or *velos* as they are called in Switzerland can be rented at nearly all of the some one thousand train stations spread throughout the country. Most are of the three-speed variety. In any case, these are just suitable for local flat country touring. Cycles can be rented at one point and returned to any participating station. If you have a ticket, rates are quite reasonable: 9 SFr. for the first twenty-four hours and then 7 SFr. for each additional day. If you don't have a ticket, you will have to pay a small surcharge.

ACCOMMODATIONS

Switzerland is the world leader when it comes to providing the best in accommodations. Hoteliers from all over come to study Swiss techniques in hotel and restaurant management. From such world-famous resorts as St. Moritz's Palace Hotel where you can spend 500 SFr. per night to comfortable farmhouses in out-of-the-way villages where you can enjoy Swiss hospitality for as little as 15 SFr. per night, the availability and selection is great. In fact, it is estimated that there is one hotel or inn for each 232 Swiss residents, one of the highest ratios in the world. No matter what you pay, you will encounter nothing but spotless facilities, a reflection of the Swiss obsession with cleanliness. A continental breakfa῾ ί is almost always included in the price of a room. Hotels belonging to the Swiss Hotel Association are graded with from one to five stars, depending on the degree of luxury.

A great way to get to know the country and to have some contact with the people is to rent a room for a week or so on a working farm. Rooms are cheap and you can take your time to explore the local region on your bike. For details, contact **Buchungszentrale** (Ferien auf dem Bauernhof, Postfach 423, 6030 Ebikon; Tel: [041] 36 87 80) or the **Swiss National Tourist Office**.

There are eighty-nine Swiss IYHA youth hostels pretty evenly spread throughout the country. There is no age limit, although when crowded, preference is given to people under 25 years of age. Reservations are recommended during July and August and should be made with the individual hostels directly. For further information, contact **Verein fur Jugendherbergen Zürich**, (Mutschellenstrasse 116, 8038 Zürich; Tel: [01] 48 24 561). A map showing the location and giving a description of all Swiss hostels is available from the Swiss National Tourist Office.

Camping is quite a popular Swiss pastime, and there are more than five hundred campgrounds, mostly concentrated around the popular tourist destinations. Campsites are generally very clean and well maintained. In keeping somewhat with the scale on which things are done here, campgrounds are usually small and *gemütlich*. Most sites are open from mid-April to early October, although many campgrounds in the higher mountain regions have a shorter season.

Free camping is generally prohibited, although this varies from canton to canton. The Canton of Ticino in the Italian part of the country has very strict regulations against any type of camping outside of an official campground. In other parts of the country, you can usually get away with putting up a tent for the night. Where possible, ask for permission.

TRANSPORTATION WITHIN THE COUNTRY

In spite of the country's mountainous terrain, Switzerland has one of the most highly developed and efficient transportation systems in the world, reaching even the smallest mountain villages. Where there is no rail service, the familiar yellow post buses travel. You can take your bike with you anywhere in the country with the exception of on the Inter-City trains.

If you have a train ticket, the cost of shipping a bike is 5 SFr. anywhere in the country. A 10-ticket pack is available for 30 SFr. The shipping charge is higher if you send the bike unaccompanied. If you think that you will be doing any significant amount of train travel within Switzerland, look into the various money-saving ticket plans available. Show up with your bike at least thirty minutes before departure. In most cases the bike will be loaded and unloaded by the station personnel. Sending the bike "unaccompanied" will cost about 15 SFr.

The Swiss National Railway (SBB) publishes a booklet in German or French only called *Velo-Bahn* that describes forty short routes in selected parts of the country. It is available at all train stations for 6 SFr.

The post buses will carry your cycle on a space available basis.

SOURCES OF ADDITIONAL INFORMATION

The **Swiss National Tourist Office (SNTO)** (608 Fifth Avenue, New York, NY 10020; Tel: [212] 757-5944 or 250 Stockton Street, San Francisco, California 94108; Tel: [415] 363-2260) can provide information for trip planning.

Local tourist offices can supply a wealth of useful information about specific regions but rarely have information about other parts of the country. In the German-speaking areas, look for *Verkehrsverein* or *Verkehrsbüro*; in the French section, look for *Office du Tourisme*; and in the Italian-speaking region, *Ente Turismo*.

The **Schweizerischer Radfahrer und Motorfahrer Bund (SRB)** (Schaffhausenstrasse 272, 8023 Zürich; Tel: [01] 31 19 220) is the main cycling organization for the German-speaking region. They have been very active in promoting the marking and building of cycle paths. They publish a booklet describing many local tours.

The **Touring Club Suisse** (9 rue Pierre-Fatio, 1200 Geneva; Tel: [022] 3712) is the largest automobile club in Switzerland and has an active section devoted to cycle touring. They maintain a number of *velo centers*, where bikes can be rented and taken on tours from these centers over marked cycle paths. They also sponsor many group cycle outings throughout the country. The equally active camping section publishes a guide to Swiss campgrounds and is involved in the management of a number of the country's better sites.

The **Union Cycliste Suisse** (4 rue de Vieux-College, 1121 Geneva 3; Tel: [022] 21 52 06) is the main cycling group in the French-speaking part of the country. Although principally concerned with racing, they do sponsor some group outings, called *brevets*, and can supply information about cycling Switzerland's many mountain passes.

ZÜRICH TO GENEVA: THE SWISS CONNECTION

START	FINISH
ZÜRICH	GENEVA

DISTANCE
405 kms/252 miles

MICHELIN MAPS
#216, Bale-St. Gall;
#217, Geneve-Berne
  (scale 1:200,000; 1 cm = 2 kms)

KÜMMERLY & FREY VCS VELOKARTE MAPS
Zürichsee-Zug;
Luzern Ob-und Nidwalden;
Bern-Freibourg;
Lausanne-Vallee de Joux;
Geneve et environs
  (scale 1:50,000; 1 cm = 0.5 kms)

For our route through Switzerland we have tried to include a representative sampling from the broad range of attractions that the country offers. We pass through all of Switzerland's major cities, with the exception of Basel, and cycle around parts of the most scenic lakes, including the Züricher See, Vierwaldstätter See, Thuner See, and Lake Geneva. As you pedal this route you will encounter a variety of attractive landscapes – the rolling pastoral farm country around the Benedictine Cloister at Einsiedeln; the spectacular snow-tipped mountains, rambling farmhouses, and chalets of the Berner Oberland; and the steep vineyard-covered hills that rise up from Lake Geneva in the French-speaking part of the country. There is quite a variety indeed for such a small country.

The route can be cycled in either direction, but there seems to be a little more downhill coasting going from Zürich to Geneva. From Kreuzlingen along the "Lake Constance Route" (as described elsewhere in this book), it's only about 50 kilometers by way of Winterthur to Zürich to connect these two routes. From Geneva you can continue along the French part of Lake Geneva to complete the tour around the lake. Geneva also serves as a good jumping-off point for touring the French alps.

Any route that goes from one end of Switzerland to the other is certainly going to include some steep sections. To get the most out of this varied route it helps to be in good condition. If you want to enjoy the scenic beauties along the way and not fight the hills, you can easily bypass the steepest stretch which crosses the Jaun Pass by taking the train from Thun to Bulle. From Bulle it's mostly downhill to Lake Geneva. The same applies to the other hilly portions from Pfaffikon on the Züricher See to Einsiedeln and the portion of the route between Lucerne and Bern. In all cases, you should have a good ten-speed bicycle, and for the mountain stretches, a three-sprocket twelve-speed or eighteen-speed bike is advisable.

The two best months for cycling this route are June, before the tourist traffic gets too heavy and you can still enjoy the sight of snow along the road at the higher elevations, and the month of September, when many of the tourists have departed and the weather is often at its finest.

Any time you tour the alps you run into the possibility of encountering snow at the higher elevations. Always check the signs at the bottom of a pass before starting your ascent to make sure that the pass is open. This is especially important in May and June and September and October. By dialing 162, you can obtain the weather report in the language of the region from which you are calling. Summer rains are a frequent occurrence but are usually of short duration. The weather can change very quickly, especially in the mountains, and sudden, often terrifying thunderstorms can literally put a damper on your cycling.

If you decide to cycle in the latter part of July and in August when the Swiss are on vacation, plan to encounter a lot of traffic in the resort areas, as well as crowded hostels and campgrounds.

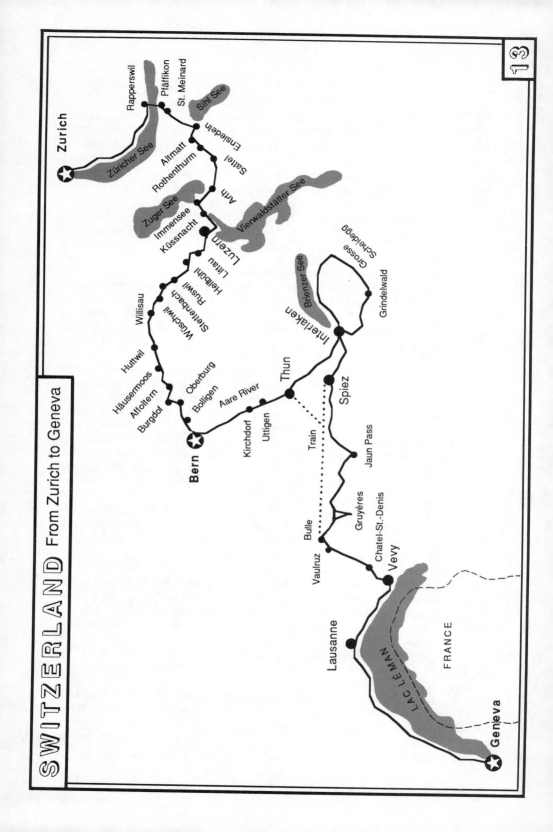

★ *LOOKING OUT OVER THE HANDLEBARS* ★

FROM ZÜRICH
TO GENEVA

CITY

ZÜRICH

ROUTE

17

DISTANCE KM	TOTAL KM
44	0

ROUTE DESCRIPTION

From the Zürich Hauptbahnhof, cross the bridge over the Limmat, and follow the road along the lake about 30 kms to Rapperswil, which has a thirteenth-century fortress perched on the rocks overlooking the lake. In the distance you can see the peaks of the alps. Cross over the Seedam Bridge, which divides the lake, and pass the Seedam shopping center in Pfaffikon. From Pfaffikon head toward Einsiedeln and climb steeply to the little settlement of St. Meinrad, gaining 500 meters in about 4 kms. (*Note:* You can avoid this climb by taking the train from Pfaffikon to Biberbrugg and then following the road into Einsiedeln.) From St. Meinrad it is an easy ride the remaining 5 kms into Einsiedeln, with a nice view of the Sihlsee.

CITY

EINSIEDELN

ROUTE

8

DISTANCE KM	TOTAL KM
48	44

ROUTE DESCRIPTION

Take the road that climbs out of Einsiedeln to Dritte Altmatt. At the Altmatt, pick up hwy 8 and follow the signs to Rothenthurm, Sattel, and then to Arth at the foot of the Zuger See, a pleasant small town with one of the finest baroque churches in the country. Follow the road along the lake to Immen See. Then cross the isthmus separating the Zuger See from the famous Vierwaldstätter See at Küssnacht and then stay along the lake shore into Luzern (Lucerne).

CITY

LUZERN (LUCERNE)

DISTANCE KM	TOTAL KM
35	92

ROUTE DESCRIPTION

From the center of Luzern, head west through the Gutschwald, following the signs to Littau. At Littau, take the road to Hellbühl. From there, continue on to Ruswil. From Ruswil the road runs through the pleasant hill country (no steep climbs), passing through the villages of Statenbach and Wüschwil into Willisau.

CITY

WILLISAU

ROUTE

23

DISTANCE KM	TOTAL KM
39	127

ROUTE DESCRIPTION

The route from Willisau winds and climbs through steep hill country first to Huttwil, and then along hwy 23 to the small town of Häusernmoos. Turn off to Affoltern. From there follow the signs into the medieval town of Burgdorf, which has a wonderful eleventh-century fortress. From Burgdorf, take the road along the Schachen River 2 kms to Oberburg. Then follow the road through the wooded hills into Bern, passing through Bolligen.

CITY
BERN

DISTANCE KM	TOTAL KM
30	166

ROUTE DESCRIPTION

From the center of Bern, take the path along the Aare River to the Wabern Campground. Then follow the river past a small airport and another campground, continuing in this direction to Kirchdorf. Then follow the signs to Thun by way of Uttigen.

CITY
THUN

DISTANCE KM	TOTAL KM
23	196

ROUTE DESCRIPTION

From Thun, follow the north shore of the Thuner See to Interlaken.

CITY
INTERLAKEN

ROUTE
11

DISTANCE KM	TOTAL KM
72	219

ROUTE DESCRIPTION

From Interlaken, you can take a beautiful 20-kms side trip into Grindelwald. Unless you take the trail over the Grosse Scheidegg and wind on back to Interlaken by way of the Brienzer See, you will have to return to Interlaken on the same road. *This is heavy-duty mountain cycling. Be sure that you are properly prepared.* To continue from Interlaken, take the road along the south side of the Thuner See to Spiez. At Spiez, turn off onto hwy 11, which after 22 kms intersects with the road to the Jaun Pass. From this point the road climbs sharply to the summit at 1,509 meters. Follow the signs down into the medieval town of Bulle for a well-deserved rest. For an interesting side excursion just before Bulle, turn off on the road to the delightful little cheese-making town of Gruyères.

Note: To avoid having to climb the pass, you can take the train from either Interlaken or Spiez to Bulle.

CITY
BULLE

ROUTE
12

DISTANCE KM	TOTAL KM
35	291

ROUTE DESCRIPTION

Leave Bulle on the road to Vaulruz. From Vaulruz, take hwy 12 which runs alongside the new autobahn, passing through Chatel-St.-Denis and continuing down a steep grade to meet up with Lake Geneva at Vevy.

CITY	
VEVY	

ROUTE	
9	

DISTANCE KM	TOTAL KM
20	326

ROUTE DESCRIPTION

From Vevy, take the busy hwy 9, which follows the lake into Lausanne.

CITY	
LAUSANNE	

DISTANCE KM	TOTAL KM
59	346

ROUTE DESCRIPTION

Leave Lausanne on the Route de Vidy, which runs along the lake. Although you may encounter quite a bit of traffic, it is possible to have an enjoyable day's cycling from Lausanne to Geneve (Geneva).

CITY	
GENEVE (GENEVA)	

DISTANCE KM	TOTAL KM
0	405

ZÜRICH TO GENEVA SIGHTS AND ACCOMMODATIONS

ZÜRICH. Switzerland's most populous city and one of the world's major banking centers, German speaking Zürich has managed to retain a charm and ambience not usually associated with such large cities. The **Limmat River** which flows through the city and empties into the **Züricher See** (Lake Zürich) is so clean that swimming areas are set aside on the river banks right in the heart of the city. The fashionable **Bahnhofstrasse** leads from the main train station past a dazzling array of exclusive shops and staid banks. The two principal churches are the **Grossmunster**, whose origins can be traced back to Charlemagne, and the **Fraumunster**, whose main attractions are the stained-glass windows by **Marc Chagall**.

Across the river from the Bahnhofstrasse is the small, well-preserved **Altstadt** (Old Town). The **Kunsthaus** (Art Museum) contains a wide cross section of European paintings and includes one of Europe's best collections of the works of the Norwegian artist, **Edvard Munch**. The **Schweizerisches Landesmuseum** (Swiss National Museum), just across from the Bahnhof, has exhibits tracing the development of Swiss civilization and culture.

Zürich's elegant shops and boutiques, especially those on the Bahnhofstrasse, offer some of the finest goods that our consumer-oriented society has to offer. The quality and selection are excellent – just bring along lots of Swiss francs. The Swiss are prepared to ship whatever you purchase, whether it's a Rolex watch or a hand-painted fondue pot, safely and efficiently. While in Switzerland be sure to pick up a handy Swiss Army knife, something no cyclist should be without.

Although Zürich is laid out so that the main attractions can be covered easily on foot or bicycle, an interesting and unusual way to tour the city is via the **Goldtimer**, a restored 1928 vintage streetcar, finished entirely in gold. The hour-long ride along the famous Bahnhofstrasse and past the city's highlights is accompanied by a multilingual guide. The cost is approximately 15 SFr. For further information and reservations, stop in at the tourist office in the main train station at the head of the Bahnhofstrasse.

Another fine way to tour the city and get a different perspective on the old **guild houses** along the river is to take the Limmat River cruise boat. Trips are scheduled every thirty minutes from in front of the Landesmuseum.

Accommodations in this world banking capital are not cheap; however, quality is high. If price is no consideration, you can rub elbows with the oil sheiks and diplomats at the conveniently located HOTEL BAUR AU LAC (Talstrasse 1, 8000 Zürich; Tel: [01] 22 11 650). Just as convenient but at less than half the price is the modest HOTEL LIMMATHOF (Limmatquai 142; Tel: [01] 47 42 20) located at the river bank near the train station. A gem of a small Zürich hotel is the FLORHOF (Florhofgasse 4; Tel: [01] 47 44 70), located in a recently renovated eighteenth-century patrician house close to the university. For an inexpensive, clean, no-frills room, try the PENSION HINTERER STERNEN (Freieckgasse 7; Tel: [01] 25 13 268).

The huge four-hundred-bed Zürich youth hostel offers dormitory accommodations in Spartan surroundings. Kitchen facilities are also provided. The IYHF JUGENDHER-BERGE ZÜRICH (Mutschellenstrasse 114; Tel: [01] 48 23 544) is located near the lake just south of the city center in Zürich-Wöllishofen.

Of the several Zürich area campgrounds, the most convenient is CAMPING SEE-BUCHT, located on the lake 2 kms from Zürich center. It is a small pleasant site with a washing machine, camp store and restaurant, open 1 May to 30 September.

EINSIEDELN. In a quiet setting nestled in the hills overlooking the **Sihlsee**, Einsiedeln was once one of the cultural centers of the German-speaking world. During the Middle Ages it was one of the main assembly points for pilgrims making the journey to Santiago de Compostela, Spain, on the Pilgrimage of St. James. The main attraction today is the Benedictine **Cloister Church of Maria-Einsiedeln**, built in the early eighteenth century; it is one of the finest examples of baroque architecture in Switzerland.

The town's top hotel is the HOTEL DREI KÖNIGE (8840 Einsiedeln; Tel: [055] 53 24 41) where a double with bath costs about 110 SFr. The HOTEL LINDE (Tel: [055] 53 27 20) is a nice modest hotel located just across from the cloister.

The most convenient campground is CAMPING CARAVANING GRÜNE, located on the Sihlsee about 5 kms east of Einsiedeln. It is open all year.

LUCERNE (Luzern). Central Switzerland's most important city, Lucerne is beautifully situated on the shores of the **Vierwaldstätter See**. It is a favorite destination of Swiss and foreign tourists. Site of many international music and art festivals, Lucerne is the cultural center of the Swiss heartland. As in many Swiss cities, the old town has been well preserved and serves as the focal point for any visit. Instead of allowing their historic landmarks to wither and decay, the practical and industrious Swiss have made a practice of utilizing many of their centuries-old architectural treasures by converting the interiors into fashionable shops and cozy restaurants while meticulously maintaining and restoring the ancient facades. A stroll through the center of Lucerne will amply illustrate this.

The covered wooden **Kappellbrücke** (Chapel Bridge) is the city's best-known landmark. Originally built in the fourteenth century, the bridge has been faithfully restored and maintained. Galleries on the bridge are full of colorful representations of scenes from both local and national history.

The **Alte Rathaus** (Old City Hall) was built in 1602 into the remnants of the ancient city walls, creating an interesting blend of Swiss and Italian architecture. It is now the site of the local **History Museum**. The **Kunst Museum** (Art Museum) is in the art and convention center at the lake, just past the Seebrücke. The largest part of the collection is devoted to Swiss painters. One of the country's most interesting museums is the **Verkehrshaus der Schweiz** (the Swiss Transportation Museum). The largest of its kind in Europe, it has a varied selection of all modes of transportation, from horse-drawn carriages to space vehicles.

The region around **Vierwaldstätter See** itself is a popular vacation area. The lake, which lies deep in the heart of William Tell country, is named after the four bordering cantons (states): Uri, Schwyz, Unterwalden, and Luzern. The marketplace in the small town of **Altdorf** at the southeast corner of the lake is the site of a statue dedicated to the legendary Swiss crossbow marksman. A small William Tell museum is located in the nearby village of **Burglen**, his presumed birthplace. Although not easily reached by cycle, you can visit there by taking the boat from Lucerne.

Built on the ruins of a thirteenth-century fortress perched on a hill overlooking the city is the delightful HOTEL CHATEAU GÜTSCH (Kanonenstrasse, 6003 Luzern; Tel: [041] 22 02 72). The hotel, which runs its own cable car from the center of town, was reputed to have been a favorite of Queen Victoria. Doubles go for 125 to 200 SFr. For a pleasant hotel in the moderate price category, try the HOTEL PICKWICK (Rathausquai 6; Tel: [041] 51 59 27), located at the river facing the Kapellbrücke. Conveniently situated near the Spreuerbrücke is the low-cost HOTEL LIGE (Pfistergasse 17; Tel: [041] 22 09 18).

The youth hostel, AM ROTSEE (Sedelstrasse 12, Tel: [041] 36 88 00), has 206 beds and provides cooking facilities. It is located at the north edge of town near the cemetery.

CAMPING LIDO is a pleasant site in a parklike setting on the Vierwaldstätter See next to the Transportation Museum. Facilities include a washing machine, restaurant, and camp store. It is open 15 March to 31 October.

WILLISAU. Located in the heart of central Switzerland, Willisau is an attractive little town with a number of fine medieval buildings that makes a convenient stopover on the route between Lucerne and Bern. If you are anywhere in this area in May it pays to pedal the extra kilometers to be in Willisau for the annual **International Jazz Festival**, which attracts a surprising number of top jazz stars to this little out-of-the-way town.

Comfortable inexpensive rooms can be found at either the cozy little HOTEL MOHREN (6130 Willisau; Tel: [045] 81 11 10) or at the HOTEL KREUZ (Tel: [045] 81 11 15).

There is no campground in Willisau; however, you should have no difficulty getting permission from a local farmer to put up your tent for a night. There is a good campground with a view of the old fortress located on the route to Bern in Burgdorf. The site is called CAMPING WALDEGG and is open 1 April to 31 October.

BERN. With a population of only 165,000, Bern is one of the smallest and most charming of Europe's capital cities. Since Bern is the dividing line between the German-speaking and French-speaking parts of the country, one often hears an interesting mixture of the two languages being spoken – sometimes in the course of a single sentence.

The old town, situated on a small outcropping and surrounded on three sides by the Aare River, is well preserved. Many of the quaint old buildings now house smart shops and charming restaurants. Like most Swiss cities, Bern is an ideal city for walking. The pedestrian area has many decorative fountains and tucked away behind some of the country's most attractive Gothic and baroque facades are a number of very chic modern shops and a variety of interesting restaurants. On the banks of the Aare by the Nydegg bridge is an area set aside for the bears that are Bern's trademark.

The **Kunstmuseum** (Art Museum) contains a large collection of the works of the twentieth-century Swiss painter Paul Klee. The **Schweizerisches Post Museum** traces the development of postal service dating back to Roman times and displays a collection of Swiss postage stamps from 1843 to the present.

The HOTEL GOLDENER ADLER (Gerechtigkeitsgasse 7, 3000 Bern; Tel: [031] 22 17 25) is a traditional old inn set in the heart of the old town. City records show that there was an inn known as the Weisses Kreuz at this location as far back as 1489. A double without a bath can be had for under 100 SFr. Another fine old inn with a good traditional restaurant is the HOTEL GOLDENER SCHLÜSSEL (Rathausgasse 72; Tel: [031] 22 02 16).

The 144-bed Bern youth hostel, the BERNER JUGENDHAUS (Weihergassee 4; Tel: [031] 22 63 16), is conveniently situated at the river below the Parliament buildings. It is one of the country's best hostels. Meals and cooking facilities are available.

There is a pleasant grassy campground on the river across from the zoo just a few minutes cycling from the center of town on a path along the Aare. CAMPING EICHOLZ has a camp store, washing machine, and restaurant. It is open 1 May to 30 September.

THUN. A delightful old town at the northwest end of the lake of the same name, Thun offers a pleasant blending of the medieval and the modern. It is a popular base for excursions into the **Bernese Oberland**. Worth a visit is the **Historical Museum** located in the tower of the imposing twelfth-century fortress that looks down over the town.

The HOTEL BEAU RIVAGE (3600 Thun; Tel: [033] 22 22 36) is a comfortable hotel nicely situated on the river. For an inexpensive room in a private house, check in with the Otto family (Gurnigelstrasse 24; Tel: [033] 22 93 72).

The closest youth hostel, the JUGEND-HERBERGE FAULENSEE (Quellenhofweg 66, 3710 Spiez; Tel: [033] 54 19 88), is 10 kms away at Spiez about halfway between Thun and Interlaken.

There is a first-rate campground located on the lake at Gwatt about 3 kms south of Thun. CAMPING BETTLEREICHE has a washing machine and snack bar. It is open 14 April to 14 October.

INTERLAKEN. In German it means between the lakes, and that is exactly what the lovely city of Interlaken is. Occupying the narrow isthmus separating the Thuner See and Brienzer See and presenting captivating alpine vistas, Interlaken offers visitors a wide range of outdoor activities from water sports to mountain climbing and hiking. The **Museum of Tourism** in Interlaken (Obere Gasse 26) shows the development of tourism in the region over the last two hundred years. During the summer months there are regular outdoor performances of Schiller's classic play, *William Tell*. What better setting than in the heart of the Swiss alps to see the dramatization of this famous Swiss legend. It's a little hokey but great fun!

From Interlaken it is about 20 kilometers by bike to the delightful village of **Grindelwald**, in one of the most spectacular settings in the alps. This is the heart of Swiss "big mountain country." The famous **Eiger**, the **Monch**, and the 4,158-meter-high **Jungfrau** tower over the village below. Numerous well-marked trails open up this region for exploration by foot and, in some cases, by bicycle. For one of the most spectacular mountain trips in the world, take the train to the 3,454-meter-high **Jungfraujoch**. Go only on a clear day, when you can see forever.

As the principal gateway to the Bernese Oberland, Interlaken has a good selection of accommodations of all kinds. The CHALET OBERLAND (3800 Interlaken; Tel: [036] 22 94 31) offers quality accommodations at moderate prices in the center of town, just down the street from the tourist office. The HOTEL TELL (Hauptstrasse 49; Tel: [036] 22 18 55) is a good inexpensive hotel in Matten at the south edge of town. Also in Matten is the delightful GASTHÖF HIRSCHEN (Tel: [036] 22 15 45) on the road to Grindelwald. This old converted twenty-five-room farmhouse has been in the possession of the same family for over three hundred years.

There is a two-hundred-bed IYHF youth hostel, the JUGENDHERBERGE BÖNIGEN (Aareweg, 3806 Bönigen; Tel: [036] 22 43 53) in Bönigen on the Brienzer See about 2 kms from Interlaken. In Grindelwald, the JUGENDHERBERGE DIE WEID (Terrassenweg, 3818 Grindelwald; Tel: [036] 53 10 09) has 144 beds.

If you are camping, you can take your pick of a large number of good campgrounds in the Interlaken-Grindelwald region. One of our favorites is CAMPING MANOR FARM, located directly on Lake Thun. Follow the signs to Campground #1. This is a large grassy site with good facilities in a magnificent setting. It is open all year.

BULLE. The small medieval market town of Bulle lies in the middle of the **Gruyères region**, one of the most enchanting parts of Switzerland. Much of the town was destroyed in an 1805 fire and the present town mostly reflects the architecture of the early nineteenth-century. Bulle is well known for its cattle market, cheese production, and the preservation of old customs and traditions. A visit to the **Musée Gruerien** (Gruyères Museum) will give you a good insight into the development of this often-missed part of Switzerland. The fortified little town of Gruyères, with its castle and broad cobblestone main street lined with fine old flower-decorated houses, is one of the reasons you came to Switzerland. It's a real gem of a town, well worth the climb up the hill to get here. Be sure to visit the magnificent **Castle of the Counts of Gruyères**, which has a fine collection of medieval furnishings and weapons. A visit to the **cheese factory** where the tasty Gruyère cheese (an essential ingredient in making an authentic fondue) is made will give you a good understanding of Swiss cheese production methods.

To enhance your enjoyment of this delightful place, spend a night at the cozy HOSTELLERIE DE ST. GEORGES (1663 Gruyères; Tel: [029] 62 246). Its fine restaurant is an excellent place to sample a cheese fondue. In Bulle, which is a little less commercial, you can get a comfortable, reasonably priced room at the HOTEL TONNELIER (1630 Bulle; Tel: [029] 27 745).

The most convenient campground is located between Gruyères and Bulle at Epagny. CAMPING LES SAPINS is about 1 km north of Gruyères on the Gruyère-Molson road. It is open 1 April to 30 September.

VEVY. The lakefront resort towns of **Vevy** and **Montreux** have been popular with visitors to Switzerland since the early days of tourism. Vevy is the center of the region's extensive wine production. Montreux is a Victorian era resort that has retained a great deal of its elegance and is today host to a number of prominent music festivals, including the **Jazz Festival** in July and the **Classical Music Festival** in August and September. The nearby **Fortress of Chillon** is a beautiful, well-preserved thirteenth-century castle, with torture chambers, medieval weapons, and the dungeon immortalized in Lord Byron's poem "The Prisoner of Chillon." The castle, which juts out into the lake, affords an excellent view of the lake and Mont Blanc.

This strip of coast, sometimes referred to as the Geneva Riviera, contains a wide range of mostly expensive accommodations. The HOTEL DU LAC (rue d'Italie, 1800 Vevy; Tel: [021] 51 10 41) is a stately first-class hotel. You can find a comfortable budget-priced room in Vevy at the PENSION BURGLE (16 rue Louis-Meyer; Tel: [021] 51 40 23).

There is a 114-bed youth hostel in Montreux: AUBERGE DE JEUNESSE MONTREUX-TERRITET (Passage l'Auberge 8, 1820 Montreux;Tel: [021] 4934).

CAMPING LA PICHETTE about 4 kms west of Vevy is a small site with access to the lake. It is open 1 May to 30 September.

LAUSANNE. Lausanne is a pleasant cultural and convention center on the north shore of the lake. The **Lausanne Cathedral** located in the center of the old city is Switzerland's largest and is the best example of Gothic church architecture in the country. A particularly unusual and interesting museum is the **Collection de L'Art Brut**, a moving and extensive collection of various art forms, all works of mentally disturbed artists.

One of Lake Geneva's classic hotels is the historic castle hotel, CHATEAU D'OUCHY (place du Port, 1006 Ouchy, Lausanne; Tel: [021] 26 74 51). At one time this was the residence of the bishops of Lausanne. Figure on spending about 150 SFr. or more per night for this romantic lakeside hotel. In the budget category, try the HOTEL PRES-LAC (ave. General Guisan, 1009 Pully; Tel: [021] 28 49 01) or the clean and

cheap LOGEMENT PRES DE VIDY
(Chemin du Bois de Vaux 36; Tel: [021]
24 24 79).

The 180-bed Lausanne youth hostel, the
AUBERGE DE JEUNESSE LAUSANNE
OUCHY (Chemin du Muguet 1; Tel: [021]
26 57 82), is nicely situated near the lake.

CAMPING DE VIDY located on Chemin
du Camping is a nice site on the lake just
south of Lausanne on the way to Geneva.
Its full facilities include a washing machine,
camp store, and restaurant. It is open all
year.

GENEVA (Geneve). Beautifully
situated at the southwest corner of **Lac
Leman** (Lake Geneva) and surrounded on
three sides by France, Geneva is a favored
location for many international agencies and
diplomatic conferences. The numerous
sumptuous lakeshore villas hidden behind
bushes and gates house a varied collection
of deposed monarchs, both famous and
infamous. Visitors are not welcome! Visitors
are, however, very welcome at the **Palais
des Nations**, the former headquarters of
the League of Nations and the current seat
of the European section of the **United
Nations**.

The city has a number of interesting
museums, including the **Musée d'Art
Histoire** (Historical Art Museum), which
has one of the best archaeological
collections in the country and an excellent
representation of Swiss artists. **The Musée
Ariana** displays porcelain and ceramics
from all over the world. The French
impressionists are well represented in the
Petit Palis (Museum of Modern Art). For
watch and clock freaks, the **Musée de
l'Horlogerie** has exhibits tracing the
development of time-telling from prehistoric
times to the present.

Geneva was once the center of the
Reformation and Calvinism. The somber
Cathédrale St.-Piere was the church of
Calvin, and from its north tower one has a
good view of the lake and the snow-clad
alps in the distance. The **Vieille Ville** (Old
Town), with its quaint houses, winding
streets, and parklike lakefront, is a delightful
place for walking and absorbing the
beautiful setting and atmosphere of Geneva.

For orientation, check in at the **Office
du Tourisme** (Tour de L'Ile) right where
the Rhone runs through the city. Pick up a
free map and copy of *This Week in
Geneva*.

The atmosphere in Geneva, although
decidedly French, has a very cosmopolitan
flair, due to the large number of diplomats
stationed there. Some of the finest cuisine
in the country is available from the more
than one thousand restaurants in and
around the city. Unfortunately, the presence
of so many diplomatic functionaries on
expense accounts has driven up prices;
Geneva is Switzerland's most expensive city.

With rooms at a premium, five-star
hotels, such as the elegant **Beau Rivage**
charge upwards of 300 SFr. for a room.
This is a good town to have your tent or
youth hostel card along. One of the town's
few bargains is to be found at the HOTEL
DES TOURELLES (2 boulevard James-
Fazy, 1200 Geneva; Tel: [022] 34 44 23),
centrally located near the river. Doubles
without bath run from 65 SFR. Another
good budget bet is the HOTEL ETOILE (17
V. Grenadiers; Tel: [022] 28 72 08). For
an affordable, first-class old town hotel, try
the HOTEL CHANDELIER (23 Grand-Rue,
Tel: [022] 21 56 88).

The large, comfortable, 266-bed hostel,
the IYHF AUBERGE DE JEUNESSE
GENEVE (rue des Plantaporrets; Tel: [022]
29 06 19) is one of your best bets in this
expensive town.

Campers can settle in at the all-year
campground, CAMPING SYLABELLE,
located at the southeast edge of the city off
the road to Veyrier.

Additional Recommended Routes

One of the country's best-kept secrets and most desirable cycling regions is the region know as the **Jura**, a lovely mountain area that runs from the north shore of Lake Geneva for some 200 kms along the French border to Basel, Switzerland's second largest city. Although some peaks reach a height of 1,600 meters, the average altitude is about 750 meters. Although lacking the spectacular vistas of the better known alpine regions, the Jura is rich in forests and contains some beautiful cycling country. With the exception of the heavily traveled road that runs from **Yverdon** at the foot of the **Lac de Neuchatel** up to the watch-making center of Biel, the Jura is quite hilly cycling.

In addition to the route around the **Bodensee** (Lake Constance) described in our "Three Country Tour," there are some other interesting cycling areas that do not require heavy-duty climbing. From Lake Constance you can ride down the entire length of the Rhine Valley, most of the way on the trail that runs along the river to Chur. From Chur you can hop on the train to bypass the mountains or, if you want to tackle some high alpine passes, you can continue up over the 2,284-meter-high **Julier Pass** into the chic resort town of St. Moritz and the beautiful Engadine Valley. From there it is less than 100 kilometers via the 1,815-meter-high **Maloja Pass** to the blue waters and Mediterranean vegetation of Italy's **Lake Como**.

Now that there are high-speed autobahns that cross the classic **St. Gottard** and **St. Bernard** passes, the original roads – hairpin turns and all – are relatively free of traffic and present cyclists with some of the best and most challenging cycling that Europe has to offer.

If you have a mountain bike and don't mind carrying it occasionally there are a number of hiking trails that lend themselves well to such mounted exploration. Be sure to have detailed maps and carry a tent, some food, and warm clothing. One particularly interesting route is from **Grindelwald** up and over the **Grosse Scheideeg** and down into the **Rosenlauital Valley**.

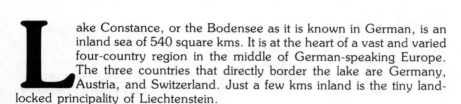

BIKING THROUGH EUROPE

LAKE CONSTANCE
A THREE COUNTRY TREAT

Lake Constance, or the Bodensee as it is known in German, is an inland sea of 540 square kms. It is at the heart of a vast and varied four-country region in the middle of German-speaking Europe. The three countries that directly border the lake are Germany, Austria, and Switzerland. Just a few kms inland is the tiny land-locked principality of Liechtenstein.

As the object of a bicycle tour, the Bodensee has a lot to offer. For one thing there is the chance to sample three countries in a short span. Even though the countries share a common language, you will notice very distinct differences in the architecture, food, and even the people from the three countries that border the Bodensee.

The lake itself is some 60 kms long and 12 kms at its widest point. It is fed by the Rhine River, which tumbles down from the Swiss alps and empties into the Bodensee at the Austrian town of Hard, near Bregenz. After running through the entire length of the lake, the Rhine exits near the picturesque Swiss town of Stein am Rhein.

Since boat traffic and the discharge of pollutants into the Bodensee are strictly regulated, the water is clear all around the lake. You can swim at any of the many beaches along the way without hesitation.

The scenery is varied enough to keep you interested over the entire circuit. Rising up from the shore on the German side, the hills are covered with vineyards and lined with medieval towns such as Meersburg, site of Germany's oldest castle. Looking over across the lake to the Swiss and Austrian side, the landscape is dominated by the snow-tipped alps, which form a perfect backdrop for the rich meadows and fruit orchards.

ROADS

Since the bicycle boom arrived well after the motorized tourist invasion, until recently, low priority was given to developing a continuous bike trail around the lake. In recent years attitudes have been changing, and it is now possible to cycle most of the way around the lake on marked trails. In many places these are narrow and must be shared with pedestrians, and on some stretches, it is necessary to take heavily traveled streets. But all in all, conditions for doing a cycle loop around the lake are very good.

MAPS

The most detailed map showing the cycle routes around the Bodensee is published by Kümmerely and Frey in conjunction with the VCS (Swiss Traffic Club) and is called the **Velokarte Bodensee-Thurgau** (scale 1: 50,000; 1 cm = 0.5 kms). The cost is 25 SFr. It is available from bookstores in Switzerland or it can be ordered from the VCS (Postfach, 3360 Herzogenbuchsee; Switzerland).

The German **ADFC Radtourenkarte** #33, Hohenzollern-Bodensee (scale 1: 100,000) shows the best cycling possibilities on the German side, but only outlines the roads in Austria and Switzerland. The map costs 10 DM and is available at bookstores in Germany.

ACCOMMODATIONS

The whole Bodensee region is very popular with vacationers from all over Europe and offers a complete range of accommodations. You can pedal the Bodensee in style, staying at first-class hotels and charming country inns, or you can enjoy the region's many attractions on a low-cost budget, staying at youth hostels and campgrounds.

SOURCES OF ADDITIONAL INFORMATION

For information about guided cycle tours around the lake, contact **Terranova** (Hirschsprung 8, 6078 Zeppelinheim, West Germany; Tel: [0611] 69 30 54) and **Velotours** (Mainaustrasse 34, 7750 Konstanz, West Germany; Tel: [07531] 52 085).

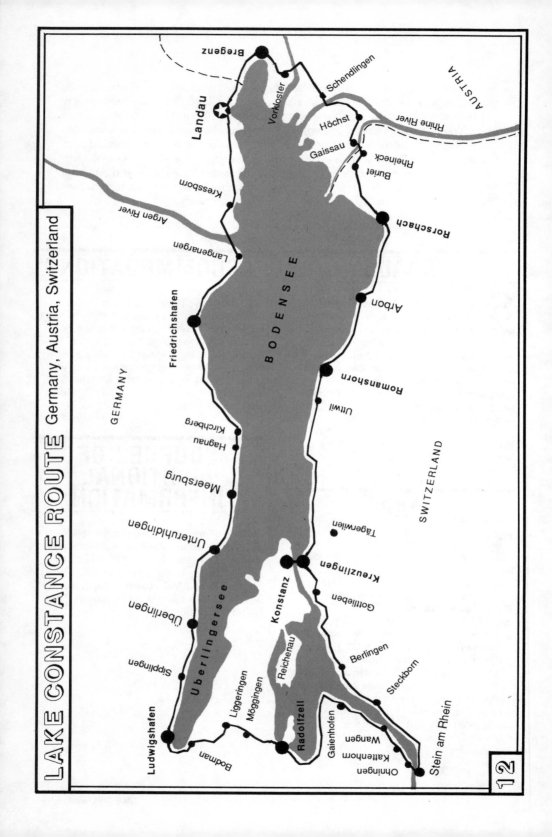

LAKE CONSTANCE ROUTE Germany, Austria, Switzerland

12

Bregenz

Schendlingen

Landau

Vorkloster

Höchst

AUSTRIA

Gaissau

Rhine River

Rheineck

Buriet

Kressbom

Rorschach

Argen River

Langenargen

Arbon

BODENSEE

Friedrichshafen

Romanshorn

GERMANY

Utwil

Kirchberg

Hagnau

Meersburg

Unteruhldingen

Tägerwilen

SWITZERLAND

Überlingen

Konstanz

Kreuzlingen

Überlingersee

Gottlieben

Sipplingen

Reichenau

Berlingen

Ludwigshafen

Liggeringen

Möggingen

Steckborn

Bodman

Radolfzell

Gaienhofen

Ohingen

Kattenhorn

Wangen

Stein am Rhein

THE LAKE CONSTANCE TOUR

START	FINISH
LINDAU, GERMANY	LINDAU

DISTANCE
181 kms/113 miles

VCS VELOKARTE MAPS
Bodensee-Thurgau (scale 1:50,000)

ADFS RADTOURENKARTE MAPS
#33, Hohenzollern-Bodensee
  (scale 1:100,000)

We start our trip around the Bodensee in Germany at Lindau and follow around the lake into Austria, traveling in a clockwise direction. But, this route can be pedaled in either direction and started anywhere along the lake.

There are several places along the way where you can connect with other routes described in this book. It's only about 50 kms from Kreuzlingen or Constance on the Bodensee to Zürich, where you can link up with our "Zürich to Geneva" route. From Bregenz or Lindau, you can do some heavy-duty mountain cycling to combine the level Bodensee tour with the "Bavarian Highlights Tour" or the Innsbruck-Salzburg "Mountains to Mozart" loop.

To include yet another country in your log book, you can easily pedal down the Rhine Valley into Liechtenstein along good cycle paths on the Austrian side of the Rhine. Don't expect too much from the Rhine at this point. It's little more than a stream, a far cry from the mighty castle-lined river further downstream.

Should you want to do an abbreviated Bodensee tour, there are passenger ferries between most of the main cities on the lake, which enable you to shorten the loop at several points along the route.

For the lake tour itself, if you stay near the lake, the terrain is flat and easy going. The only slightly hilly portion of our route is the stretch that divides the Untersee and the Überlingersee parts of the lake. This is a comfortable, relaxed route with plenty of places to stop and eat, stay overnight, or just enjoy the surroundings.

With respect to the weather, July and August are the best months for doing this loop; however, expect big crowds wherever you go. Our favorite time for doing this trip is early September when the lake is still warm enough for swimming and the high season crowds have departed.

THE LAKE CONSTANCE ROUTE

CITY
LINDAU

ROUTE
B31 190

DISTANCE KM	TOTAL KM
9	0

ROUTE DESCRIPTION

From the Lindau train station, leave the island via the cycle path along the railroad bridge. On the mainland, follow the signs toward Bregenz and pick up B31, the Bregenzer Strasse, which runs to the Austrian border. After crossing the border, stay on the main street (hwy 190) until you can cross the railroad tracks and take the bike path that runs along the tracks all the way to the Bregenz train station.

CITY
BREGENZ

DISTANCE KM	TOTAL KM
37	9

ROUTE DESCRIPTION

Leave Bregenz and follow the path along the lake past the Festspielhaus and stadium to Vorkloster. Then continue along the river to cross the bridge at Schendlingen. Take the bike path along the road to Höchst, and continue across the Rhine to the Swiss border. Do not cross the border here! Just before the bridge, take the bike path along the Alter Rhein to the border crossing at Gaissau. Cross over to the Swiss town of Rheineck and follow the signs to Buriet. At Buriet, cross under the autobahn and continue along the lake to Rorschach. From Rorschach, follow the road along the lake through Arbon and then into Romanshorn.

CITY
ROMANSHORN

DISTANCE KM	TOTAL KM
19	46

ROUTE DESCRIPTION

From Romanshorn, follow the sometimes narrow path along the lake, passing through a little developed area of fields and orchards into Kreuzlingen (Switzerland) and Konstanz (Germany).

Note: To do the short version of this route: from Konstanz (Constance), follow the signs to the island of Mainau and from there take the boat to Unteruhldingen. From Unteruhldingen, continue with the main route which leads to Meersburg.

CITY
KREUZLINGEN/KONSTANZ (CONSTANCE)

DISTANCE KM	TOTAL KM
26	65

ROUTE DESCRIPTION

From the old Rhine bridge in Konstanz, follow the river to the autobahn bridge and then to the Gottlieben Swiss border crossing. Do not follow the signs to Kreuzlingen or Zürich! Continue on the Gottlieben Strasse for about 700 meters in the direction of Tägerwilen. Then turn toward the Rhine and follow the path into Gottlieben, a picture-postcard little settlement of half-timbered buildings. The path continues along the part of the lake called the Untersee past Berlingen to the medieval town of Steckborn. Stay along the lake, sometimes on the road and sometimes on the path next to the train track the rest of the way into Stein am Rhein.

CITY
STEIN AM RHEIN

DISTANCE KM	TOTAL KM
55	91

ROUTE DESCRIPTION

From Stein, cross the border back into Germany just before Ohningen. Stay on the path along the lake to Kattenhorn and then continue along the road to Wangen past the Castle of the Bishops of Constance at Gaienhofen. At Gaienhofen, pick up the cycle/pedestrian path that runs close to the lake through a nature preserve, and into Radolfzell. Take the road from Radolfzell to Möggingen. Then there is a short climb up to Liggeringen. Continue across the ridge and then coast downhill to rejoin the lake at Bodman. From there follow the trail along the shore to Ludwigshafen.

Note: The highway between Ludwigshafen and Sipplingen is narrow and often has heavy traffic. You can avoid this stretch by taking the boat from Ludwigshafen to Überlingen or taking the side roads through the hills.

From Ludwigshafen, take the coast road to Überlingen and continue past the Prehistoric Museum at Unteruhldingen to Meersburg.

CITY
MEERSBURG

ROUTE
B31

DISTANCE KM	TOTAL KM
35	146

ROUTE DESCRIPTION

From the lakefront at Meersburg, take the path running alongside the lake to Hagnau. Then continue on the bike trail that runs along the main highway (B31) past the castle at Kirchberg and on to Friedrichshafen. Take the bike path past the youth hostel and campground. Then turn off to the lake and take the trail through the marsh lands to Langenargen. After crossing the Argen River, the path continues to Kressborn. From there follow the little-traveled lake road into Lindau.

CITY
LINDAU

DISTANCE KM	TOTAL KM
0	181

LAKE CONSTANCE SIGHTS AND ACCOMMODATIONS

LINDAU (Germany). Although this one-thousand-year-old Bavarian jewel has spread out and now reaches up into the hills above the lake, Lindau remains an island city, an enclave of fine medieval buildings clustered together on a tiny island in the Bodensee and tethered to the shore by two bridges. The views of the Swiss and Austrian alps across the lake are nothing short of spectacular. The old thirteenth-century **lighthouse** which once guarded the entrance to the compact harbor, is now a part of the city's fortifications. The present harbor is home to a fleet of white excursion boats that ply the lake's waters and is dominated by a nineteenth-century lighthouse and the proud Bavarian lion, a remainder that Lindau is very much a part of the state of Bavaria. The recently restored fifteenth-century **Altes Rathaus** (Old Town Hall) with its richly decorated facade is one of the finest Renaissance buildings in the region. The ground floor houses the municipal archives and the 18,000-volume former Imperial town library, with some manuscripts dating back to the fourteenth century. The nearby **St. Peter's Church** is the oldest building on the lake. Now a war memorial chapel, it contains some rare frescoes by Hans Holbein the Elder. The tower with a turreted roof across the way is the **Diebsturm** (Thieves Tower), which was a prison in medieval times.

Be sure to take some time during your Lindau stop to sit at an outdoor café and enjoy a good Bavarian beer or a glass of *Spitalhalde* (the fine local wine) while taking in the view.

With its overwhelming charm, it is little wonder that this small island is virtually overrun with visitors during the peak July and August months. If you want to stay on the island itself, make your reservations well in advance or, better yet, plan your visit for June or September.

The island's number one hotel, located right on the Seepromenade overlooking the harbor, is the HOTEL BAYERISCHER HOF (Seepromenade, 8990 Lindau; Tel: [08382] 5055). You can get a comfortable double with a bath at the attractive little HOTEL GASTHOF STIFT (Stiftsplatz 1; Tel: [08382] 5516) for 60 DM. The hotel is conveniently located on the quaint marketplace in the middle of the pedestrian zone. There are also many inexpensive pensions in the "mainland" part of Lindau.

The two-hundred-bed JUGENDHERB-BERGE LINDAU (Herbergsweg 11a; Tel: [08382] 5813) is located 1 km northeast of the Seebrücke in a pleasant old house.

There is a first-class, expensive campground located on the lake 4 kms from Lindau on the way to Bregenz. CAMPING-PLATZ LINDAU-ZECH is open from 26 April to 6 October.

BREGENZ (Austria). Since Austria lost so much of its territory following World War I, Bregenz is now the only Austrian city with frontage on an international body of water. The administrative capital of the mountainous province of Vorarlberg, Bregenz is the gateway to a vast region of tall mountains, tumbling streams, and picturesque alpine villages.

The town of Bregenz has several interesting attractions, the most famous of which is the **Bregenzer Festspiel**. During the summer, outdoor plays, concerts, and operas are performed on an impressive stage built on a platform in the lake. The region's history and art are well represented in the **Vorarlberg Museum**. For an impressive view of the lake, take the cable car from the town center to the 1,063-meter-high **Pfänder**. From Bregenz it's just a short ride along well-marked cycle paths down the Rhine valley to Liechtenstein.

For a first-class Bregenz hotel, check in at the HOTEL WEISSES KREUZ (6900 Bregenz; Tel: [05574] 22 488). If you are looking for a nice little budget-priced inn down by the lake, try the GASTHOF SEEHOF (Tel: [05574] 22 824).

The 176-bed JUGENDHERBERGE BREGENZ (Belrupstrasse 16a; Tel: [05574] 22 867) is located in the center of town near the cable car station, just a few minutes up the hill from the train station.

SEECAMPING BREGENZ is a large site on the lake with a washing machine, restaurant, and camp store. It is open 15 May to 15 September.

ROMANSHORN (Switzerland).
In a beautiful lakeside park setting, Romanshorn, once a medieval fishing village, is today a modern city and one of the Bodensee's principal ferry ports.

As you cycle between Bregenz and Romanshorn, take an extra day and visit **St. Gallen** about 15 kms inland from Rorschach. The cultural and economic center of eastern Switzerland, St. Gallen was founded in 612 by the Irish monk St. Gall. Wander through the busy old town quarter and be sure to see the **cathedral** and elegant baroque **Stiftsbibliothek** (cathedral library).

You can find comfortable accommodations in Romanshorn at the HOTEL ANKER (8590 Romanshorn; Tel: [071] 63 17 32) by the train station just across from the ferry landing and at the inexpensive six-room HOTEL SONNE (Tel: [071] 63 12 03).

There are youth hostels in Romanshorn and St. Gallen: JUGENDHERBERGE ROMANSHORN (Gottfried-Keller Strasse 6; Tel: [071] 63 17 17) and JUGEND-HERBERGE ST. GALLEN (Juchstrasse 25; Tel: [071] 24 34 44).

Although there is no campground in Romanshorn, there are several in Utwill a few kms farther along in the direction of Constance (Konstanz). For a nice site right on the lake, try CAMPING STRANDBAD AMRISWIL. It is open from 15 April to 20 September and facilities include a washing machine, camp store, and restaurant.

KREUZLINGEN (Switzerland)/ Konstanz (Constance) (Germany).
Except for the fact that they are in two separate countries with border controls in between, the Swiss city of Kreuzlingen and the German city of Konstanz could easily be a single city. With the exception of a recently restored **rococo church**, there is not much of interest in Kreuzlingen. The lakefront and the old quarter of Konstanz are pleasant for strolling, and the **Rosengarten Museum** in a lovely, well-preserved fifteenth-century hall is of particular interest.

The **Island of Mainau**, often referred to as the "flower island" is just a few minutes cycling distance away. The island, which is owned and operated by a relative of the Swedish royal family, is a 110-acre paradise of subtropical gardens complete with a baroque palace and church.

One of the most romantic hotels along the Bodensee is the INSEL HOTEL (Auf der Insel 1, 7750 Konstanz; Tel: [07531] 25 011), a fourteenth-century monastery that has been tastefully converted into a luxury hotel. Another gem of a romantic hotel in nearby Gottlieben, just 2 kms across the border in Switzerland is the lovely half-timbered HOTEL DRACHEN-BERG-WAAGHAUS (8274 Gottlieben; Tel: [072] 69 14 14).

There are youth hostels in Konstanz and Kreuzlingen. The 207-bed hostel in Konstanz is in the northern suburb of Allmansdorf about 3 kms from the center of Konstanz. JUGENDHERBERGE OTTO MOERICKE TURM (Zur Allmannshohe 18; Tel: [07531] 32 260) is open from 1 March to 31 October. In Kreuzlingen, look for JUGENDHERBERGE VILLA HORNLI-BERG (8220 Kreuzlingen; Tel: [072] 75 26 63) located at the lake.

The best of the area's campgrounds is CAMPING FISCHERHAUS, a pleasant site located near the youth hostel and just a few meters from the lake. It is open 1 April to 31 October.

STEIN AM RHEIN (Switzerland).
Situated on both banks of the Rhine at the point where the river emerges from the Bodensee, Stein am Rhein is an enchanting little town of steeply gabled medieval houses with decoratively painted facades. The ornate **Rathaus** (Town Hall) dates back to 1539. The former monastery has been converted into a **museum** where you can get a good idea of what the early monks' lives were like. On a hill just north of the town is the imposing twelfth-century **Hohenklingen Castle**, which has a tower that offers a superb view of the town and lake.

The LANDGASTHOF BACCHUS (8260 Stein am Rhein; Tel: [054] 41 24 05) is a comfortable country inn with a homey restaurant.

The 113-bed youth hostel, JUGEND-HERBERGE STEIN AM RHEIN, (Nieder-feld; Tel: [054] 85 255), is located along the river about 1 ½ kms downstream from Stein am Rhein.

There is an all-year campground located just a few meters from the German border crossing near Ohningen called CAMPING GRENZSTEIN.

MEERSBURG (Germany). With its steep winding streets lined with a delightful assortment of half-timbered houses, Meersburg fulfills even the most romantic notions of what an ancient German city should look like. For more than three hundred years Meersburg was the residence of the Bishops of Constance and many of the town's finest buildings were built during that period. Situated at the upper reaches of the town with an inspiring view of the lake and the Swiss alps in the distance is Germany's **oldest occupied castle**, which was built in 628.

In the nearby town of **Unteruhldingen** is a reconstruction of a Stone Age set-tlement. There are a number of interesting buildings set on pilings in the lake and a small museum.

The HOTEL ZUM WILDER MANN (Bismarckplatz 2, 7758 Meersburg; Tel: [07532] 9011) is a small, traditional, family hotel nicely situated at the lakefront. In the moderate price range, try the newly remodeled GÄSTEHAUS CLAUDIA (Seepromonade 8; Tel: [07532] 5090).

The closest campground, a large site at the lake, is in Hagnau about 5 kms in the direction of Lindau. It is open Easter to 15 September.

BIKING
THROUGH
EUROPE

TOURING IN ADDITIONAL COUNTRIES

In addition to the major cycling countries already described, Europe is full of interesting bicycle touring possibilities. In this section we would like to tell you about cycling in some of these other countries.

Greece

Although Greece's reputation has suffered as a result of the onslaught of mass tourism, a cycle tour of this intriguing cradle of western civilization affords the opportunity of actually experiencing the country in a way available to few bus-bound tourists. If you steer clear of the tourist traps and time your visits to the major attractions (such as the Parthenon and Delphi) for the early morning hours before the tour buses disgorge their cargoes, you will find a cycle tour of Greece can be a fascinating and rewarding experience.

See Athens because it's an important part of Greece and should be seen. But, don't even think about riding your bike in Athens with its horrendous traffic, poorly maintained streets, and choking air pollution. After that cyclist's nightmare, head out into the countryside and discover the real Greece. Once away from the tourist enclaves, you can enjoy pedaling through sleepy villages of dazzling white stone houses that sparkle under the hot Mediterranean sun. Stop in at a friendly *taverna*; the Greeks, especially in the out-of-the-way parts of the country, are very hospitable. Choose your meal from the bubbling pots in the kitchen as is the Greek custom, then perhaps take a mid-day nap under the shade of a gnarled olive tree, also a widely observed Greek custom, before venturing on down the road.

If you are cycling along the coast, a pretty likely possibility since Greece, including its 1,400 islands, has some 9,000 miles of coastline, you can take a refreshing dip in the sea before moving on. Such are the joys of cycling in Greece.

The best time for getting the best out of the Greek islands without getting trampled by masses of tourists are the months of June and September when the sun has plenty of strength without the broiling intensity experienced in July and August, and the ocean is ideal for swimming. The interior regions are best for touring in April and May when for a short time the countryside is a symphony of colorful spring blossoms. July and August are too hot for comfortable cycling unless you can stay near the water.

TOURING REGIONS

The **PELOPONNESE**. The large, jagged peninsula known as the Peloponnese separated from the mainland by the narrow Corinth Canal, contains a superb combination of the types of attractions that have been drawing visitors to Greece for centuries. For students of antiquities, there are such jewels as **Epidaurus**, which has a fine open-air theater, the spectacular finds at **Mycenae**, which under Agamemnon was once Greece's most important city, the ancient city of **Sparta**, and, in the western part of the peninsula, **Olympia**, site of the original Olympian Games. The archaeological site at **Delphi** in a magnificent setting at the foot of **Mount Parnassus** is located on the mainland, just a day's cycling from the Corinth Isthmus.

The Peloponnese coast, hostile and rocky at some points and tranquil and inviting at others, offers a pleasant respite when you've had enough of ancient temples and amphitheaters. The interior is rugged with some peaks reaching a height of 2,000 meters (6,517 feet). The caves at **Piros Dirou** on the Mani peninsula, the middle of the three fingerlike extensions at the southern end of the Peloponnese, are the country's greatest natural wonder.

THE ISLANDS. No visit to a country with 1,400 islands would be complete without at least some island hopping. You'll find it easy to commute between islands on the swarm of ferry boats that fan out from the busy port of **Piraeus**. Although there is some inter-island traffic, Piraeus, which is the port for Athens, serves as the hub for most ferries.

Each island has its own mood and personality; the only unifying factor is that they are all overflowing with tourists in July and August. Many, such as **Hydra** and **Mykonos**, are so small that you hardly have time to shift gears before you've run out of road, while others, like **Rhodes** and particularly **Crete**, offer more extensive touring possibilities. Crete has some magnificent ruins, including the ancient Minoean city of **Knossos**, fine beaches, rugged gorges, and isolated mountain villages. It is well worth the twelve-hour ferry trip from Piraeus.

MAPS

For planning purposes and for cycling between major points, use the **Michelin map #980, Greece** (scale 1:700,000). Place names are given in both the Greek and Roman alphabets. The map also has a transcription of the Greek alphabet, as well as a number of key phrases in Greek and English.

The slightly more detailed **Kümmerly & Frey map, Greece** (scale 1:500,000) is also good for planning and cycling.

For cycling the Peloponnese, the **Freytag & Berndt map, Peloponnese** (scale 1:300,000) is the best available.

The **Greek National Survey series** (scale 1:200,000) are very detailed and are excellent for off-road cycling and exploring remote areas. All notations are in Greek only. Detailed maps of many of the more popular islands can be obtained from the local tourist police.

ACCOMMODATIONS

Hotels are regulated and classified by the tourist police. There are six categories, starting with luxury, followed in descending order by classes "A" to "E". In addition there are many pensions, *tavernas*, and private rooms available. These are usually less expensive than the "E" category hotels. There are substantial price reductions available in off season. The local tourist police can be very helpful in securing accommodations at all levels.

With only thirty hostels in the country, it is not possible to plan a trip based upon staying at youth hostels only.

Campers have a choice of some 250 official sites, most of which are located along the coast and at the major tourist attractions. Although free camping is prohibited, there are many places where you can inconspicuously set up a tent. In the more remote regions no one really seems to mind.

ROADS

Many who have never been there picture Greece as a country of romantic islands and broad sandy beaches. In reality, some 80 percent of the country is mountainous; in some places, particularly in the North, there are peaks in the 2,500-meter (8,146-feet) range. Surfaces on the main roads are generally good, but the more scenic secondary roads are no place to take a lightweight racing bike. For touring Greece's rough, back-country roads, a mountain bike is ideal.

Although you will probably encounter heavy traffic on the main roads in the vicinity of the major cities, traffic density in Greece is generally much lower than in the rest of Europe.

Greek drivers take some getting used to. Fast reckless driving with plenty of horn honking and bazouki music blaring from speakers mounted on car rooftops seems to be a national pastime. There are no bike paths on which to take refuge.

While not essential, a knowledge of the Greek alphabet is a big help when trying to find your way in the more remote regions where the infrequent signs are usually written in Greek symbols.

BICYCLE SHOPS AND RENTALS

Outside of Athens and Thessaloniki, it's difficult to find a well-stocked bike shop, although many small towns have some sort of repair facility, often a multipurpose fix-it shop. Bike touring is not a Greek avocation; however, you will often see packs of colorfully clad Sunday club riders out for a spin.

Rental bikes suitable for short local excursions are available at most of the popular resort areas.

TRANSPORTATION WITHIN THE COUNTRY

Bikes can be carried on most Greek trains free of charge, although in some cases you could probably pedal the distance in a shorter time. Delays are frequent and service, especially in the western part of the country, is very limited. Bring your bike to the baggage counter at least one hour before departure.

Greece has an extensive network of intercity buses that reach even the most remote regions of the country. Most buses will transport bikes on a space available basis, although the final determination is made by the driver.

For a small charge, you can take your bike on all of the inter-island ferries.

SOURCES OF ADDITIONAL INFORMATION

Greek Youth Hostels Association
4 Dragatsaniou Street
Athens 105-59
Tel: [01] 32 34 107

Greek Cycling Federation
(the national cycle racing organization)
28 Bouboulinas Street
Athens 147
Tel: [01] 88 31 414

Italy

There is not much that Italy doesn't have. What it does have includes fantastic art treasures, towering mountains, incredible pollution, horrendous traffic snarls, the leaning tower of Pisa, Pompeii, the Mafia, great food, the best in modern design, the Vatican, pickpockets, terrorists, communists, capitalists, the canals and palaces of Venice, picturesque mountain villages, pristine mountain lakes, the murky slums of Naples, and, of course, Italy's most unique asset, the Italians themselves! There is not much that you can't find in this fascinating Mediterranean enigma of a country. The problem with cycle touring in Italy is picking out what you want to see from this colossal antipasto of attractions and leaving the rest. It's quite a challenge, but also a lot of fun.

Although the Italians are great bicycle enthusiasts – in fact cycling is one of the national pastimes – the emphasis is on racing. As a cyclist with a fully packed touring bike you will be the object of much friendly curiosity. Cycling through the Italian countryside is a great way to meet the locals.

TOURING AREAS

The **DOLOMITES AND THE LAKE DISTRICT**. Spectacular vistas, lung-bursting ascents followed by breathtaking descents, and enough hairpin curves to last a lifetime are all a part of cycling in the Dolomites, the towering limestone peaks that make up Italy's most rugged and popular mountain range. Located in the northeastern portion of the country, the Dolomites are part of the province of South Tyrol, which before World War I belonged to Austria. In many parts of the region German is still widely spoken, and most signs and place names are in both Italian and German.

The town of **Bolzano** (Bozen in German), just over the Brenner Pass from Innsbruck, makes a good starting point for exploring the region. If you can stick to the secondary roads and avoid the heavily traveled Dolomite Road, which runs from Bolzano to the resort town of Cortina d'Ampezzo, traffic should not be a major problem.

After a heavy-duty workout cycling in the mountains, a tour of the Italian Lake District offers a pleasant change of scenery and a chance for a bit of more relaxing biking. **Lago di Garda** (Lake Garda), the largest of the Italian lakes, is also the closest to the Dolomites. It's less than 100 kms from Bolzano to Riva at the north end of the lake. The eastern shore, which has the best sandy beaches, is also the most suitable for cycling. Be sure to stop and visit **Verona**, the lovely city of Romeo and Juliet. It is only a short ride from the southern shore.

Still further east, about 100 kms of fairly flat cycling from Verona, is the slowly decaying but still romantic city of **Venice**. Bikes are not allowed in the city!

Roughly 150 kms west of Lake Garda, surrounded by a surprising assortment of Mediterranean flora, lie the deep, finger-shaped lakes so often praised in literature and poetry, the most popular of which are **Lago di Como, Lago di Lugano**, and **Lago Maggiore**. Although the lakes are crowded in the summer, you will still be able to find space on the roads for your bike and a place on the lakeshore sands for your body. Take advantage of the numerous ferries that crisscross the lakes to avoid the congestion. The combination of the deep blue waters and semitropical vegetation viewed against a backdrop of the snow-tipped alps is worth braving the crowds for.

A trip through the Italian Lake District combines nicely with a tour of Switzerland; in fact, Lago Maggiore and Lago di Lugano are partly in Switzerland. About 75 kms of pedaling will take you from Lago di Como, over the 1,815-meter (5,914-foot) **Maloja Pass**, to **St. Moritz** in the heart of Switzerland's magnificent **Engadin Valley**.

TUSCANY AND CENTRAL ITALY.
While the broad central plain on both sides of the Po River is flat and makes for easy cycling, the region itself is heavily industrialized and, to put it kindly, uninspiring. If you are after easy pedaling terrain, Holland is the place for you. It's infinitely cleaner and more interesting. On the other hand, the investment of your time and energy exploring the hills and valleys of the Toscana (Tuscany), as well as the provinces of Umbria and Latium, will be amply rewarded. From art to architecture to cuisine, this region offers more of the romance and beauty that have attracted travelers to Italy for centuries than any other part of the country. **Florence**, the art capital of Italy, is a good place to start. From there it's just a day's pedaling to **Siena**, another living art museum. Your tour should also include the medieval fortress town of **San Gimignano**, as well as **Lucca**, which has a striking assortment of architectural styles. From Lucca, it will take you less than an hour to cycle to **Pisa's famous leaning tower**.

THE ITALIAN RIVIERA.
Although there is a lot of romance associated with the Italian Riviera, this is definitely one of those parts of the world whose time has come and is now gone. There is very little, in our opinion, to recommend cycling along this stretch of the Italian coast. The roads are congested, the architecture undistinguished, the water polluted, and the beaches jammed packed and dirty. The best way to enjoy this part of the country is from the window of a speeding train.

ROADS AND TERRAIN

With the exception of the flat Po River valley, the "heel" of Italy's distinctive boot in the south, and much of the some 4,000 miles of coastline, most of the rest of the country is very rugged and mountainous. Finding good roads on which to cycle involves a constant trade-off between the better paved, but very congested main roads and the often neglected, poorly surfaced, but less heavily traveled secondary roads. Where toll roads or *autostrada* have been built, it is often possible to cycle with relatively little traffic on the parallel main roads. In many villages and towns long stretches of cobblestone streets still exist. Generally speaking, road conditions are better in the prosperous northern parts of the country, where many of the main roads have paved shoulders suitable for cycling.

Cycling in an Italian city is a bit like trying to thread your way through a maze of bumper cars. Between the onslaught of horn-tooting Fiats and whizzing motor scooters, all of which seem to be piloted by frustrated Grand Prix drivers, the poor cyclist hasn't a ghost of a chance.

Don't take offense at the horn honking and arm waving motorists, more often than not they are just saying hello and showing their approval of what you are doing.

BICYCLE SHOPS AND RENTALS

While the large cities have a sufficient number of bike shops, finding one in the smaller towns and villages is a problem. When you do locate a shop, you will find that the emphasis is primarily on racing equipment.

Cycle rentals are rarely available outside of the major tourist areas.

ACCOMMODATIONS

With its long tradition of attracting tourists, Italy has built up an extensive network of accommodations at all levels. Although there is an official hotel classification, experience has shown that with the obvious exception of helping to differentiate between a luxury hotel and a cheap flop, your best bet for avoiding unpleasant surprises is to inspect the room and confirm the "total" price before registering. "Supplementary" charges can add as much as 30 percent to your bill. It is required that prices be posted in each room.

In the more remote central and southern regions, the choice of accommodations may be quite limited. For inexpensive lodgings, look for a *pensione*, *albergo*, or the Italian equivalent of a bed and breakfast, a *soggiorno*. With just slightly more than fifty youth hostels spread throughout the country, Italy is not conducive to doing a hostel oriented tour.

Campers fare quite a bit better. Along the coast and in all the major tourist areas there are plenty of official campgrounds ranging from super modern camping cities that accommodate thousands of campers and offer a full range of activities to tiny backyard-size sites with primitive facilities. Free camping is possible in most parts of the country; however, it is a good idea to get permission whenever possible.

MAPS

There are several good maps available for planning, including the **Michelin map #988, Italy/Switzerland** (scale 1:1,000,000) and the more detailed **Kümmerly & Frey, Italy** (scale 1:500,000).

For cycling, use the **TCI Touring Club Italiano series** (scale 1:200,000), which covers the country in fifteen detailed maps. The maps show scenic routes, steep grades, and some unsurfaced roads. The **Kompass Wanderkarten series** (scale 1:50,000) is excellent for off-road cycling in the Dolomites and the rest of South Tyrol.

TRANSPORTATION WITHIN THE COUNTRY

The Italian railroads seem a bit chaotic at first sight, but after you've used them for a while you will learn to deal with the chaos. You may take your bike as accompanied baggage on all but the express trains (*Rapido*), although the charges are relatively high, especially over short distances. Bikes are loaded and unloaded by the station personnel and it is necessary to have the bike at the baggage office (*bagagli portenze*) at least thirty minutes before the train leaves. Allow a little longer during the summer months.

Some intercity buses will carry bikes.

SOURCES OF ADDITIONAL INFORMATION

Associazione Italiana Alberghi per la Gioventu
(the Italian Youth Hostel Federation)
Palazzo della Civilta del Lavo
Quadrato della Concordia 9
00144 Rome
Tel: [06] 59 13 702

Federazione Ciclistica Italiana
(the country's principal cycling organization)
Via Leopoldo Franchetti 2
00100 Rome
Tel: [06] 36 85 72 55

Luxembourg

Entering Luxembourg we had the feeling that perhaps we should be buying admission tickets. There is a certain Disneyworld feeling about this miniature country, which is smaller than the state of Rhode Island. Despite its Lilliputian size, the Grand Duchy of Luxembourg has all of the components of a full-size country, including a head of state (the Grand Duke) and a bicameral legislature. The country is a constitutional monarchy with a trilingual population who speak Luxembourgeois, French, and German. English is also widely spoken. The diversified economy is based on steel production, agriculture, and tourism. Although the Grand Duchy shows the influence of its neighbors France, Belgium, and Germany, it nevertheless makes a point of preserving its identity, as expressed in the national motto, "We wish to remain what we are."

For cycle touring, Luxembourg is made to order. Medieval castles, charming villages, and a diverse landscape with rolling farmlands, lush forests, and steep hills and valleys formed by winding rivers are all packed into an area that is just 110 miles long by 125 miles wide. A tour of Luxembourg combines well with cycling in Belgium to the west or Germany to the east.

Cyclists who like to "collect" countries can take advantage of the unique opportunity to cycle in five countries in a single day. By carefully studying your maps, it's possible to plan a cycle route through parts of Holland, Belgium, Germany, Luxembourg, and France while covering just a little more than one hundred miles.

Note: The Belgium franc can be used interchangeably with the Luxembourg franc in Luxembourg; however, the reverse is not true. It is difficult to exchange Luxembourg currency outside of the country.

TOURING AREAS

After a sightseeing tour of the one-thousand-year-old capital, Luxembourg City, a pleasant blend of modern and medieval architecture, cycle through the area of peaceful rolling hills, curious rock formations, and forests just north of Echternach along the German border known as **Little Switzerland**. The medieval village of **Vianden** has a particularly fine castle perched on a hill overlooking the town. The hilly **Oesling region** in the west is an extension of the Belgian Ardennes.

TRANSPORTATION WITHIN THE COUNTRY

Although the size of the country makes it unlikely that you will be taking your bike on the train with you, should you decide to use the **CFL (Chemin de Fer Luxembourgaise)**, you will find it an efficient outfit with good connections to the rest of the continent. Bikes may be carried as accompanied baggage on a space available basis at a very reasonable flat rate. The procedure is to buy a bicycle ticket at the ticket counter and to load and unload the bike yourself. When shipping the bike unaccompanied, the loading and unloading is done by the CFL staff.

Buses do not transport bicycles.

ROADS

Although it's a small country, Luxembourg has a surprisingly good network of quiet secondary roads, which are ideal for cycling. The excellent condition of the roads reflects the country's high standard of living. There are bike paths between Luxembourg City and Hesperange, Vianden, and Echternach by way of Diekirch and between Echternach and Junglinster, with more paths planned. The tourist offices in Luxembourg City, Diekirch, and Mersch can furnish pamphlets detailing cycle tours on roads with little traffic.

MAPS

Since it's so small, Luxembourg is usually shown as part of maps of Belgium, France, and Germany. **Michelin map #409 Belgium/Luxembourg** (scale 1:350,000) is suitable for planning tours in both countries. **Michelin map #214 Mons-Luxembourg** (scale 1:200,000) which also includes southern Belgium, is the standard map for touring Luxembourg, and shows all paved roads, scenic routes, and steep hills.

Even more detail is the **Geokart #64, Grand Duche de Luxembourg** (scale 1:100,000), which includes unpaved roads and footpaths. It is available at bookstores in Luxembourg.

BICYCLE SHOPS AND RENTALS

With neighbors like the French and Belgians, it's hardly surprising that cycling is very popular in Luxembourg. Well-stocked bike shops are found throughout the country, and you should have no trouble obtaining parts and service for touring bikes, although the emphasis is on metric equipment.

Bikes suitable for local touring can be rented at the major tourist centers throughout the country.

ACCOMMODATIONS

There are hotels, *auberges*, and pensions for all budgets throughout the country. Standards of service and cleanliness are generally high. The cuisine reflects the influence of the neighboring countries, providing a pleasant blending of the best of French and German cooking. The local wines from the Moselle region are excellent.

Youth hostelers can build a tour around the nine conveniently situated hostels. All hostels are heated and provide hot showers and meals.

The country's small size is conducive to touring from a fixed base. For that purpose, the **Gites d'Etape Luxembourgeois** (23 boulevard Prince Henri, 1724 Luxembourg: Tel: 23 698) maintains a series of rest houses with kitchen facilities throughout the country. A rest house is similar to a youth hostel, but is less formal. There are no membership requirements. Married couples are not admitted except as group leaders.

With some 120 campgrounds distributed throughout this small country, you will never be more than a short cycling distance from a campsite. Free camping is not permitted; however, even in Luxembourg you can find places where you can inconspicuously pitch your tent for the night. When camping on private land, be sure to obtain the owner's permission.

SOURCES OF ADDITIONAL INFORMATION

Centrale des Auberges de Jeunesse Luxembourgeoises
(the national youth hostel organization)
18 place d'Armes
BP 374, Luxembourg City
Tel: 25 588

Union Luxembourgeoise de Cyclotouristes
(the country's cycle touring organization)
39 rue de l'Etoile
F-57190 Florange

Portugal

At the southwest corner of the European continent occupying most of the western portion of the Iberian peninsula, Portugal is a delightful little country of picturesque villages, brightly colored flowers, beautiful beaches, and warm sunshine. Since the bloodless revolution of 1974, Portugal, western Europe's poorest country, has been struggling to make up for lost time and catch up with the mainstream of contemporary European life after more than forty years of a standstill dictatorship. The country's 1986 entry into the European Common Market was a very positive step in that direction. However, in spite of this desire for things modern and the mushrooming of tourist developments along its sparkling coastline, Portugal remains one of Europe's most attractive and friendliest corners.

Just a few kms away from the busy tourist centers, village life goes on with few concessions made to the twentieth century. While cycling through the countryside it's not unusual to pass traditionally attired peasants on the way to market riding colorfully painted donkey carts or to encounter women washing clothes at a river bank. Even though Portugal is no longer the well-kept travel secret that it was just a few years ago, and more and more tourists are "discovering" the country, the genuinely warm and friendly reception that travelers to Portugal have always enjoyed remains the same.

One of the nice things about touring Portugal, in addition to the pleasant climate and excellent beaches, is its small size. Since it's only about 350 miles long and 100 miles wide, you can cycle through the country without having to endure the seemingly endless monotonous stretches that characterize bicycle touring in neighboring Spain.

TOURING AREAS

LISBON AND THE NORTH. For practical purposes we can consider the river Tagus, which forms the expansive harbor at Lisbon, as the dividing line between north and south. Lisbon itself, sprawled out on a series of hills overlooking the bay in a setting reminiscent of San Francisco, is definitely worth seeing. Park your bike and spend some time strolling the narrow, winding labyrinth of streets that make up the **Alfama**, the city's old quarter.

The country north of the Tagus contains the most rugged terrain, with the most challenging cycling in Portugal found in the lovely **Serra da Estrela mountains** east of the ancient university city of Coimbra. Roads climb to a height of 1,500 meters (4,888 feet) or more. The highest point in the country reachable by road is the 1,991-meter (6,487-foot) **Torre Summit** between Covilha and Seia.

Porto, Portugal's second largest city situated at the mouth of the Douro River, is itself a rather drab place, but has achieved world renown as the center for the production and distribution of port wines. A ride along the **Douro**, particularly in the fall when the grapes grown on the steep terraced vineyards are harvested, is one of the high points of a tour of Portugal. The **Tras os Montes** region, which translated means the land beyond the mountains, in the northeast corner of the country is a lovely, little developed area not often visited by tourists. The highlights of this region include the fortified town of **Braganca**, **Vila Real-Mateus**, the home of the famous Mateus wines, and **Lamego**, a pleasantly situated town with a number of fine sixteenth-century and eighteenth-century houses.

The northern coastal region contains some fine stretches of dune and forest-backed beaches; however, the beaches on the more sheltered southern coast are more suitable for swimming. Although it's a favorite tourist stop, the fishing village of **Nazare** is nevertheless worth visiting. The best views are obtained from the little town of **Sitio** atop the cliff, where you can watch the small fishing boats brave the crashing surf.

Although much of hilly northern Portugal offers tough cycling, you can still enjoy a great deal of this pleasant country by pedaling the coastal roads and those that follow the river valleys.

SOUTH OF LISBON. The region south of Lisbon encompassing the provinces of **Alentejo** and **Algarve** is sparsely settled, with the exception of tourist developments along the Algarve coast. Although not as mountainous as the north of the country, there are plenty of hills, especially in the interior regions. The Alentejo, the country's largest province, is also its breadbasket. It is a region of large farms and occasional stands of cork oak, interspersed with villages of dazzling whitewashed houses. Offering little shade and with summer temperatures in excess of 100 degrees F., the Alentejo is best cycled in spring or autumn. The provincial capital, the walled town of **Evora**, with its Roman and Moorish features, is one of the country's most attractive cities.

The **Algarve**, Portugal's southern province, contains some of Europe's finest beaches along its southern shore, which stretches some 100 miles from the river Guadiana at the border with Spain to Cape St. Vincent, Europe's most southwesterly point. Unfortunately for cyclists, the only through road runs several kms inland for most of the way, affording only occasional glimpses of the ocean. To get to the ocean it is necessary to take the numerous feeder roads that connect the beaches and picturesque fishing towns with the main highway. The best beaches and the least developed areas are west of the ancient town of Lagos. The Algarve is blessed with a mild winter climate so that cycling is possible throughout the year.

ROADS

If its roads were better, Portugal could be one of Europe's best cycle touring countries. Unfortunately, even though much is being done to improve road conditions, there is a decided lack of roads suitable for cycling. Most of the secondary roads and many of the main highways are very narrow and poorly surfaced, making riding a hazardous, bone-jarring experience. There are no bicycle paths. In many areas, there are still long stretches of cobblestone roads. The one saving grace is the fact that, with the exception of a few heavily traveled main arteries, Portuguese roads have a very low traffic density. Often you can ride the back roads for hours encountering little traffic other than an occasional donkey cart.

Portuguese motorists tend to drive fast and are not accustomed to sharing the road with cyclists. The highway accident rate is one of the highest in the world.

The poor road conditions and many unpaved dirt roads make Portugal a country well suited to mountain bike touring.

TRANSPORTATION WITHIN THE COUNTRY

The rail system, the **Caminhos de Ferro Portugueses (CP)** is not known for its efficiency or extensive network. However, with enough time and patience you and your bicycle will eventually wind up at your destination. Take the bike to the baggage office (*bagagem*) at least thirty minutes before the train is scheduled to leave. If there is no *bagagem*, which is often the case, take it to the ticket office. The bike will be loaded by the station personnel, and you will be given a claim check, without which you will have difficulty retrieving the bike. The shipping charges are minimal and bikes can be taken as accompanied baggage on most trains.

It's possible to ship a bike on some of the intercity buses; however, since policy varies from place to place it's best to check locally.

ACCOMMODATIONS

Portuguese hotels are generally of good quality and are reasonably priced, except at the beach resorts in high season. Hotels are graded with from one to five stars, and prices are posted in each room. Breakfast is generally included. A pension or boarding house is called a *pensao* and can usually be counted on to provide clean, inexpensive lodging. *Pousadas* are government-controlled inns, most in historic buildings and scenic locations, while a privately run *estalagem* is a typical Portuguese inn.

There are fourteen youth hostels in the country. They are known in Portuguese as *Pousadas de Juventude*.

Portugal has just over one hundred campgrounds, most of which are located along the coast. Free camping usually presents no problem, although it's best to be discreet in built-up areas and in the popular tourist areas.

BICYCLE SHOPS AND RENTALS

Outside of the major cities, bicycle shops are a rarity. Bicycling is not a major Portuguese pastime, and most of the shops just carry a limited supply of parts for racing equipment and children's bikes. Because of Portugal's close trade ties with England, some shops carry 27-inch tires and tubes. But don't count on it. Bring along a spare tire and tube.

Rentals are limited to the major tourist areas and good touring bikes are not available.

MAPS

For planning purposes, you can use the same map for both Spain and Portugal: **Michelin map #990 Spain/Portugal** (scale 1:1,000,000). The best all-around map for cycling is **Michelin map #37, Portugal** (scale 1:500,000). The more detailed **Instituto Geografico e Cadastral series maps** (scale 1:200,000) cover the country in eight maps, but they are difficult to find and are often out-of-date. The **Mapa Turistico Algarve** (scale 1:200,000) issued by the Automovel Club de Portugal is quite good for finding your way around the Algarve.

SOURCES OF ADDITIONAL INFORMATION

Associacao Portuguesa de Pousadas de Juventude
   (the Portuguese Youth Hostel Association)
Rua Andrade Corvo 46
1000 Lisbon
Tel: [01] 57 10 54

Federacao Portuguesa de Ciclismo
   (the National Bicycle Racing Federation)
Rua Barros Quieros 39-1 Esq. 1100 Lisbon
Tel: [01] 32 62 15

Spain

Spain, western Europe's second largest country, offers an incredible variety of attractions which reflect the country's long and complex history. Prehistoric cave paintings, Roman amphitheaters, graceful Moorish palaces, an abundance of spectacular cathedrals and monuments, as well as a number of fine beaches are but a few of Spain's drawing cards. However, this vast and fascinating assortment of places to visit presents the cycle tourist with somewhat of a problem. While France, its larger neighbor to the north, boasts an extensive network of secondary roads and many places of interest are conveniently clustered together, Spain is quite a different story. For one thing, the country, which occupies the major portion of the Iberian peninsula is more mountainous than any other European country, with the exception of Switzerland. The relatively flat but narrow coastal shelf that follows Spain's more than two thousand miles of shoreline is heavily built up, and the main roads, especially in the summer months, are badly congested. Spain just doesn't have the miles of secondary roads and quiet, backcountry lanes found elsewhere. However, if you are willing to brave the crowds along the coast and don't mind the long, desolate mountainous stretches through the interior, a Spanish cycling trip can be a rewarding experience – but one that is not recommended for inexperienced cyclists or first-time travelers to Europe.

TOURING AREAS

The **PYRENEES AND THE BASQUE REGION**. For centuries the massive range of mountains running along Spain's border with France served to isolate the country from the mainstream of European life. These rugged mountains, which are dotted with quaint villages of stone houses, fertile orchards, and rich pasture lands, are somewhat reminiscent of parts of Switzerland. This is a great region in which to enjoy some challenging summertime mountain cycling, without having to fight the crowds and traffic that plague the alps in July and August.

The popular beach town of San Sebastian on the Bay of Biscay, just a few kms from the French border, makes a good jumping-off point for a tour of the Pyrenees. Be sure to include a visit to **Nationalpark Ordesa** in your itinerary. The park, a rugged valley carved out of the limestone mountains by the river Arazaz, contains some of the most spectacular scenery in this part of Spain. Also worth a visit is the fortified town of **Jaca**, the ancient capital of Aragon.

As a pleasant change of pace from the strenuous mountain cycling, pedal along the **Costa Verde**, the pleasant region extending westward from San Sebastian, which contains some of Spain's finest sandy beaches. Although the beaches are crowded in July and August, the crowds are nothing compared to those along the Mediterranean coast. **Santillana del Mar** only a few kms from the well-known prehistoric caves at **Altamira** is one of Spain's best-preserved medieval towns.

Another excellent opportunity for mountain cycling is offered by the **Picos de Europa**, a jagged range of mountains that extend inland between Santander and Oviedo. This entire mountain region is crisscrossed by a series of jeep trails (*pista para jeeps*) that are ideal for mountain bike excursions.

The northern coast, the Pyrenees, and the Picos de Europa are among the few places in Spain where you can enjoy cycling without having to contend with the blistering heat that bakes the rest of the country in the summer.

ANDALUSIA. More than any other region of this vast country, Andalusia, which contains Spain's southern provinces, personifies the romance and allure that has captured the hearts of generations of travelers. It is here that the Moorish influence is most strongly felt. Particularly fine examples of Arabic architecture can be found in Seville, Cordoba, and Granada, whose fourteenth-century **Alhambra** is one of the highlights of a visit to Spain.

The best times for touring Andalusia are in spring and autumn. Murderous temperatures in the interior and horrendous crowds, especially along the Costa del Sol, are enough to deter all but the most fool-hardy from cycling this part of the world in July and August.

The **Sierra Nevada Mountains** near Granada offer a great opportunity to test legs and machine in making the 55-km ascent to the top of the 3,392-meter (11,052-foot) **Pic Veleta** on Europe's highest road. On a clear day you can almost see forever. The inspiring view extends across the Strait of Gibraltar to the Riff Mountains of Morocco.

MADRID AND CENTRAL SPAIN. After visiting the country's bustling capital, where the best place for your bike is at the train station or your hotel, you can take in the highlights of the **Plains of Castile** by cycling a loop that passes through **El Escorial** (burial place of the Spanish kings), **Segovia** (whose 900-foot-long aqueduct is one of the best-preserved Roman remains in the world), the ancient fortified city of **Avila** (at an elevation of 4,000 feet, it is Spain's highest provincial capital), the old university city of **Salamanca** (the Plaza Mayor is the finest classical square in Spain), **Merida** (an important Roman city with many interesting ruins), and fabulous **Toledo**, the city of El Greco.

This land of castles and *conquistadores* is not easy cycling country. A good part of the region is high plateau where the temperatures soar in the summer and plunge to freezing cold in the winter. The only sensible time of the year to be caught on a bike here is in the spring and autumn. In addition to the inhospitable weather, there are also several mountain ranges and long desolate stretches to contend with.

ROADS

Although in recent years there has been a tremendous improvement in the quality of Spanish roads, from a cyclist's viewpoint they still have a long way to go. Most of the improvements have been made on the major heavily traveled "N" routes. The network of secondary "C" roads is sparse compared to the central European countries, and many of these roads are in poor shape, some with more patches and potholes than paved surface. While many of the main roads have paved shoulders suitable for cycling, actual bicycle paths are nonexistent.

MAPS

For planning purposes and a good overall view of the country, use **Michelin map #990 Spain/Portugal** (scale 1:1,000,000).

For cycling purposes, we like the **Michelin Regional 400 series** (scale 1:400,000). At present the following maps are available: #42, Burgos-St. Sebastian; #43, Zaragoza-Barcelona; #441, Northern and Western Spain; #442, Northern Spain; #443, Northern and Eastern Spain; #444, Central Spain; #445, Central and Eastern Spain; #446, Southern Spain; #447, Central and Western Spain.

For the most popular tourist areas along the Mediterranean coast, there are more detailed maps available, including those from **Firestone Hispania** and **Die General Karte series** published by Mair.

For off-road cycling, the detailed **Mapa Militar de Espana series** (scale 1:50,000) is excellent.

TRANSPORTATION WITHIN THE COUNTRY

If you travel at all by rail in Spain, the letters **RENFE**, which stand for *Red Nacional de los Ferrocarriles Espanoles*, the Spanish rail network, will soon become very familiar to you. Although service and efficiency have improved greatly in recent years, RENFE has a long way to go before it can be considered to be in the same league as such model operations as the Swiss or German railways.

Spanish trains are classified by speed and comfort. The fastest and most comfortable type of train is the *Talgo*, and then in descending order come the *Expresso*, *Rapido*, and *Correo*, or mail trains. Bikes can be taken as accompanied luggage at no cost on the mail trains, which run at night. Some of the faster daytime trains will also carry bikes, but the policy seems to vary from station to station. It is best to arrive early and ask several people if necessary.

ACCOMMODATIONS

While the most popular tourist regions, particularly those along the coast, are well supplied with all levels of accommodations, the same cannot be said of the rest of the country. Be prepared for long stretches between even the simplest of villages, and don't expect to find a wide choice in many of the smaller towns. Accommodations are classified and regulated by the government and are designated with anywhere from one to five stars, depending on the amenities provided. Starting at the bottom of the price/amenities scale, the classification proceeds as follows: *fondas*, *casas de huespedes*, *hospadajes*, *pensiones*, *hostales*, and *hotels*. Establishments are required by law to display prices in each room, as well as a blue plaque identifying the type of establishment. In addition, a number of historic sites have been converted into government-run inns called *paradores*.

There are approximately 120 inexpensive youth hostels (*albergues de la juventud*) spread among the most popular tourist areas.

Rooms in private homes are referred to as *casas particulares* and are best found by asking at local tourist offices.

Campers can chose from some six hundred official sites, most of which are located in the coastal regions and the major tourist areas in the interior. Spain's vastness lends itself well to free camping; however, it's best where possible to get local permission. Free camping is not allowed in built-up tourist areas, near official campgrounds, and within 150 meters of a drinking water source.

BICYCLE SHOPS AND RENTALS

Bicycle racing is a popular sport, with most of the interest concentrated in the wealthy northern part of the country. Bike shops can be found in the larger cities, but the emphasis is on racing equipment. Forget about finding nonmetric tires and parts.

While it's possible to rent clunker-type bikes for day trips in some of the more popular tourist regions, good touring bikes are virtually impossible to rent.

SOURCES OF ADDITIONAL INFORMATION

Red Espanola de Albergues Juveniles
(the official youth hostel organization)
Jose Ortega y Gasset 71 Madrid 28006
Tel: [91] 40 11 300

Federacion Espanola Ciclismo
(the Spanish national cycle-racing organization)
Ferraz 16-5
Madrid 8
Tel: [91] 24 20 421

BIKING THROUGH EUROPE

APPENDIX

NATIONAL TOURIST OFFICES IN THE U.S.

ANDORRA
Sindicat d'Iniciativa de les Valls d'Andorra
1923 W. Irving Park Rd.
Chicago, IL 60613
Tel: [312] 472-7660

AUSTRIA
Austrian National Tourist Office
500 Fifth Ave.
New York, NY 10110
Tel: [212] 944-6880

BELGIUM
Belgian National Tourist Office
745 Fifth Ave.
New York, NY 10151
Tel: [212] 758-8130

BULGARIA
Bulgarian Tourist Office
161 E. 86th St.
New York, NY 10028
Tel: [212] 722-1110

CZECHOSLOVAKIA
CEDOK, Czechoslovak Travel Bureau
10 E. 40th St.
New York, NY 10016
Tel: [212] 689-9720

DENMARK
Danish Tourist Board
655 Third Ave.
New York, NY 10017
Tel: [212] 949-2333

FINLAND
Finnish Tourist Board
655 Third Ave.
New York, NY 10017
Tel: [212] 949-2333

FRANCE
French Government Tourist Office
610 Fifth Ave.
New York, NY 10020
   (for mail inquiries only)
   or 628 Fifth Ave.
New York, NY 10020
Tel: [212] 757-1125

EAST GERMANY
Embassy of the German Democratic
   Republic
1717 Massachusetts Ave. NW
Washington, DC 20036
Tel: [202] 232-3134

WEST GERMANY
German National Tourist Office
747 Third Ave.
New York, NY 10017
Tel: [212] 308-3300

GREAT BRITAIN
British Tourist Authority
40 W. 57th St.
New York, NY 10019
Tel: [212] 581-4700

GREECE
Greek National Tourist Organization
Olympic Tower, 5th Floor
645 Fifth Ave.
New York, NY 10022
Tel: [212] 421-5777

HUNGARY
Hungarian Travel Bureau [IBUSZ]
630 Fifth Ave., Room 520
New York, NY 10111
Tel: [212] 582-7412

IRELAND
Irish Tourist Board
590 Fifth Ave.
New York, NY 10036
Tel: [212] 869-5500

ITALY
Italian Government Travel Office
630 Fifth Ave., Suite 1565
New York, NY 10111
Tel: [212] 245-4822

LIECHTENSTEIN
See Switzerland

LUXEMBOURG
Luxembourg National Tourist Office
801 Second Ave.
New York, NY 10017
Tel: [212] 370-9850

MONACO
Monaco Government Tourist and
   Convention Bureau
845 Third Ave.
New York, NY 10022
Tel: [212] 759-5227

MOROCCO
Moroccan National Tourist Office
521 Fifth Ave., Suite 2800
New York, NY 10017

NETHERLANDS
Netherlands National Tourist Office
576 Fifth Ave.
New York, NY 10036
   (for mail inquiries only)

437 Madison Ave.
New York, NY 10022
Tel: [212] 223-8141

NORWAY
Norwegian Tourist Board
655 Third Ave.
New York, NY 10017
Tel: [212] 949-2333

POLAND
Polish National Tourist Office
500 Fifth Ave., Suite 328
New York, NY 10110
Tel: [212] 391-0844

PORTUGAL
Portuguese National Tourist Office
548 Fifth Ave.
New York, NY 10036
Tel: [212] 354-4403

ROMANIA
Romanian National Tourist Office
573 Third Ave.
New York, NY 10016
Tel: [212] 697-6971

SPAIN
Spanish National Tourist Office
665 Fifth Ave.
New York, NY 10022
Tel: [212] 759-8822

SWEDEN
Swedish Tourist Board
655 Third Ave.
New York, NY 10017
Tel: [212] 949-2333

SWITZERLAND
Swiss National Tourist Office
608 Fifth Ave.
New York, NY 10020
Tel: [212] 757-5944

TURKEY
Turkish National Tourist Office
500 Fifth Ave.
New York, NY 10036

USSR
Intourist Travel Information Office
630 Fifth Ave.
New York, NY 10111
Tel: [212] 757-3884

YUGOSLAVIA
Yugoslav National Tourist Office
630 Fifth Ave., Suite 280
New York, NY 10111
Tel: [212] 757-2801

Packing Checklist

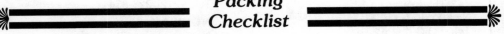

The following items are listed to serve as reminders of things which you might want to take. Your requirements will vary with the type of trip you are taking, and it is not intended that anyone take everything on the list.

PERSONAL
Passport
Appropriate visas
Youth hostel card
Camping carnet
International student identity card
Medic Alert or similiar I.D.
Credit cards
Travelers checks

CAMPING GEAR
Tent
Sleeping bag
Foam pad
Sheet sleeping bag
Butane stove
Cooking kit (nesting type)
Frying pan
Mess kit with eating utensils
Water bottles
Matches (waterproof)
Can opener
Multipurpose knife (Swiss army)
Corkscrew
Scouring pads
Detergent

TOILET ARTICLES
Soap
Shaving gear
Toothbrush
Tooth paste
Deodorant
Shampoo

CLOTHING
Shorts
Long pants/skirt
Sweater
Sweatshirt
T-shirt
Underwear
Socks
Cycling/walking shoes
Waterproof jacket
Rain gear
Hat
Sunglasses
Gloves
Bathing suit
Towel

TOOLS AND SPARES
Allen wrenches
Spoke wrench
Wrenches
Screw driver
Pliers
Tube repair kit
Spare tube
Spare tire
Wire
Spokes
Lamp bulb batteries
Tire levers
Tire pump

MEDICAL AND FIRST AID

Band aids
Antiseptic
Triangular bandage
Pressure pads
Sun screen
Water purifying tablets
Scissors
Safety pins
Insect repellent
Spare glasses
Medications and prescriptions
Spare denture
Lomotil or similar medication for diarrhea
Pain medication

MISCELLANEOUS

Maps
Guidebooks
Pen/notebook
Diary
Compass
Camera and film
Plastic bags
Bike lock
Money/passport pouch
Bungie cords
Sewing kit
Magic marker
Travel alarm/watch

 # Mail Order Suppliers of Bikes and Accessories

Bike Nashbar
4111 Simon Road
Youngstown, OH 44512
Tel: [800] 345-BIKE

Cycle Goods
2735 Hennepin Ave. South
Minneapolis, MN 55408
Tel: [612] 872-7600

The Camper's Companion to Southern Europe
A Campground & Roadside Travel Guide

The Camper's Companion to Southern Europe
A Campground & Roadside Travel Guide

by Dennis & Tina Jaffe

More than just campground directories, these travel guides share the best of each country off-the-beaten path. The Jaffes rate over 700 campgrounds covering all of Northern Europe in one volume, Southern and Eastern Europe and Northern Africa in the other volume. Country-by-country campgrounds.

300 pages, 6 x 9, maps, tables
Quality paperback, $13.95

How To Import A European Car
The Gray Market Guide

by Jean Dugay

Here's everything you need to know to purchase a car in Europe, drive it on your vacation, and ship it legally into the United States. You can save up to 25% on foreign car purchases – at the very least pay for your whole trip in savings! Names, addresses for reliable European dealers, best U.S. conversion centers, shippers. Covers DOT, EPA, customs, financing, bonding. Cost comparison for 200 models. Authoritative.

192 pages, 8½ x 11, illustrated, tables
Quality paperback, $13.95

Guide To Free USA Attractions

by Don Wright

Ghost towns, gold mines, caverns, zoos, museums, historical sites, natural wonders, tours, exhibits. They're all here in Don Wright's up-to-date unique guide to over 3,000 of the best FREE attractions in the USA.

640 pages, 5½ x 8½, maps, photos
Quality paperback, $14.95

Guide To Free USA Campgrounds

by Don Wright

Here is the only directory to the 6,300 free campgrounds in the USA. Indispensable for the millions of campers and their families who enjoy the beauty of noncommercial campgrounds.

544 pages, 8 x 11, maps
Quality paperback, $14.95

International Careers:
An Insider's Guide

by David Win

If you long for a career that combines the excitement of foreign lifestyles and markets, the opportunity to explore your own potential, the promise of monetary and personal reward, then learn from David Win how to get off the stateside corporate ladder and into the newly emerging areas of international careers. Now's the time!

224 pages, 6 x 9, charts
Quality paperback, $10.95

Dining On Deck:
Fine Foods for Sailing & Boating

by Linda Vail

For Linda Vail a perfect day's sail includes fine food – quickly and easily prepared. She offers here 225 outstanding recipes (casual yet elegant food) with over 90 menus for everything from elegant weekends to hearty breakfasts and suppers for cool weather sailing. Her recipes are so good and so varied you'll use her cookbook year-round for sure!

160 pages, 8 x 10, illustrated
Quality paperback, $9.95

After College
The Business of Getting Jobs

by Jack Falvey

Wise and wonderful . . . don't leave college without it. Filled with unorthodox suggestions (avoid campus recruiters at all costs!), hands-on tools (put your money in stationery, not in resumes), wise observations (grad school? - why pay to learn what others are paid to learn better). You've already spent a fortune on textbooks. Now for only $10 you can have the most valuable book of all.

192 pages, 6 x 9
Quality paperback, $9.95

What's Next?
Career Strategies After 35

by Jack Falvey

Falvey explodes myths right and left and sets you on a straight course to a satisfying and successful mid-life career. Bring an open mind to his book and you'll be on your way. A liberating book to help us all get happily back into work.

192 pages, 6 x 9
Quality paperback, $9.95

Golde's Homemade Cookies
by Golde Hoffman Soloway

"Cookies are her chosen realm and how sweet a world it is to visit."
Publishers Weekly

Over 100 treasured recipes that defy description. Suffice it to say that no one could walk away from Golde's cookies without asking for another . . . plus the recipe.

144 pages, 8¼ x 7¼, illustrations
Quality paperback, $7.95

Simply Elegant Country Foods:
Downhome Goes Uptown
by Carol Lowe-Clay

An outrageously good cook brings country cooking to its pinnacle. A cookbook that's not fussy, not trendy - simply elegant. Everything from country fresh Pizza Rustica to Crumbed Chicken in Wine Sauce, Country Pork Supper, Sweet Cream Scones with Honey Butter to Whipped Cream Cake with Almond Custard Filling. Over 100 recipes capturing the freshness of the moment!

160 pages, 8 x 10, beautifuly illustrated
Quality paperback, $8.95

Ice Cream!
The Whole Scoop
by Gail Luttmann

Ice cream lovers rejoice! Here are over 250 unbelievably delicious, homemade ice cream recipes including frozen custard, tofutti, ices, sherbets, sorbet, low-fat, low-cholesterol ice cream, sauces, ice cream cakes, ice cream for diabetics, and more. For every kind of ice cream freezer!

220 pages, 8 x 10, photos
Quality paperback, $9.95

TO ORDER

At your bookstore or order directly from Williamson Publishing. We accept Visa or Mastercard (please include number, expiration date and signature), or send check to **Williamson Publishing Co., Church Hill Road, P.O. Box 185, Charlotte, Vermont 05445**. (Phone orders: 802-425-2102.) Please add $1.50 for postage and handling. Satisfaction guaranteed or full refund without questions or quibbles.